On Dangerous Ground

On Dangerous Ground

America's Century in the South China Sea

GREGORY B. POLING

OXFORD
UNIVERSITY PRESS

OXFORD
UNIVERSITY PRESS

Oxford University Press is a department of the University of Oxford. It furthers
the University's objective of excellence in research, scholarship, and education
by publishing worldwide. Oxford is a registered trade mark of Oxford University
Press in the UK and certain other countries.

Published in the United States of America by Oxford University Press
198 Madison Avenue, New York, NY 10016, United States of America.

Library of Congress Control Number: 2022000760

ISBN 978–0–19–763398–4

DOI: 10.1093/oso/9780197633984.001.0001

1 3 5 7 9 8 6 4 2

Printed by LSC Communications, United States of America

CONTENTS

ACKNOWLEDGMENTS

I have often been warned that book writing is a long and lonely process. This was certainly no exception. That I came out the other side with an actual book to my name is because of the generous support and advice of many friends and colleagues. At the Center for Strategic and International Studies, my home for over a decade now, Michael Green saw value in the project and ensured I had the resources and flexibility to see it through. Conor Cronin was the first to push me toward the undertaking. Murray Hiebert was a valuable mentor, as he has been throughout my career. Harrison Prétat helped keep the lights on in the Asia Maritime Transparency Initiative while I dove into research. And several capable research interns at AMTI helped me track down sources, including Charlotte Adams, Jillian Lope, Grace Headinger, and Camille Bismonte. My longtime collaborator Paul Franz turned my years of GIS tinkering into the elegant maps in this volume. John Schaus, Jude Blanchette, and Gregory Winger all read early versions of chapters and gave valuable feedback.

I am immensely grateful for the collaboration and generosity of fellow scholars in the South China Sea research community, without whom this would have been an impossible undertaking. Jay Batongbacal pointed the way to valuable early sources on American and Philippine discussions about the South China Sea. Marites Vitug helped answer follow-ups on her excellent volume on the Philippine arbitration case, *Rock Solid*. Alex Vuving lent his singular expertise on the confusing sequence of Vietnamese occupations in the Spratlys. Bill Hayton allowed me to endlessly needle him with questions about early Chinese claims and sources from his seminal *The South China Sea*. James Kraska gave me the missing ingredients for the law of the sea chapters by recommending Ann Hollick's *U.S. Foreign Policy and Law of the Sea*. Many others have helped me along this path through generous conversations over drinks on the conference circuit over the years. I won't try to list them all, as I will inevitably miss some, but you will find much of their valuable research filling the notes in this volume.

I also owe a great debt to the teams at Oxford University Press and Newgen Knowledge Words, including David McBride, Emily Benitez, and Nirenjena Joseph, for shepherding this book through the review, editing, and production process.

Finally, I never would have made it through this process without the support and considerable patience of my wife, Nicole Poling, and daughter, Ella. They put up with plenty of weekend and late-night writing sessions. Now each has a stack of IOUs for missed playtimes and date nights and postponed home repairs coming due. I am very happy to pay up.

Interests That Abide

China is creating a great wall of sand, with dredges and bulldozers, over the course of months. When one looks at China's pattern of provocative actions towards smaller claimant states—the lack of clarity on its sweeping nine-dash line claim that is inconsistent with international law and the deep asymmetry between China's capabilities and those of its smaller neighbors—well it's no surprise that the scope and pace of building man-made islands raise serious questions about Chinese intentions. . . . And we're all hopeful that China will become a contributor to stability, not a source of insecurity. But as we like to say in Navy circles, hope is not a strategy.

—U.S. Pacific Fleet Commander Adm. Harry Harris, Remarks at the Australian Strategic Policy Institute, March 31, 2015[1]

Have the United States and its allies and partners "lost" the South China Sea? It is a common refrain. China has steadily militarized the contested waterway while squeezing out its neighbors. U.S. policy has failed to halt, or even markedly slow, that process. And that failure has dented American standing. But what exactly is there for the United States—a non-claimant located an ocean away—to win or lose? What, if any, critical U.S. interests are at stake? Those questions need to be answered before policymakers can craft strategy and judge success or failure.

The South China Sea is home to not one but two different kinds of disputes. Together they make it the most politically and legally contested body of water in the world. First, there are territorial disputes over hundreds of rocks and reefs that dot the sea. In the northwest lie the Paracel Islands, which are occupied by China but claimed by Taiwan and Vietnam. In the south are the Spratlys, which are claimed in whole by those three and in part by Brunei, Malaysia, and the Philippines. Control over Scarborough Shoal to the northeast is disputed by China, Taiwan, and the Philippines. And Pratas Reef, just off China's coast, is held by Taiwan and claimed by China. There are also many underwater features

On Dangerous Ground. Gregory B. Poling, Oxford University Press. © Oxford University Press 2022.
DOI: 10.1093/oso/9780197633984.003.0001

that don't belong to any of the island groups, though China and Taiwan claim them anyway.

The second set of disputes covers the water, seabed, and airspace around those islands. Brunei, Indonesia, Malaysia, the Philippines, and Vietnam claim offshore rights based on the United Nations Convention on the Law of the Sea (UNCLOS). Those entitlements generally include a 12-nautical-mile territorial sea and economic rights over water and seabed 200 miles from the coast.[2] The convention also grants a territorial sea, and potentially more, around each island. That web of overlapping claims would already make the South China Sea the world's most contested body of water. China and Taiwan further complicate the situation. They don't restrict themselves to the boundaries set by international law. In addition to the maritime zones allowed by UNCLOS, Beijing and Taipei seek special rights over nearly the entire South China Sea. They do this with an ill-defined boundary, often dubbed the "nine-dash line" in the case of China and the "U-shaped line" with regard to Taiwan (see Figure I.1).

The United States, like other outside parties, remains neutral on the sovereignty disputes. It has little interest in wading into historical arguments over who first administered which rock or reef. But on maritime disputes, Washington has consistently voiced opposition to excessive claims. That is especially true of the nine-dash line. And many other non-claimants, including Australia, New Zealand, Japan, India, and members of the European Union, have joined in that criticism. But why should they care? What makes arguments over water and seabed half a world away so important to the United States and like-minded partners?

For decades, U.S. policymakers have been drawn time and again to two abiding interests in the South China Sea.

Freedom of the Seas

The first and oldest American interest at stake is the freedom of the seas and maritime law. U.S. leaders have seen maintenance of the free seas as vital to national prosperity and security for more than two centuries. Few interests have been as abiding over the course of American history. This commitment drove the young United States to launch its first military forays abroad. And by the middle of the nineteenth century, it carried the U.S. Navy across the Pacific for the first time to defend the perceived rights of American merchants and missionaries. It is impossible to understand U.S. interests in the South China Sea absent its historical relationship with the freedom of the seas and the international law defining it.

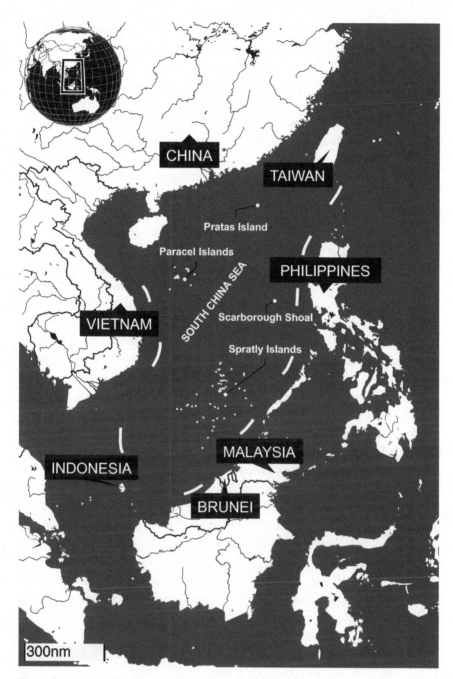

Figure I.1 South China Sea islands and nine-dash line. Created using Mapcreator and OpenStreetMap.

For most of history, freedom of the seas was a given. Governments exercised authority over people, whether citizens or subjects. And people live on land. Nations might try to control inland waterways. The most ambitious could exert some authority over waters just offshore. But the seas were mostly an ungoverned and largely unused space. Fisherfolk stayed close to shore. Traders hugged the coast or kept to established routes *between* spheres of government authority, dodging the marauders who preyed on those sea lanes. Navies used the same routes to launch attacks against rival nations but had no incentive to control the empty spaces between. Only the boldest sailed the uncharted oceans. And even then, their goal was to trade, raid, or exploit the resources of lands beyond, not control the sea itself.

The thought that a ruler might lay claim to the open oceans first emerged in Europe at the end of the fifteenth century. Advances in shipbuilding and navigation had allowed first Portugal and then Spain to claim far-flung colonies and open new trade routes across the high seas. They called on the pope in Rome to broker a peace. The resulting papal bull of 1493 purported to divide the world along a line of longitude running through the Atlantic Ocean and the eastern part of South America. All non-Christian lands *and waters* to the west were reserved for Spain's use, and those to the east for Portugal's. In the Treaty of Tordesillas the following year, each nation recognized the other's right to navigate its waters. But that right wasn't extended to third parties. Naturally, this held only so long as no third party rose to challenge it.

By the late sixteenth century, the Dutch and British were looking to develop their own colonial and commercial empires. When Francis Drake sailed into the Pacific, Spain's ambassador to England complained about this violation of the papal bull. Queen Elizabeth I was dismissive: "The use of the sea and air is common to all; neither can any title to the ocean belong to any people or private man."[3] In 1609, Dutch jurist Hugo de Groot, known as Grotius, published his famous exposition on the *Mare Liberum*, or free seas. He argued that neutral vessels should have unrestricted rights to use the high seas. This was a self-serving argument for Grotius's patrons in the Dutch East India Company, but it was also the way the oceans had been treated for most of human history.

Britain continued to support the free seas in principle, but it also had a parochial interest in protecting its domestic fishing industries. This led King James I to decree in 1609 that all foreigners fishing within view of the British coast must obtain a license from the crown. His successors Charles I and Charles II declared outright sovereignty over the seas around Britain. To justify these claims, jurist John Selden developed an argument for a *mare clausum*, or closed seas, which he published in 1635.[4] But by the early eighteenth century, the British had walked back most of these claims. A consensus then emerged in

Europe that a state's authority extended as far from shore as it could effectively exert power; the high seas beyond were free to all. And the clearest limit to a coastal state's power was thought to be the range of its cannons: about 3 miles. The 3-mile territorial sea, known as the "cannon shot rule," gained wide acceptance in Europe and was carried to its colonies. There were variations, of course. Scandinavian states, for example, claimed 4 miles, the width of a Scandinavian "league."[5]

The United States inherited this European position. In 1793, Secretary of State Thomas Jefferson informed London and Paris that the new nation would fix its territorial sea at 3 miles. Congress passed a law to that effect a year later, making the United States the first country to cement the 3-mile limit in domestic legislation.[6] This reflected how tightly the American states were enmeshed in European trading networks. By the early nineteenth century, wealthy American merchants were supplementing this with direct trade with China.[7] This commerce was vital to the new country's prospects. And it required unfettered access to the seas around Europe and Asia. By midcentury, the booming whaling and guano industries also became important voices demanding government protection for their maritime rights. In response, U.S. diplomats consistently asserted American prerogatives at sea. And though the young republic was far from a major naval power, it quickly proved willing to use force to defend freedom of the seas when possible.

The United States had scarcely gained independence before facing its first international crisis over maritime rights. The North African states of Morocco, Algiers, Tunis, and Tripoli had regularly seized merchant vessels for ransom in the Mediterranean—not wholly unlike the use of privateers by European powers. The British paid tribute to avoid seizure of their ships, but American vessels lost that protection when they declared independence in 1776. As a result, the Barbary States began seizing American ships in the 1780s, and Algiers declared war in 1785. Under the Articles of Confederation, the U.S. government could neither raise a navy nor pay sufficient tribute to stop the practice. In 1784, the United States negotiated a treaty with Morocco. But Algiers continued to prey on American merchants. The colonies finally adopted the new U.S. Constitution in 1789, creating a federal government capable of doing something about the problem. Five years later, Congress directed funds to build the first six ships of the U.S. Navy. Algiers, along with Tunis and Tripoli, signed treaties the very next year agreeing to stop harassing American ships in exchange for tribute. But in 1801, Tripoli demanded larger payments and declared war. President Thomas Jefferson responded by dispatching the new navy and marine corps to the Mediterranean—the country's first expeditionary military action. They defeated Tripoli's forces, and the First Barbary War ended with a new treaty in 1805.[8]

Fighting between Britain and France from 1792 through 1814 created another dilemma for the United States. Britain repeatedly blockaded French ports and refused to recognize the trading rights of neutral parties like the United States. Washington regularly voiced opposition to this policy, but there was little it could do about it. Tensions grew as the British began boarding American ships and pressing sailors into service. This included both native-born American citizens and those who had been naturalized after fleeing Britain. These violations of American maritime rights led to growing U.S. hostility against Britain and greatly contributed to the outbreak of war in 1812.

Hostilities between Britain and the United States afforded some of the Barbary pirates an opportunity. With encouragement from London, Algiers repudiated the 1795 treaty, declared war on the United States, and began seizing American merchant vessels again. The United States had to endure those outrages until 1815. Less than a month after ratifying the Treaty of Ghent, which ended the fighting with Britain, Congress declared war on Algiers and dispatched a U.S. Navy squadron to the Mediterranean. It quickly defeated two Algerian warships. Algiers signed a new treaty ending the demand for American tribute. Tripoli and Tunis did the same. When Algiers repudiated the treaty a few months later, Washington sent a second squadron and a nearly identical treaty was signed.[9]

Before long, this desire to protect the nation's maritime rights drew the U.S. Navy into the Pacific Ocean. The United States sent the first warships of a new East India Squadron to the western Pacific in 1835. Their task was to protect U.S. commercial interests and ensure that American merchants need not rely on the British for protection. Except for a brief interlude during the American Civil War, U.S. naval vessels have operated continuously in Asia ever since.[10] By midcentury, the United States was determined to enjoy the same rights to navigation and trade as the European powers. And that often led it to emulate European disregard for Asian and Pacific Island opinions on the matter. In the most famous example, Cmdre. Matthew Perry steamed into Edo (Tokyo) Harbor in 1853 and forced Japanese officials, under threat of bombardment, to open direct trade relations with American merchants.

A year after Perry's famous use of gunboat diplomacy, the East India Squadron undertook its first patrols on the Yangtze River. They were there to protect American commercial rights in the treaty ports that China was forced to open after the Opium Wars with the United Kingdom. The Yangtze patrols continued until World War II. In 1868, the East India Squadron was folded into the new U.S. Asiatic Squadron. And in 1898, Cmdre. George Dewey sailed that squadron into Manila Bay, defeated a Spanish fleet, and began more than a century of direct U.S. involvement in the South China Sea.

The Asiatic Squadron, upgraded to the Asiatic Fleet in 1902, remained relatively small. But after 1919, it was always led by a four-star admiral to ensure that the ranking U.S. officer in Asia could negotiate on an equal footing with the envoys of other powers. This was a recognition that the navy was the primary representative of both American security and commercial interests in the region. The fleet's role was mostly constabulary: protecting the rights of American missionaries, diplomats, and especially merchants under international law.[11] Defense of U.S. maritime rights remained the fleet's primary mission right up to the eve of hostilities with Japan. In the postwar decades, U.S. interests in the Pacific grew along with the country's power, but freedom of the seas always remained high on the list.

Balancing Alliance Commitments

The second abiding U.S. interest in the South China Sea, at least since the end of World War II, has been to uphold defense commitments without being dragged into the arguments of U.S. allies over disputed sovereignty. The U.S. alliance network, along with American territories in the region, have made the United States a resident power and helped maintain stability in Asia. They allow the country to forward-deploy significant military forces thousands of miles from the homeland, deterring aggression and quickly responding to regional security challenges. This in turn keeps the United States and its allies safe and their shared interests protected.

Much of this U.S. security network traces its roots to America's early pursuit of freedom of the seas, or at least its interpretation of it. By the end of the nineteenth century, the commitment to defend maritime and commercial freedoms was an important factor in Washington's contradictory stances on colonialism. In 1899, Secretary of State John Hay formulated the Open Door Policy, which declared that America would ensure China remained independent from European colonization and free to trade with all countries equally. Yet from 1898 to 1899, the United States took possession of the Philippines and Guam from Spain, annexed Hawaii, and agreed with Germany to carve up Samoa. America's decision to become a colonial power was controversial at home. But in each case, one of the arguments used to justify the Faustian bargain was the navy's need for coaling stations and other facilities to defend American commercial rights.

America's earliest involvement in the South China Sea sprung from its colonial presence in the Philippines. It grew anxious about Japanese designs on Pratas Reef, the Spratly Islands, and especially the expanse of nearby reefs known as the "Dangerous Ground." Being more conflicted about its colonial status than were its European counterparts, the U.S. Congress passed legislation in 1932 establishing a pathway for Philippine independence. From 1935 until the outbreak of World War II, the transitional Commonwealth of the Philippines ran

most domestic affairs. Formal independence came in 1946. But with the Cold
War spinning up and fear of Soviet encroachment in Asia, neither side wanted
American forces to leave. They inked a Military Bases Agreement in 1947 and
a Mutual Defense Treaty (MDT) in 1951, creating America's earliest security
alliance in the Pacific. This was the first step in the creation of the U.S. alliance
system that persists in Asia to this day.

The United States soon inked similar defense treaties with Australia, New
Zealand, the Republic of China (ROC), Japan, and South Korea. Then came
semiformal alliances with Thailand and South Vietnam—formally the Republic
of Vietnam. Among this club, the Philippines, ROC, and South Vietnam all
staked claims to disputed islands in the South China Sea. During this time, the
top U.S. priority in the disputes was to maintain credibility without alienating
any of the three allies. And that meant remaining neutral and urging calm.

That changed over the course of the 1970s. Saigon fell, the victorious forces
of North Vietnam moved into the Spratlys, the People's Republic of China
(PRC) violently expanded its footprint in the Paracels, and the United States
abrogated its treaty with the ROC on Taiwan. In the span of a few years, Manila
found itself the only American ally left in the dispute, facing potential aggression from either Hanoi or Beijing. At the same time, perceived abandonment of
South Vietnam and Taiwan raised worries about the credibility of other U.S. defense commitments. Philippine officials wondered if the alliance had become
a one-way street—were they making themselves a target by hosting U.S. bases
without even a credible American commitment of support in the South China
Sea, where they faced potential violence? This kicked off a cycle of negotiations
over the scope and value of the alliance. In many ways, that cycle continues to
this day.

Over the past four decades Washington has slowly clarified that the U.S.-
Philippines MDT applies to any attack on Philippine forces in the South China
Sea. It continues to balance that commitment with its long-standing neutrality on territorial claims. There have been some close calls on both sides, but
Washington has determined over and over that its oldest alliance in Asia is too
valuable to let slip away. Manila has repeatedly reached the same conclusion. The
U.S.-Philippine relationship is at once vital and conflicted. It is built on more
than a century of cultural interchange, deep personal connections, shared sacrifice, and common interests. But it is also clouded by the history of colonization, political interference, unequal economic relations, and a huge disparity in
power. The last leaves one side often fearing abandonment and the other entrapment. For more than a century, U.S. policy in the South China Sea disputes has
most often followed from its relationship with the Philippines, first as colonizer
and then as ally. Today, upholding its alliance commitments remains one of the
two primary American interests in the disputes.

Manila would find it all but impossible to defend its maritime rights from growing Chinese encroachment without U.S. military support. And were the United States to be seen as abandoning the Philippines to Chinese aggression, it would ripple well beyond the South China Sea. The ability of the United States to project power and respond to crises in Southeast Asia would be severely compromised if it lost access to Philippine territory. Other allies and partners would naturally question the U.S. capability and will to remain a regional security provider. The American alliance network would face a crisis, of both confidence and capability, at a time when it is needed most. The rise of Chinese power, and its clear revisionist intent, would make the rapid diminution of U.S. influence in Asia far more destabilizing than it was in the 1970s.

Pulling Together the Threads

Secretary of State Hillary Clinton, at the behest of Southeast Asian leaders, declared freedom of navigation and peaceful resolution of disputes in the South China Sea a U.S. national interest in 2010.[12] That was a crystallizing moment, but it only elevated positions that U.S. officials had voiced many times over the years. Defending maritime rights and preventing violence against or between allies had long been the primary American interests in the South China Sea. Understanding how that came to be requires tracing three converging narratives. One of those covers the U.S. relationship with the law of the sea; another the evolution of U.S. alliances, especially with the Philippines; and a third the development of the South China Sea disputes themselves. At times, these historical threads ran parallel; at others they intersected and then diverged. This book traces each to the present day, where they are more interwoven than ever.

The United States has been involved in the South China Sea disputes almost from their conception. That has occasionally taken the form of clear-eyed, proactive defense of American interests. But more often, policymakers have been entangled by circumstance. Their attention elsewhere, they would be unexpectedly roused by a crisis or the demands of regional allies. They would need to quickly assess the national interest. And then the disputes would return to the margins of U.S. policy until the next crisis. The results were unsurprisingly mixed.

This time, the stakes are higher and the South China Sea disputes are not going to fade into the background. If the United States is going to secure its national interests, it will need to be more deliberate about identifying and pursuing them. It has long defended the freedom of the seas and a credible alliance network in Asia. The maintenance of both has helped ensure the national security and prosperity of the United States and its partners. Those interests were from time to time challenged in the South China Sea. But now China's actions in the disputes threaten to fatally undermine them. Facing this challenge from a peer competitor—the first in decades—the United States must hold to a realistic assessment of its own interests. That will allow American leaders to compromise where they can, stand firm where they must, and tell the difference between the two.

1

Seeds of Discord

1800–1951

> While the shoal appears outside the limits of the Philippine archipelago
> as described in Article III of the American-Spanish Treaty of Paris of
> December 10, 1898, it would seem that, in the absence of a valid claim
> by any other government, the shoal should be regarded as included
> among the islands ceded to the United States by the American-Spanish
> treaty of November 7, 1900.
>
> Accordingly, in the absence of evidence of a superior claim to
> Scarborough Shoal by any other government, the Department of State
> would interpose no objection to the proposal of the Commonwealth
> Government to study the possibility of the shoal as an aid to air and
> ocean navigation.
>
> —Secretary of State Cordell Hull, letter to Secretary of War Harry
> Woodring concerning Scarborough Shoal, July 27, 1938[1]

For more than a century, the United States has engaged in a careful balancing act
in the South China Sea. It takes no position on most sovereignty questions while
insisting that they be pursued peacefully and in accordance with international
law. This is predicated on the reality that no side has an airtight case and that
Washington would gain little by wading into messy historical debates. Refusing
to pick sides was necessary from the beginning, as the disputes quickly pitted
against each other nations friendly to the United States. That gave Washington
an incentive to oppose the use of force or coercion but not much else. This situation changed only when one party's expanding claims clearly threatened international law and the security of American territory in the Philippines.

On Dangerous Ground. Gregory B. Poling, Oxford University Press. © Oxford University Press 2022.
DOI: 10.1093/oso/9780197633984.003.0002

In the Beginning

For centuries, the South China Sea has been an important artery for commerce and one of the most productive fishing zones on the planet. Historically, vessels from across Southeast Asia, southern China, and the Arab world freely plied its waters. The islands and reefs of the South China Sea were used by regional fishers for rest and replenishment, while most other mariners knew them only as hazards to navigation. But with few exceptions, the South China Sea's land features remained beyond the administration and often the awareness of governments.

The first documented moves to claim and administer some of these far-flung islands took place during the early nineteenth century. The Spanish, as the colonial power in the Philippines, undertook occasional surveys of Scarborough Shoal from 1800 onward. Spain never made a formal declaration of sovereignty over the feature but included it on some maps as part of the Philippine archipelago.[2] Emperor Gia Long, who founded the Nguyen dynasty in Vietnam, declared sovereignty over the Paracel Islands in 1816.[3] Prior to that, Vietnamese authorities had been officially sanctioning salvage operations in the islands for several decades.[4] Vietnam continued to make occasional use of the islands during the 1830s and 1840s, after which official interest lapsed.[5]

In 1843, Captain Richard Spratly aboard the British whaler *Cyrus* claimed to be the first to discover the island that bears his name. Eventually the entire island group would come to be known as the Spratlys. The British East India Company had been conducting surveys of the islands from the late eighteenth century, and in 1868 the British Admiralty compiled the results of those efforts into a new nautical chart of the South China Sea. That map displayed nine distinct islands and reefs in the western portion of the grouping, including Spratly Island itself. In the east, it showed a largely empty expanse of water dotted with reefs whose existence could not be confirmed. The chart labeled this area "Dangerous Ground," a nickname it still bears. The map was revised in 1881 and reproduced by nearly every country with an interest in the South China Sea, including the United States. It would remain the standard chart of the area until the 1950s.[6] No government showed much interest in the islands themselves until 1877, when the British colonial authorities in Labuan, North Borneo, registered a claim to Spratly Island and Amboyna Cay on behalf of London. Those two features were listed as possessions by the British Colonial Office from 1891 to 1933, though the British never vigorously pursued the claim.[7]

Despite later revisionism, Qing dynasty documents and actions show that Chinese officials considered Hainan Island to be the southernmost limit of their authority.[8] There is no record of any Chinese objections to Gia Long's annexation of the Paracels or subsequent Vietnamese activity there. When German and Japanese ships carrying insured British copper wrecked on the islands in 1895 and 1896, Chinese authorities foreswore any responsibility for them. Chinese fishers had salvaged the wrecks, prompting the insurance company to demand compensation from those responsible. This was transmitted through the United Kingdom's embassy in Beijing and its consul in Hoihow (modern Haikou). In response, Chinese officials in Liangguang—supervising Guangxi and Guangdong provinces, including Hainan—insisted the islands were unclaimed as far as they were concerned.[9] China's disinterest began to change only in the early twentieth century in response to Japanese and French activities.

The Qing government ceded Taiwan, or Formosa, to Japan in the 1895 Treaty of Shimonoseki ending the First Sino-Japanese War. This gave Japan a foothold on the edge of the South China Sea and helped kick off a decades-long expansion of Japanese commercial interest in maritime Southeast Asia. Starting in 1902, Japanese business interests began surveying Pratas Island and nearby reefs off the southern Chinese coast for possible exploitation of fisheries and guano.[10] Several of these individuals called on Tokyo to annex the island, either directly or as part of Taiwan. Then in 1907, a private Japanese guano miner named Nishizawa Yoshiji came ashore with 105 workers. He christened the feature "Nishizawa Island" and claimed it on behalf of Japan.[11] His operations sparked concerns among some Chinese and American officials that Tokyo would make a formal claim and establish a naval presence on the feature. The U.S. secretary of war William Howard Taft raised the issue with the Qing government. He was presumably concerned about a Japanese base so near the Philippines, of which he had recently been the first American governor. Authorities in Washington reportedly fretted about whether they should recognize Chinese sovereignty over Pratas to preempt a Japanese claim.[12] But this proved unnecessary. While the imperial court in Beijing was unconcerned, authorities in Canton (modern-day Guangzhou) engineered a boycott of Japanese goods in 1909. That convinced Tokyo to enter negotiations and recognize Chinese sovereignty over Pratas in exchange for a sizable payment to Nishizawa.[13]

That same year, China's Adm. Li Zhun caught wind of another island group to the south: the Paracels. He undertook an expedition to survey the islands and formally declared their annexation.[14] This prompted a debate among French authorities, which had consolidated their control over Indochina two decades earlier, on whether to assert a competing claim based on Vietnam's earlier activities. The French consul in Canton, Jean-Joseph Beauvais, wrote, "France has as many rights to the islands as China." But he urged caution after seeing how local officials had reacted to Nishizawa's actions on Pratas. Beauvais counseled Paris that declaring sovereignty would arouse Chinese nationalism, which could be "more damaging to us than the possession of the Paracel Islands would be useful."[15] This also led to the first of many ambiguous U.S. reactions to sovereignty claims in the South China Sea. Unsure of the merits of China's claim, the 1915 version of the U.S. Navy's *Asiatic Pilot* noted that the Paracels had been "annexed by the Chinese government."[16] The wording was purposeful; "annexation" wasn't necessarily lawful.

Chinese authorities seemingly forgot about the Paracels in the chaos that followed the 1912 collapse of the Qing dynasty. But Japanese and French interests continued to grow. Several Japanese businessmen surveyed the islands beginning in 1917 and unsuccessfully petitioned the imperial government to annex them as part of Japan. One of them, Hirata Sueji, informed the Japanese government that the Paracels were unclaimed, declared them the "Hirata Archipelago," and filed an application with Tokyo to mine for phosphate. Hirata, along with the Mitsui Corporation, extracted guano and phosphate from the islands until 1920. By then he had learned of the 1909 Chinese claim and sought advice from the Japanese Foreign Ministry and its consulate in Canton. In 1920, Tokyo was again informed of China's claim by both the British government and its own consulate in Hong Kong. This might have dissuaded Japan from annexing the islands, but it continued to allow Japanese citizens to exploit them. In 1921, Hirata established a joint venture called the Paracels Archipelago Industries Company Unlimited with two partners from China and Macau. The company surveyed and extracted phosphate from the islands until 1926.[17]

These Japanese activities seem to have gone unnoticed by China and France, which had no physical presence in the Paracels. In March 1921, the governor of Kwangtung (modern Guangdong province) declared that his government would incorporate the Paracels as part of Hainan. This prompted the French governor for the colonies to send a letter to Paris suggesting that it might consider recognizing Chinese sovereignty in exchange for "a formal commitment from the sovereign Government never to set up a military or naval base there and to install no facilities to that end."[18]

Japanese business interests, meanwhile, had begun to make their way farther south to the Spratlys. Hirata surveyed several of the islands and claimed them for Japan in 1917. He was followed by a series of Japanese entrepreneurs who would petition Tokyo to recognize their discovery and rights to various islands. The most influential was the Lhasa Phosphates Company led by Tsunefuji Noritaka. The company landed a survey team on five of the largest islands in 1918 and expanded its footprint from there. By 1924, it had constructed dormitories for as many as two hundred Japanese and Taiwanese workers engaged in fishing and guano extraction on Itu Aba, the largest of the islands. It conducted similar activities on several other islands in the grouping until 1929, at which point the business might have fallen victim to the Great Depression.[19]

Despite multiple petitions by Lhasa Phosphates and other stakeholders, Tokyo held off on formally annexing the islands. This may have been due to concerns about upsetting relations with the United Kingdom. From 1926 to 1928, Japanese authorities asked their embassies to look into competing claims to the Spratlys. They determined that neither China nor the United States (via the Philippines) had made claims, but two features—Spratly Island and Amboyna Cay—were shown as British territory on some maps.[20]

Japan's economic exploitation of the Paracels and Spratlys had gone largely unopposed thanks to domestic turmoil in China and a lack of interest by other parties. But by the late 1920s, neither of those conditions still held. In 1928, the same year Chiang Kai-shek established the new Nationalist government in China, an expedition departed Canton for the Paracels.[21] It discovered that Japanese business interests had been operating since at least 1919 and that French authorities from Annam had landed on Woody Island, the largest of the chain, in 1925 and 1926. The French formally claimed the islands in 1932 as part of the protectorate of Annam, arguing that Vietnamese rulers had exercised sovereignty over them since the early nineteenth century.[22] Chinese officials objected, insisting that the Paracels were the southernmost territory of China. This strongly suggests that the central government wasn't yet considering a claim to the Spratly Islands farther south.[23]

The French, however, were. A French naval commander took possession of the eponymous Spratly Island in 1930. Paris then informed the press that it claimed sovereignty over all islands and reefs within a set of coordinates covering the western portion of the Spratlys. France issued a communiqué to the other great powers announcing its occupation of the islands on the grounds that they were *terra nullius*, or unclaimed land.[24] This prompted the United Kingdom, which since 1877 had maintained a claim on paper to Spratly Island and Amboyna Cay, to demand clarification from France over exactly which features it was claiming. Paris responded in 1933 by formally annexing Spratly and Amboyna Cay, along with Itu Aba, Loaita Island, Thitu Island, and Le Deux Iles (The Two Islands), consisting of Northeast and Southwest Cays (collectively called North Danger Reef in English). It also annexed their "dependent islets" (see Figure 1.1).[25] The British Foreign Office then decided it had insufficient grounds to contest the French claim. It quietly removed Spratly Island and Amboyna Cay from its official list of colonial possessions.[26]

The initial Chinese response again came from provincial authorities in Canton. They mistakenly accused the French of having annexed islands belonging to the Paracels.[27] The Nationalist government moved more cautiously. It ordered the Chinese consul in Manila to ask the U.S. Coast and Geodetic Survey office there about the islands. Upon learning they were an entirely different group, he reported back that the Cantonese authorities were in error.[28] But voices in China,

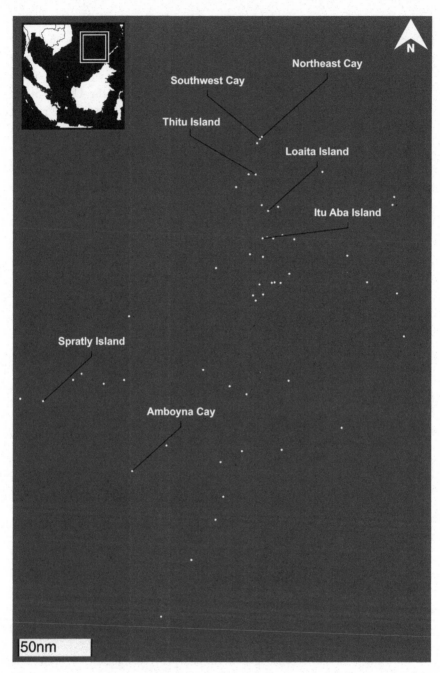

Figure 1.1 Spratly Islands annexed by France, 1933. Created using Mapcreator and OpenStreetMap.

including from Canton and the navy, still called on the government to stake its own claim to the Spratlys.[29] In August 1933, the Nationalist government notified the French that "pending a thorough investigation of the matter, it 'reserved its rights' with respect to the said French occupation."[30] But despite later claims, it appears that authorities in Nanjing chose not to formally object to France's claim.[31] This decision to keep quiet was likely influenced by a secret report from the Chinese Military Council. It examined the 1912 *China Sea Pilot* prepared by the U.K. Royal Navy, which detailed Chinese fishing around the islands. The council concluded that the document "does not provide evidence of any Chinese administration, the presence of an official representative of China, or Chinese equipment and infrastructure [on the Spratlys]. In conclusion, we have only one piece of evidence, our fishermen from Hainan, and we have never done anything on these islands."[32]

At the same time, Chinese authorities were planting the seeds of an even thornier problem. The ROC Land and Water Maps Review Committee, a group of officials and cartographers, met for the first time in 1933. One of their missions was to codify the country's claims to land features in the South China Sea. Lacking documentation of any historical claim or the capacity to undertake their own surveys, they collected foreign sailing charts to identify islands and reefs. In the case of the Spratlys, that meant relying on the 1881 map produced by the British Admiralty. The group translated or transliterated the English names of islands, reefs, and undersea features on this map into Chinese. In 1934, this resulted in the "Table of Chinese and English Names for All of the Chinese Islands and Reefs in the South China Sea."[33] A year later, the committee published a map with these 135 newly named "islands."[34]

The list included a great many errors that continue to complicate the South China Sea disputes to this day. Most were caused by a combination of mistranslation and the committee's unfamiliarity with the area. The most infamous is probably James Shoal, which schoolchildren in both China and Taiwan are still taught is the southernmost territory of China. James Shoal is more than 60 feet under water; the supposed "territory" is a myth. The error occurred because the committee members were thrown by the English word "shoal," meaning a raised area of seabed, and translated it as *tan*, meaning a "beach" or "sandbank."[35] The same error was repeated across many underwater reefs and banks which Beijing and Taipei continue to treat as if they were dry land. Other features claimed by the committee didn't exist at all; they would be removed from subsequent British charts as a result of later surveys.[36]

In addition to Pratas Island, the Paracels, and the Spratlys, the committee's list of islands and reefs included Scarborough Shoal and Macclesfield Bank. These were lumped together as the Nansha Islands (despite being neither islands nor geographically related). In 1936, a Chinese geographer named Bai

Meichu published his own adaptation of the committee's map, featuring a solid line around all the islands. This was the earliest version of the U-shaped line. Despite the committee's work, the ROC government didn't immediately annex any of the newly named islands and reefs, beyond the already claimed Pratas and Paracels. But the list would resurface after World War II. And in 1946, two of Bai's students would place a version of his line, this time drawn as eleven dashes, on an official map for the first time.[37]

Unlike the Nationalist authorities in China, Japan's government quickly delivered a note of protest in response to Paris's annexation of the Spratlys. Tokyo had not formally claimed the islands, but Japanese business interests led by Lhasa Phosphates had been operating on them until just a few years before. The issue was temporarily settled in 1934. After six rounds of negotiations, France pledged not to use the islands for military purposes and to respect the economic interests of Japanese companies.[38] But the deal wouldn't hold for long.

The French annexation also sparked the first expression of Philippine interest in the Spratlys. This came as Filipino legislators were negotiating with the American colonial government for a transition to independence. In August 1933, former Philippine senator Isabelo de los Reyes sent a letter to Governor General Frank Murphy suggesting that the United States claim the features annexed by France, which he called "Las Corales."[39] De los Reyes told the press, "It would be a grave carelessness to permit that France or Japan has power over these islets to fortify and arm them against ourselves within our own territory."[40] A few years later, Japan would indeed use Itu Aba to launch attacks against American and Filipino forces.[41] In the meantime, authorities in September 1933 proposed that Senator Elpidio Quirino chair a parliamentary committee to study possible annexation. Quirino would be the leading proponent of a Philippine claim to the islands for the next two decades.

In response to this Philippine interest, American authorities did quietly explore whether the United States might have a claim. The director of the U.S. Coast and Geodetic Survey office in Manila determined that, while they could be strategically valuable, the Spratlys were not covered by the 1898 Treaty of Paris, under which Spain had ceded the Philippines to the United States.[42] The State Department agreed. In October, it informed the territorial government, "These islands are therefore at considerable distances and outside the limits of the Philippines."[43] This didn't deter Quirino, who became interior secretary of the newly established Commonwealth of the Philippines in 1935. Concerned that France and Japan were both angling for advantage in anticipation of war, he reportedly filed an official claim with the U.S. State Department in 1937. Washington, however, took no action.[44] A year later, he told the press that the Philippines would eventually claim the islands to safeguard its national security.[45]

Washington's refusal to support a Philippine claim was consistent with its South China Sea policy up to that point. The United States had taken no position on the prior competing claims of China, France, and the United Kingdom, insisting only that they accord with international law. And it could find no rationale to make a claim of its own. But Washington came to a very different legal conclusion about another South China Sea territory: Scarborough Shoal. This triangular reef about 120 nautical miles west of Luzon includes a few rocks that poke above water at high tide. It went largely unnoticed during the rush to claim the larger island groups and wouldn't become a flashpoint until the 1990s. The Treaty of Paris drew a set of lines around the Philippines, denoting the territory ceded by Spain. Scarborough falls outside of those lines. But in 1900, Spain and the United States negotiated an addendum: the Treaty of Washington. This pact clarified that Spain ceded any other territories it had administered as part of the Philippines, regardless of their location. As it happened, Spanish authorities had undertaken several surveys of Scarborough Shoal and included it on some maps and documents describing Philippine territory.[46]

As a result, U.S. authorities in the Philippines began including the feature in official documents, including a 1918 census of the Philippine islands.[47] In 1938, the government of the Commonwealth of the Philippines requested permission from American authorities to study the shoal for the possible construction of an aid to navigation. Unlike Quirino's claim to the Spratlys, which the State Department had politely ignored, this request got an answer. The Departments of State, War, and Commerce quickly agreed that in the absence of any other legal claim, Scarborough should be considered American territory under the Treaty of Washington.[48] After the Republic of the Philippines gained independence in 1946, U.S. authorities would consistently treat the shoal as uncontested Philippine territory. That surety, which has softened in recent years, sets Scarborough Shoal apart from all other disputed South China Sea territories.

The South China Sea at War

The Second Sino-Japanese War began on July 18, 1937, when Chinese and Japanese forces clashed on the Marco Polo Bridge near Beijing. Most of the region would be engulfed in the Second World War two years later. As hostilities spread, the islands and reefs of the South China Sea took on new strategic importance. They were positioned along vital sea lanes which had been dominated by British, French, and, to a lesser degree, American naval forces for a century. On September 3, the Japanese Navy occupied Pratas Reef, as Taft had feared they would three decades earlier. This facilitated Japanese control of both ends of the Luzon Strait (the other being anchored by Taiwan and the Ryukyus).

Japan thus controlled the most important passages between the Northeast and Southeast Asian theaters. Two days later, the Japanese Third Fleet announced a blockade of the entire coast of China. And on September 17, it commenced bombing Hainan Island.[49] This worried London and Paris, which believed that a Japanese conquest of Hainan would endanger their naval operations and the safety of their colonies in Hong Kong and Indochina.

Japan's strategy from 1937 to 1939 focused on strengthening its control over China and crushing the Nationalist government's resistance while avoiding outright hostilities with the West. That involved a lot of brinksmanship to try to intimidate the Americans, British, and French. All three were actively supporting the Nationalist forces and refused to recognize Japanese administrative efforts. Beginning in late 1937, Japanese forces demanded the right to board and inspect American and other foreign vessels to enforce their blockade of the Chinese coast. They also requested prior notice of the movements of American ships in Chinese coastal waters. And after seizing control of the Yangtze River, they sought to restrict foreign access to China's inland waterways. All of this was in violation of treaties governing the rights of European and American vessels in Chinese waters.[50]

For the next two years, the Imperial Japanese Navy and the U.S. Asiatic Fleet played a high-stakes game of chicken with echoes of today's Sino-U.S. tensions. Japanese naval officers made increasingly brazen demands, risked the safety of American mariners, and occasionally used low-level force. The Asiatic Fleet consisted of thirty-nine outdated ships and five thousand sailors and marines. Under the command of Adm. Harry Yarnell, it doggedly carried out an official U.S. policy of "standing adamantly on all American rights of property and person." Yarnell deployed navy vessels to the front wherever Japanese actions threatened American lives or sought to restrict U.S. access. He regularly interposed his ships between American commercial interests on shore and larger, better-armed Japanese vessels, daring them to use force. Yarnell also issued continuous diplomatic missives to Japanese counterparts signaling American resolve.[51] The riskiness of this strategy was laid bare in December 1937, when Japanese bombers and fighters sank the gunboat USS *Panay* along with three Standard Oil tankers outside Nanjing. Tokyo apologized, insisting the incident was an accident, and paid an indemnity.

Even before the war in China started, France and the United Kingdom were increasingly worried about a potential Japanese occupation of the Paracels and Spratlys. In early 1937, with British encouragement, France began preparations to militarily occupy both island groups. This would have violated its 1934 deal with Japan. In July, the British Air Ministry reported a Japanese presence on Itu Aba and Spratly Island. French and Vietnamese troops landed on Itu Aba in early December and confirmed that a small number of Japanese citizens—fishers from

Taiwan—had established a settlement.[52] This prompted France to issue a series of diplomatic messages between December 1937 and August 1938 restating its claim to the Spratlys.[53]

The British, fearing French inaction, proposed leasing Itu Aba and Spratly Island from Paris to construct air strips before the Japanese could. But France worried about Japan's reaction if it evicted the Taiwanese fishers. London grew even more concerned when it heard additional reports of Japanese civilians on Spratly Island. In fact, small groups of French Vietnamese and Japanese Taiwanese civilians were now living side by side on both islands.[54] The British government held an interdepartmental meeting in March 1938 to consider the issue. It decided that Japan must not be allowed to establish air or submarine bases and that it would be best if all Japanese citizens were evicted from the islands. British authorities then began to review how they could support French efforts to those ends.[55] Paris sent another warship to Itu Aba in April to repair sovereignty markers on the island.[56] But then its attention was pulled north.

Japan had quietly established a military presence in the Paracels, on Woody Island, in January 1938. It set up another outpost on nearby Lincoln Island in April. France responded two months later, deploying a mission to Woody and Pattle Islands to establish lighthouses and leave Vietnamese police behind on each. This was a concession to the fact that France claimed the Paracels on behalf of its protectorate of Annam, whereas it claimed the Spratlys for itself. Paris informed Chiang's government of the plan beforehand and assured it that the operation would have no impact on the eventual determination of sovereignty. Two Japanese warships met the French forces at Woody Island but allowed them to land. The sides exchanged pleasantries, both asserted that the island belonged to them, and then the French hoisted their flag. From that point until the end of the war, Japan and France both maintained military garrisons on Woody Island. They apparently never came to blows. As planned, French Vietnamese forces also occupied Pattle Island, which they had all to themselves.[57] Paris formally announced its occupation of the Paracels in July (Figure 1.2). And it pointedly informed the Japanese Foreign Ministry that the only country with which it would discuss sovereignty over the islands was the ROC.[58]

At first Japan only monitored these French maneuvers, not wishing to expand the conflict beyond China. Chiang had moved his Nationalist capital further inland to Chongqing in October 1937, and Japan was trying to convince Paris to block alternate supply routes to the beleaguered Chinese forces. The most important of these ran from the Vietnamese port of Haiphong along the Gulf of Tonkin through Nanning in southern China. But by late 1938, the Japanese government was frustrated. Its coastal blockade had failed to suffocate Chiang's forces. Tokyo decided to turn the screws on Paris and set the stage for

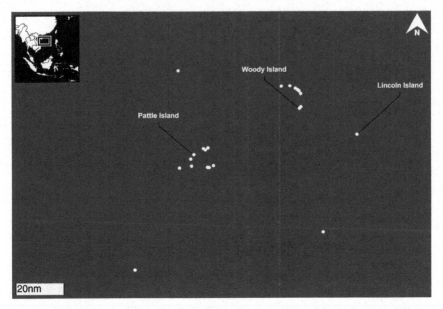

Figure 1.2 Paracel Island occupations, January–June 1938. Created using Mapcreator and OpenStreetMap.

an occupation of Hainan, which would bring both Nanning and Hanoi within range of Japanese bombers. Japanese warships visited Itu Aba on October 30 and again on December 7. Later that month, Tokyo announced the annexation of the Spratlys and Paracels. They were placed under the jurisdiction of Taiwan. When Paris protested, Japan's Foreign Ministry insisted that its actions were necessary to protect the life and property of Japanese citizens on the islands. France proposed taking the matter to third-party arbitration; Japan refused.[59]

Europe, meanwhile, was moving toward all-out war. In 1938, France began diverting naval forces from Indochina to Djibouti in preparation for an Italian attack on its North African colonies. By early 1939, the German and Italian governments were urging Japan to occupy Hainan as part of a larger strategy against France. It was becoming clear that Tokyo could not continue the campaign against Chiang's forces while maintaining positive relations with Paris. Once the decision was made, it moved quickly: Japan invaded Hainan on February 28, announced the military occupation of the Paracels on March 1, and landed troops on Itu Aba on March 30. The next day, the Japanese government officially renamed the Paracels and Spratlys the New South Archipelago (Shinnan Gunto).[60] Japan allowed the French Vietnamese civilians to stay for the time being. They wouldn't be evicted from Itu Aba until October 1940, likely to make room for the submarine and seaplane base Japan would build on the island.[61]

Paris and London immediately protested these occupations. On May 17, the U.S. State Department summoned Japan's ambassador in Washington to register its displeasure. The United States reiterated its neutrality but called on Japan to resolve disputes by negotiation rather than force. Washington labeled Tokyo's actions illegitimate and denied that the Paracel and Spratly Islands were a single archipelago.[62] The United States would not pick sides between competing claims made within the bounds of international law, but it rejected those made outside that framework.

Washington found Tokyo's claim particularly threatening because of its scope. The Shinnan Gunto included not just the islands claimed by France but also the vast expanse of reefs and rocks known as the Dangerous Ground. American authorities had recently developed an interest in this area off the Philippine island of Palawan, and they were undoubtedly worried about a hostile power controlling it. The area remained poorly understood, and commercial maps still echoed those published by the British Admiralty half a century earlier. But the United Kingdom, United States, and Japan were secretly vying to find navigable sea lanes through it. Success would grant two important advantages: it would offer hidden anchorages where most other navies couldn't operate, and it would open a shortcut from the Philippines or British Borneo to points south and west. The British had begun searching in 1925 and finally found a north-south route through the Spratlys in 1934. They continued annual surveys until 1938, producing the most detailed charts of the area. The U.S. Asiatic Fleet based in Cavite was focused on finding a path through the Dangerous Ground to Singapore, which it finally managed in 1935.[63]

The Imperial Japanese Navy started surveying the Spratlys in 1936, right under France's nose. It drew detailed charts which proved crucial when it converted Itu Aba into a submarine base—exactly the kind of thing that worried the Americans. In May 1939, Cdr. Unosuke Kokura wrote:

> A remarkable fact is that the whole of the Spratly islands can be considered as a kind of fortified area, because it is known as a dangerous area on all the maps of the world. . . . But because of a laborious work of our Imperial Navy, this area is not a dangerous area at all for us. Our warships and commercial ships can sail freely through these groups of islands and take shelter behind the reefs.[64]

French historian François-Xavier Bonnet interviewed the purported author of a U.S. Navy memorandum drawn up days after Japan's declaration of the Shinnan Gunto. The memo reportedly argued that the United States must be free to continue surveying the eastern part of the Spratlys and to develop any of the reefs or islands in the area. As such, it recommended that Washington remain neutral over the competing claims in the western Spratlys but strongly oppose the Japanese claim to the Dangerous Ground in the east.[65] Washington never publicly made this distinction. But the secretary of state sent a note to the Japanese ambassador stating that Washington did not consider all the rocks and reefs claimed by Japan to be part of a single island group.[66]

By late 1939, Admiral Yarnell's strategy of asserting American rights along China's coasts and rivers was becoming increasingly fraught. And hostilities in Europe soon spilled over into Asia. Germany invaded France in May 1940, toppling the government in Paris by the end of June. With the colonial administration of French Indochina in chaos, Tokyo pressed the governor general to close all supply routes to the Nationalists. Unable to defend against a potential Japanese invasion, he complied. Tokyo immediately went farther, demanding a complete closure of the border and basing rights for Japanese forces in Indochina.

By the end of June, French colonies were under the control of the new Vichy puppet government, which opened negotiations with Tokyo. Germany refused to intervene on behalf of its French client. Japan set a late September deadline for France to meet its demands, or else. Just before the clock ran out, the government of French Indochina agreed that a few thousand Japanese troops could be stationed in Tonkin and the Japanese Army could move through the protectorate on its way to China. Despite the concessions, Japan launched a four-day offensive into Tonkin, humiliating the French defenders. The operations made it painfully clear that Indochina was at the mercy of the Imperial Japanese Army. On September 27, the day after hostilities ended, Japan signed the Tripartite Pact with Nazi Germany and Fascist Italy.

U.S.-Japanese tensions were escalating quickly, and Yarnell's successor, Adm. Thomas Hart, saw no choice but to begin removing the Asiatic Fleet to the Philippines. He later recalled:

> By mid-October, 1940, I became convinced that the place for me was with the Fleet, and for the Fleet in the Philippines, that our main job was to get ready for war; that being on the China Coast protecting American interests and all that was not reduced in importance, but it was no longer the main issue; that as such it must be dropped; that I myself should get south with the Fleet and get ready for the war which I felt more and more every day was coming.[67]

Hart was right. The drive to war accelerated in mid-1941 as Japan decided to drive south and seize the valuable oil, rubber, and other resources of the Dutch East Indies. Japanese leaders determined this was the only way to withstand growing economic pressure from the United States and fuel the war in China. In preparation, large numbers of Japanese forces moved from Tonkin into Annam and Cochinchina in July 1941. Tokyo then forced the Vichy government to sign an agreement legitimizing this de facto occupation. French civilian authorities would be allowed to retain nominal control until early 1945. Japan's moves into southern Indochina provoked exactly the economic retaliation that Tokyo feared: Washington froze Japanese assets in the United States on July 2 and established an oil embargo on August 1.

Hostilities seemed inevitable by late November, and the United States began pulling most remaining forces out of China. On November 27 and 28, the 4th Regiment of the U.S. Marine Corps, known as the China Marines, pulled out of Shanghai's International Settlement. They boarded the *President Madison* and the cruise liner *Harrison* and sailed out into the East China Sea. The *Harrison*, the last to leave, was menaced on its way by patrol planes and ships of the Imperial Japanese Navy before the Asiatic Fleet arrived to escort it into the South China Sea and on to Subic Bay in the Philippines.[68] The marines would be sent to Corregidor, Gen. Douglas MacArthur's island fortress in Manila Bay. Most spent the next four months in foxholes weathering artillery bombardments and guarding the island's beaches against an amphibious assault that never came.[69]

The remaining gunboats of the Yangtze Patrol, including the *Panay*'s sister ships *Luzon* and *Oahu*, made a run for the Philippines at the end of November. The vessels were never intended for the open seas but rendezvoused safely with the Asiatic Fleet on December 3 and were escorted into Manila Bay. The *Mindanao* was the last, and least seaworthy, to make the South China Sea crossing. It had remained in port at Hong Kong until receiving confirmation that the others reached Manila. The boat set out in a storm on December 4 and immediately picked up an unwanted escort of Japanese destroyers. It was forced to turn north along the coast toward Taiwan before tacking south again. Along the way it released its empty lifeboats into the storm, hoping that the pursuing Japanese would spot them and assume the ship had sunk. The ruse seemed to work. The *Mindanao* limped into Cavite Naval Yard in Manila Bay on December 10 to find the war already underway and the Philippines besieged.[70]

The war erupted with nearly simultaneous attacks across the Pacific on December 7 and 8, 1941. First Japan invaded British Malaya, starting with the bombardment of Kota Bharu just after midnight on December 8, local time. Less than an hour later, a surprise attack hit American naval forces at Pearl Harbor (it was still the morning of December 7 in Hawaii). Meanwhile, Japanese troops invaded Thailand from French Indochina. They rapidly overcame Thai resistance, crossed the border into Malaya, and sped toward the British colony of Singapore. The Japanese Navy began shelling the city around 11:00 p.m., providing cover for the first battalions of Imperial Army troops to cross the Johor

Strait from Malaya. At the other end of the South China Sea, Japanese troops launched an assault on British forces at Hong Kong around 8:00 a.m., local time.

Bombing raids hit Iba and Clark Airfields in the Philippines at just past noon. They wiped out more than half of the U.S. Far East Air Force, whose bombers and fighters were still on the ground. The American aircraft were fueling up for retaliatory raids on Taiwan. According to U.S. war plans, they should have taken off hours earlier in response to the attack on Pearl Harbor. The delay was disastrous. Nearly all surviving American planes in the Philippines would be destroyed in a matter of days. The first Japanese invasion forces hit the beaches of Luzon in the afternoon.

By the time London and Washington declared war that same day, Japan had already scattered Allied air and naval power in the Pacific, and American and British troops were under assault on three sides of the South China Sea. The waterway would become, in effect, a Japanese lake for the next three years. Hong Kong fell on Christmas Day 1941. Singapore held out until February. After a harried retreat into the Bataan Peninsula, American and Filipino troops kept Japanese forces bogged down until April. Gen. Jonathan Wainwright surrendered on Corregidor on May 6, ordering all remaining American troops in the Philippines to do the same.

As for Hart's outgunned Asiatic Fleet, most escaped the initial Japanese offensive against the Philippines. But they could offer little support to the troops pinned down in Singapore and Bataan. The bulk of the fleet withdrew to the south and was thrown into the disastrous Battle of the Java Sea in February 1942. Many were lost there or in the string of Allied naval defeats that followed. A few submarines continued to make the dangerous run to Corregidor until it fell. In February and March, they helped spirit Philippine president Manuel Roxas, General MacArthur, and their families out of the island fortress to safety in Australia. Some of the smaller gunboats of the Yangtze Patrol, like the *Mindanao*, wouldn't have survived the open ocean escape from the Philippines and so were trapped. They did what they could in the defense of Bataan and Corregidor. The last were sunk by enemy fire or scuttled in early May.[71]

The turning point for the Allies came a month after Corregidor's surrender, when the U.S. Pacific Fleet defeated the Japanese Navy at the Battle of Midway. Allied forces spent the next two years making their way back across the Pacific in a grinding island-hopping campaign. Then, in late October 1944, U.S. and Australian forces returned to Philippine waters and broke the back of the Imperial Japanese Navy at the Battle of Leyte Gulf. During the battle, the American submarine USS *Darter* ran aground on Bombay Shoal in the Spratly Islands while pursuing a Japanese destroyer, joining generations of vessels wrecked on the Dangerous Ground.[72] The naval victory paved the way for the liberation of the Philippines and reestablished Allied naval and air dominance in the South China Sea. It also sealed the fate of the isolated Japanese units in the Spratlys and Paracels and on Pratas Island.

For the remainder of the war, U.S. submarines and the Flying Tigers of the Fourteenth Air Force—the successor of Gen. Claire Chenault's famous American Volunteer Group in China—wreaked havoc on Japanese vessels in the South China Sea. In February 1945, the American submarine USS *Pargo* quietly deposited two Australian commandos on Woody Island. They belonged to Z Special Unit, which consisted of mostly Australian special forces who specialized in reconnaissance and sabotage behind enemy lines. The commandos reported only two Japanese and one European civilian living on the island beneath a French flag. The *Pargo* collected the commandos and shelled all the buildings before steaming off. A month later, U.S. bombers targeted radio installations on Woody and Pattle Islands. When another submarine, the USS *Cabrilla*, visited Woody Island in July, it reported a white flag of surrender flying above the French one. In the Spratlys, American planes strafed and bombed the Japanese base on Itu Aba on May 1. They used a newly developed weapon—napalm— with devastating effect. It is unclear when the Japanese garrison left, but when a U.S. reconnaissance mission returned in November, after the war had ended, they found the island deserted.[73]

Then there was the "conquest" of Pratas Island, which marked the first and only time that U.S. forces physically occupied a disputed feature in the South China Sea. On May 4, the American submarine USS *Bluegill*, which like the *Pardo* carried a group of Z Unit commandos, approached Pratas. Its crew suspected the island was still being used as a radar and meteorological facility by Japanese forces and bombarded it overnight. But before the commandos could attempt a landing, the *Bluegill* was called away to search for American airmen downed during raids on Taiwan. It returned to Pratas on May 26 and took up a position offshore. Two days later, it bombarded the island again with the assistance of a U.S. Navy Catalina patrol-bomber. Two Australian commandos splashed ashore in the early hours of May 29. Other than some decoys set up to look like guards, they found the island abandoned. A U.S. Navy landing party joined them a few hours later. They estimated that the garrison had left less than two weeks earlier. The sailors raised the American flag and set up a plaque commemorating their capture of the island, which they renamed Bluegill Island. After loading up the most valuable equipment, ammunition, and souvenirs, they leveled the remaining buildings with explosive charges and returned to their submarine. Cdr. Eric Barr wrote an Action Report envisioning a future American base on the island. He reportedly sent a self-congratulatory message to navy brass in Pearl Harbor that ended, "Please have invasion medals struck immediately."[74] That didn't happen, and the brief American occupation of Pratas Island was largely forgotten.

Postwar Irresolution

In November 1943, Chiang Kai-shek, U.K. prime minister Winston Churchill, and U.S. president Franklin Roosevelt met in Cairo and declared as part of their war aims that "Japan shall be stripped of all the islands in the Pacific which she has seized or occupied since the beginning of the First World War in 1914, and that all the territories Japan has stolen from the Chinese, such as Manchuria, Formosa [Taiwan], and the Pescadores [Penghu], shall be restored to the Republic of China. Japan will also be expelled from all other territories, which she has taken by violence and greed."[75] This commitment was reiterated in the Potsdam Declaration issued by Chiang, Churchill, and Roosevelt in July 1945.[76] To this day, China and Taiwan maintain that the Cairo Declaration intended for the Paracel and Spratly Islands to be included among the territories "stolen from the Chinese." It is hard to say whether this was really Chiang's position at the time. But if so, it wasn't shared by the other allies. In May 1943, six months before Cairo, the U.S. State Department had drawn up document T-324 relating to the South China Sea islands. It determined that they could not be left to Japan but took no stand on their eventual disposition. In December 1944, another U.S. government document, CAC-301, recommended that the Spratly Islands be placed under the trusteeship of the planned United Nations, assuming France could be convinced to support the plan. After all, as far as the Allies could tell, the ROC government had never formally claimed the Spratlys. CAC-308 offered three options for the more complicated situation in the Paracels: a trusteeship, a Sino-French deal, or support for China's claim if France could not provide stronger evidence of Annam's. The United States didn't push for any of these solutions after the war, likely seeing that France wouldn't play ball.[77] But the documents show that the Allies were not of one mind when it came to the fate of the islands.

After Japan's surrender, France and the ROC raced to assert sovereignty over the islands. Pratas was the easiest, as all the Allies recognized the ROC's claim to it. Nationalist forces set up a meteorological station on the island and have occupied it ever since.[78] The fate of the Paracels and Spratlys, on the other hand, was unclear. A French infantry platoon arrived in the Paracels aboard the *Savorgnan de Brazza* in May 1946 and accepted the surrender of Japanese forces stranded on Pattle and Woody Islands.[79] But the French didn't stay. In October 1946, Gen. Alphonse Pierre Juin, French chief of staff of national defense, urged the Committee on Indochina to reoccupy the Paracels: "It is of the utmost importance for France to prevent any sign of occupation by a foreign power of the islands which command access to the future base at Cam-Ranh and dominate the sea route Cam-Ranh–Canton–Shanghai. If it transpires that the occupation

of the Paracels leads to a resumption of the discussion on our rights of sovereignty, it will ... consolidate our position in any future legal debate on this matter
between France and China."[80] The French government ordered its high commissioner in Indochina, Adm. Georges Thierry d'Argenlieu, to reestablish a presence in the Paracels on behalf of Vietnam. But d'Argenlieu was distracted. Ho
Chi Minh, leader of the Viet Minh, had declared the independent Democratic
Republic of Vietnam (DRV) in September 1945. French forces had returned to
Indochina soon after, and by March 1946 the two sides had negotiated a shaky
agreement for Vietnam to become a free state within the French Union. But relations deteriorated quickly, and in November d'Argenlieu attempted to eliminate
the DRV by bombarding the city of Haiphong, where Vietnamese nationalists
had established their own customs post. The first Indo-China War started a
month later when fighting broke out in Hanoi. The delay in the Paracels proved
costly.[81]

As for the Spratlys, a French minesweeper briefly visited Itu Aba in October
1946 and erected a stone marker. Unlike the Paracels, which it continued to
claim on behalf of Vietnam, Paris asserted its own sovereignty over the Spratly
Islands.[82] ROC forces landed on Itu Aba two months later and did the same.
The Chinese sailed aboard two former U.S. Navy vessels: the *Taiping*, formerly
the USS *Decker*, and a tank landing ship rechristened the *Zhongye*.[83] The landing
marked the first time any Chinese official stepped foot in the Spratlys. The
French never returned, but the Chinese soon would.

On January 4, 1947, ROC forces took advantage of French distraction and
landed on Woody Island in the Paracels. As with the expedition to Itu Aba a
month earlier, they sailed on two recently donated American naval vessels: the
Yongxing, formerly the USS *Embattle*, and the *Zhongjian*, formerly the USS LST-
716.[84] France issued an official protest, and d'Argenlieu finally took action. He
deployed the warship *Le Tonkinois* with instructions to occupy Woody as well as
Pattle Island. On January 17, *Le Tonkinois* arrived at Woody Island to find it held
by more than sixty Chinese troops. Its captain tried to cajole, coerce, and even
bribe them to leave, but to no avail. The ship then fired warning shots into the
air. When the Chinese garrison radioed Nanjing for instructions, the ROC government was irate. Paris backed down and *Le Tonkinois* sailed away, depositing a
small French Vietnamese force on Pattle Island as ordered.[85] The two sides held
a series of talks in Paris from February to July 1947 but made little progress. As
it had earlier with Japan, France suggested that they take the issue of the Paracels
to third-party arbitration; the ROC refused.[86]

Even as it planted flags on Itu Aba and Woody Island, the ROC government
internally debated the scope of its claims. Two former students of Bai Meichu,
the man who had sketched a U-shaped line around the islands a decade earlier,
worked to legitimate their mentor's invention. In September 1946, they placed

a dashed version of the line on a "Location Sketch Map of the South China Sea Islands." This map was created for an interagency meeting at the ROC Ministry of the Interior. Its task was to decide which islands the government should demand from Japan.[87] Chinese officials were united on the Paracels. But some, including the commander of the Itu Aba expedition in December, were more ambivalent about claiming the Spratlys. In April 1947, the Ministries of Interior, Foreign Affairs, National Defense, and the Navy finally agreed that James Shoal should be declared the southernmost point of Chinese territory, as shown on the maps created by Bai and others. So they decided the ROC would claim both island groups and urged the navy to permanently station personnel on them.[88] Chinese forces already occupied Woody Island; they soon returned to Itu Aba and established a permanent garrison.

In May 1947, the ROC Parliament passed a resolution calling for the government to "recover" the Paracels from France and more clearly "delimit our territory." The Geography Department of the Ministry of Internal Affairs took up the latter task. It began updating and adding to the list of 135 "islands" described by Chinese cartographers in 1935. Many of the more obvious transliterations of British names were replaced with new Chinese titles. Itu Aba and Woody Island were renamed Taiping and Zhongye in honor of the ships that had recently carried the first Chinese troops to them. Some translation errors were fixed, with a newly invented term, *ansha* (literally "hidden sand"), replacing *tan* (beach or sandbar) for those features called "shoal" in English. But this didn't change the official mythology of underwater James Shoal (Zengmu Ansha) as China's southernmost territory. And confusingly, *tan* continued to be used for the deeper features labeled "bank" on English maps. The island groups themselves were given their modern Chinese titles: the Paracels and Pratas were confirmed as Xisha (West Sand) and Dongsha (East Sand); the Spratlys were given Macclesfield Bank's old name, Nansha (South Sand); and Macclesfield and Scarborough Shoal were rechristened Zhongsha (Middle Sand).[89] In December 1947, the ROC government officially released this new list of 159 "islands" and placed them under the administration of Hainan province. It was the first formal claim of Chinese sovereignty beyond Pratas Island and the Paracels.

In February 1948, the ROC Ministry of Internal Affairs published a Location Map of the South China Sea Islands with eleven dashes descended from Bai's map. It didn't explain what they meant, but there is no evidence that it was intended as a territorial or maritime boundary. During the interagency meeting two years earlier, Bai's students had presented the map only as a way of identifying which islands China should claim. The PRC would officially adopt the list of 159 islands along with the dashed line in 1952, following the Chinese Civil War. A year later, in a sign of fraternity with Ho's insurgent DRV government, the PRC removed the two dashes in the Gulf of Tonkin.[90] From that point, the PRC's map would be known internationally as the "nine-dash line." The ROC authorities on Taiwan have maintained the original, which they prefer to call the "U-shaped line." There is still no explanation for the map from either government, but it has evolved well beyond its original meaning, especially in Beijing.

The Philippines also renewed its interest in the islands at this time. The United States officially granted the commonwealth its independence on July 4, 1946. Elpidio Quirino, who had advocated for annexing the Spratlys a decade earlier, became vice president of the republic. Within a month of taking office, he told the Manila press corps that the country would claim the Spratlys as a matter of national security.[91] He may also have sent a letter to General MacArthur at this time claiming them "based on the geographical propinquity of the islands to the Philippines and the vital importance of the same to our national defense."[92] But this is up for debate. The letter is known only from press reports a decade after the fact, and there is no record of it in the archives of MacArthur's correspondence. If it was sent, neither MacArthur nor the U.S. government responded. Quirino's public remarks in 1946 did, however, draw the attention of Paris. The French consul in Manila met with the vice president in August 1947 and claimed that Quirino was surprised to learn that the Spratlys were the same islands claimed by France in 1933. The consul then assured Paris, incorrectly, that the matter had been put to rest.[93]

Despite being elevated to the presidency in 1948, Quirino refrained from formally claiming the Spratlys. Two concerns likely held him back: the absence of American support and a desire to avoid confrontation with the ROC. Since 1946, the Nationalists had been fighting an increasingly desperate civil war with U.S. backing. As a result, they were finding it difficult to justify the maintenance of remote garrisons on Woody Island and Itu Aba. In 1949, most of Chiang's forces fled to Taiwan, and Mao Zedong declared the founding of the PRC. Nationalist forces held out on Hainan until the beginning of May 1950. Two weeks after their defeat there, President Quirino spoke to the press, apparently troubled by what the Communist victory meant for Philippine security. He reiterated his long-held view that the Spratly Islands were strategically important and lamented that the Americans had not acted on a request in 1946 to help establish a foothold there—an apparent reference to his letter to MacArthur. He then declared, "[A]s long as Nationalist China is holding them, there is no necessity for the Philippines to seize control." But he insisted that Manila would assert its rights if the Chinese Communists threatened to take the islands.[94] He seemed unaware that the ROC had already withdrawn from Itu Aba and Woody Island, presumably finding the garrisons too isolated after the fall of Hainan.[95] Quirino's fears of a PRC presence in the Spratlys, however, wouldn't be realized for almost forty years.

The fate of the Paracel and Spratly Islands was debated, without resolution, during the 1951 San Francisco Peace Conference. Neither the ROC nor the PRC attended due to disagreement over which government should represent China. France appeared to defer to the representatives of its client, the State of Vietnam, allowing them to assert sovereignty over the Paracels and Spratlys. On September 7, Prime Minister Tran Van Huu declared, "As we must frankly profit from all the opportunities offered to us to stifle the germs of discord, we affirm our right to the Spratly and Paracel Islands, which have always belonged to Vietnam."[96] PRC foreign minister Zhou Enlai declared from Beijing, "Whether or not the U.S.-British draft treaty [San Francisco Treaty] contains provisions on this subject, and no matter how these provisions are worded, the inviolate sovereignty of the PRC over Nanwei [Spratly] Islands and Hsisha [Paracel] Islands will not be in any way affected."[97] And the head of the Soviet delegation, Deputy Minister Andrei Gromyko, intervened on the PRC's behalf, asserting, "[I]t is an indisputable fact . . . Taiwan (Formosa), the Pescadores [Penghu Islands], the Paracel Islands and other Chinese territories, should be returned to the Chinese People's Republic." Gromyko unsuccessfully proposed an amendment to the treaty specifying that Japan renounced all claims to the Paracels, Spratlys, and Macclesfield Bank in favor of China.[98]

The Philippines did not raise its interest in the islands during the conference. It is unclear whether Manila and Washington communicated on that point. But the United States had repeatedly shown President Quirino that it would not champion his claim. Without a powerful backer, as Vietnam had in France and the PRC in the Soviet Union, a Philippine claim would not have gained any traction. It must also have been obvious that the conference would not resolve the issue. Facing so many competing demands, the United States and other Allies refused to address sovereignty over the islands in the final text. As a result, the treaty said that Japan gave up any claim to the Paracels and Spratlys but did not specify to whom. In the bilateral Treaty of Taipei one year later, Japan again agreed to cede the islands. And while it would be reasonable to assume Japan was ceding them to the ROC as the only other party to that agreement, that text too is not explicit. In addition, France and the other Allies were not parties to that treaty, and in an exchange of notes afterward, Japanese authorities assured their counterparts in Paris "that the new treaty had not, in the view of Japan, entailed any change in relation to the San Francisco Treaty."[99]

The Treaty of San Francisco allowed the United States and other parties to maintain their neutrality, but at the cost of the disputes lingering for decades. In the years that followed, successive Vietnamese governments would demand all the islands as successors to the French, the Philippines would formalize its claim to much of the Spratlys, and eventually Malaysia would do the same.[100] For the next quarter-century, three U.S. allies would lay competing claims to the islands: the Philippines, the ROC, and France (followed by its successor state, the Republic of Vietnam). Washington recognized from the outset that no side had an airtight claim, and it was not prepared to alienate one ally in favor of another with the Cold War heating up.

America and the Free Seas, Part I

1930–1966

> Extension of the boundary of a State beyond the 3-mile limit would directly conflict with international law, as the United States conceives it, and may, moreover, precipitate developments in international practice to which this Government, in the national interest, is clearly opposed. A number of foreign states are at present showing a clear propensity to extend their sovereignty over considerable areas of their adjacent seas. This restricts the freedom of the sea, and the freedom of the sea has been and is a cornerstone of the United States policy because it is a maritime and naval power.
>
> Any change of position regarding the 3-mile limit on the part of the United States is likely to be seized upon by other states as justification or excuse for broader and even extravagant claims over their adjacent seas. Indeed, this is just what happened when this Government made its proclamation of 1945 regarding the resources of the Continental Shelf. It precipitated a chain reaction of claims generally going beyond the terms of the United States proclamation, including claims of sovereignty extending to 200 miles from shore.
>
> —Letter from Assistant Secretary of State Thruston B. Morton to
> Senator Henry Jackson, March 6, 1953[1]

At this point, there was still no such thing as a "South China Sea dispute." There were arguments about ownership of the Paracel and Spratly Islands, but no government claimed the sea itself. It was still taken for granted that beyond a narrow band of territorial waters along coasts and islands, the South China Sea was open to all. The seeds of future maritime claims were, however, planted during the interwar years. Cracks began to show in the global consensus on the extent of the *mare liberum*, or free sea. They widened to fissures after World War II as more postcolonial states gained a seat at the table and sought changes to the customary rules written by Europeans.

On Dangerous Ground. Gregory B. Poling, Oxford University Press. © Oxford University Press 2022.
DOI: 10.1093/oso/9780197633984.003.0003

Technological advances in the first half of the twentieth century made a regime of maritime law based almost entirely on a 3-nautical-mile territorial sea unworkable. New fishing techniques and the advent of offshore oil and gas drilling were creating novel industries ever farther from shore. The oceans were no longer just a transit route for trade; they were an increasingly valuable resource to be exploited. Coastal states inevitably sought greater control over the riches off their coasts. The disagreements started small—over the width of the territorial sea and whether, as the British jurist John Selden had once argued, states should be able to control foreign fishing some distance beyond that. But they quickly spiraled into legal realms previously unimagined.

New frameworks were badly needed to manage offshore competition. U.S. officials understood that and were as eager as anyone to claim a piece of the growing maritime pie. But the United States, and especially its navy, remained as committed as ever to the gospel of the freedom of the seas. And Washington watched the fracturing of the global consensus around the "cannon shot rule" with growing anxiety. It argued, internally and abroad, over where limits should be placed between economic rights and long-standing maritime freedoms. And it was a central player in the long, and in some sense ongoing, process of answering that question through the international institutions that emerged from the world wars. This evolution in the law of the sea and U.S. maritime policy is as important to understanding current American involvement in the South China Sea disputes as any jostling over the Paracel and Spratly Islands.

Moving beyond the Territorial Sea

Argentina was the first to push the envelope, claiming a 10-mile fishing zone in 1907. It took a while for others to follow. But in 1923, Colombia demanded exclusive rights to fish and drill for oil within 12 miles of its coast. Four years later, the Soviet Union became the first to declare a 12-mile territorial sea. Mexico went almost as far, first claiming sovereignty to 20 kilometers (10.8 miles) from shore before settling in 1935 on a distance of 9 miles.[2]

The cracks in the colonial maritime consensus were modest, but they were spreading. The newly minted League of Nations tried to step in and settle the matter. It convened a Conference for the Codification of International Law in The Hague in 1930, which included a committee tasked with maritime boundaries. Members from forty-eight countries debated whether the territorial sea should extend to 3 miles, as had been the norm; 4, as in Scandinavia; or even a more expansive 6. But there was no consensus. The participants were also divided on the size of a proposed "contiguous zone" for customs and immigration enforcement beyond the territorial sea. And some followed Argentina and Colombia in wanting this zone to include jurisdiction over fishing.[3]

The United States played a major role in this debate as it increasingly broke ranks with the Europeans. This reflected the personal preferences of President Franklin Delano Roosevelt, inaugurated in 1933, to extend American rights farther from shore. The proposals explored by his administration irrevocably changed the global debate on maritime law. Roosevelt's successors would spend the next three decades trying to bottle up the genie that he helped release. The system needed to adapt, but Roosevelt's unilateral approach to rulemaking threatened anarchy rather than a new global consensus. Other states would use his policies to justify even more extensive maritime claims. It was a lesson in unintended consequences that would leave successive U.S. administrations chastened. Not until the Reagan administration in the 1980s would the United States reembrace unilateralism in maritime law, and then more for obstruction than new claim making.

In 1935, Congress passed legislation allowing the United States to conduct antismuggling operations up to 62 miles from shore. Previous U.S. law dating to 1790 had allowed such operations only within 12 miles of the coast. When hostilities erupted in Europe in 1939, the United States and Latin American nations issued the Declaration of Panama, establishing a zone of neutrality around the Western Hemisphere (excluding Canada). In some places, this zone covered the high seas more than 300 miles from shore. Foreign states were warned not to engage in any belligerent activity in the area. The declaration was never enforced, or enforceable for that matter. And it was set aside when the United States entered the war two years later. It would, however, be recalled by later governments in Latin American looking for precedents to defend their new resource claims.

But natural resources, not national security, were the primary impetus for the Roosevelt administration to toy with more expansive maritime claims. The president had been elected to guide the country out of the Great Depression, and any proposal that might strengthen long-term economic health could expect a favorable reception at the White House. On the fishing front, the U.S. salmon industry spent the 1930s lobbying Washington to do something about the recent arrival of Japanese boats off Alaska. U.S. fishers worried that the entry of the Japanese fleet into this traditionally American and Canadian fishery would lead to overexploitation. They also insisted that salmon caught in the waters off Alaska should be considered a uniquely American resource because they relied on U.S. rivers for spawning.

In response, Roosevelt personally floated several ideas. At one point, he suggested temporarily closing the waters off Alaska to all salmon fishing—American, Canadian, and Japanese—to protect stocks. He also considered declaring the seas from the Pacific coast to a depth of 600 feet to be "territorial waters" in which foreign fishing would require a license from the United States. This would have extended to 200 miles in some places—a claim that most officials considered unthinkable. The State Department's legal counsel talked him down, telling the president it would set a dangerous precedent and still wouldn't effectively protect salmon stocks. That didn't stop the Senate in 1937 from considering a bill that would have given Roosevelt this authority. But Secretary of State Cordell Hull personally stepped in and spiked that legislation. He warned Congress that if the United States took such a step, "it would find it difficult to object to the application of the principle against our own nationals and vessels" in distant waters.[4]

Meanwhile Roosevelt's secretary of the interior, Harold Ickes, was leading a charge to extend federal control over seabed resources. The first offshore oil well had been drilled in 1898 and development off the California coast had taken off around 1928. Interest in drilling in the Gulf of Mexico began to build in the late 1930s. Most extraction took place close to shore, but it was only a matter of time before it became profitable to drill wells beyond the territorial sea. The navy backed the Interior Department, urging Roosevelt to declare the nation's continental shelf a naval petroleum reserve. They found the president not just receptive but overeager. In 1938, he instructed Ickes to explore whether he could issue an executive order declaring such a reserve "extending halfway across the oceans." Interior was forced to tell the president that would exceed his legal authority. But Roosevelt didn't easily abandon an idea once it had seized him. In July 1939, he instructed the attorney general and secretaries of state, navy, and interior to study how to introduce legislation in Congress claiming the continental shelf beyond the territorial sea. He wrote, "I am still convinced that . . . federal jurisdiction can well be exercised as far out into the ocean as it is mechanically possible to drill wells. I recognize that new principles of international law might have to be asserted but such principles would not in effect be wholly new, because they would be based on the consideration that inventive genius has moved jurisdiction out to sea to the limit of inventive genius."[5]

The effort to make new seabed claims ran into trouble in Congress. The states believed they, not the federal government, should have jurisdiction over the continental shelf. But the State Department didn't push back as it had against proposed fisheries limits. This was because seabed claims were a wholly new legal concept, seemingly divorced from traditional freedom of the seas. And they concerned a largely hypothetical activity, unlike fishing. In this way, the debates within the Roosevelt administration previewed future international negotiations on the law of the sea. It would, at first, be easier to reach agreement on a new regime for the continental shelf than to adjust the older rules concerning the territorial sea and fishing rights. But once "inventive genius" made drilling on the shelf possible, that consensus would fracture.

After the United States entered the war in December 1941, Roosevelt had bigger things to worry about than fishing and seabed claims. But he didn't forget about the issue, and neither did Ickes. In June 1943, the interior secretary sent Roosevelt a letter arguing that war needs made it even more important to claim the resources of the continental shelf and the waters above it. Roosevelt agreed. In May 1944, he directed the Departments of State, Interior, and Justice to consider the question. Interior took the lead in crafting a draft proclamation on the continental shelf. The State Department did the same for fisheries conservation. State again worried about the effect that any unilateral declaration would have on the rights of American fishing vessels off distant shores. It based its work on the draft of a regional fisheries agreement already being negotiated with Canada and Newfoundland. Most within the department, especially in the Office of Economic Affairs, thought it essential that the United States get the concurrence of these countries and other partners before making any unilateral declaration.

The draft proclamation on fisheries would allow the United States to establish conservation zones in areas of the high seas beyond the territorial sea to preserve fish stocks. The rights of other states whose nationals had historically fished in such areas would be preserved, but new entrants could be barred. This seemed tailor-made to exclude Japan, but not Canada, from the Alaska salmon fishery. The State Department was careful to assure foreign governments that these conservation zones would remain high seas in all other respects. The continental shelf proclamation would allow the United States to claim the resources of the seabed adjacent to its coast to a depth of 600 feet (a point known as the 200-meter isobath). And again, State was careful to insist that the high seas status of the waters above would be unaffected.

Edward Stettinius, who replaced Cordell Hull as secretary of state in December 1944, officially recommended against making the continental shelf and fisheries declarations unless State could confirm that other countries were favorably disposed to the new policies. But Ickes worried more about further delay than about upsetting allies. He made a counterproposal that, after securing Roosevelt's approval, State would be given two months to consult with foreign governments before the proclamations would be automatically sent to the president for signature. Stettinius was pulled away to prepare for the upcoming Yalta Conference. So it fell to Acting Secretary Joseph Grew to sign off on Ickes's plan, with which he was hardly familiar. President Roosevelt approved it on March 31, 1945. He died less than two weeks later.

President Harry Truman assumed office with much weightier matters on his plate than the pending fishery and continental shelf proclamations. Since they were already approved by Roosevelt, he would have found it difficult to reverse course. But the transition gave State some extra time to seek concurrence from allies and partners. It didn't help. Foreign officials understood that they were being informed, not really consulted. The clock was ticking, and the declarations would be made no matter what. Twelve governments were briefed, and only Cuba offered clear support. The British government sent a note strongly disassociating itself from the American proclamations. Canada and Newfoundland were irate that the United States was acting unilaterally instead of finalizing the regional fishery policy they had been negotiating. Every other government consulted was noncommittal. The president signed what became known as the Truman Proclamations on September 28, 1945.[6] The entire process had been out of step with Washington's broader postwar focus on multilateral cooperation. And though the U.S. government never tried to implement the fisheries proclamation, there was no stopping the repercussions. The short-term effect of the declarations was to irritate American allies. Over the long term, they set off a chain reaction of claims that went far beyond what their drafters had envisioned. But that, in turn, helped bring the international community to the table for the first UN Conference on the Law of the Sea.

Seeking an International Approach

By 1947 the State Department had lost all interest in implementing the fishery proclamation. Instead, it focused on regional approaches to managing fishing beyond the territorial sea. The first step was the convening of an international whaling convention in Washington in December 1946. This resulted in the International Convention for the Regulation of Whaling and establishment of the International Whaling Commission. But multilateral cooperation otherwise proved difficult, especially in Latin America. The Truman Proclamations had served as the starting gun in a race to claim waters and seabed in the region. This coincided with the rapid rise of U.S. tuna fishing up and down the Pacific coast of the Americas. These countervailing forces led to frequent seizures of U.S. boats and rising diplomatic tensions throughout the 1940s and 1950s.

The first dispute arose between Mexico and the United States. The 1935 Mexican claim to a 9-mile territorial sea was already a source of tension. The two countries were negotiating a bilateral fishing treaty when the Truman Proclamations threw a wrench into the process. One month after the proclamations, Mexico's president took things a step further. He announced that the continental shelf to a depth of 200 meters was part of Mexican territory. The Truman Proclamations, by contrast, had claimed economic rights but not full sovereignty over the shelf. The Mexican president also declared that, just as the United States had claimed for itself, Mexico could unilaterally establish fishery conservation zones in the waters above the shelf. In December 1945, the Mexican government went further, amending the constitution to declare all waters over the continental shelf national property. But the amendment was never approved by the requisite number of states.

Panama moved next. In 1946 it claimed the continental shelf to an unspecified distance as national territory and asserted jurisdiction over all fishing above it. That same year, Argentina declared national sovereignty over a continental shelf of undetermined size and much of the waters above it (what it called the "epicontinental sea"). In 1947, Chile and Peru became the first states to do what Roosevelt had considered and claim jurisdiction over all fishing within 200 miles of shore. They used both the Truman Proclamations and the 1939 Declaration of Panama to justify these claims. The next year, Costa Rica declared sovereignty over the continental shelf and waters up to 200 miles from shore. The resulting concern from and lobbying by U.S. tuna fishers operating off Costa Rica led to one of the most successful negotiations of this period. In 1949, Costa Rica walked back the sovereignty claim to waters and sought to regulate fishing within only 6 miles of the coast. Then Costa Rica and the United States hammered out the Convention for the Establishment of the Inter-American Tropical Tuna Commission to help conserve stocks.[7] In the years since, more than twenty countries have joined the commission.

The flurry of new claims in Latin America put pressure on the U.S. State Department to clarify U.S. international fishery policy. The Office of the Special Assistant to the Secretary for Fisheries and Wildlife was established in 1947–48. Then in July 1948, identical letters were sent to Argentina, Chile, and Peru protesting their recent proclamations. The State Department said it rejected declarations of sovereignty beyond the territorial sea and found that the new claims "differ in large measure from those of the United States [Truman] Proclamations and appear to be at variance with the generally accepted limits of territorial waters."[8] This was the start of a policy of issuing public protests against excessive maritime claims, which continues to this day. The department would soon conclude that it was more constructive to object privately and go public only when quiet diplomacy failed. The United States was joined in these protests by many of the maritime nations of Europe.

Multilateral cooperation was much easier to find in the North Atlantic. In January 1949, the United States invited Canada, Denmark, France, Iceland, Newfoundland, Norway, Portugal, Spain, and the United Kingdom to a conference to manage and conserve fish stocks in the area. The participants concluded the Northwest Atlantic Fisheries Convention, which built on the draft agreement that Canada, Newfoundland, and the United States had been negotiating before the Truman Proclamations. All ten countries ratified the convention by 1953 and the Soviet Union acceded in 1958. Eventually the commission it created would be replaced by today's North Atlantic Fisheries Organization.[9]

In the northern Pacific, Canada, Japan, and the United States finally negotiated a fisheries convention in 1952 to manage salmon and other fish stocks. The International North Pacific Fisheries Commission would remain in operation until 1992, when it would be replaced by a new convention that brought in Russia and South Korea.[10] A major component of the convention was that all sides agreed to voluntarily abstain from fishing any stocks that were already being exploited to the maximum and subject to conservation programs by the other parties. In other words, Japan would keep out of the traditional U.S.-Canadian salmon fishery. Washington would try to have this principle of voluntary abstention from fully exploited fisheries included in future UN negotiations on the law of the sea, but without success. And within a decade, Japan grew tired of observing a principle that no one else was following and demanded major revisions to the 1952 convention.[11]

More maritime zones popped into being in Latin America between 1950 and 1951. Nicaragua and Brazil laid claim to the continental shelf to an unspecified distance. Ecuador did the same to a depth of 200 meters, declared its right to regulate fishing over the shelf, and expanded its territorial sea to 12 miles. Honduras issued a similar claim to seabed and fishing rights to 200 miles and a territorial sea of 12 kilometers (6.5 miles). And El Salvador dispensed with legal pretense and simply declared a 200-mile territorial sea, though it pledged to allow freedom of navigation through it. The U.S. protest to the Salvadorian proclamation was almost immediate. Five years later, El Salvador pared its claim back to a 12-mile territorial sea and exclusive fishing zone. The race for more expansive maritime zones came to Asia in August 1952, when the Republic of Korea declared a 60-mile conservation zone and 200-mile fishing zone.

By 1952, Chile, Ecuador, and Peru had begun to coordinate efforts to promote the legitimacy of claims up to 200 miles. Failing to make headway in bilateral or regional negotiations, Washington sought to internationalize the issue. European states needed little encouragement to publicly denounce the 200-mile claims. The Soviet Union, which was eagerly promoting its distant-water fishing fleet, did the same. The United States also proposed submitting the disagreements for arbitration by the International Court of Justice but was rebuffed. The only real hope for resolving the disagreements was through the new United Nations. The UN International Law Commission had been tasked with codifying customary international law on the territorial sea and high seas in 1949. The United States eagerly supported this process along with parallel efforts on fisheries under the auspices of the new Food and Agriculture Organization. The State Department initially wanted the UN General Assembly to take up the continental shelf as a separate issue, but it eventually agreed to an Icelandic proposal to have the International Law Commission consider it as part of deliberations on the high seas.[12]

Fisheries and territorial sea claims would remain hotly contested for decades, as European and American governments dug in their heels on well-established norms. But reaching consensus on the continental shelf, a relatively new concept, was easier The United States and the United Kingdom were among the first to declare rights over seabed resources. Following the Truman Proclamations, the United Kingdom claimed a continental shelf for itself and many of its dependencies in the Caribbean between 1948 and 1950. Ten Middle Eastern states under British protection did the same in 1949.[13] Other countries followed suit. And the United States and European countries were careful not to object to Latin American claims to the shelf, only to the waters above it. As a result, by the early 1950s the international community was in general agreement that states should control the resources of their continental shelves. There were still different opinions on how far the shelf extended and which resources belonged to it, but these paled in comparison to the arguments over waters.

The Truman administration, having kicked off this series of seabed claims, ironically lacked legal authority to implement its proclamation on the continental shelf. This became an issue in the 1952 presidential elections when Republican candidate Dwight Eisenhower publicly sided with Congress in asserting that it should be the states, not the federal government, that controlled seabed resources. After Eisenhower won the presidency, Truman made a last-ditch attempt to circumvent Congress. Four days before leaving office, he issued an executive order declaring the entire U.S. continental shelf a naval petroleum reserve, as Roosevelt had considered fifteen years earlier. But Eisenhower immediately overturned the order.

Despite the new president's stated position, fissures emerged within the Eisenhower administration regarding the continental shelf. The attorney general and State Department considered bills introduced in the Senate to be excessive. One area of disagreement was over how the territorial sea and continental shelf should be measured. Many of the states argued for the right to draw straight baselines between points on the coast, rather than following the natural low-water line, as the starting point for measuring offshore jurisdiction. This would allow them to connect offshore islands and avoid indentations in the coastline. The effect would be to extend the territorial sea beyond its traditional limits. The baselines issue was a major sticking point for State and the navy. Both worried about setting a precedent that would let others close off parts of the high seas. Countries might seek to ban passage through vast new internal waters by connecting offshore islands. Even worse, they might seek to close important international straits by drawing baselines across them.

The International Court of Justice had set an important precedent in 1952 by ruling that Norway could use straight baselines to measure its fisheries zones. But the State Department refused to budge. In March 1953, Assistant Secretary of State for Congressional Relations Thruston Morton wrote to Senator Henry Jackson, warning, "Any change of position regarding the 3-mile limit on the part of the United States is likely to be seized upon by other states as justification or excuse for broader and even extravagant claims over their adjacent seas."[14] The department had learned the lesson of unintended consequences following the Truman Proclamations. The baselines question would be an important sticking point in future law of the sea negotiations. And excessive straight baselines remain a frequent target for U.S. objections to this day, including in the South China Sea.

The U.S. Congress passed the Submerged Lands Act in April 1953, and President Eisenhower signed it into law a month later. The act gave the states ownership of the seabed beneath their territorial seas. Should that be deemed unconstitutional, the law also gave them the right to exploit seabed resources over which the federal government held title. The territorial sea was to be measured from the low-water line, as the State Department had urged. But the department's concerns were ignored when it came to the breadth of the territorial sea. A floor amendment set the maximum size of a state's boundaries at 3 miles in the Atlantic and Pacific but up to 9 miles in the Gulf of Mexico, where lawmakers sought to keep up with Mexican claims.

A few months later, Congress passed and the president signed the Outer Continental Shelf Lands Act. This authorized the federal government to lease the continental shelf beyond the territorial sea for the first time. An early version of the bill sought to declare U.S. "sovereignty" over the shelf, but that was replaced with "jurisdiction, control, and power of disposition," following objections from the State Department. The law defined the limits of the outer continental shelf as "the point where the continental slope leading to the true ocean bottom begins," at an approximate depth of 200 meters. And Congress carefully specified that the act "does not in anywise affect the character as high seas of the waters above that seabed and subsoil nor their use with respect to navigation and fishing."[15] This is where the United States and most European partners would try to hold the line: a narrow territorial sea (despite Congress mucking about in the Gulf) and economic rights to the seabed up to a depth of 200 meters, but no rights to the waters above it.

The Organization of American States convened a special conference in March 1956 to discuss the continental shelf and law of the sea. The United States was clearly outnumbered; nearly all Latin American governments had by that time claimed sovereign rights over waters well beyond the territorial sea. U.S. negotiators therefore insisted that the conference make no decisions without unanimous consent. The participants reached only one major substantive agreement, on a definition for the continental shelf: "The sea-bed and subsoil of the continental shelf . . . adjacent to the coastal state, outside the area of the territorial sea, and to a depth of 200 meters or, beyond that limit, to where the depth of the superadjacent waters admits of the exploitation of the natural resources . . . appertain exclusively to that state and are subject to its jurisdiction and control."[16] That language was forwarded to the International Law Commission of the United Nations, which incorporated it into its final report on the territorial sea and high seas presented a few months later.

The International Law Commission's report included seventy-three articles covering customary international law and state practice regarding the territorial sea, contiguous zone, continental shelf, and high seas. The most important issue on which the members failed to reach agreement was the width of the territorial sea. They could say only that the limit was somewhere between 3 and 12 miles.[17] The commission recommended that the United Nations organize an international conference to discuss the law of the sea and draw up relevant conventions. After some debate, in February 1957 the General Assembly voted to hold the first United Nations Conference on the Law of the Sea, since dubbed UNCLOS I.

Successes and Failures in Geneva

Roughly seven hundred delegates from eighty-six countries gathered in Geneva from February to April 1958 to debate the International Law Commission's findings. Prince Wan Waithayakon of Thailand was chosen as president of the convention.[18] Indonesia, the Philippines, the Federation of Malaya, and the ROC all took part. So did the Republic of (South) Vietnam by virtue of membership in several UN agencies (though it had been denied a seat in the General Assembly in 1957). The Democratic Republic of (North) Vietnam and the PRC were excluded. The Soviet Union and the nonaligned states protested their absence, along with those of East Germany and North Korea, but without success.

UNCLOS I attempted to hammer out agreement on all the issues that had plagued the law of the sea for the past several decades. The United Nations Secretariat established the rules of procedure, setting up four committees to review components of the report drafted by the International Law Commission. A fifth committee was added at the insistence of landlocked states to deal with their access to the sea. The committees arrived at decisions by a simple majority. Proposals were then voted on in the main conference, where they required two-thirds support for passage.

The conference was hampered by disagreements between three major factions: the West, the Soviet bloc, and the newly independent nations of Asia and Africa. The U.S. delegation entered the negotiations determined to set narrow limits on the territorial sea and fishing zones. American negotiators had limited flexibility on these issues. The U.S. distant-water fishing lobby would reject any coastal state jurisdiction beyond a 12-mile contiguous zone. The U.S. Navy might grudgingly recognize a territorial sea of 6 miles, but no more. Anything larger would entirely cover key straits in the Mediterranean, Southeast Asia, and Japan. Ships would still be able to pass through such international straits, but aircraft could not. And submarines would be required to transit on the surface. This was unacceptable, not least because it would compromise America's new submarine-based nuclear deterrent.

In effect, the United States was willing to accept what had seemed like radical positions just a quarter-century earlier at the League of Nations' international law conference. Unfortunately, what would have been good enough in 1930 would prove insufficient in 1958. The Europeans generally shared the U.S. view, though some were more determined to hold the line on a 3-mile territorial sea. But the newly constituted North Atlantic Treaty Organization (NATO) didn't agree on everything. Canada, for instance, endorsed the liberal use of straight baselines over U.S. objections. And Iceland broke ranks entirely by supporting a 12-mile territorial sea.

The Soviet bloc, which controlled eleven votes, wanted more. It was firmly committed to a 12-mile territorial sea and opposed to compulsory dispute settlement in any agreements. Its members also clashed with the U.S. and European participants over the rules governing "innocent passage," meaning a vessel's right to pass through a country's territorial sea for the sole purpose of transit. The Soviets demanded that foreign warships be required to obtain permission before undertaking innocent passage through the territorial sea.[19]

The newly independent states of Africa and Asia were loosely bound by a demand for change in the customary international law crafted by their colonizers. They were also generally opposed to compulsory dispute settlement. But beyond that, there was considerable variety in their negotiating positions. The ten Arab states were firmly united behind a 12-mile territorial sea, while others were more ambivalent. The Philippines and Indonesia opposed nearly every territorial sea proposal, insisting on a wholly new concept: that archipelagic states be able to draw baselines connecting their various islands, and that the space between these baselines should be internal waters. The idea was originally Indonesia's, where, a year earlier, Prime Minister Djuanda Kartawidjaja had declared a 12-mile territorial sea measured from baselines connecting the archipelago's islands. He asserted that all the space within those lines was Indonesia's internal waters. The United States, European countries, and the Soviet Union had all decried the declaration.[20] Indonesia and the Philippines found little support for the archipelagic concept at the Geneva conference. But they would eventually be vindicated.

Latin American states also presented a variety of views and didn't fit neatly into any of the major factions. Some favored expansive maritime rights. But it was clear from the start that the proponents of a 200-mile fishing zone were isolated. The International Law Commission had based its fisheries recommendations on the outcomes of a 1955 International Technical Conference on the Living Resources of the Sea convened by the Food and Agriculture Organization. That conference had agreed that coastal states had a special interest in conserving fish stocks near their shores. The wave of regional fisheries conventions over the previous decade proved there was wide agreement on that point. But regional conservation agreements were one thing; exclusive fishing rights for the coastal state were quite another. The NATO and Soviet blocs were united in opposing such rights beyond 12 miles, at the most.[21]

Given these divisions, it was no small feat that the conference reached agreement on four treaties. The first and most difficult was the Convention on the Territorial Sea and the Contiguous Zone. The treaty confirmed that states had sovereignty over a territorial sea measured from their coastlines and island territories. It laid out the methods for establishing baselines from which to measure that territorial sea. And it provided guidelines for delimiting overlapping boundaries between states. Notably, the treaty permitted straight baselines, including across historic bays up to 24 miles. This was a major concession by the United States, which had sought much more restrictive rules.[22]

But the conference failed to settle the size of the territorial sea. The camps were hopelessly far apart on this question, as well as the related debate over fishing zones. U.S. negotiators tried to forge a compromise. First, they proposed a 3-mile territorial sea and an additional 9-mile contiguous zone in which the coastal state would have exclusive fishing rights. But the Soviet bloc and most developing states were too entrenched in their support for a 12-mile territorial sea. Meanwhile many of the Europeans along with the United States' own distant-water fishing interests opposed exclusive fishing rights that far from shore.

On a second attempt, the U.S. team proposed a 6-mile territorial sea and an additional 6-mile contiguous zone in which historical fishing rights by other states would be recognized. Three other proposals competed for support in the committee. Canada tweaked the American plan by seeking exclusive fishing rights in the contiguous zone. The Soviet Union again demanded a 12-mile territorial sea, eliminating the need for such a zone. And a coalition of Latin American and Asian states, including Indonesia, proposed that countries be able to claim any combination of territorial sea and contiguous zone up to a combined 12 miles. None of these won passage in the committee. They were all reintroduced in the plenary, where they failed again. The American plan received the most support but fell seven votes short of a two-thirds majority.[23] In the end, negotiators could agree only on a limited contiguous zone—a band of high seas in which states could exercise customs and immigration control. This granted no jurisdiction over fisheries. The new zone started at the edge of the territorial sea, which was left undefined, and ended 12 miles from shore.[24]

The rules governing foreign warships undertaking innocent passage through the territorial sea also provoked heated debate. The International Law Commission had suggested that "the coastal state may make the passage of warships through the territorial sea subject to previous authorization or notification."[25] The U.S. and European delegates fiercely opposed a requirement for "authorization." They narrowly won two-thirds support in the plenary to have it stripped from the text. The Soviet Union and others rallied an even larger majority against the text only mentioning "previous notification." So both were scrubbed from the convention. This was ironic since a supermajority of states clearly supported *at least* prior notification from foreign warships passing through the territorial sea. Had they codified that in 1958, such transits might not cause so much friction in the South China Sea and other waterways today.[26]

The second treaty negotiated at UNCLOS I was the Convention on the High Seas. Participants agreed that "the high seas being open to all nations, no State may validly purport to subject any part of them to its sovereignty."[27] There was considerable debate about which high seas freedoms should be listed in the treaty. The International Law Commission's draft report included four: the freedoms of navigation, fishing, overflight, and laying submarine cables and pipelines. These provoked some debate, with Peru trying to have fishing removed and others trying to add other rights. But no proposal gained enough support, so the list remained unchanged in the final convention. A Soviet effort to ban nuclear testing on the high seas met strong U.S. and European opposition. The disagreement threatened to stall progress on the convention until India forged a compromise. The nuclear testing question was referred to the General Assembly along with a resolution noting that many countries worried it threatened high seas freedoms.[28]

Next up was the Convention on Fishing and Conservation of the Living Resources of the High Seas. Negotiations were relatively amicable. States had already agreed to most of its underlying principles during the 1955 Technical Conference on Living Resources of the Sea. The convention declared it the responsibility of all states to prevent overfishing and conserve the "living resources of the high seas." The only contentious debate was over whether coastal states could impose unilateral conservation measures without negotiating with distant-water fishing nations. A compromise was reached that required a six-month negotiating period. If negotiations failed, unilateral conservation measures by coastal states could remain in effect while an arbitral commission decided the issue. The convention also prohibited parties from declaring reservations to its key components.[29] As a result of the compulsory arbitration process, the Soviet bloc refused to sign, though it indicated support for the substance of the convention.

Finally, there was the Convention on the Continental Shelf. This codified the right of countries to exploit the mineral resources of the shelf beyond their territorial seas. The convention adopted the definition of the shelf that the Organization of American States had reached two years earlier. The only successful amendment came from the Philippines, which specified that it applied equally to coastal states and islands.[30] Countries were to have exclusive rights to the seabed to a depth of 200 meters *or* to the maximum depth at which it was possible to exploit resources. The distinction was mostly academic given the technical barriers to mining at greater depths. If the continental shelves of adjacent states overlapped, they should negotiate a boundary. Failing that, the boundary should be the median line between their coasts unless "special circumstances" applied.[31]

Among the countries bordering the South China Sea, only the ROC signed all four of the treaties in 1958. Indonesia and the Philippines refused to endorse the Convention on the Territorial Sea and the Contiguous Zone because it didn't include their concept of archipelagic waters and baselines. Indonesia signed the other three; the Philippines did not.[32] South Vietnam had taken part in the debates within the continental shelf committee and objected to the clause allowing claims deeper than 200 meters based on exploitability.[33] It didn't sign any of the four conventions. Neither did the Federation of Malaya, though it soon acceded to all four.[34]

The first UNCLOS was successful in many respects. It codified much of the customary law of the sea and formally established the new regime of the continental shelf. But it failed to answer a fundamental question: the breadth of the territorial sea. Before heading home, negotiators recommended that the United Nations hold a second conference to try again. Following their advice, UNCLOS II convened two years later. Representatives from eighty-eight countries gathered for the short negotiation from March to April 1960. Prince Wan Waithayakon again presided over the conference.[35] The only topics of discussion were the breadth of the territorial sea and contiguous fishing zone. All debates happened in a single Committee of the Whole.

Few countries had made new claims or adjusted their negotiating positions. The initial discussions rehashed familiar debates over the same proposals introduced two years earlier. But then the United States and Canada brought forward a compromise around which most of the maritime powers and distant-water fishing states rallied. They proposed a 6-mile territorial sea and 6-mile contiguous fishing zone in which historic rights would be respected, but under more stringent rules. To claim historic rights, a country would need to have fished the area for at least five years. And those rights would be phased out over a ten-year period. The Soviet Union backed a counterproposal by eighteen mostly developing nations that would allow states to fix the limit of either their territorial sea or fishing zone at 12 miles. The U.S.-Canadian scheme was adopted by the Committee of the Whole, while the eighteen-nation proposal was narrowly defeated.

Debates then moved to the plenary, where another effort to establish a 12-mile territorial sea was easily defeated. The U.S.-Canadian proposal also failed to get the two-thirds majority needed. But Washington's hopes had already shifted to a third option. Brazil, Cuba, and Uruguay had proposed an amendment to the U.S.-Canadian proposal that would grant coastal states preferential fishing rights in the high seas beyond the 6-mile territorial sea and 6-mile contiguous zone. The United States supported the amendment despite its prior opposition to such claims and outcries from the distant-water fishing lobby. The American delegation's top priority was arresting the spread of 12-mile territorial sea claims. And the only path to a two-thirds majority would be by combining the NATO-aligned votes with those pushing for 200-mile fishing zones. The lobbying got so intense that letters from President Eisenhower were hand-delivered to key foreign leaders.[36]

Washington thought it had the votes right up to the end. Japan initially voiced support but then abstained in the face of fierce opposition from its domestic fishing industry. Ecuador pledged to abstain if Washington would lift fines levied against it by Congress for seizing American fishing vessels; negotiators couldn't guarantee that, so Ecuador voted no. Chile also said it would abstain, but it needed permission from neighboring Peru. The two had signed a treaty pledging to uphold their respective 200-mile claims in international negotiations. Peru said no. The final tally was fifty-four to twenty-eight, with five abstentions—one vote shy of a two-thirds majority.[37]

UNCLOS II had failed by the narrowest, most idiosyncratic of margins. But it might have been doomed anyway. Had a joint proposal succeeded, states already claiming 12-mile territorial seas would have been loath to walk them back. And many countries that voted yes did so reluctantly. Ratification would have been difficult across the board, not least in the United States. Still, it leads to some interesting hypotheticals. Could the Americans and Europeans have eventually gained global acceptance of the 6-mile territorial sea? Or would it have become yet another rift in the Cold War, preventing further progress on the law of the sea? And would preferential fishing rights have satisfied developing coastal states? Or were exclusive rights, which eventually took the form of today's exclusive economic zone, inevitable?

Between Conferences

The divisions that doomed UNCLOS II—between the Western and Soviet blocs, maritime powers and developing states, and coastal and distant-water fishing nations—also slowed adoption of the four treaties signed in 1958. The pacts needed only twenty-two ratifications, but they took years to hit that mark. The U.S. Congress ratified all four in April 1961. Malaya had done the same in December 1960. But the other parties to the South China Sea disputes remained ambivalent. Indonesia ratified the Convention on the High Seas in August 1961 but with a reservation that it still considered the seas within the archipelago to be internal waters. This provoked another round of objections from Australia, Europe, and the United States. Jakarta never ratified the other two conventions it had signed. In 1970, the ROC finally ratified the Convention on the Continental Shelf but not the others, despite having signed them.[38]

The least controversial of the treaties, the Convention on the High Seas, reached twenty-two ratifications in 1962. The territorial sea and continental shelf treaties entered into force in 1964. The Convention on Fishing and Conservation of the Living Resources of the High Seas didn't secure the necessary ratifications until 1966. By that time, UN membership had expanded to 122 countries, most of which were either unhappy with key components of UNCLOS I or had taken no part in it. The treaties provided an important codification of international maritime law to that point, but they also highlighted how much was left unsettled.

The immediate effects of UNCLOS I and II were modest. States continued to declare territorial seas and contiguous zones at the same uneven pace as before. One of these was the PRC. While it had no seat at the table, Beijing watched the negotiations in Geneva closely and generally followed Moscow's lead. A few months after the first conference, the Second Taiwan Strait Crisis erupted. In the middle of the fighting, the PRC declared a 12-mile territorial sea from its coast, including "the Dongsha [Pratas] Islands, the Xisha [Paracel] Islands, the Zhongsha [Macclesfield Bank and Scarborough Shoal] Islands, the Nansha [Spratly] Islands and all other islands belonging to China."[39] It is, however, debatable how much officials in Beijing actually intended to claim with this declaration.

The PRC had adopted the ROC government's list of 159 South China Sea "islands" in 1952, but it seems absurd to think that it intended to claim 12-mile territorial seas around all of them. Anyone looking at the list could see that many of the entries were underwater shoals (*ansha*) and banks (*tan*).[40] A lot of the others were ambiguously named reefs (*jiao*) at which Beijing had no way to tell if there was dry land. The PRC had a clear idea of conditions only in the eastern Paracels, where in 1955 it had landed forces on Woody Island. It likely knew something of the geography in the rest of the Paracels and at Pratas Reef, though how much is unclear. And surely someone in power knew that Macclesfield Bank was underwater. But PRC officials had a very fuzzy picture of the Spratlys. It would be decades before they knew exactly what they were claiming there. All in all, when the PRC issued its territorial sea declaration, it could know for sure only that it was claiming 12 miles around Woody Island, a few other features in the Paracels, and Pratas. At most, it could have added to the list the seven Spratlys that France annexed in 1933.

Despite later revisionism, this 1958 declaration was the first Chinese claim to waters within the South China Sea. The PRC did not claim any maritime rights beyond the territorial sea. Neither did the ROC. Although Beijing had adopted the nine-dash line along with Nanjing's list of islands in 1952, there is no evidence that Chinese leaders saw it as a claim to waters or seabed. It is not mentioned in the 1958 declaration or any other maritime laws or statements from this period. Neither did the Chinese government assert "historic rights" over the South China Sea or use any of the other language that today serves as a stand-in for the nine-dash line. The dashes were a convenient depiction of China's territorial claim to islands, not to the waters around them.

Indonesia in 1960 reiterated its claim to a 12-mile territorial sea and internal waters within a network of straight baselines.[41] The Philippines followed suit in 1961, declaring its own baselines and internal waters between islands. But this hardly registered because at the same time, Manila took an even more controversial step. It formally expanded its territorial sea all the way to the limits of the 1898 Treaty of Paris between Spain and the United States. Those limits extended up to 300 miles from the Philippine coast in the Pacific. They weren't quite that excessive in the South China Sea, but still went far beyond 12 miles. Manila would subsequently claim that the 1898 treaty had always been recognized as ceding waters as well as land. But that was never the interpretation of the U.S. government. The Philippines had first voiced this controversial position in a 1955 note to the International Law Commission.[42] And when that was roundly criticized during the UNCLOS I negotiations, the Philippine Foreign Office's legal advisor had indicated that Manila would reverse course.[43] The subsequent decision to forge ahead would hobble Philippine efforts to cast itself as a good actor on the international maritime stage for decades.

For the South China Sea littoral countries, new claims broke down along more obvious Cold War lines. North Vietnam in 1964 joined the rest of the

Soviet bloc in declaring a 12-mile territorial sea. South Vietnam, by contrast, followed the U.S. lead and in 1965 reiterated its commitment to a 3-mile territorial sea.[44] The ROC also stuck with 3 miles. Malaya (Malaysia after 1963) did too until 1969, when it expanded its claim to 12 miles ahead of boundary talks with Indonesia.[45]

3

Settling on Dangerous Ground

1954–1974

HENRY KISSINGER, SECRETARY OF STATE: What are those, the Spratlys? (Pointing to the map.)

ADM. THOMAS MOORER, CHAIRMAN OF THE JOINT CHIEFS OF STAFF: No, the Spratlys are south of the Paracels.

WILLIAM COLBY, CIA DIRECTOR: The problem is that the Spratlys are claimed by everybody.

SECRETARY KISSINGER: We have never taken a position on these islands?

KENNETH RUSH, DEPUTY SECRETARY OF STATE: Are they occupied?

MONTEAGLE STEARNS, DEPUTY ASSISTANT SECRETARY OF STATE: Yes, we think there is a garrison on them.

MR. RUSH: Who has troops?

MR. STEARNS: There is a Philippine garrison on them, I think.

SECRETARY KISSINGER: How did the fight get started? Who started the fight over the Paracels?
—Minutes of Washington Special Action Group Meeting, January 25, 1974[1]

In the wake of World War II, U.S. policymakers concluded that it was necessary to maintain a forward military presence in Asia. This would help maintain regional stability, deter potential adversaries (the Soviet Union and PRC), and ultimately guarantee U.S. national security and prosperity. But the U.S. Pacific territories were not sufficient for the task. It was made possible only through mutual defense pacts forged in the postwar years. These included alliances with the Philippines, Australia, New Zealand (until 1986), the Republic of China (until 1979), Japan, South Korea, and Thailand.[2] Its allies provided the United States access and support that no adversary could match. In exchange, those allies expected the protection of the U.S. security umbrella.

On Dangerous Ground. Gregory B. Poling, Oxford University Press. © Oxford University Press 2022.
DOI: 10.1093/oso/9780197633984.003.0004

This system persisted through the tumultuous decades of the Cold War and into the present day. It survives because the remaining allies, along with security partners like Singapore, continue to see the U.S. presence as a regional stabilizer. And for all that time, the need to maintain the "hub-and-spokes" alliance network has been a central factor in U.S. decisions regarding the South China Sea. Until the 1970s, most of the parties to the disputes were U.S. allies, and so Washington had to balance credibility with each against fears of entrapment in a conflict that could pit one ally against another.

U.S. policy was also constrained by the nature of the claims, particularly in the Spratly Islands. No party had an airtight case. The United States hadn't picked sides during the earlier arguments between France, Japan, and the ROC— at least, not until Tokyo's claims passed beyond the limits that Washington considered legally justifiable. The United States had even less incentive to weigh in after the war. This balance between alliance credibility and official neutrality would eventually shift. The number of allies involved would dwindle, the threat of violence would grow, and new maritime claims would cross the long-standing U.S. commitment to freedom of the seas. But it would be a gradual and uncomfortable evolution for Washington—one that would never quite satisfy its first and last ally in the disputes, the Philippines.

The Paracels Divided

None of the parties to the South China Sea disputes was happy with the status quo left by the 1951 San Francisco Peace Conference, but all had bigger concerns in its immediate aftermath. China was consumed by civil war and the cross-Strait hostilities that followed. France was facing a much more tenacious insurgency in Vietnam than it had expected. This meant neither had much attention to spare for the islands of the South China Sea. When the ROC had withdrawn from Woody Island and Itu Aba in 1950, the small French Vietnamese garrison on Pattle Island contained the only occupants left in either island group. But Paris made no effort to extend its control to the eastern half of the Paracels or to reestablish a foothold in the Spratlys.

In May 1954, Viet Minh forces handed France a humiliating defeat during the Battle of Dien Bien Phu, ending Paris's hopes of reestablishing colonial dominion over Indochina. Two months later, France and Ho Chi Minh's government in northern Vietnam signed the Geneva Accords, along with China, the Soviet Union, and the United Kingdom. The agreement temporarily divided Vietnam along the 17th parallel pending national elections to be held two years later. The French-backed State of Vietnam in the south refused to sign. So did the United States, which had supported France's fight against the Viet Minh. Both pledged not to undermine the agreement, but that didn't last long. Less than a year later, the United States supported the establishment of a new Republic of Vietnam government based in Saigon.

In 1956, after refusing to hold the elections mandated by the Geneva Accords, this government of South Vietnam officially declared itself the successor to France's claim to the Paracels and Spratlys. The Paracels connection was clear: Paris had always maintained that it was acting on Annam's behalf in claiming the Paracels based on Emperor Gia Long's annexation of 1816. In 1950, Paris had formally transferred authority over the Paracels to the State of Vietnam, though French troops remained on Pattle Island.[3]

The PRC entered the fray in August 1955 when it quietly occupied Woody Island.[4] From that point on, Chinese forces maintained control over the eastern half of the Paracels, called the Amphitrite Group, but left the Crescent Group in the west to the French and Vietnamese. In April 1956, South Vietnamese troops relieved the French garrison on Pattle Island.[5] They soon occupied nearby Robert and Money Islands as well.[6] The South Vietnamese government also issued a license to a Saigon businessman to extract phosphate from all three islands—a practice that continued until 1963.[7] In early 1959, South Vietnam occupied Duncan and Drummond Islands, evicting eighty Chinese fishers from the former (see Figure 3.1). A year later, the first Vietnamese civilian officials were posted to the Paracels to administer the islands, which were given the status of a *xa*, or village, under Quang Nam province.[8]

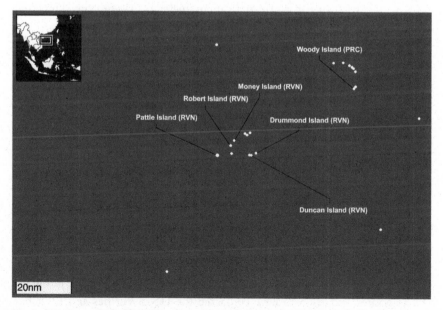

Figure 3.1 Paracel Islands, 1959. Created using Mapcreator and OpenStreetMap.

Freedomland and Its Discontents

To the south, France made no effort to reassert control over the seven Spratly Islands it had once annexed. Nor did it seek to transfer administration over them to the State of Vietnam. French authorities had administratively attached the islands to Cochinchina's Ba Ria province in 1933.[9] But Cochinchina was a directly administered French colony, not a protectorate like Annam and Tonkin. That created uncertainty over whether Paris's claim automatically transferred to the independent State of Vietnam and its successors. Saigon said yes; France said no. In a September 1955 diplomatic note, Paris unequivocally recognized Vietnamese sovereignty over the Paracels but said it still claimed the Spratlys as part of the French Union.[10]

The argument seemed academic, as the Spratly Islands had sat unoccupied since ROC forces abandoned Itu Aba in 1950. But two private citizens, one American and one Filipino, were hatching quixotic plans that would upend that status quo. The first was Morton Meads, an American living in Manila.

Meads and his collaborators would later declare that he was the inheritor of an independent state in the Spratly Islands called the Kingdom of Humanity. They would trace his claim to a supposed British forebear, James George Meads, captain of the *Modeste*. According to these stories, the elder Meads had discovered the Spratlys in the late 1870s. He had dubbed the area the Humanity Sea and given his own name to Itu Aba. Then in 1914, Franklin Meads, son of James, had returned and established the Kingdom of Humanity on "Meads Island" along with several British and American compatriots. Title to the "kingdom" eventually passed to Franklin's grandson, Morton, in 1946.[11]

The truth is that Meads was a confidence man whose tall tales changed considerably over the years. He was discharged from the U.S. Army in Manila in 1946 and engaged in various business ventures, mainly the sale of army surplus. The first public reports of his claim to the Spratlys appeared in the Manila papers in early 1955. At this point the stories, presumably spread by Meads himself, claimed that he had first traveled to Itu Aba in 1945. There he found the Kingdom of Humanity, already home to thousands of happy citizens who inexplicably named Meads their consul and commercial agent. Only decades later would the origin story be retconned to make him royalty.

Meads had "official" stamps from the kingdom printed for sale and attempted the same with paper money. The newspaper stories soon caught the attention of the Philippine military, which dispatched a patrol bomber to have a look. As expected, it found the islands empty. Meads was arrested on criminal and civil charges related to his business practices, though these were eventually dropped. His associates also seem to have contacted the U.S. Securities and Exchange

Commission in 1955 and 1956 to try to stake a claim to resource rights over the islands.[12]

Meads and company likely never stepped foot on the Spratly Islands. And for the most part, they have been written off as a salacious footnote in South China Sea history. But that judgment might be too hasty. Their activities drew the attention of powerful people. And they may have unwittingly set the stage for Filipino businessman Tomás Cloma, whose exploits less than a year later would spark a race to occupy the Spratlys. In response to the "Kingdom of Humanity" stories, prominent Filipino military officers and politicians began to take up Elpidio Quirino's old argument for Manila to claim the Spratlys on national security grounds. One of these was Vice President Carlos Garcia, who would champion the cause for the next few years.[13] He also became Cloma's most important booster.

It must have been an open secret that Filipino leaders were debating a claim at this time. The ROC ambassador in Manila responded by announcing that Taipei would contest any Philippine claim.[14] This is corroborated by a 1956 U.S. State Department intelligence report, stating that the ROC ambassador sent a note to Philippine officials after the Meads episode insisting that any ships visiting the Spratlys would be violating Chinese territorial waters.[15] The report's authors disavowed official American backing for Meads's actions, suggesting rumors to that effect. And they drew a direct connection between his scheme and the more famous events of the following year. The report says, "The recent scramble to claim the islands first began in June 1955 [with Meads's claim]."[16]

The person at the center of those events, Tomás Cloma, was familiar with the South China Sea. As a young man in 1933, he had taken a job as an assistant shipping editor with the *Manila Bulletin*. In 1947, he and his brother Filemon had founded the Visayan Fish Corporation with a small fleet of decommissioned American navy tugs converted into fishing boats. That year, Filemon had reportedly been fishing off Palawan when a storm drove him to seek shelter in the Spratlys. Afterward, according to the brothers, they began developing plans to commercially exploit the islands, much as Japanese business interests had in the 1920s and 1930s. They hoped to develop fish canneries and phosphate mines.[17] But first they needed a legal basis to do so. And despite the interest shown by President Quirino and others, the Philippines had made no formal claim to the islands.

Cloma would later claim to have returned to the Spratlys in 1948 and found them unoccupied. That is possible; ROC forces weren't on Itu Aba at the start of the year.[18] But he would also say he was unable to find the islands, much less evidence of prior claims, on any map.[19] That is hard to believe, especially given his background in the shipping and fishing industries and access to senior

Philippine officials. Regardless, Cloma declared that the islands were unclaimed and free to whoever was bold enough to take them.

In early 1956, he undertook a thirty-eight-day expedition to several of the islands and declared them "The Free Territory of Freedomland."[20] His expedition was not officially sanctioned by the Philippine government, but it had the blessing of several prominent politicians. Foremost was Vice President and Foreign Secretary Carlos Garcia, a friend of Cloma's who attended the expedition's farewell party.[21] And Cloma made clear that he saw Freedomland as a territory of the Philippines, not an independent country. On May 21, he sent a note to Garcia explaining this and asking the government to back his claim.[22] Garcia supported Cloma's activities but couldn't win President Ramon Magsaysay to his cause.[23]

Cloma's expedition provoked outcries from Beijing, Saigon, Paris, and Taipei. The PRC issued an official objection in May. This was followed by a Declaration of Sovereignty over the Nansha (Spratly) Islands, which insisted, "China's legitimate sovereignty over the Nansha Islands shall under no circumstances be violated by any country on any ground or by any means."[24] But Beijing wasn't ready to pursue the matter further. Saigon issued a declaration on June 1 reiterating its claim to the Spratlys. Paris did the same on June 7, repeating its position that the Paracels belonged to Vietnam but the Spratlys remained French.[25]

But the ROC had the most forceful response. In early June, it dispatched naval ships to patrol the Spratlys. A month later, Taiwanese troops were redeployed to Itu Aba after a six-year absence.[26] To patch things up with Taipei, Magsaysay's office issued a communiqué insisting that Cloma had acted in his private capacity and the Philippines was not officially claiming the Spratlys.[27] Cloma now realized that Manila wasn't going to back him. In early July, he declared the establishment of the independent state of Freedomland with himself as president.[28] President Magsaysay was irate and, according to press reports, ordered Garcia to "cut short Cloma's comic opera before it got really serious."[29]

In August, South Vietnam dispatched a navy cruiser, though it only erected a sovereignty marker on Spratly Island before sailing home.[30] Two months later, Saigon officially placed the Spratlys under the administration of Phuoc Tuy province. Things took a dangerous turn in October when two ROC Navy ships boarded one of Cloma's vessels near North Danger Reef. It was captained by his brother Filemon. The Taiwanese sailors seized his ship's weapons and maps, forced Filemon to sign a statement apologizing for trespassing in Chinese territory, and then dismantled all the structures Cloma's people had set up on nearby islands.[31] In an act of either hubris or desperation, Cloma traveled to New York to lodge a formal complaint at the United Nations. But Philippine diplomats there informed him that he had no standing to do so and wouldn't receive support from Manila.[32]

In December, Cloma wrote to President Magsaysay, pleading one last time for government support. The reply, which came from the vice president, took three months. Garcia wrote to his old friend, agreeing that the features within Freedomland were previously unclaimed. Cloma had carefully drawn the borders of his new state to exclude Spratly Island itself. That allowed him, and Garcia, to pretend that Freedomland was distinct from the islands contested by China, France, and South Vietnam. But it was a weak gambit. Freedomland covered every island France had claimed in 1933 *except* Spratly, which it missed by only 15 nautical miles (Figure 3.2).

Garcia also supplied Cloma with a second justification for his actions; he wrote that in the opinion of the Philippine Department of Foreign Affairs, the San Francisco Treaty had placed the western Spratlys—those annexed by France and then controlled by Japan—under the trusteeship of the Allies, including the Philippines. As a Filipino, Cloma was welcome to exploit them.[33] The Philippine government would eventually recycle these rationales when it made its official claim to the islands a decade and a half later. But Cloma wasn't looking for legal advice; he needed physical and diplomatic protection from the ROC. His government was offering none, and that effectively killed his dream of a commercial empire turned free state.

These developments prompted the United States to reexamine its position on the South China Sea. In August 1956, the State Department had drafted a

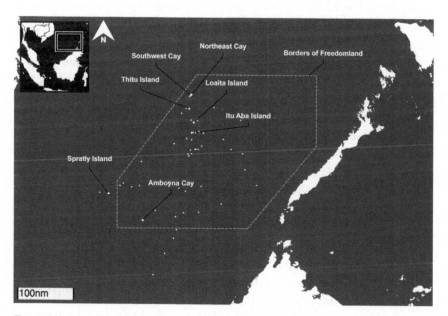

Figure 3.2 French annexations and the borders of Freedomland, 1956. Created using Mapcreator and OpenStreetMap.

classified intelligence report titled "Islands of the South China Sea." It showed a clear and mostly accurate understanding of the history and geography of the territorial disputes, and prior U.S. policy toward them. That clarity would often dissipate in the years that followed, as the South China Sea faded into the background of regional geopolitics. But Washington would rediscover the report during future crises. It provided a foundation on which American analysts and policymakers would build as the disputes evolved. That foundation is best captured in the report's abstract:

> The international status of these islands has never been settled. The United States has neither advanced claims of its own in the area *nor made any official determination of the merits of the respective claims of others.* Despite their small size and apparently limited usefulness, their strategic location and the nationalist sensitivities of the several claimants make it likely that these island groups will continue to attract international attention from time to time, and, as long as they continue to be visited or garrisoned by the contending parties, there remains the possibility of armed clashes.[34]

More than sixty years later, this assessment still holds true. Washington remains neutral regarding sovereignty, and one of its primary concerns is that the disputes could escalate into violence. The territorial disputes are still primarily driven by nationalism and a competition for strategic geography, though competition for resources has also played an important secondary role that couldn't be foreseen in 1956.

But not everything in the State Department report was so clear. For one thing, it refused to nail down the geographic scope of the dispute, saying that "there is no internationally-recognized definition of precisely what is referred to by the term 'Spratly Islands.'"[35] This left the U.S. government some wiggle room to distinguish between the Spratlys in the west and the Dangerous Ground in the east. Philippine officials seem to have been aware of this ambiguity in the U.S. position. And it helps explain their dogged insistence that Freedomland and the Spratlys were distinct entities. Interestingly, the State Department report claimed that the Foreign Office of the Philippines had considered formally claiming some of the islands in 1955 and 1956, perhaps to preempt Cloma, but held off because it lacked U.S. support.[36]

Amid all the position papers, diplomatic notes, and physical patrols that followed Cloma's expedition, one party was notably silent: the government of North Vietnam. Hanoi's position seems to have been intentionally unclear. This was due to its heavy reliance on Chinese support during its wars, first against France and then against South Vietnam and the United States. Ho's regime couldn't afford to alienate its patron, so it kept silent. Chinese authorities would later claim that during a conversation with a Chinese official in June 1956, North Vietnam's vice foreign minister Ung Van Khiem conceded that "according to Vietnamese data, the Xisha and Nansha Islands are historically part of Chinese territory."[37] Vietnam disputes that account. But even if it never recognized Beijing's sovereignty over the islands, Hanoi didn't make any claim of its own. In fact, it would spend the next decade and a half avoiding the issue. And when avoidance was no longer possible, North Vietnamese authorities would say what needed saying to keep the PRC on their side.

The most problematic example was in 1958, when China declared its 12-mile territorial sea.[38] Beijing made this claim from "all territories of the People's Republic of China, including . . . the Dongsha Islands, the Xisha Islands, the Zhongsha Islands, the Nansha Islands and all other islands belonging to China."[39] In response, North Vietnam's premier Pham Van Dong wrote to his Chinese counterpart Zhou Enlai, "We have the honour to solemnly inform you . . . that the Government of the Democratic Republic of Viet Nam recognizes and supports the declaration of the Government of the People's Republic of China on its decision concerning China's territorial sea. . . . The Government of the Democratic Republic of Viet Nam respects this decision and will instruct the responsible state organs that . . . they should strictly respect the decision that the breadth of China's territorial sea is twelve miles."[40] Unlike Khiem's alleged statement in 1956, Vietnam doesn't dispute the contents of this letter, but it insists that China misinterprets it. Addressing the matter in 1988, the Vietnamese Ministry of Foreign Affairs would write:

> [T]he nation was embroiled in a desperate war for survival when the statements were made; therefore what appeared to be a concession of the Truong Sa [Spratly Islands] to the PRC was actually just a strategic move to deny the United States use of the archipelago and the East Sea. Hanoi believed that any PRC sovereignty over the Truong Sa would be temporary: Viet Nam trusted China in all sincerity and believed that after the war all territorial problems [between the two countries] would be suitably resolved.[41]

In Beijing's eyes, the letter recognized China's claim to the Paracels and Spratlys. But according to Hanoi, Dong said the bare minimum to appease his Chinese allies without formally ceding anything. According to this interpretation, the final sentence referenced the breadth of China's territorial sea but not the claim to islands because North Vietnam was committing to respect the former without ceding the latter.

Manila and Saigon Join the Party

Official Philippine interest in the Spratly Islands waned following Cloma's exploits. In March 1957, the widely admired president Magsaysay was killed in a plane crash and Cloma's old friend Garcia succeeded to the office. But Garcia seemed to have lost his enthusiasm for the Spratly Islands. He never pushed a Philippine claim during his nearly five years in office, at least not publicly. Neither did his successor, Diosdado Macapagal. Perhaps Garcia was chastened by the fallout from the Cloma expedition. It had certainly shown that Manila couldn't pursue a claim without provoking a strong response from Taipei and Saigon. And with Taiwanese forces now on Itu Aba and the South Vietnamese Navy patrolling the islands, it was even riskier for the Philippines to try to move in. Finally, while Garcia and Macapagal weren't as close to Washington as Magsaysay had been, they were surely hesitant to pick a fight with South Vietnam or Taiwan—fellow American allies—and risk a U.S. backlash.[42]

South Vietnam was more active. It stepped up its naval presence and made symbolic landings on several islands. Between 1961 and 1963, South Vietnamese naval forces erected sovereignty markers and hoisted their flag over six of the seven islands claimed by France in 1933: Amboyna Cay, Loaita Island, Northeast Cay, Southwest Cay, Spratly Island, and Thitu Island. The seventh, Itu Aba, was in ROC hands. So the Vietnamese forces raised a flag as close as they could get, on Namyit Island, about 12 miles south. Saigon would continue to send regular naval patrols around these features throughout the 1960s but held off on permanent occupation.[43]

While the Philippines under Garcia and Magsaysay held back from active participation in the Spratly Islands dispute, it began to exercise more physical control over another feature farther north: Scarborough Shoal. Manila had continued the American practice of claiming the reef as part of the Philippines but paid it little attention in the postwar years. Then in the early 1960s, authorities began conducting surveys and cracked down on local smugglers who had been using the reef as a base of operations. In 1963, the Philippine Navy bombed piers and a warehouse that a criminal syndicate had constructed on the shoal. Two years later, the Philippines built a lighthouse on the reef along with a flagpole flying the national colors.[44]

Neither Taipei nor Beijing objected to these activities—a sharp contrast to how they responded to developments in the Paracels and Spratlys. In fact, they seemed to pay the shoal no mind at all. It had been included in the updated list of 159 "islands" claimed by the ROC in December 1947, at which point it had been renamed Minzhu Jiao (Democracy Reef). The PRC, finding that too subversive, would eventually change it to Huangyan Dao (Yellow Rock Island). But their claims to it would remain largely hypothetical until the 1990s.

In late 1965, Ferdinand Marcos assumed the presidency of the Philippines. More ambitious than his predecessors, he would finally realize Quirino's desire to formally claim part of the Spratly Islands. He ordered troops to visit several of the islands beginning in 1968. Two years later, Philippine forces quietly set up the country's first permanent outpost on Nanshan Island. They quickly occupied five more in 1971: Loaita Island, Northeast Cay, Southwest Cay, Thitu Island, and West York Island. Only then did Manila publicly announce what it had done. The government declared that securing the islands was necessary for national security and, more broadly, "to protect the interest of the state and its citizens."[45] The interests Marcos had in mind seemed about economics as much as security. In 1968, just before he dispatched troops to the islands, the Economic Commission for Asia and the Far East had speculated that the South China Sea might contain significant oil and gas deposits.[46] And as Filipino forces were landing on the Spratlys in 1970 and 1971, the country was undertaking its first surveys for oil off Palawan.[47]

These developments also brought an unexpected epilogue to the story of Morton Meads and his compatriots. In 1968, presumably hearing the rumors about oil and gas resources, they unsuccessfully petitioned the U.S. Board of Geographic Names to recognize their claim. By then, their kingdom had been rechristened the Kingdom of Humanity/Republic of Morac-Songhrati-Meads. Its self-appointed representatives said this was due to a dramatic series of events involving the breakup and reconstitution of their imagined state. That September, the assistant geographer of the U.S. State Department's Office of Strategic Research wrote to the kingdom's "ambassador extraordinary." It was strange that the State Department responded at all. The letter mainly restated U.S. neutrality regarding sovereignty over the islands. More interesting, it again drew a distinction between the Spratly Islands and the Dangerous Ground, suggesting Washington's position remained as ambiguous on this point as it had been in 1939 and 1956.[48]

In October 1971, just a month after the Philippine government announced that it had occupied part of the Spratlys, the U.S. Embassy in Manila received a formal affidavit from the assistant secretary of state security for the Kingdom of Humanity/Republic of Morac-Songhrati-Meads detailing the evidence of its claim. The next year, Meads himself reportedly wrote to President Marcos, Chiang Kai-shek, and UN Secretary General Kurt Waldheim asserting his rights. But the scheme ended in tragedy that June when a boat carrying most of the kingdom's self-appointed leaders sank in a typhoon off the Philippine coast, killing all aboard. Meads himself wasn't on the boat, but he never again pursued a claim to the Spratlys.[49]

As expected, the Philippine occupations reignited tensions with the ROC and South Vietnam. These developments put Washington in an awkward position: not only were all the parties U.S. allies; they were all supporting the war in Vietnam. Taiwan provided logistics and training support to South Vietnam. The Philippines had begun deploying medical and humanitarian personnel to the country in 1964. From 1966 to 1969, thousands of Filipino noncombat forces served in South Vietnam as part of the Philippine Civic Action Group. Most important, U.S. Naval Base Subic Bay and Clark Air Base in the Philippines were vital to the American war effort. But perhaps it was this interdependence that assured Marcos he could move into the Spratlys without too much risk. The United States and South Vietnam both needed the Philippines, and Washington would discourage Taipei from reacting too forcefully.

Still, the United States had to be concerned about potential violence between its allies, whether intentional or not. That danger became clear in July 1971, when Marcos accused Taiwanese forces on Itu Aba of firing on a boat and plane owned by Philippine congressman Ramon Mitra.[50] Then in 1973, a combination of security and economic concerns drove South Vietnam to establish its first base on Namyit Island, one of the seven islands on which it had planted sovereignty markers a decade earlier. Filipino troops had already occupied four of the others, and Saigon likely worried that they weren't done yet.[51] Potential seabed resources also created new incentives for South Vietnam to strengthen its position in the Spratlys. The same month that it occupied Namyit, the South Vietnamese government awarded its first offshore oil concessions to Mobil, Exxon, and a Shell subsidiary in Canada (Figure 3.3).[52]

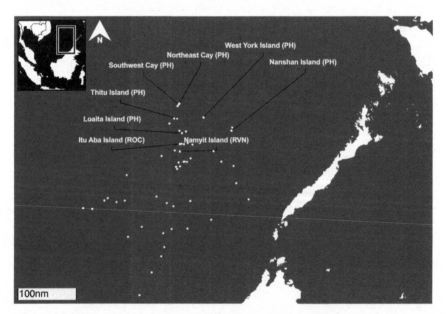

Figure 3.3 Spratly Islands occupied by the ROC, South Vietnam (RVN), and the Philippines, 1973. Created using Mapcreator and OpenStreetMap.

Philippine officials were still formulating legal justifications for their actions. They settled on a version of the arguments made by Cloma and Garcia. Manila insisted that the islands it had occupied didn't include those Spratlys legitimately claimed by other states. It asserted sovereignty over them based on Cloma's original declaration that Freedomland was unclaimed territory annexed on behalf of the Philippines.[53] The argument was shaky, but not crazy. No government had ever administered the islands occupied by the Philippines. France had annexed four of the six, but never occupied them; Nanjing and Tokyo had listed them among the Nansha Islands and the Shinnan Gunto, but that was just on paper. The argument for disaggregating the "Spratlys"—distinguishing those few islands which France, Japan, and most recently the ROC had physically administered from the many they had not—wasn't new. The United Kingdom had rejected France's attempt to claim all features within an arbitrarily drawn box. Several states had objected to Japan's attempt to claim the entire Shinnan Gunto as a single archipelago. The U.S. government in 1939 considered the Dangerous Ground a separate, unclaimed group of islands and reefs. And it still seemed open to that interpretation.

But the reliance on Freedomland as a basis for the official Philippine claim was also problematic. It suggested a claim far larger than just the islands Manila controlled. The borders of Freedomland as drawn by Cloma included Itu Aba, which had been occupied by France, Japan, and the ROC in turn, and Namyit Island, which was now in South Vietnamese hands. The claim also required selective amnesia since the Philippine government under Magsaysay had expressly disavowed Cloma's actions. In January 1974, Cloma himself weighed in. He publicly called on the government to support his claim to Freedomland before the International Court of Justice. But bringing himself to Marcos's attention was a mistake. The president invited him to Malacañang Palace, where Cloma reportedly agreed to sell his title to the islands.[54] But when negotiations dragged on for months, Marcos lost his patience. The seventy-year-old Cloma was placed under arrest in late October, one of his ships was confiscated, and the government threatened to charge him with illegally impersonating a naval officer. On December 4, 1974, after fifty-seven days in a cell, Cloma signed over the title to Freedomland to the Philippine government for one peso.[55]

The Battle of the Paracels

For almost twenty years, control of the Paracel Islands had been divided. The PRC controlled the eastern Amphitrite Group from its base on Woody Island. It also kept smaller garrisons on nearby Rocky Island and isolated Lincoln Island to the southeast.[56] South Vietnam maintained a smaller footprint in the western

Crescent Group, with a mostly civilian presence on Pattle Island. For most of that time, both countries had neglected their holdings. South Vietnam had stopped garrisoning Robert, Money, Duncan, and Drummond Islands. But China became more active in 1970, surveying nearby features and starting construction on a new harbor at Woody Island.[57] Within a few years, dwindling U.S. support for Saigon presented Beijing with an opportunity to upend the status quo.

On January 27, 1973, the United States and South Vietnam signed the Paris Peace Accords with North Vietnam and its southern client, the Provisional Revolutionary Government. Although Hanoi and Saigon violated the agreement early and often, it provided Washington the exit the American public demanded after more than a decade of fighting. Nearly all U.S. forces were withdrawn from Vietnam by March. The United States pledged continued support for the South Vietnamese military, and the Nixon administration left open the possibility of a renewed air campaign if Hanoi restarted hostilities. But the administration couldn't back up those promises. In June 1973, Congress overwhelmingly passed the Case-Church Amendment prohibiting military involvement in Vietnam without legislative approval. Washington still provided financial support to the South Vietnamese military, but Congress quickly began cutting those funds. Meanwhile, the North geared up for the war's final campaign.

That same year, the Chinese government tapped future leader Deng Xiaoping to organize an operation to seize control of the Paracels.[58] In December 1973, and perhaps as early as October, Chinese fishing vessels began operating around unoccupied islands in the western Crescent Group. They raised flags on a few and physically occupied at least one, Duncan Island. Chinese sources paint these as uncoordinated civilian activities. They also claim that in November, the South Vietnamese Navy began ramming these fishing boats and arresting their crews.[59] There is probably some truth to these accounts, but the Chinese boats were neither uncoordinated nor simply fishing. The PRC seems to have been purposely using them to establish beachheads as the first step toward a planned seizure of the western Paracels.

The U.S. Army Special Research Detachment would later conclude that the PRC had been preparing for an amphibious assault "at least by December 1973, and possibly as early as September 1973."[60] This was based on eyewitness reports from Guangxi province's Beihai Port, where hundreds of Chinese commandos were seen leaving aboard fishing trawlers each day for training exercises.[61] Nominal civilians would play a critical role in the operation—a forerunner of the professionalized maritime militia that operates across the South China Sea today. Fishing boats would be the first on the scene, depositing the Chinese vanguard before the battle. A larger militia force would reinforce them and draw first blood in the fighting.

On January 14, 1974, authorities in Saigon received reports of more Chinese boats congregating in the area. They sent a navy frigate to check. Upon arriving, the HQ-16—formerly the seaplane tender USS *Chincoteague*—confirmed two Chinese fishing vessels trying to establish a presence on unoccupied Robert Island. Vietnamese sources describe them as steel-hulled, armed militia boats. HQ-16 drove them away while South Vietnam rushed fourteen commandos to the scene aboard the HQ-4, which had once been the destroyer escort USS *Forster*. An American advisor, former Green Beret Gerald Kosh, accompanied them. Kosh had served in Vietnam before taking a civilian job with the U.S. Embassy as a regional liaison officer.[62]

Kosh's after-action report in combination with Chinese accounts seem to provide a complete account of the ensuing battle.[63] On January 16, he and the commandos arrived to find PRC forces already holding Duncan and Drummond Islands. Whether they were regular army units or militia is unclear. A small group of South Vietnamese meteorologists and guards still controlled Pattle Island. Over the next day, Vietnamese commandos were deposited on nearby Money and Robert Islands as well. Each side reinforced its naval presence, with South Vietnam dispatching the frigate HQ-5 and minesweeper HQ-10, both recommissioned U.S. Navy ships. Two Chinese submarine chasers, No. 271 and No. 274, arrived on the scene after picking up supplies and militia troops on Woody Island. They were soon joined by minesweepers No. 389 and No. 396.[64]

In the early hours of January 18, the PRC ships landed forty additional militia personnel on Drummond, Duncan, and Palm Islands (Figure 3.4). That evening,

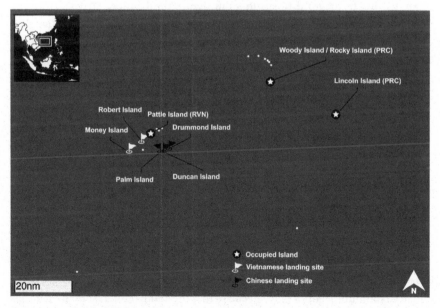

Figure 3.4 Battle of the Paracels starting positions, January 18, 1974. Created using Mapcreator and OpenStreetMap.

after a failed attempt to land his own forces on Duncan Island, the commander of the Vietnamese flotilla sent Kosh and a few other noncombatants to Pattle for safety. The next day, while the ships maneuvered around each other, twenty Vietnamese commandos succeeded in reaching Duncan and Palm Islands. They were greeted at the beaches by Chinese fire. Two were killed and the rest fell back, with several injured.

The four South Vietnamese Navy ships retaliated by opening fire on their Chinese counterparts. After this initial salvo, the smaller PRC vessels closed the distance, negating the advantages of the better armed but lumbering Vietnamese ships. The ensuing fight was intense, and two of the Chinese ships were seriously damaged. No. 389 had to be beached on Duncan Island after catching fire and taking on water. But they carried the day. HQ-10 was crippled after its magazine exploded, and the other three Vietnamese ships were forced to pull back after sustaining damage. Two more Chinese sub chasers belatedly arrived and fell upon HQ-10, sinking it near Antelope Reef.

The three surviving South Vietnamese Navy ships limped back to Danang, leaving the troops on Money, Robert, and Pattle Islands to their fate. The Chinese shelled the islands while patrol craft arrived with two companies of regular infantry. On January 20, they loaded the soldiers onto rafts and made for the beaches. Kosh and the mostly civilian occupants of Pattle were taken without a fight. The commandos on Robert, outnumbered more than ten to one, surrendered after a brief stand. Their fellows on Money Island had already done the math; they put to sea in a raft before the Chinese arrived. A fishing boat rescued them off the Vietnamese coast nine days later.[65] The PRC had completed its takeover of the Paracels with minimal losses, compared to more than one hundred Vietnamese killed or wounded and forty-nine personnel, including Kosh, captured.

Washington Plays Catch-Up

The clash caught the U.S. government by surprise. Records of many discussions by senior officials have since been declassified. They show an administration scrambling to gather basic facts about the South China Sea and unsure why violence had occurred, how much it mattered, or what might come next. The CIA on January 18 told President Gerald Ford that a clash "may have" occurred two days earlier. Word of the Vietnamese commandos rushing to confront PRC forces likely prompted this premature warning. But details were scarce. The intelligence community could only speculate that the sudden interest in the Paracels "may have been prompted by the prospect of finding oil on them or under the surrounding waters."[66] The next day Ford received a more accurate picture of the battle just hours after it had actually occurred. This indicates that American military and intelligence officials in Saigon were being informed of developments in near real time. But the president was incorrectly told that South Vietnam had pulled its personnel from the islands, not abandoned them to capture. And there was no mention of Kosh.

At this point, the intelligence community speculated that South Vietnam had somehow set off the clash by restating its claim to the Spratlys a few months before. That was probably the most recent time the South China Sea had come across American analysts' desks and so was the first thing they reached for when pressed for an explanation. In reality, Beijing had been preparing to seize the western Paracels since at least 1970. But the CIA had a much better idea of what both sides would do next: "The South Vietnamese are unlikely to seek further combat in view of the apparent Chinese determination to use force. Each side will accuse the other of starting the fighting, but it is unlikely that either seeks a prolonged military confrontation over the islands."[67]

Ford learned about Kosh on January 21. His daily intelligence briefing reported that "the South Vietnamese [had] abandoned their troops on the islands," along with the American liaison officer. Part of this section of the briefing remains classified, but it ended with yet another inaccurate guess at the reason for the clash: "Until recently, the South Vietnamese had maintained a presence only on Pattle Island. The appearance of Saigon's troops on neighboring islands may have provided the stimulus for Peking military actions."[68] In truth, Chinese troops had taken Duncan and Drummond first and attempted to occupy Robert Island as well. That the CIA considered Saigon's version of events unreliable isn't surprising. South Vietnam's government was working hard to spin the story of defeat into something more heroic.[69] Had it been responsible for starting the fight, it likely would have spun that too. The CIA may also have been too confident in assuming Beijing wouldn't risk its détente with Washington over what seemed like small stakes.

But China had astutely read the political environment. It gambled that it could engage in limited military action against South Vietnam without triggering a direct American response. During the crisis, the senior South Vietnamese Navy officer in charge had made two formal requests for assistance from the U.S. Seventh Fleet. He received no reply.[70] On January 21, a U.S. Department of Defense spokesperson confirmed that American forces were ordered not to get involved, while denying that Saigon had asked for help. He also insisted, incorrectly, that Kosh had been dispatched to the islands on a routine technical mission with no knowledge of the impending clash.[71]

South Vietnam called on the other parties to the 1973 Paris Peace Accords—the United States, North Vietnam, and its client Provisional Revolutionary Government of South Vietnam—to help organize an emergency session of the

UN Security Council, but to no avail. The North Vietnamese government would say only that it "deplored the use of force."[72] The Provisional Revolutionary Government was at pains to express concern without unduly upsetting Beijing. Its resulting statement explained that, "considering the complex nature of the problem, it needed to be examined on the basis of the principles of equality, mutual respect, friendship and good neighbourliness and settled by negotiation."[73]

It had been less than two years since Nixon's historic visit to Beijing and only eight months since the two sides had opened liaison offices in each other's capitals. In the days after the clash, top American officials focused on securing Kosh's release while minimizing the damage to the budding Sino-American relationship. This necessarily meant distancing themselves from the South Vietnamese position, which was made easier by their mistaken suspicions that Saigon started the fight. On January 23, Secretary of State and National Security Advisor Henry Kissinger met with Han Xu, acting chief of the PRC Liaison Office in Washington. He told the de facto Chinese ambassador:

> The South Vietnamese government is making a number of representations to international organizations, to SEATO [the Southeast Asia Treaty Organization] as well as to the United Nations. We wanted to let you know we do not associate ourselves with those representations. We are concerned, however, about the prisoners, and we noted that your government has indicated that the prisoners will be released at an appropriate time. We wanted to urge that this appropriate time be very soon, especially as there is an American included in that group. And that would certainly defuse the situation as far as the United States is concerned. That's really all I wanted to say about that issue.[74]

Kissinger also assured Han that Washington took no position on the competing sovereignty claims over the islands and repeated the story that Kosh's presence on the islands was an unfortunate coincidence having nothing to do with the South Vietnamese operation.[75]

Two days later, Kissinger chaired a meeting of the Washington Special Action Group, which brought together the leadership of the National Security Council, Joint Chiefs of Staff, CIA, and Departments of State and Defense to respond to crises. It was the first time the collective attention of the U.S. executive branch had ever focused on the South China Sea disputes. Kissinger set the tone early on when he pointed to a map of the Paracel Islands and asked if they were the Spratlys. He wasn't alone; most of the participants had probably never heard of the islands until that week. And their departments hadn't been given much time to round up the relevant decades-old records on past U.S. policy. The leadership was mostly flying blind.

The only exceptions were Adm. Thomas Moorer, chairman of the Joint Chiefs of Staff, who had previously served as commander-in-chief of the Pacific Fleet, and William Colby, director of the CIA and former station chief in Saigon. Moorer gave the participants a rough sketch of the South China Sea's geography and history and details of the recent clash, and Colby jumped in to offer insights. Still, basic questions went unanswered. When Kissinger asked for confirmation that Washington had never backed Saigon's claim—something he had already assured Han—no one answered. Deputy Secretary of State Kenneth Rush asked whether any country had troops in the Spratlys. He and Kissinger both worried about the fight moving there. Monteagle Stearns, the deputy assistant secretary of state for East Asian and Pacific affairs, said he thought the Philippines had one garrison. He was either unaware of the ROC and South Vietnamese facilities or considered them irrelevant.[76]

After informing the group for the second time that U.S. forces had been ordered to stay away from the islands, Admiral Moorer asked, "That's our policy, right?" Again, no one answered. As the group began to move on to other topics, he tried once more: "My instructions have been to stay clear of the whole area. That's what you want, right?" Kissinger and Rush finally approved this policy, which was good because the Pentagon had already announced it to the press. Acting Defense Secretary Bill Clements jumped into the conversation only once. A Texas oil magnate before entering government, Clements knocked down a suggestion by Colby that the North Vietnamese might be drawn into the dispute by a desire for oil: "Let's not get carried away on the possibility of oil in those islands. That is still a pie-in-the-sky. There is nothing there now, it's all in the future. Oil there is not realistic now. It's only a potential."[77] Despite rumors to the contrary, he was right: the seabed around the Paracels has little commercially viable oil and gas.

Before moving on, Kissinger asked the CIA to draft a report on the Spratly Islands, presumably concerned that they might see violence next. Colby promised to do so for the entire South China Sea.[78]

Kissinger and Rush weren't the only ones thinking that violence might spread south. William Sullivan, the U.S. ambassador to the Philippines, cabled the State Department on January 23 and again on January 26 to relay his concerns. Based on the failure of U.S. military intelligence in the Paracels, Sullivan worried about being blindsided by a surprise PRC attack in the Spratlys. He asked four things of Washington: an authoritative interpretation on whether the U.S.-Philippines Mutual Defense Treaty obligated the United States to defend Filipino troops in the Spratlys; a démarche to Beijing warning that it did; the authority to consult with Manila on what actions each was taking in that context; and assurances that the U.S. military was adequately surveilling the approaches to the Spratly Islands. He seems to have received none of these. Sullivan also told Washington that he was avoiding asking Filipino officials how many troops they had in the Spratlys and where. He wanted to know whether the United States would be obligated to defend them first. He ended with a colorful sign of his irritation: "It is now three days since I sent previous cable. . . . If completed action impossible at this time, kindly send up a flare so that I will have the impression someone is thinking of us back there."[79]

President Ford kept apprised of developments. On January 29, he was told the Chinese government had agreed to release Kosh and five wounded South Vietnamese captives in Hong Kong two days later. The other forty-three Vietnamese prisoners would follow in batches.[80] The CIA also updated the president on the difficult position in which Hanoi found itself. North Vietnamese leaders refused to recognize or act in concert with authorities in Saigon, but they didn't want to be accused of abandoning Vietnamese sovereignty over the islands. Their solution was to pass the buck by deferring to the Provisional Revolutionary Government as the legitimate representative of South Vietnam. (Of course, that government answered to Hanoi.)[81]

Then Washington's attention was drawn to the Spratly Islands. On January 31, the president was told of South Vietnamese press reports claiming Saigon had dispatched three ships and two hundred troops to make landings in the islands. The CIA believed this was "an effort to save face after losing the Paracels." And while the landings could spark further clashes with China, the agency thought that unlikely. It noted, "Peking would have to move naval units into the area and would have to operate beyond the range of its fighter aircraft and at the outer range of its tactical bombers."[82] But to be safe, Graham Martin, the U.S. ambassador to South Vietnam, was trying to convince Saigon to cancel the landings.

This was all sound reasoning. But as with the Paracels, the intelligence community was struggling to gather accurate information. The CIA warned the president that South Vietnam's moves could lead to confrontation with Taiwan and the Philippines because they both occupied some of the islands. But the agency wasn't sure how many. It knew ROC forces were on one of them, and it believed the Philippines had troops on only "two or three," when the real number was six. According to the Saigon press, the Vietnamese were under orders to avoid a fight with the Taiwanese. The CIA assumed this also applied to the Filipinos, but believed that the islands they held were targeted for landings by South Vietnamese troops.[83]

By the next day, the intelligence community had made some calls but was still missing important information. Ford was told that three Vietnamese Navy ships had deposited 136 men in five locations: Sin Cowe Island, Spratly Island, Amboyna Cay, Sand Cay, and Northeast Cay. They were wrong about Amboyna and Northeast. It seems that Vietnamese troops were dispatched to the former but deemed it too small to maintain a garrison. The latter was already held by

Filipino forces. The CIA was clearly unaware of that, since it made no mention of it while asserting that the South Vietnamese were under orders not to attempt landings on occupied islands.[84] But Vietnamese soldiers did occupy Spratly Island, Sin Cowe Island, and Sand Cay, which is next door to Itu Aba. Saigon now had four outposts in the Spratlys. On February 5, the agency sent a memo to the White House titled "Wrap-Up on Spratlys." This time the analysts said South Vietnamese troops had been "garrisoned for many years" on Namyit and had now deployed to "five additional islands."[85] In reality, Namyit had been occupied just a few months earlier. The agency soon corrected that mistake, but it never got the total count of South Vietnamese bases right.[86]

Fear that China would repeat its aggression had provided South Vietnam a justification to expand its footprint in the Spratlys. But the CIA was probably right that the operation was mostly to save face. That officials crowed about it to the Vietnamese press suggests as much. The CIA informed Ford that Beijing, and to a lesser degree Manila, had complained about the Vietnamese occupations. But they reiterated that military action was unlikely due to the difficulty China would have in projecting air and naval forces so far from its coast. That conclusion would hold for another decade. The incident also led the agency to speculate, as it had earlier regarding the Paracels, that a desire for oil might have motivated South Vietnam. Saigon was in desperate need of foreign exchange and had recently moved up its timetable for inviting foreign bids on offshore oil concessions elsewhere, mainly in the Gulf of Thailand.[87] Maybe hopes of a future oil discovery in the Spratlys did add weight to arguments for reinforcing its position. But as Bill Clements had said, that possibility remained "pie in the sky." Wounded pride and worries about further Chinese aggression were more immediate.

For three weeks, American leaders stumbled through the aftermath of the Paracels crisis while consistently misunderstanding facts on the ground and the motives involved. Why did the intelligence community struggle so much? For starters, the South China Sea disputes had previously commanded Washington's attention in 1956. Since then, U.S. officials had taken note of new occupations and claims when they happened, but those were buried in two decades' worth of cables and reports. It seems that no one had been tasked with keeping a coherent record of those developments. This was most obvious in the Spratlys, where officials were vaguely aware that there had been new occupations, but not how many or by whom.

In the Paracels, occupation had been mostly static over the years, and U.S. military intelligence had reason to keep an eye on any major changes to China's footprint. As a result, policymakers at least knew who held which island on the eve of the clash. But they were missing context and a clear understanding of motives. They correctly judged the Paracels to be of marginal strategic and economic value. Not understanding the national pride and mythmaking that had gone into the claims, especially on the Chinese side, they struggled to grasp why either would risk military confrontation. And American intelligence didn't realize until much later how long the PRC had been preparing for the operation. It couldn't independently confirm who started the fighting until Kosh was debriefed following his release. Most of the information Washington did have came from the government in Saigon, which was considered suspect as Vietnamese officials sought to shift blame and put the best spin on an embarrassing defeat. All of this led U.S. leaders to treat the clash like a diplomatic kerfuffle that got out of hand rather than an act of aggression against an ally.

It is hard to imagine the U.S. government ordering the Seventh Fleet to go to South Vietnam's aid even if it had immediately understood what had happened. Neither Congress nor the American people had any appetite for renewed military involvement in Vietnam, much less over disputed islands they had never heard of. And the United States had no mutual defense treaty obligating it to defend South Vietnamese territory or personnel, as it did with the ROC and the Philippines.[88] The main legal rationale for American military involvement in Vietnam had been the latter's inclusion as a territory under the protection of SEATO. But the Paracel Islands had never been recognized as Vietnamese territory by any member of SEATO except France. When Saigon turned to the organization after the battle, it found no support.

Had Washington more clearly understood what happened and why, it might have offered Saigon more diplomatic support, including backing at the United Nations. Maybe it would have demanded Beijing return to the status quo ante or make other concessions. Rapprochement with the United States was a top priority for China's leaders, and there is no telling what effect such demands might have had. At the very least, American policymakers would have weighed the reputational costs more carefully had they recognized the clash as a well-planned attack on an ally. In Saigon, U.S. inaction was certainly seen as a disappointment bordering on betrayal. But there was little opportunity for the clash to damage American credibility beyond Vietnam. It was largely forgotten amid the much larger tragedy visited on Saigon a year later.

4

The Great Alliance Debate

1975–1979

> Marcos' request that we give him a written guarantee that we will de-
> fend his forces in the Reed Bank area poses a dilemma. The Mutual
> Defense Treaty requires us to react to attacks against Philippine ter-
> ritory, islands or "on its armed forces, public vessels or aircraft in the
> Pacific." As disputed areas, the Spratlys and the Reed Bank can be de-
> fined as territory to which the treaty would not apply. However, the
> broader reference to forces, vessels or aircraft "in the Pacific," could be
> interpreted to cover Philippine units attacked in either the Spratlys or
> the Reed Bank....
>
> Essentially there are three responses we can give to Marcos on this
> issue: an affirmative one clearly extending our commitment to cover
> Philippine units attached [*sic*] in the Reed Bank; a negative one defi-
> nitely excluding the area from our defense commitment; or an ambig-
> uous one restating our overall defense commitment to the Philippines
> but leaving unanswered whether we would respond to all attacks on
> Philippine units in the area.
>
> —Memo from National Security Advisor Brent Scowcroft to President
> Gerald Ford, October 1976[1]

By invading the western Paracels, China brought the South China Sea disputes
to the attention of senior American leaders for the first time in two decades. For
most of the twentieth century, Washington had successfully balanced its neutrality on the sovereignty disputes with a commitment to defend freedom of the
seas, support international law, and, after 1951, uphold its defense commitments
to allies. The last time it really had to pick a side in the South China Sea was
in 1938, when it had opposed the Japanese annexation of the Shinnan Gunto.
Nearly all the parties to the San Francisco Peace Conference had been happy
to avoid the issue, and Washington had largely stayed above the fray during the
adventures of Morton Meads and Tomás Cloma. Despite occasional tensions
during the 1950s and 1960s, the Philippines, South Vietnam, and Taiwan were

On Dangerous Ground. Gregory B. Poling, Oxford University Press. © Oxford University Press 2022.
DOI: 10.1093/oso/9780197633984.003.0005

all American allies and had avoided a fight for the islands. But now that status quo had ended.

The Battle of the Paracels was a sign of the times. From 1975 until the end of the decade, the political and security landscape of Asia underwent momentous change. Those shifting geopolitics were reflected in the South China Sea. New players entered the fray, the hunt for oil and gas fueled disputes, a whole new regime of maritime claims took form, and allies openly debated U.S. credibility. For American policymakers, this all came together in the context of the U.S.-Philippines alliance. At times, the U.S. relationship with its former colony seemed unlikely to survive the tumult. The debates and decisions made during this period shaped the next forty years of U.S. involvement in the South China Sea.

Saigon's Fall and Its Aftershocks

Saigon and Manila had one last round to play in their game of one-upmanship in the Spratly Islands. The Philippines had controlled Southwest Cay since 1971. It treated the islet as a satellite of its larger military facility on Northeast Cay, just 1.5 nautical miles away. The closest feature under Vietnamese control was Sand Cay, over 60 miles to the south. One evening in early 1975, the Filipino garrison on Southwest motored over to Northeast Cay for the evening, as they often did. They returned later than usual the next day. One rumor holds that they had joined their comrades for a party and were nursing hangovers. The more likely explanation is that they had to wait for a storm to clear before heading back to Southwest Cay. Whatever the truth, they returned to find the South Vietnamese flag flying over the island—the first time a country had taken one of the Spratlys from another since the end of World War II. After some debate, the Filipinos decided it would be foolhardy to attempt a landing with the Vietnamese already dug in.[2] That decision avoided hostilities between the two American allies. But South Vietnam didn't have long to enjoy its prize.

At the start of 1975, Hanoi launched its spring offensive. It didn't plan for this to be the final push toward Saigon, but by March, South Vietnam's forces were being routed and the North pressed its advantage. In April, its troops drove south as Saigon's army collapsed. At the same time, Hanoi launched a campaign to take the South's bases in the Spratly Islands. Unlike Saigon, it had very little navy to speak of, so it took a page out of Beijing's paramilitary playbook. On April 14, several fishing trawlers carrying North Vietnamese commandos approached Southwest Cay. During the early hours of the morning, they paddled ashore in rubber rafts, taking the South Vietnamese garrison by surprise. The defenders put up a fight but were quickly overwhelmed.

Three days later, a South Vietnamese soldier escaped his captors and swam the 1.5 miles to Philippine-held Northeast Cay. He threw himself on the mercy of the same troops he had helped hoodwink a few months earlier. Luckily, the Filipinos were in a forgiving mood, and the soldier was given refuge in the Philippines. The rest of the South Vietnamese captives were shipped off to Danang.[3]

On April 25, North Vietnamese special forces conducted a nearly identical assault on Sand Cay. They again took the island after a brief fight. Hanoi would claim to have killed eight and captured more than fifty soldiers in these two operations. The next day, Saigon ordered the navy to evacuate its remaining troops and withdraw from the Spratlys. The noose was tightening on the capital, and every ship and soldier was needed for the defense. By the time North Vietnam launched its final assault on Saigon on April 29, its forces had already waded unopposed onto Namyit, Sin Cowe, and Spratly Islands.[4] Like the South Vietnamese a year earlier, they also tried to land on Amboyna Cay but gave up the attempt, reportedly due to rough weather.[5] Around noon on April 30, North Vietnamese tanks broke through the gates of the Presidential Palace in Saigon (Figure 4.1).

The official Vietnam News Agency announced the capture of the islands a week later, falsely including Amboyna in the list.[6] But no one was checking on such details. With the war over, authorities in Hanoi quickly changed their tune on the South China Sea. They no longer felt it necessary to defer to their patron in Beijing. In May 1975, they declared that the Paracel (Hoang Sa) and Spratly (Truong Sa) Islands were Vietnamese territory. In March 1976, the Spratlys were incorporated into Dong Nai Province.[7] That July, the governments of North Vietnam and the Provisional Revolutionary Government in the south officially merged to form the Socialist Republic of Vietnam. Ever since, Hanoi has maintained that it is the lawful inheritor of all previous Vietnamese and French claims to the islands.

For the other occupants of the Spratlys, as well as the United States, 1975 marked a serious deterioration in the security environment. To that point, the status quo between the Philippines, South Vietnam, and Taiwan had been tense but manageable. The entry of this new player suddenly made the disputes much more dangerous, especially for the claimant with the weakest military: the Philippines. As a result, Washington and Manila began to struggle with whether and how their alliance applied in the case of an attack in the South China Sea.[8]

The 1951 U.S.-Philippines MDT uses language that is nearly identical to other American security pacts, especially the Australia–New Zealand–U.S. (ANZUS) treaty negotiated at the same time.[9] Article IV requires both parties to act to meet the "common danger" of an attack on the other. Article V specifies that this includes attacks on the "metropolitan territory of either of the Parties, or on

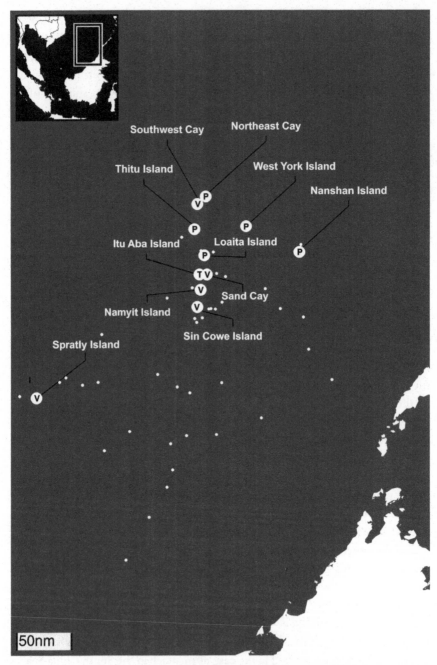

Figure 4.1 Spratly Islands occupied by the Philippines (P), Taiwan (T), and Vietnam (V), 1975. Created using Mapcreator and OpenStreetMap.

the island territories under its jurisdiction in the Pacific or on its armed forces, public vessels or aircraft in the Pacific."[10] Whether and how this applies in the Spratly Islands has always been debatable. Manila hadn't yet claimed the islands when the treaty was concluded, and the United States never recognized them as being part of the Philippines or under its "jurisdiction." More likely, Manila might invoke the final part of Article V, covering an attack on Philippine "armed forces, public vessels or aircraft in the Pacific," despite U.S. neutrality on the sovereignty question. But it was unclear whether Washington would agree that clause applied to attacks on disputed territory.

Today comparisons are often made between the U.S.-Philippines and U.S.-Japan defense treaties regarding disputed territories. But there are important differences between the Article V language in the two documents. The term "island territories under its jurisdiction" was included in the U.S.-Philippines and ANZUS pacts specifically to cover the UN Trust Territories established in the Pacific after World War II. These included Nauru and Papua New Guinea, administered by Australia; Samoa, administered by New Zealand; and modern-day Palau, the Federated States of Micronesia, and the Republic of the Marshall Islands, administered by the United States. The language was also seen as covering Okinawa, for which the United States fruitlessly hoped to secure a formal UN trusteeship. Japan's post–World War II pacifist constitution made similar language impossible. It could not commit to defend American forces abroad, whether on U.S. soil, in the Trust Territories, or anywhere else in the Pacific. So Article V of the 1960 U.S.-Japan treaty was simplified to cover "territories under the administration of Japan."[11]

This difference in language had an unintended effect when it came to disputed territories. The United States has subsequently argued that it can be neutral regarding the sovereignty of an island but still recognize an ally's de facto administration. This is the case with the Senkaku Islands in the East China Sea, which are administered by Japan but claimed by China and Taiwan. "Jurisdiction," on the other hand, was very specifically intended to signal a legal right recognized by an international body like the United Nations. The Philippines administers some of the Spratlys, but its "jurisdiction" has never been recognized by any international body.

These questions had been weighing on Ambassador William Sullivan ever since China's invasion of the Paracels the year before. Sullivan had arrived in Manila in August 1973 as one of the most respected officers in the foreign service. He was also one of its most outspoken and controversial. Sullivan's early postings included Thailand, India, and Japan. He caught his big break when Averell Harriman, President John F. Kennedy's assistant secretary of state for East Asian and Pacific affairs, recognized his talents and made him his deputy. He served briefly in Saigon before being appointed ambassador to Laos from 1964 to 1969. There Sullivan had direct control over the U.S. "Secret War," the largest sustained bombing campaign in history. He went on to serve as Kissinger's chief deputy at the 1972–73 Paris peace negotiations with North Vietnam. This complicated legacy made Sullivan a divisive figure. It also made him one of America's most knowledgeable Southeast Asia hands.

On April 16, two days after the North Vietnamese assault on Southwest Cay, Ambassador Sullivan wired Washington. Filipino troops on Northeast Cay had been uncomfortably close to the fighting. They had heard the early-morning gunfire and explosions just 1.5 miles away. Sullivan predicted that Manila would soon demand to know whether the MDT provided protection for Filipino troops in the Spratlys. He urgently asked the State Department for an answer.[12]

On the morning of April 25, Sullivan met with President Ferdinand Marcos to discuss the North Vietnamese assault on Saigon's bases in the Spratlys. Whether they knew that Hanoi's forces had just taken Sand Cay earlier that morning is unclear. But Marcos already feared Hanoi would seek to conquer the entire island group. Sullivan told the Philippine president that North Vietnam likely wanted to preempt any Chinese attempt to take advantage of Saigon's impending fall to occupy the islands itself. He added that Washington expected Hanoi had little appetite for a fight with the Philippines or Taiwan.[13]

After the meeting, Sullivan wired the State Department again. He told Washington that while Marcos hadn't mentioned the MDT, Sullivan had taken the opportunity to remind him that the United States didn't officially recognize the Philippines' claim. He said, "Marcos agreed situation was nebulous and let matter drop there." But Sullivan expected the issue to come up again. As he had the previous January, the ambassador asked for clearer guidance regarding the treaty.[14] He would again be disappointed.

The East Asian and Pacific Bureau penned a response from Kissinger on May 5. In its estimation, the Philippine government probably expected Washington would refuse to extend the MDT to the Spratlys and therefore wouldn't ask. That was just as well because the department's "preferred legal position" was that the treaty didn't apply. But Sullivan was warned not to communicate that to the Filipinos. Instead, he should avoid the issue. If pressed, he was only to repeat that the United States was neutral regarding sovereignty over the islands and supported peaceful resolution of disputes. The department realized how unsatisfactory this was, writing, "We recognize this is thin gruel but it is our carefully considered policy."[15] But Manila wasn't going to let it drop. And neither would Sullivan.

On May 20, the ambassador sent Washington an exasperated response. He warned that if the contents of Kissinger's previous telegram, which he sarcastically labeled "our firm, unflinching policy on the Spratlys," were ever known to the Philippine government, it "would confirm their worst fears and suspicions concerning value of U.S. treaty commitments." He urged the secretary to recall all copies of the memo and restrict its distribution to need-to-know officials. Then he caustically asked the State Department to look beyond territorial sovereignty and consider how Article V would apply to an attack on Filipinos at sea:

> When you review contingencies, please examine situation in which Philippine naval vessel, on high seas, attempting to reach Spratleys [*sic*] for purpose extracting Philippine garrison comes under attack or threat of attack from Vietnamese naval vessels and seeks U.S. naval and air protection. I think I can imagine what the "preferred legal position" would be, but have the uneasy feeling that such a contingency is far more palpable than Washington would like to assume.[16]

The ambassador concluded with a prescient warning. The two sides had been tentatively renegotiating their 1947 Military Bases Agreement for the past several years. If Washington failed to address Philippine concerns about its treaty commitments, Sullivan cautioned, Manila would likely demand the withdrawal of American bases from the country.

On June 9, the State Department's deputy legal advisor George Aldrich responded on behalf of Kissinger. He wrote Sullivan a detailed explanation of exactly *why* the department didn't think that Article V of the MDT covered the Spratly Islands. They weren't part of the "metropolitan territory" of the Philippines as recognized by the United States, which remained neutral on their ultimate sovereignty. That could change if Philippine sovereignty over the islands ever became uncontested. But the only way for that to happen would be through international arbitration—a very distant prospect. As for the second clause of Article V, it was meant to cover territories under the jurisdiction but not the sovereignty of the parties, such as the UN Trust Territories in the Pacific. Neither the United Nations nor any other international body had recognized Philippine jurisdiction over the Spratlys. On that point, Aldrich even took the time to knock down the old theory, floated by Carlos Garcia and some of Tomás Cloma's supporters, that the Treaty of San Francisco had placed the Spratlys under the joint trusteeship of the Allies.

Then came the kicker: Aldrich said the State Department didn't think Filipino troops stationed on the islands were covered by the "armed forces, public vessels or aircraft" clause. The treaty was meant for mutual defense; in that spirit, the third part of Article V should be interpreted as covering "an attack on forces deployed for defensive purposes where they have a clear international law right to be." This included ships in international waters and troops in third countries under a UN or other legal mandate. While the State Department didn't see the

Philippine occupation of the Spratlys as necessarily illegal or aggressive, it wasn't purely defensive either. Otherwise, Aldrich argued, allies would be able to deploy troops to purposely "bootstrap" a defense obligation in territories not otherwise covered by the MDT. The department worried what that could mean in places like North Borneo, where the Philippines disputed Malaysia's sovereignty, or Cyprus, where both Greece and Turkey might call for protection under NATO. Again, Sullivan was instructed to keep all of this to himself.

But Aldrich left the State Department some wiggle room. For one thing, he specified that his legal reasoning didn't cover a situation like the one Sullivan had laid out, involving an attack on ships attempting an evacuation. So even if Filipino troops on the islands weren't covered by the MDT, sailors in international waters near them still might be. Aldrich also admitted that "contrary arguments could be made." But they would have to wait for the political winds in Washington to shift. Otherwise, the administration would be making promises it couldn't keep: "As a practical matter, we see precious little chance that Congress or the American people would support US intervention in Spratly dispute. If the Phil [sic] garrisons ever were attacked, it seems to me less harmful politically to deny our obligations on legal grounds, than to leave unfulfilled an acknowledged commitment."[17]

While the embassy bickered with Washington, Manila and Hanoi were playing an odd game of cat and mouse. Philippine officials feared an impending North Vietnamese attack in the Spratlys. They were especially worried about how vulnerable their troops on Northeast Cay were. The South Vietnamese soldier who had escaped Southwest Cay in April had carried a warning; he claimed to have overheard his captors discussing plans to launch an attack on the Philippine base a few days later. That attack never came. But in May, the Philippines withdrew its garrison in the dead of night. They left the national flag flying and waited to see what would happen when the North Vietnamese realized they were gone. Meanwhile Manila reinforced its other, presumably more defensible bases. Soon enough, Vietnamese troops sailed over to Northeast Cay and hauled down the Philippine flag. But then they too left. By August, the Filipinos had returned, seemingly convinced that Hanoi wasn't planning the immediate conquest of the Spratlys.[18]

Oil and American Bases

Sullivan spent the next year dodging questions about the MDT, as instructed. But that was becoming more and more difficult. First there was the emerging problem of Reed Bank. Shorthand for a cluster of underwater banks and shoals (only one of which is the eponymous Reed Bank), this area of shallow sea is located between the occupied Spratly Islands and Palawan. Whether these features were part of the Spratly Islands dispute depended on who was asked. The ROC and PRC listed them among the Nansha Islands—another legacy of the failure of Chiang Kai-shek's early cartographers to distinguish between submerged features and islands. According to international law, underwater banks were not eligible for sovereignty claims; instead they were part of the continental shelf of the nearest state.

The right of coastal states to the resources of their continental shelves had become almost universally recognized by this point (though there was still disagreement on the size of the shelf). The Philippines, about 100 miles away, was the closest coastal state and so probably had the best claim to Reed Bank. But there was a wrinkle. China, Taiwan, and Vietnam all claimed islands close to Reed Bank, and islands were also entitled to continental shelves, though the international community was still debating the details. Ironically, the Philippines had been the one to cement this concept by pushing through its amendment to the 1958 Convention on the Continental Shelf.[19]

None of this mattered so long as there were no resources to be exploited at Reed Bank. But technological advances were creating new opportunities for offshore exploration, and since 1968 regional governments had been hoping to strike it rich by finding oil in the South China Sea. The Philippines had issued exploration licenses to several foreign and local companies to explore Reed Bank in the early 1970s. In 1975, these companies formed a consortium led by Sweden's Salen Group and increased surveys around Reed Bank. The U.S. Embassy grew worried that they would soon draw the interest of American companies and asked Washington for advice. Ambassador Sullivan was instructed to discourage U.S. firms from wading into the dispute.[20] In November 1975, the Salen Group obtained a seven-year service contract from Manila to drill exploration wells around Reed Bank. This became a real headache for Sullivan in March 1976, when Salen contracted the *Brinkerhoff II*, a ship owned by a Denver-based company of the same name, to sink its first well. They tried to keep their activities quiet, but word soon got out.[21]

The Philippines also stepped up aerial patrols around Itu Aba and the Vietnamese outposts in preparation for the drilling. In mid-May, Vietnamese troops on Southwest Cay fired on a Philippine reconnaissance plane, seriously raising concerns in Washington that the situation might get out of control.[22] Luckily, other than this incident, the claimants kept their objections to the diplomatic arena. Taiwan was the first to officially complain, insisting in May that Reed Bank was part of the Nansha Islands claimed by the ROC government. Vietnam was next, objecting to any other state exploring for oil in the "area of the Spratly Archipelago." China waited until July, when the Philippine press publicly reported on the drilling for the first time. Beijing then declared that "China has indisputable sovereignty over these islands and their adjacent sea areas and that the resources there belong to China."[23]

The U.S. Embassy suspected that Manila had engineered the *Brinkerhoff* contract to purposely entangle Washington in the disputes. It had tried, unsuccessfully, to warn the company away. In a wire to the State Department in May, Sullivan noted that the Philippine government had already tried to entice two major American oil companies to explore Reed Bank. U.S. firms were probably the only ones with the technical capacity to operate in those waters. But Sullivan was also convinced that Marcos was trying to corner Washington into recognizing Philippine claims and, ultimately, extending its mutual defense obligations to disputed areas. And while Marcos hadn't spelled it out yet, Sullivan saw a connection to another ongoing headache: the renegotiation of the 1947 Military Bases Agreement.[24]

The agreement was last amended in 1966, shortening its term to twenty-five years from the original ninety-nine. But just three years later, the Marcos government had demanded new talks. Sovereignty issues, especially concerning criminal jurisdiction over American service members, created a perpetual demand in the Philippines for changes to the pact. But from 1969, Manila had a new and more pressing reason to reopen negotiations: concerns about U.S. defense commitments. This started with the testimony of James Wilson, deputy chief of mission at the U.S. Embassy in Manila, before the "Symington Subcommittee," officially the Subcommittee on United States Security Agreements and Commitments Abroad, chaired by Senator Stuart Symington. Responding to questions about the scope of MDT commitments, Wilson offhandedly declared that the treaty did not exist "for the defense of the Philippines as such." The remark was little noted in Washington but became a fixation for years in Manila, where it was seen as hinting that the United States would act only if its own bases were attacked.[25]

This skepticism was amplified by President Nixon's Asia doctrine, the passage of the War Powers Act, and the eventual fall of Saigon. Born from the need to get the United States out of Vietnam, the Nixon Doctrine called on American allies to be the main providers of their own security. The United States would uphold its treaty commitments and provide a nuclear umbrella. Washington would also offer military and economic assistance to build up allied armed forces. But in exchange, allies were expected to take the lead in defending themselves against conventional attack. This was particularly worrying to the Philippines, which had underfunded its military for decades and relied overwhelmingly on the United States for external defense.[26]

The Nixon Doctrine continued into the Ford administration, as did the on-again, off-again talks on the Military Bases Agreement. In 1973, as American ground forces withdrew from Vietnam, the U.S. Congress passed the War Powers

Act. This legislation sought to constrain the ability of the U.S. president to wage war without the consent of Congress. This concerned Philippine officials, who worried that a need for congressional authorization would prevent American forces from coming to the timely defense of the Philippines.[27]

In 1975, a new round of formal negotiations on the Military Bases Agreement started to build momentum. By the end of the year, they hinged on two demands. First, Manila wanted Washington to commit to a generous stream of military aid to help modernize its armed forces. This was important since the Nixon Doctrine made clear that the Philippines was expected to be the primary guarantor of its own conventional security. Second, Marcos wanted assurances that the War Powers Act wouldn't stop the United States from fulfilling its Article IV and V obligations in the event of an attack that didn't directly threaten American bases.

This is where Sullivan got worried. Reed Bank presented the same complication as the Spratlys did to the mutual defense question. The ambassador repeated his warning of a year earlier: if Washington categorically denied that Article V covered disputed areas, including Reed Bank, it would be seen as a "treacherous abandonment of U.S. treaty obligations." And Marcos was explicitly linking those treaty obligations to permitting the continuation of U.S. bases in the Philippines. Sullivan already knew that the State Department wouldn't give any positive assurances, so he urged Washington to say nothing at all. He concluded, "Much will depend on the outcome of drilling by the Brinkerhof [*sic*] rig. If no rpt [repeat] no reasonable oil deposits are found, this whole issue will probably evaporate quietly. If real oil is hit, we can expect the problem to amplify to a new dimension which we will doubtless have to address as a major policy issue, regardless of any legal parsing of our treaty obligations."[28]

As it turned out, the *Brinkerhoff* found mostly natural gas. This was disappointing since the technology and market forces of the day made it unlikely that anyone could profitably extract gas that far from shore. But it was also a promising sign that there might be oil in the area. It meant there would be more exploration in the future.[29] The early results were enough to attract the attention of Standard Oil of Indiana, better known as AMOCO, despite warnings from the U.S. Embassy. The company bought a 38 percent stake in the Salen-led consortium and took over the exploration operations.[30] Manila had finally drawn in a major American oil company.

The service contract with Manila required that AMOCO drill two more wells by the end of 1977. In July 1976, the company asked Philippine officials whether Nanshan and nearby Flat Island were occupied and by whom. These were the easternmost of the Spratlys and the closest to Reed Bank. They were also 50 miles from the well drilled by the *Brinkerhoff*. The U.S. Embassy took this as a sign that AMOCO wanted to drill its second well in more hotly contested waters near the islands.[31] The Philippines had occupied Nanshan since 1970. Flat Island was unoccupied, but not for much longer. In September, Ambassador Sullivan met with senior AMOCO representatives in Manila. He warned them again about the dangers of exploring Reed Bank and asked that they at least not use an American drilling ship again. They were receptive but made no promises.[32]

Meanwhile talks on the Military Bases Agreement continued. But as Sullivan feared, the Philippines began to link further progress to a clarification of U.S. defense obligations in the Spratlys and Reed Bank. During negotiations in July, Philippine officials pressed the ambassador on how the United States would respond to an attack on vessels at Reed Bank. Sullivan dodged the question, as instructed.[33] This only angered Marcos. It reinforced his concerns that ambiguities in the MDT would allow Washington to dodge its responsibilities unless an attack directly threatened American bases. On August 6, Marcos handed visiting Deputy Secretary of State Charles Robinson a note to carry back to Washington. It listed his concerns bluntly and demanded "a most authoritative and specific statement of the US government regarding its obligations under the [MDT] . . . whether in the Reed Bank or in any part of this country."[34]

Washington finally got it: there would be no agreement on continued basing without clearing up the MDT issue. But there were still differing opinions on how much Marcos really cared about the answer. Some thought he was just buying time in the hopes of getting a better deal if Jimmy Carter won the upcoming U.S. presidential elections. Brent Scowcroft, who had replaced Kissinger as national security advisor a year earlier, was told that it probably didn't matter. Washington wasn't prepared to extend protection to disputed territories, so a deal was unlikely.[35] The Office of Management and Budget, which already objected to the assistance packages being discussed, wanted to suspend negotiations since Manila wouldn't get the answer it needed anyway.[36]

But the most vigorous debate was at the State Department, where Kissinger was still secretary. He pulled together the department's senior officials on August 16 to discuss Marcos's demands. Dismissing the other areas of disagreement as "minor league stuff," he zeroed in on the MDT. Kissinger didn't buy that Marcos was just stalling and thought he needed to be given a real answer from a senior U.S. official. He seemed to understand the political pressures facing the Philippine leader. The anxieties that started with the Nixon Doctrine and the passage of the War Powers Act had only been heightened with the fall of Saigon. And dictator or no, Marcos needed to assure Filipinos that American bases were more than a liability.

The discussion grew tense. At one point, Kissinger snapped at Deputy Secretary Robinson, "Don't be an idiot. The guy is sitting out there, with Viet-Nam having gone down the drain, having the only U.S. bases there. He needs something to justify our being there." Under Secretary for Political Affairs Philip Habib insisted that Washington didn't need to "knuckle under" because

Marcos couldn't afford to alienate the United States, But Kissinger shot back, "That is not the point. It is spectacularly not the point. It is that mentality that has gotten us into difficulty." Ambassador Sullivan also came in for criticism. The secretary complained about his "series of objections" on the MDT, which Kissinger considered too myopic: what Marcos needed was a statement of American fidelity to use as political cover. The details of that commitment were less important.[37]

Kissinger thought he could hash the whole thing out if he could just get Marcos in a room. But that was politically difficult, maybe impossible, before the November elections.[38] As a first step, Philippine foreign secretary Carlos Romulo was invited to Washington in early September to help determine if a return visit by Kissinger and Deputy Defense Secretary Bill Clements might do the trick. Marcos, however, refused to allow Romulo to meet Kissinger until the Americans gave him an affirmative answer on the MDT commitment. This heightened the debate over the U.S. negotiating strategy. The White House saw little hope of a deal before the elections and thought Marcos was trying to extract further concessions by making them impatient. Kissinger still thought the two sides could make a breakthrough, and that doing so before the polls would be best. But for the time being, the administration decided to wait and see how Sullivan's next round of negotiations in Manila went.[39]

Marcos relented, partially. Kissinger and Romulo would meet in early October on the sidelines of the annual UN General Assembly debate in New York. Ahead of the meeting, Scowcroft updated President Ford on the Philippines' demands and the haggling over military and financial assistance. He told the president, "Marcos' request that we give him a written guarantee that we will defend his forces in the Reed Bank area poses a dilemma." Scowcroft admitted that the Article V reference to "armed forces, public vessels or aircraft in the Pacific . . . could be interpreted to cover Philippine units attacked in either the Spratlys or the Reed Bank."[40] So there were three options.

The administration could deny Article V protection in the South China Sea, which would probably sink the basing negotiations. In fact, Secretary of Defense Donald Rumsfeld had already counseled the president that the risks of this option "are so great as to rule it out of consideration."[41] Option 2 was for Washington to unconditionally affirm that the treaty applied, which Scowcroft warned would "bear at least equal risks." It would raise tensions with China and Vietnam, face opposition from Congress and a war-weary public, and potentially encourage the Philippines to assert its claims more aggressively. The third choice would be to offer an ambiguous commitment. This was the preference at both the State Department and the Pentagon, and Scowcroft agreed.

He recommended telling Manila that Article V would cover an attack on Filipino forces at Reed Bank "as long as their presence is consistent with the provisions of the Mutual Defense Treaty, particularly Article I regarding peaceful settlement of disputes and refraining from the threat or use of force." State Department lawyers had used the same logic a year earlier to contend that Article V probably didn't cover Filipino forces in the Spratlys. What it meant for Philippine vessels at Reed Bank was unclear, which was the point. President Ford agreed; State and Defense were instructed to deliver the message.[42]

On October 6, Kissinger met with Foreign Secretary Romulo and Defense Secretary Juan Ponce Enrile in New York. He was accompanied by Sullivan. Romulo opened the meeting by reading a statement that demanded the United States commit to repelling any attack on the Philippines, not just defending American bases. Romulo said he understood that the Spratlys issue might make the U.S. government hesitant to offer such a commitment. So, on the authority of President Marcos, he assured Kissinger that Manila "has no intention of involving the United States in the resolution of the Spratlys question because the GOP [government of the Philippines] feels it can resolve the issue on the basis of understanding with the parties involved, without the need of U.S. assistance." This didn't mean the Philippines wouldn't expect help if attacked in disputed areas, just that it wouldn't start a fight to draw the Americans in. Kissinger said he had no problem assuring Manila that Article V covered the entire metropolitan Philippines, not just U.S. bases. But he warned, "If, however, the GOP insisted on dragging in the Spratlys, we would have to include complicated formulations and escape clauses which would cause more problems than they settled." He didn't relay the complicated formulation the president had approved regarding Reed Bank. Romulo agreed that "controversial areas could be excluded."[43]

Then they moved on to Manila's second concern: military assistance. Secretary Enrile asked for a five-year assistance program starting at $500 million in the first year. Kissinger dismissed that as unrealistic and asked instead for a list of equipment Manila would like prioritized. The meeting got a bit tense when Romulo shot back that Kissinger should consider how important the bases really were to the United States. The secretary answered that they were important, but America could manage without them. Kissinger then warned that if Manila wanted a deal soon, they would need to iron out the main points before the U.S. elections on November 2. He would consult with President Ford and the National Security Council on how much total assistance they thought the administration could wring from Congress. Manila would have to take that number as their "final offer." Then the two sides could announce an agreement in principle. Kissinger would travel to Manila after the elections to settle the remaining details with Marcos. Romulo agreed, and the press was told the two secretaries had made "good progress."[44]

Kissinger and Romulo met again in New York on October 28. Kissinger handed over a note providing written assurances that the United States considered Article V to cover the entirety of the metropolitan Philippines. It also expressed gratitude that Manila didn't seek to involve America in resolving its sovereignty disputes. It said nothing about the South China Sea, just as the two secretaries had agreed.[45] Kissinger then presented Romulo with the "final offer" he had promised on military and economic aid. Washington was willing to provide $900 million over five years.[46] Despite Kissinger's insistence that the deal had to be accepted before the polls or wait for the next administration, Manila took its time considering the offer. Five days later, Carter narrowly beat Ford in the presidential elections.

On November 23, Romulo called on Kissinger in Washington. He passed along a note rejecting the proposed economic package and demanding greater clarity on the Article V commitment. On the former, Manila demanded $2 billion over five years. On the latter, Marcos was willing to accept that disputed territories weren't part of the "metropolitan Philippines" covered by the treaty. But he wanted a clear commitment under the "armed forces, public vessels or aircraft in the Pacific" clause of Article V. The note said, "We would like to have a more precise definition of the term 'Pacific Area.' For example, would the South China Sea form part of the Pacific Area? From our point of view, we believe the South China Sea should be included in the Pacific Area." It seemed that Romulo had exceeded his authority when he agreed to exclude "sensitive areas" from the discussion. And as an additional hurdle, Marcos wanted assurances that any attack on the Philippines "would be instantly repelled." He still believed that the War Powers Act would impose unacceptable delays on any response.[47]

Kissinger told Romulo that the definition of the "Pacific Area" could be "handled," along with most other issues. But $2 billion in assistance was out of the question. If that was Manila's bottom line, he said, then it would have to take it up with the Carter administration.[48] When informed of these demands, Sullivan cabled Washington with his interpretation. The note seemed to him "deliberately designed to be unacceptable to us" and therefore suspend the negotiations. Marcos was already signaling through intermediaries that he wanted to ink a deal with Carter rather than Ford so the incoming president would feel personally invested. In the meantime, the ambassador believed that Manila was trying to make it easier to reach agreement once negotiations restarted. Rather than specifics on the Spratly Islands and Reed Bank, it was narrowing its MDT demands to the question of automaticity and the South China Sea being part of the "Pacific Area."[49]

Everyone else thought time was up, but Kissinger and Romulo were too invested. They wanted to give it one last shot. During a November 28 stopover in Acapulco, Kissinger received a message from Romulo seeking a meeting.[50] They were both heading to the inauguration of Mexico's new president, José López Portillo, and agreed to meet in Mexico City two days later. There, Romulo

informed Kissinger that Marcos would accept a new American offer of $1 bil-
lion over five years. He suggested that should cover only military assistance, with
broader economic aid to be discussed later. Kissinger insisted it would have to
cover both, and Romulo demurred. The two agreed to meet again on December
4 in Washington, where they would announce a deal in principle.

Then things went sideways. Romulo arrived in New York on December
3. American officials quickly sought him out and shared the draft text of the joint
announcement. He said he would need to clear it with Marcos. Later that evening, he called Under Secretary of State Habib to say that Marcos had rejected
the deal and demanded $1 billion in purely military assistance. After conferring
with Kissinger, Habib informed Romulo that was unacceptable. The planned
announcement ceremony was hastily scrapped. Unfortunately, the administration had already briefed members of Congress, and someone went to the press.[51]
On December 5, the *New York Times* broke the story. It blamed Romulo for
abandoning the deal and questioned why Kissinger had tried to rush it through
before Carter took office.[52]

Romulo gave his own version of events in an Associated Press interview,
blaming the whole thing on Washington. He insisted he hadn't seen the details of
the announcement until a U.S. official ambushed him at the airport and tried to
pressure him to agree. Sullivan thought it likely that Romulo never told Marcos
he had already reached agreement with Kissinger in Mexico City. Instead, he
likely presented it as a U.S. proposal, confident Marcos would accept. When the
president didn't bite, Sullivan surmised, Romulo had to pin it on the Americans
to "save his own skin."[53] The State Department was incensed but wanted to avoid
any more public bickering. It encouraged Sullivan to privately share the full story
with Marcos to help smooth things over. And then everyone agreed that it was
best to hit pause until Carter took office.[54]

New Beginnings, New Occupations

Jimmy Carter was inaugurated on January 20, 1977. Five days later, Marcos
told the press that when talks on the bases agreement restarted, he would demand a stronger commitment from the new American president to defend the
Philippines. But he was in no hurry, saying, "I don't think it's seemly for the
Philippines to rush in when the president is barely getting acquainted with his
new home."[55]

Luckily for new secretary of state Cyrus Vance and his team, the previous administration had done much of the heavy lifting on the MDT problem. The legal
and political debates of the previous two years hadn't entirely satisfied either
side, but they had narrowed the scope of disagreement. And the U.S. bureaucracy

had neared consensus. The United States would defend any part of the metropolitan Philippines from attack. The Spratly Islands and Reed Bank were not to be considered part of that area. Nonetheless, Article V should cover attacks on Filipino "armed forces, public vessels, or aircraft" at Reed Bank, so long as they hadn't started the fight. That principle applied to contested water, but not necessarily land. The State Department was still resistant to extending protection to Filipino forces on disputed islands. It admitted, however, that this was open to reinterpretation. That final point would remain ambiguous for another forty years, but the rest was effectively settled. And it remains U.S. policy to this day.

Marcos now understood what was politically possible in Washington. The two treaty clarifications he still sought were mostly consistent with the new consensus in the State Department. He wanted an explicit statement that the South China Sea was part of the "Pacific Area" in which the "armed forces, public vessels, or aircraft" clause of Article V applied. And he wanted to know that the United States wouldn't let its "constitutional processes," referenced in the MDT, delay the response to an armed attack. These were manageable. But Marcos had a bigger problem. He had grossly misjudged the likelihood of getting a better financial deal from the new administration. Soon after taking office, President Carter moved to cap the total value of U.S. arms transfers abroad and supported the Congress in cutting security assistance to the Philippines as punishment for Marcos's human rights abuses.[56] It was clear that the level of U.S. assistance would be a much tougher sticking point in the new negotiations. Getting back to Kissinger's offer of $1 billion over five years might be impossible.

Despite their differences, by late 1977 both sides wanted progress. In late September, First Lady Imelda Marcos was dispatched to New York, accompanied by Secretaries Romulo and Enrile, to meet with Carter, Vance, and other officials. They were treated to a lengthy presentation on the War Powers Act by the State Department's deputy legal counsel, which seemed to assuage their concerns about an automatic American response to any attack.[57] U.S. chargé d'affaires Lee Stull concluded that Marcos knew he couldn't extract much more on the MDT. Stull advised Washington that a statement of U.S. commitment to Article V with an "embellishment" indicating that the "Pacific Area" included the South China Sea would finally put the issue to bed.[58]

It probably helped that the threat of a crisis over Reed Bank was subsiding. That made a public commitment less risky for the United States. The consortium led by Salen and AMOCO was contractually obligated to drill two more wells by the end of 1977. AMOCO had contracted an American-owned and -operated ship, the *Glomar Tasman*, to drill the first from late March. If AMOCO really had been interested in drilling closer to Nanshan and Flat Islands, as the embassy feared, it thought better of it. The new well was 30 miles north of the *Brinkerhoff*'s drill site and stayed just as far from the islands. At the end of May, the *Glomar*

Tasman moved 11 miles southeast—even farther from any claimed islands—and drilled its second well.[59] In July, James MacDonald, president of AMOCO's Philippine subsidiary, told the embassy the exploratory wells were "the three most rank wildcats he had ever seen."[60] AMOCO would need to go back to the drawing board and was in no rush. In October, the members of the Reed Bank consortium agreed that new seismic surveys were needed to find a more promising site and asked the Philippine government to defer their obligation to drill another well in 1978.[61] In March 1978, AMOCO resigned as operator, though it remained invested in the consortium. Salen would drill additional wells in 1978, 1979, and 1981 but wouldn't find any commercially viable deposits (Figure 4.2). By the mid-1980s, Canada's Denison Mines would take over operations, but with no better luck. That would put a halt to oil and gas exploration at Reed Bank for the next two decades.[62]

While the focus on Reed Bank was dissipating, the status quo in the Spratly Islands continued to shift. AMOCO might have lost interest in the waters near Nanshan and Flat Islands, but the Philippine government was still worried about them. Filipino troops had been regularly visiting Flat Island, just 5 miles from their base on Nanshan.[63] In June 1977, they quietly established an outpost on the small cay, giving the Philippines its sixth base in the Spratlys.[64] It seems likely that Manila garrisoned Flat Island to make sure Vietnamese or Chinese forces couldn't do so first, which would have allowed them to menace Nanshan or future drilling operations at Reed Bank.

A new party also began to show interest in the disputes at this time. The Malaysian government was preparing to formally claim rights over the waters and seabed up to 200 miles from East Malaysia, comprising the states of Sabah and Sarawak. In this, Kuala Lumpur was keeping pace with the ongoing Third United Nations Conference on the Law of the Sea. Negotiators there were nearing consensus that the continental shelf along with a new entity called the exclusive economic zone (EEZ) should extend 200 miles from each state's coast. Kuala Lumpur knew there were numerous submerged reefs and possibly a few islets within that distance from Sabah and Sarawak. But no one could say exactly how many. The area was poorly mapped and rarely surveyed.

For the U.S. government and many other observers, these reefs were part of the Dangerous Ground but not necessarily the Spratly Islands. The PRC and ROC, on the other hand, listed them among the Nansha Islands. And the Philippines and Vietnam would probably claim *some* of them, even if they couldn't say how many. The coordinates outlining Cloma's Freedomland in 1956 certainly overlapped with Malaysia's desired claim to waters and seabed. So did the coordinates in France's original 1930 annexation announcement. The current governments in Manila and Hanoi were likely to claim sovereignty over any islands within those boundaries. In late 1977, the Malaysian government asked

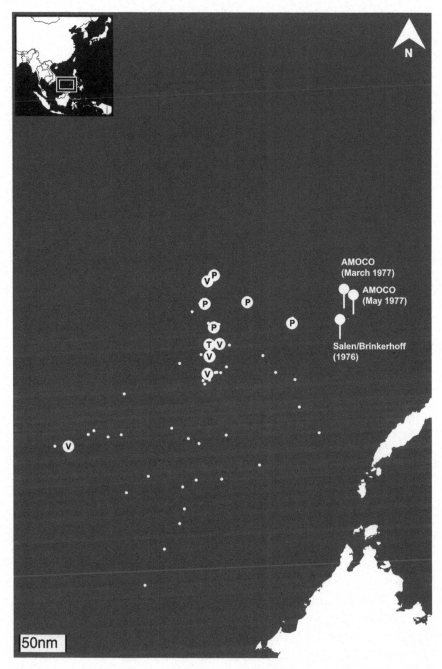

Figure 4.2 Reed Bank drilling sites, 1976–77, with islands occupied by Philippines (P), Taiwan (T), and Vietnam (V). Created using Mapcreator and OpenStreetMap.

the U.S. Embassy in Kuala Lumpur for documentation on the extent of claims in the South China Sea. Washington passed along some academic treatises and sanitized versions of its own studies.[65] But those didn't have the answers either. The State Department's Bureau for Intelligence and Research had just concluded earlier that year that no one knew the full extent of the territorial claims nor the boundary between the Spratly Islands and the Dangerous Ground.[66]

To help find answers, Malaysia undertook a survey of the waters and reefs off Sabah and Sarawak. It needed to confirm whether any contained real islands and, if so, whether they were occupied. The U.S. Embassy suspected, with good reason, that Kuala Lumpur was considering occupying any islands it found to keep them out of the hands of other parties. This would have made sense. Islands were entitled to their own territorial seas, and potentially continental shelves and EEZs. Any that were occupied, or even claimed, by other states would complicate Malaysia's plan to assert rights to the waters and seabed in the area.

As it turns out, there were seven pieces of dry land in the section of the Dangerous Ground that Malaysia would eventually claim. But none was occupied in 1977, and only one had received any previous attention from other claimants: Amboyna Cay. During the survey, Malaysian personnel visited the cay and found it vacant. When a Malaysian official shared that with the U.S. Embassy, it was the first time Washington realized that North Vietnamese troops hadn't actually occupied the cay in 1975.[67] Malaysia followed this up in early 1978 by sending a detachment of navy commandos there. They quietly erected sovereignty markers and left.[68]

A few months later, in March 1978, the Philippines followed its occupation of Flat Island by building an outpost on the even smaller Loaita Cay.[69] This sandbar had nothing to recommend it other than its proximity to Philippine-occupied Loaita Island about 5 miles away. And, as with Flat Island, Manila likely wanted to make sure no one could use it to threaten the more important base nearby. Marcos and other officials at first insisted that Filipino troops had been on the island since 1971, but they eventually abandoned that story. When Filipino troops landed on Loaita Cay and dubbed it Panata Island, the feature didn't even appear on most charts of the Spratly Islands. But nearby Lankiam Cay, which is on the other side of Loaita Island, was known to international cartographers. As a result, when the Philippines' official mapping service updated its charts to reflect the new occupation, it mistakenly stuck the "Panata Island" label on Lankiam rather than Loaita Cay.[70] The Philippine government didn't fix its charts until the early 2000s. And Manila still misleadingly lists its English name as "Lankiam Cay." As a result, most maps continue to place Panata in the wrong spot. This is especially silly at a time when any Google Earth user can spot the bright red, white, and blue Filipino flag painted on the roof of the Loaita Cay facility, while Lankiam is an empty, shifting sand bar.[71]

Hanoi responded to these developments in the same way Saigon had in the past: it grabbed more land to shore up its position in the disputes. Between March and April 1978, Vietnamese troops built new outposts on Grierson, Pearson, and Central Reefs and finally occupied Amboyna Cay. That short-circuited whatever plans Malaysia had for the island.[72] Grierson was on the opposite side of Union Banks from Sin Cowe Island, allowing Vietnam to keep watch over both ends of that large reef structure. Central Reef was the first outpost built in the London Reefs, just over 200 miles from the Vietnamese coast; only Spratly Island was closer. Pearson Reef was within 200 miles of the Malaysian coast and may have been included in its 1977 survey. It was just outside the continental shelf Malaysia would claim a year later, but Vietnam didn't know that yet. Vietnamese troops also briefly occupied Barque Canada Reef near Amboyna Cay. They left in May after finding it too difficult to build a permanent structure on the few dry rocks there.[73] This left Vietnam in control of nine islands and reefs compared to the Philippines' seven. Taiwan remained content with Itu Aba (Figure 4.3).

In June, Manila formally annexed the islands it occupied along with all others inside the borders of Cloma's Freedomland. This included Itu Aba, all the features held by Vietnam except Spratly Island itself, and most of the reefs and rocks being eyed by Malaysia. The Philippine government dubbed these the Kalayaan Islands Group, *kalayaan* meaning "freedom" in Tagalog.[74] In the decree establishing the Municipality of Kalayaan, Marcos tried to weave to-gether the various legal justifications that Philippine officials had made over the years. These included geographic proximity, national security, and the lack of prior claims to some (but not all) of the islands: "[M]uch of the above area [the Kalayaan Islands Group] is part of the continental margin of the Philippine archipelago. . . . [B]y reason of history, indispensable need, and effective occu-pation and control established in accordance with the international law, such areas must now deemed to belong and subject [*sic*] to the sovereignty of the Philippines. . . . [W]hile other states have laid claims to some of these areas, their claims have lapsed by abandonment."[75] The decree also laid claim to the seabed and airspace within the borders of Freedomland, though no justification was offered for this legally dubious proposition.

Even as the Philippines and Vietnam expanded their presence in the Spratlys and Malaysia dipped its toe in the disputes, a warming diplomatic environment was leading most of the parties toward a new equilibrium. Relations between China and the United States continued to improve, which helped facilitate closer ties between Beijing and Manila (as well as the other anti-Communist states of Southeast Asia). Tectonic shifts were also taking place within the Communist Party of China. The decade-long tumult of the Cultural Revolution had finally ended in late 1976 with the death of Chairman Mao and the ouster of his dep-uties known as the "Gang of Four." In July 1977, former vice chairman Deng

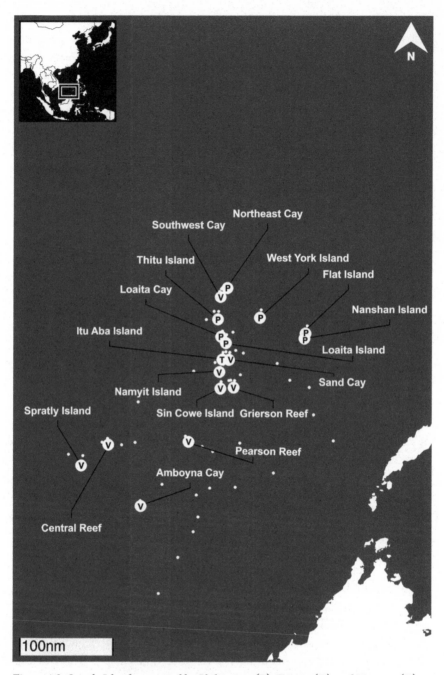

Figure 4.3 Spratly Islands occupied by Philippines (P), Taiwan (T), and Vietnam (V), 1978. Created using Mapcreator and OpenStreetMap.

Xiaoping had been restored to his office after more than a year in the political wilderness. He had begun to spearhead a program of economic reform and greater openness.

In March 1978, PRC vice premier Li Xiannian visited Manila. The press had just learned of the occupation of "Panata Island," and Marcos worried it would put a damper on the visit. He blasted the media for misreporting the issue and insisted, falsely, that Filipino troops had been on the cay for years.[76] More important, he claimed to have reached previously undisclosed agreements with both Beijing and Hanoi to peacefully negotiate the South China Sea disputes. According to Marcos, he and Deng had reached such an agreement in June 1975 during his first visit to Beijing to open diplomatic relations.[77] Li reaffirmed China's commitment to this policy during his trip.[78]

Marcos said a similar accord had been reached in 1977 with Vietnam's deputy prime minister Nguyen Duy Trinh.[79] Vietnam and the Philippines came to a more public agreement in September 1978 during Prime Minister Pham Van Dong's groundbreaking visit to Manila. He and Marcos issued a joint statement that pledged to resolve disputes, which both understood to include the Spratly Islands, through peaceful means. Philippine officials touted the successful visit as a model for how their fellow anti-Communists in the Association of Southeast Asian Nations (ASEAN), which also included Indonesia, Malaysia, Singapore, and Thailand, could improve relations with Vietnam.[80]

A month later, Deng visited Tokyo, followed by Kuala Lumpur, Bangkok, and Singapore. He met with Japan's prime minister Takeo Fukuda on October 25, and the two discussed the territorial dispute over the Senkakus, called Diaoyu Islands in China. During the press conference that followed, Deng previewed his vision for managing such disputes, which would become known as "setting aside disputes and pursuing joint development": "We believe that we should set the issue aside for a while if we cannot reach agreement on it. It is not an urgent issue and can wait for a while. If our generation do not have enough wisdom to resolve this issue, the next generation will have more wisdom, and I am sure that they can find a way acceptable to both sides to settle this issue."[81] Chinese officials formally suggested joint development of resources around the Senkakus a few months later. It would take another decade for China to make a similar offer around the Spratlys.[82] But by late 1978, it was clear that Beijing was prepared to downplay territorial disputes in both the East and South China Seas for the sake of improving relations abroad. During the December 1978 Third Plenum of the Central Committee of the Communist Party of China, Deng stepped forward as the country's clear leader. This was a watershed moment and accelerated his reform agenda.

On January 1, 1979, the United States formally switched its diplomatic recognition from the ROC on Taiwan to the PRC in China, ahead of Deng's official visit to Washington later that month. That same day, the Carter administration announced the abrogation of the 1954 Mutual Defense Treaty between the United States and the ROC. The pact would formally end one year later, on January 1, 1980. In the meantime, Taipei and its allies in the U.S. Congress mobilized to try to salvage the relationship. More than a dozen lawmakers, led by Senator Barry Goldwater, had already filed a court case in 1978 arguing that President Carter needed congressional approval to withdraw from the treaty. The case reached the U.S. Supreme Court but would be dismissed in late 1979 on jurisdictional grounds.

With little hope of saving the defense treaty, Congress moved quickly to protect the political and economic relationship with Taiwan. In March 1979, it passed the Taiwan Relations Act, which Carter signed into law on April 10. It established the nonprofit American Institute in Taiwan as a de facto U.S. embassy in Taipei and declared that Taiwan, while no longer recognized as an independent state, would be treated the same as other "foreign countries, nations, states, governments, or similar entities" under U.S. law. The act requires the U.S. government to make available to Taiwan the weaponry and other materiel necessary for its defense. And it declares that the president and Congress shall take "appropriate actions" to respond to any threats to Taiwan, though what exactly those would be are purposely ambiguous. Like the 1954 MDT, the act defines "Taiwan" as the island itself and the nearby Pescadores. It doesn't cover any other territories and, unlike the MDT, provides no way to expand that coverage.[83]

For the entire postwar period, the United States had in one form or another been allied to most of the parties involved in the South China Sea disputes: France, South Vietnam, the Philippines, and the ROC. As of January 1, 1979, the Philippines was the only one left. And the future of that alliance was still being negotiated.

Toward a New Status Quo

The U.S. and Philippine governments had restarted formal negotiations on the Military Bases Agreement in early 1978. Talks had continued throughout the year, and for most of that time the political questions surrounding MDT application had been set aside. Negotiators instead focused on nuts-and-bolts issues like the balance between Philippine sovereignty and U.S. operational control on base, criminal jurisdiction over American service members, and, of course, military and financial assistance. But in late 1988, Marcos unexpectedly reintroduced the Spratlys problem. He asked for written answers to several questions about Articles IV and V, including the definition of the "metropolitan

Philippines." None of the questions was directly about the South China Sea, but the State Department was wary. U.S. officials thought these problems had been resolved. In December 1988, the department approved draft responses for the U.S. Embassy to share with Marcos. And Washington offered to have Secretary Vance make a formal statement on the scope of the MDT for public release. But he would do so only as part of a "comprehensive agreement" on basing renewal. The department also sent a warning: "Any further questions, particularly if they were of a hypothetical nature, would have to be answered very legalistically, and would have to emphasize the limits of our commitment so that the answers could be clearly justified to and accepted by Congress. Formal written responses thus tend to be less forthcoming than would our actual response if a real crisis were to arise."[84] This was the same thing Kissinger had told Romulo two years earlier. If Manila pushed for more, the lawyers and politics in Washington would make the answer a convoluted, unsatisfying word soup. This time, Marcos relented. U.S. and Philippine negotiators met on January 2 and reached agreement on the remaining issues. The U.S. Embassy worried that Marcos might reconsider and make new demands if given enough time. The new ambassador, Richard Murphy, urged Washington to move quickly.[85]

The embassy handed Marcos a letter from President Carter two days later. It promised that the White House would make its "best effort" to secure $500 million in security assistance for the Philippines over five years.[86] It was half of what the Ford administration had offered, but Marcos knew it was the best he could get out of Carter or the Democrats in Congress. Three days later, Romulo received a letter from Vance. As promised, it gave some official clarification on the geographic scope of the MDT and promised that the War Powers Act would not constrain the ability of the United States to respond to an attack. It also added the "embellishment" suggested by Stull: "An attack on Philippine armed forces, public vessels or aircraft in the Pacific would not have to occur within the metropolitan territory of the Philippines or island territories under its jurisdiction in the Pacific in order to come within the definition of Pacific Area in Article V."[87] In other words, the South China Sea wasn't *excluded* from the MDT commitment.

The internal consensus at State was a little clearer than this public position. Article V was assumed to cover unprovoked attacks at sea, including around Reed Bank. But violence against Filipino troops on disputed territory was still a gray area. So far, only China and Vietnam had resorted to force in the disputes. But the Philippines had engaged in lower level provocations of its own. And that gave Washington reason to fear being dragged into a fight that might not be entirely defensive. This would be the consensus on MDT application in the South China Sea for the next forty years.

It was good enough. The Philippine government released Vance's letter to the press and signed the renewal of the Military Bases Agreement on January

7. During a press conference a few weeks later, Romulo assured a reporter that he was satisfied with how the letter had dealt with the islands dispute.[88] Of course, that language had been on the table two years earlier, along with a more generous assistance package. So what had changed between 1976 and 1979 to make the deal acceptable to Marcos now? Domestic politics and his own personality certainly played a role—Marcos was convinced he had gotten all he could from Carter and wanted to improve relations with the administration while also declaring himself the protector of Philippine sovereignty.[89] And it helped that the new agreement included an automatic renegotiation every five years, so Manila could push for more concessions the next time around.

But Ambassador Murphy also credited the shifting geopolitics in Asia with helping seal the deal. He told the State Department that Marcos feared the United States would see less value in its Philippine bases following normalization with China. The absence of a threat from Beijing might reduce Marcos's leverage if negotiations dragged on. At the same time, the Philippine president was hearing from fellow ASEAN member-states and China how important the U.S. bases were for regional stability, especially at that time. Vietnam had just invaded neighboring Cambodia at the end of December 1978 and swiftly toppled the Khmer Rouge government. (The new People's Republic of Kampuchea was formally established one day after the bases renewal was signed.) Despite putting an end to Pol Pot's genocidal regime, Vietnam's invasion made it a pariah. ASEAN members saw it as a case of Communist aggression backed by Vietnam's ally, the Soviet Union. Thailand, which shares a border with Cambodia, was so worried that it allowed an alliance of rebel forces, including the Khmer Rouge, to regroup and launch guerrilla attacks from its territory. It had implicit American backing. China, the Khmer Rouge's main patron, was apoplectic. And everyone, including Marcos, feared that the Soviets would turn the situation to their advantage.[90]

These fears were confirmed in late January 1979, when the Soviet Union dispatched a naval task group to the South China Sea, consisting of a cruiser, frigate, minesweeper, three intelligence collection ships, and several support vessels. A smaller task group of three ships steamed into the East China Sea the next month.[91] They had anticipated the coming Sino-Vietnamese conflict, which broke out in mid-February. Around 200,000 Chinese soldiers invaded northern Vietnam in response to Hanoi's operations in Cambodia. The Soviets intercepted Chinese communications and rushed military equipment to Vietnam.[92] But despite the abysmal relations between Beijing and Moscow, neither wanted a direct conflict. China purposely limited the war by keeping its navy and air force out of the fighting. Hanoi, meanwhile, refused to divert most of its forces from Cambodia and met the Chinese invasion mainly with border militia. The fighting wreaked havoc on Vietnam's northern provinces. Both sides suffered thousands of casualties, though most non-Chinese sources agree that Beijing's untested troops got the worst of it. By mid-March, China declared that it had accomplished its political objectives and withdrew.

China and Vietnam remained on the brink of hostilities for months. Both reinforced their positions along the border. Hanoi launched a renewed offensive against pockets of Khmer Rouge control in Cambodia.[93] And in April, Vietnamese gunboats fired on a Chinese patrol ship in the Paracels. The Soviet Union, meanwhile, gained greater access to Vietnam—something for which it had been unsuccessfully petitioning Hanoi for years. In late March, U.S. officials revealed that three Soviet ships had pulled into Cam Ranh Bay Naval Base for the first time. The Americans knew how valuable that real estate was; they had built the base during their war in Vietnam.[94] When two Soviet long-range patrol aircraft landed in Danang around the same time, Washington and Tokyo both feared that Moscow planned to permanently station air and naval forces in the country.[95] They were right.

Soviet ships, submarines, and planes would continually patrol the South China Sea from Cam Ranh Bay from that point on.[96] It presaged a new era of Vietnamese-Soviet cooperation, and Soviet competition with China and the United States, that would dominate Southeast Asia for the next decade. The diplomatic opening between Vietnam and its ASEAN neighbors in 1977–78 was all but forgotten. Indonesia and Malaysia even offered to send troops to Thailand if it were attacked by Vietnam, an offer which Bangkok rejected. Marcos called the suggestion "untimely and improper" but agreed ASEAN should support Thailand in other ways while keeping up a dialogue with Vietnam.[97] Marcos believed that Hanoi wanted to avoid hostilities. But by late 1979, he also worried that it might grant the Soviets access to bases in the Spratlys, which they could use to threaten the Philippines just as Japan had during World War II.[98] Within a year, the Soviet Union would begin rotating pairs of long-range patrol and anti-submarine warfare aircraft through Cam Ranh Bay to keep an eye on Chinese and American operations in the South China Sea. The base soon housed the largest concentration of Soviet naval power outside of the USSR. And in late 1983, Moscow would begin the long-term deployment of bombers at Cam Ranh Bay, which could hold both southern China and American facilities in the Philippines at risk.[99]

At the same time, a related crisis was playing out all across the South China Sea. Political repression and economic turmoil had steadily worsened in Vietnam since 1975. In late 1978, desperate citizens had begun putting to sea in small boats in the hope of escape. By the summer of 1979, tens of thousands were arriving each month on the shores of China, Hong Kong, Indonesia, Malaysia, the Philippines, and Thailand. Tens of thousands more drowned trying to cross the rough waters of the South China Sea and Gulf of Thailand. The scale of the refugee crisis quickly overwhelmed regional capacity to respond. In Malaysia, which received more arrivals than anywhere else, authorities began towing vessels back out to sea.[100] China and Indonesia warned offshore oil and gas operators, mostly American companies, not to aid refugee boats.[101] Commercial vessels became hesitant to render assistance because they might be refused entry to regional ports.

Something had to be done. The United States, Canada, Australia, and European countries agreed to take in more of the refugees. In late July, the Philippines announced that it would open a massive refugee processing center to help take pressure off Malaysia and its other neighbors. Under intense international pressure, Vietnam agreed to set up the Orderly Departure Program in partnership with the United Nations High Commissioner for Refugees. The program would allow Vietnamese citizens to apply for resettlement without having to escape from the country first. The U.S. 7th Fleet, meanwhile, launched search-and-rescue patrols in the South China Sea to aid the refugee boats.[102] This angered Hanoi, which said the operation only encouraged more people to risk the journey. Vietnamese officials also insisted that the American patrols violated their country's territorial integrity and threatened its security. During an October meeting in New York, Vietnam's vice foreign minister Phan Hien accused the United States of "gunboat diplomacy" and invoked the 1964 Gulf of Tonkin incident in calling the patrols "a dangerous act." Assistant Secretary of State Richard Holbrooke defended the operation as "in keeping with the best traditions of the US and in accord with international naval tradition . . . and stressed that the sole aim of the operation was to save lives."[103] By the end of the year, the rollout of the Orderly Departure Program and other steps to reduce the flow of refugees was having an effect. Vietnamese citizens would continue to flee the country by boat for the next several years, but at nowhere near the levels seen in 1979.

By the end of 1979, the territorial disputes in the South China Sea had reached a new status quo. Vietnam was too busy managing the fallout from the invasion of Cambodia to worry much about the Paracel and Spratly Islands. China had neither the ability nor the desire to physically assert its claims beyond the Paracels. The wave of new occupations in the Spratlys had crested, though a quieter competition would soon emerge over reefs closer to the Philippines and Malaysia. The crisis in the U.S.-Philippine alliance had passed, at least for a while. And that debate had forced Washington to reexamine its South China Sea policies. The United States remained committed to neutrality on most territorial questions. There was nothing to be gained and potentially a lot to lose by wading into that historical morass. It wouldn't necessarily help the Philippines, its last ally in the disputes, if territorial claims led to a fight. But it would respond if Filipino forces came under unprovoked attack at sea. And when it came to the waters and airspace of the South China Sea, the U.S. military had clear primacy despite the new Soviet presence.

But as the 1970s gave way to the 1980s, a new legal regime was taking hold. Even before negotiations concluded on the United Nations Convention on the Law of the Sea, member-states had begun staking claims to water and seabed under the new rules. The contest over islands had stabilized, but a new set of disputes were emerging over the sea itself.

5

America and the Free Seas, Part II

1967–1982

> As man's uses of the oceans grow, international law must keep pace. The
> most pressing issue regarding the law of the sea is the need to achieve
> agreement on the breadth of the territorial sea, to head off the threat of
> escalating national claims over the ocean. We also believe it important
> to make parallel progress toward establishing an internationally agreed
> boundary between the continental shelf and the deep seabeds and on a
> regime for exploitation of deep seabed resources.
>
> —President Richard Nixon, First Annual Report to the Congress on
> U.S. Foreign Policy, February 18, 1970[1]

By the late 1960s, it was clear that the regime of maritime law codified in Geneva
in 1958 needed to change. The United States was at the center of these debates,
but so were most of the South China Sea claimants. It would take decades to reach
consensus on new rules better suited to the modern world. What emerged was
the most ambitious and inclusive piece of international law ever created. Unlike
so much of the postwar international system, the United Nations Convention on
the Law of the Sea (UNCLOS) was not forged by Western powers or the Soviet
bloc; it required the consent of all, and so represented the interests of both developed and developing states. But an innovative legal regime also meant new
disagreements. And by the late 1970s, the South China Sea was becoming home
to a web of disputes over water and seabed. These interacted with but were distinct from the older territorial disputes. And unlike arguments over rocks and
reefs, the contest for maritime space touched directly on the interests of outside parties. These included the historic American commitment to freedom of
the seas.

On Dangerous Ground. Gregory B. Poling, Oxford University Press. © Oxford University Press 2022.
DOI: 10.1093/oso/9780197633984.003.0006

A Time of Change

Following the narrow failure at UNCLOS II in 1960, Canada, the United Kingdom, and the United States continued lobbying for their compromise package of a 6-nautical-mile territorial sea and 6-mile contiguous zone. But by 1962, they had given up on the multilateral approach. Meanwhile new fishing technologies, especially purse seining, were increasing the reach and intensity of distant-water fishing fleets. The Soviet Union was heavily subsidizing the expansion of its fleet and Japanese fishers were heading farther afield. As a result, the United Kingdom led most of Europe to adopt a regional variant of the 6-plus-6 scheme in 1964. Canada stuck with a 3-mile territorial sea but added a 9-mile fishing zone that year. Under pressure from struggling coastal fishing fleets, the United States did the same in 1966. But London, Ottawa, and Washington still refused to recognize claims beyond 12 miles from shore, except to the seabed as agreed in the Convention on the Continental Shelf. And the U.S. government advised Americans not to purchase fishing licenses beyond that limit from states making 200-mile claims. Predictably, this led to increasing seizures of American tuna boats off Latin America.

By the mid-1960s, the split between developed and developing nations had supplanted NATO-Soviet rivalry as the most important dividing line on the law of the sea. At the first meeting of the United Nations Conference on Trade and Development, in 1964, nonaligned developing countries announced the establishment of the "Group of 77" to promote their interests. The group soon took up the cause of 200-mile maritime zones, driven largely by the Latin American proponents who stood to benefit most. That coalition would eventually fracture when it became clear that expansive claims didn't benefit all countries equally. But it held for about a decade.

By the late 1960s, the United States and Soviet Union were each publicly accusing the other of interfering with its navy in international waters. But Soviet investments in naval, fishing, merchant marine, and oceanographic capabilities were also driving it closer to the U.S. positions on most law of the sea issues. Soviet officials approached their American counterparts in 1967 to express concern over the trend of ever more expansive coastal state claims. This kicked off discussions that eventually led the superpowers to a new consensus. The Americans could accept a 12-mile territorial sea. But in exchange, ships, submarines, and aircraft would need to be guaranteed normal transit rights, not just innocent passage, through international straits. And the two recognized that coastal states would need to be granted preferential, but not exclusive, fishing rights beyond the territorial sea. They drew up draft articles on these points and took them to their respective allies. But they ran into considerable resistance. It was a sign of the debates to come.[2]

Seabed technology, meanwhile, was advancing more slowly than many had predicted. In 1968, the UN Economic Commission for Asia and the Far East speculated that the South China Sea might contain significant oil and gas deposits. This fueled newspaper coverage and speculative exploration but produced few results. The story was much the same around the world. And with little immediate hope of commercial production far from shore, there was no incentive for most states to define the outer limits of their seabed claims. The Convention on the Continental Shelf didn't require them to do so. The exceptions were those countries, such as Indonesia and Malaysia, whose shelves overlapped in shallow waters with immediate commercial prospects. Jakarta and Kuala Lumpur in 1969 negotiated territorial sea and continental shelf boundaries on either side of the Natuna Islands at the southern edge of the South China Sea, as well as in the Strait of Malacca.

Still, it was widely assumed that a deep seabed resource boom was around the corner. By the end of the 1960s, the deepest producing oil well was under just 340 feet of water. But exploratory drilling had occurred at 1,300 feet, well beyond the depths envisioned by the 1958 Convention on the Continental Shelf.[3] And that raised problems. First, the convention had left the outer limit of the shelf open to interpretation. Second, there was no consensus on what regime should govern seabed activities beyond that fuzzy boundary. In 1967, Malta stepped into the breach. Its ambassador to the United Nations, Arvid Pardo, proposed that the seabed beyond the territorial sea and continental shelf be declared the "common heritage of mankind" under the supervision of an international authority. The idea was meant to guarantee all states, not just those with the technical capacity for deep seabed mining, a piece of the pie. It would also ensure that economic activity under the high seas occurred sustainably. Pardo also proposed including fish stocks beyond the territorial sea in this category but was rebuffed.[4] The General Assembly voted to establish an ad hoc committee to consider the issues raised by Malta. It was replaced by a permanent Seabed Committee in 1968. The discussions there would lead to the historic Third Conference on the Law of the Sea a few years later.

Preparing for UNCLOS III

Washington had trouble deciding how to respond to the Maltese proposal. The U.S. ambassador to the United Nations, Arthur J. Goldberg, was initially supportive and encouraged the General Assembly to take up the effort. But Congress and the Interior Department were less welcoming. More than twenty resolutions were introduced in the House of Representatives opposing the establishment of any international jurisdiction over the seabed. Many lawmakers attacked the idea out of an ideological hostility toward the United Nations. Others were more open, and it received a fairer hearing in the Senate. The Interior Department, meanwhile, backed oil industry calls for the most expansive possible definition of coastal state rights. Industry groups argued that the limit of the shelf should be the point where it reached the abyssal ocean floor. And it opposed any international machinery to regulate mining in the deep seabed beyond.[5]

On the other side were the Department of Defense and, especially, the navy. They were heavily influenced by reports like the 1969 *Our Nation and the Sea*, written by the National Commission on Marine Science, Engineering and Resources chaired by Julius Stratton. The "Stratton Commission" concluded that expansive continental shelf claims would likely lead to exclusive claims to the waters and airspace above them, just as the Truman Proclamations had. It argued, "Such developments are obviously contrary to the traditional U.S. policy to limit national claims to the sea in the interest of the maximum freedom essential to the multiple uses, including military uses, which the United States makes of the oceans."[6] This fear of "creeping jurisdiction" led the Defense Department to prefer narrow coastal state jurisdiction over the continental shelf and the establishment of an international authority to regulate mining beyond.

The State Department was internally divided and so offered little guidance at first. By late 1969, it had forged a shaky compromise between the navy and Interior to propose an international registry for deep seabed mining. But there was still no internal consensus on the limits of the continental shelf. State came up with a clever proposal for an intermediate zone between the 200-meter isobath and the edge of the continental margin. The coastal state would have the right to license drilling but would otherwise guarantee international uses of the seabed and adjacent waters. And it would pay a small percentage of the profits to an international development fund. Interior was amenable, but the Defense Department rejected the proposal. In early 1970, Under Secretary of State Elliot Richardson tweaked the proposal. Rather than exercising sovereign rights in the intermediate zone, he proposed that the coastal state be empowered to license resource extraction as a trustee of the international community. This flipped the Interior and Defense positions. The former vehemently opposed the new compromise; the latter grudgingly accepted it.

As Washington struggled to forge an internal consensus, the international demands for change grew ever louder. Moscow had similar trouble. The two had agreed on the broad outlines of a territorial sea and fisheries compromise, which would carry over to their negotiating positions in the United Nations. But each had more trouble adopting a new continental shelf policy. This led to accusations that the superpowers were standing in the way of progress in the

Seabed Committee. The Americans and Soviets also preferred to keep seabed negotiations separate from other law of the sea issues, believing a broader debate would be unmanageable. But by December 1969, developing states were tired of waiting. The General Assembly overrode U.S. and Soviet objections and approved a four-part resolution. It called for all member-states to be polled on whether to convene a new law of the sea conference, instructed the Seabed Committee to submit draft articles for consideration, asked the secretary-general to study international means for governing the deep seabed, and declared a moratorium on mining in such areas.

The momentum behind a third conference had become unstoppable, and it put considerable pressure on the United States to get its house in order. New, more expansive maritime claims were also creating a sense of urgency. In March 1970, Brazil declared a 200-mile territorial sea. At the same time, Canada was debating legislation to regulate shipping within 100 miles of shore.[7] If Washington wanted international agreement on narrower maritime zones, it first needed to break the logjam in the Seabed Committee. A few months earlier, President Nixon had highlighted the problem during his first foreign policy report to Congress: "The most pressing issue regarding the law of the sea is the need to achieve agreement on the breadth of the territorial sea, to head off the threat of escalating national claims over the ocean. We also believe it important to make parallel progress toward establishing an internationally agreed boundary between the continental shelf and the deep seabeds, and on a regime for exploitation of deep seabed resources."[8] But the White House itself was divided. The president's domestic affairs advisors were backing the Interior Department, while Secretary of State Kissinger and the National Security Council supported the navy and Under Secretary Richardson. At the end of April, Nixon made the call. He approved a version of the Richardson proposal as the official U.S. negotiating position. The continental shelf should extend to the 200-meter isobath. Beyond that should be a "trusteeship zone" to the edge of the continental margin. And in the deep seabed beyond, an international authority should regulate exploitation and collect "significant mineral royalties" to be disbursed to developing countries.

A few months earlier, the State Department had established an Interagency Task Force on the Law of the Sea led by Legal Advisor John Stevenson. Once the White House announced its new continental shelf policy, the task force set about drafting detailed proposals to take to the UN Seabed Committee. Bernard Oxman led the five-person drafting committee, which managed to put together a model treaty in just a month. Despite opposition from the oil industry, Interior and Commerce Departments, and much of Congress, the United States submitted the proposed treaty—dubbed a "working paper" to appease critics— to the committee in August. U.S. allies had been given almost no notice and offered little support on its substance. But the proposal showed that the United

States was finally ready to negotiate. A month later, the General Assembly voted to convene UNCLOS III in a little over two years' time, 1973.

The General Assembly assigned the preparatory work for UNCLOS III to the Seabed Committee, chaired by Hamilton Amerasinghe of Sri Lanka. The committee more than doubled in size to eighty-six member-states and got to work in early 1971. Three subcommittees were established to draft articles and an agenda for the conference. The first tackled international regulation of the deep seabed, the second took on everything relating to the territorial sea and fisheries, and the third was tasked with environmental and scientific issues.[9] This division of labor would continue throughout the UNCLOS III process. In December, five more states joined the Seabed Committee, including the PRC.[10] The General Assembly had voted a few months earlier to recognize Beijing rather than Taipei as the official representative of China in the United Nations.

The three subcommittees met throughout 1972. In the first, a thirty-three-nation working group under Sri Lanka's Christopher Pinto began drafting articles for the deep seabed. The second devolved into contentious arguments between the maritime powers and the Group of 77 over which topics should be listed on the negotiating agenda. Though they eventually reached agreement, it was an omen of the difficult work ahead. The third subcommittee made more progress and began drafting articles on the marine environment and scientific research. In late 1972, the General Assembly voted to convene the first session of UNCLOS III in one year's time. That meeting would tackle organizational matters, followed by a substantive negotiation in mid-1974, and a concluding session no later than 1975. It was a wildly optimistic timeframe given the long list of disagreements identified by the Seabed Committee.

Preparatory work continued in 1973, with the working groups on the deep seabed and the marine environment making considerable progress on draft treaty language. Subcommittee II set up its own working group to begin drafting articles but lagged far behind the others. In Washington, new structures were established to lead the negotiations. The Interagency Task Force on the Law of the Sea was formally housed within the National Security Council, but it remained under the leadership of the State Department, which established the new Office of Law of the Sea Negotiations. John Stevenson was made an ambassador and appointed to lead the U.S. delegation to the conference. And John Norton Moore replaced him as chair of the task force. They would serve in those critical roles for the next three years.[11]

Despite the uneven progress on preparations for the conference, the General Assembly voted in November 1973 to move forward with its ambitious timeframe. UNCLOS III was to start with an organizational meeting in New York a month later and conclude by 1975. All members of the United Nations and its agencies were invited to participate. Special invitations were also extended to nonmembers Guinea-Bissau and North Vietnam.[12] Taiwan was the only party to the South China Sea disputes at that time that wouldn't have a hand in crafting the new constitution for the oceans. Unlike its predecessors, UNCLOS III was a truly global effort. The first two conferences had included 86 and 88 countries, respectively. They had been about evenly divided among Asian, Latin American, and NATO-aligned delegations, with the smaller Soviet bloc punching above its weight. But only 6 African states had been present. UNCLOS III turned that on its head: delegates came from 147 countries, including 41 each from Africa and Asia.[13] The Group of 77 could easily claim the most votes when it was able to hold its diverse coalition together. The maritime powers represented by the much smaller NATO and Soviet blocs still held considerable influence; no law of the sea treaty could succeed without their concurrence. But they couldn't override coastal and developing nations' preferences.

Equally important were the like-minded groups that formed around specific issues. Many from Latin America still wanted a 200-mile territorial sea, but they were in the minority. Most other coastal states favored exclusive resource rights but not sovereignty over the continental shelf and adjacent waters. The maritime states pushed for preferential rather than exclusive rights over fisheries and drew a firm line on the right of normal transit through international straits. Those countries with the most advanced maritime capabilities—the United States, Soviet Union, United Kingdom, Japan, and France—came to be known as the Group of 5, though they were often at odds. Indonesia and the Philippines weren't going to leave without the recognition of archipelagic baselines they had been denied in 1958. Those countries with the largest continental margins—colorfully dubbed the "Margineers"—sought to extend the shelf beyond 200 miles. And the landlocked and geographically disadvantaged states (LL/GDS) opposed expansive seabed rights and championed the oceans as a global commons.[14] Given this diversity, every part of the convention involved difficult compromises. And in the final product, the developing world gave at least as good as it got.

Forging a New Law of the Sea, Phase 1

The first session in New York failed to settle all the procedural questions surrounding the conference. Those continued to be debated well into the second session in Caracas, which began in June 1974. Hamilton Amerasinghe was asked to continue his leadership as president of the conference. When the delegates finally got down to substantive negotiations, the Group of 77 made sure all the real work would take place in the three main committees where their superior numbers ensured the greatest influence. The division of labor mirrored that in the Seabed Committee, and the committees' leadership reflected the global nature of the conference. Paul Engo of Cameroon chaired the first committee, tasked with deep seabed mining. Christopher Pinto from Sri Lanka continued to lead its working group, and Singapore's Tommy Koh headed negotiations on financial arrangements for the new seabed regime. Leadership of Committee II, which handled all issues related to the territorial sea, fisheries, and the continental shelf, alternated between Galindo Pohl of El Salvador and Andres Aguilar of Venezuela. Bulgaria's Alexander Yankov chaired Committee III, handling marine pollution and scientific research.

The rules of procedure finally adopted in late June included a "gentleman's agreement" that all decisions should be reached by consensus. Failing that, substantive decisions required a two-thirds vote *twice*—first to agree that consensus was impossible and then again on the matter at hand. This process intentionally made votes so divisive that delegates avoided them in favor of compromise.[15] Consensus-based decision-making would prove one of the keys to success. There was no voting on individual provisions and therefore no perceived winners and losers. No article made it into the final convention until everyone had concurred. And the entire treaty was made a package deal—states had to take it or leave it. This helps explain why the process took so long and why it achieved almost universal acceptance. But sometimes that process also required negotiators to write "constructive ambiguities" into the convention, leaving them open to interpretation. This was often a result of political compromises during the negotiating process.[16]

By the time delegates met in Caracas for the second session, it was clear that negotiations would take much longer than expected. The Group of 77 was fractured by disagreements between coastal states seeking more expansive claims and the LL/GDS group opposing them. The concerns of the thirty landlocked states were self-explanatory. The geographically disadvantaged were a diverse set of countries eventually numbering twenty-five. They either had very narrow maritime zones, like Singapore, or were highly dependent on resources in their neighbors' waters. The LL/GDS group had gathered in the spring and released the Declaration of Kampala, which laid out their demands. These included access to the sea for landlocked states, the right to exploit the coastal resources of their more geographically blessed neighbors, and international stewardship of all seabed resources beyond 200 miles. Developing coastal states rejected most of these and refused to even recognize the idea of geographic disadvantage; they would negotiate concessions only for the landlocked. The LL/GDS group was further isolated in Caracas when the Soviet Union, United States, and United Kingdom broke ranks with some of the other maritime states and endorsed a 200-mile fishing zone.

Deliberations on the deep seabed in Committee I immediately hit a wall. It was here that the divide between developed and developing nations was clearest.

The most technologically advanced knew their companies were the only ones that could hope to tap mineral resources beyond the continental shelf, and so sought to limit the role of any international governing body. They proposed that an international seabed authority be created to issue licenses to qualified companies. Those firms would pay a fee in return for exclusive rights to a site for a defined period. The Group of 77 had different ideas. They knew that most benefits in such a system would accrue to the wealthiest nations, especially the United States. Instead, they wanted the proposed seabed authority to conduct all exploration, exploitation, and research itself. They allowed that it might contract work to private companies when necessary.

Committee II was both messier and more productive. With such a broad set of issues to tackle, coalitions were more malleable and concessions on one point could be traded for consensus on others. Heading into Caracas, seventy-six countries had already claimed a territorial sea of at least 12 miles, and many more were just waiting for the conference to formalize this emerging consensus.[17] But the maritime powers would not commit unless they were guaranteed the right to transit normally through straits covered by such a regime. A year earlier, Indonesia and several others had proposed draft articles allowing straits states to regulate transit. Foreign warships would be required to gain prior authorization before passing through, submarines would have to navigate on the surface, and special rules could be applied to other kinds of vessels, including those carrying nuclear weapons or powered by nuclear energy. There was no chance the maritime powers would agree. Most states were in the middle, favoring a much lighter hand for regulation by straits states. But the issue was left unresolved.

Discussions on the 200-mile fishing zone, which most were now calling the EEZ, broke down along a predictable spectrum. At one extreme were the LL/GDS, which opposed the concept altogether unless they were guaranteed an equal share in the resources. At the other were those Latin American states still lobbying for a 200-mile territorial sea. And in the middle were competing models for the new EEZ. The United States, Soviet Union, and United Kingdom had conditioned their support on the zone remaining part of the high seas. They proposed that the coastal state be allowed to regulate certain economic activities but have no authority over other issues, including foreign naval operations. And if a coastal state's own fleet couldn't fully exploit a fishery, the maritime powers wanted foreign vessels to be licensed to catch the surplus. Many coastal states, especially in Africa and Latin America, wanted to reverse that formula. They demanded exclusive rights within the zone. Foreign fleets would be allowed in only at the coastal state's discretion. And they argued that the treaty should list the freedoms guaranteed to foreign countries in the EEZ; anything not on the list would be under coastal state control.

Three other issues troubled the Committee II discussions in Caracas. On the continental shelf, the battle lines had been drawn well in advance. The LL/GDS, Japan, and some African coastal states wanted to set the limit at 200 miles. The Margineers wanted their rights to extend all the way to the abyssal ocean floor. Some of them endorsed revenue-sharing schemes like the "trusteeship zone" proposed by the United States. Others, including Australia and the United Kingdom, saw no need.

Then there were the demands by archipelagic countries to be allowed to establish a new legal regime in the waters between their islands. This concept of "archipelagic waters" was more sophisticated than the vast internal waters originally claimed by Indonesia and the Philippines. They now proposed that foreign warships could transit through archipelagic waters in innocent passage, just as they could through the territorial sea. The maritime powers still weren't enthusiastic, however, and sought to guarantee more normal passage.

And finally, delegates were undecided on whether islands should generate all the same entitlements as continental landmasses, including to territorial seas, continental shelves, and an EEZ.[18] That would become a much more difficult discussion in subsequent sessions. And of course, it would have a special relevance in the South China Sea.

In summing up the committee's work at Caracas, Ambassador Aguilar declared:

> The idea of a territorial sea of twelve miles and an exclusive economic zone beyond the territorial sea up to a total maximum distance of 200 miles is, at least at this time, the keystone of the compromise solution favoured by the majority of States participating in the Conference. . . . Acceptance of this idea is, of course, dependent on the satisfactory solution of other issues, especially the issue of passage through straits used for international navigation, the outermost limit of the continental shelf and the actual retention of this concept, and, last but not least, the aspirations of the [LL/GDS].[19]

Committee III made comparatively little progress on the marine environment and scientific research. This was partly because it had to wait for more clarity from Committee II on where maritime zones would lie. But it also suffered from the same divisions between developed and developing states, and between the LL/GDS and everyone else, that were slowing progress in the other committees. As the Caracas session neared its end, Ambassador Pohl brought together about thirty countries from across the regional blocs to informally discuss the dispute settlement chapter of the convention. They produced a working paper which would inform later negotiations. Dispute settlement mechanisms would continue to be debated outside of the three committees.

Delegates reconvened in Geneva in the spring of 1975. After another two months of negotiations, the committee chairmen managed to produce the Single Negotiating Text. Full of omissions and alternative texts, it was a far cry from the final treaty the General Assembly had expected to see that year. Seabed mining was the toughest nut to crack, and it would hold up the convention for several more years. The deep seabed debate didn't concern oil and gas, which are concentrated on the continental shelf. It focused instead on strategic minerals like manganese, nickel, and cobalt, which develop in nodules on the deep ocean floor. By the 1970s, a handful of multinational consortia and wealthy nations were developing technology to extract these manganese nodules. Commercial production was widely expected by the 1990s; decades later, however, the world is still waiting in vain for this prophesied seabed mining boom. That makes the acrimonious debates at UNCLOS III, and in the years that followed, almost tragic.

Despite what we now know, the delegates gathered in Geneva were certain that manganese nodules would be the next big thing. And developing nations had no interest in letting early adopters from the United States, Soviet Union, Japan, and Europe corner the market. The two sides had been diametrically opposed in Caracas. The Group of 77 had insisted that the mooted international seabed authority undertake exploration and mining itself. The United States and other maritime powers had demanded that it be merely a licensing body for exploitation by individual companies or governments, which would pay for the privilege. In Geneva, moderate voices in both camps sought compromise. Christopher Pinto's working group drafted a proposal for a parallel system in which some sites would be reserved for direct exploitation by an international authority and others for joint ventures from individual countries. The United States had already offered to consider such a system. But once it was in writing, many members of the Group of 77 revolted, and the committee ended the session back where it had started.

Discussions in Committee II were again more fruitful. The consensus on the 12-mile territorial sea continued to solidify. Delegates agreed that states could use straight baselines to measure the territorial sea in cases where the coastline was unstable. They also agreed that such baselines could be drawn to low-tide elevations near the coast, meaning reefs, rocks, or sandbars that are dry only at low tide. Both represented compromise by the United States, which had long championed the low-water margin as the only acceptable point from which to measure maritime zones. Committee II also saw a breakthrough on straits passage and archipelagic waters, which were closely linked.[20] Fiji and the United Kingdom convened an informal group of fifteen delegations to forge a compromise on straits. The United States, Soviet Union, and the three major straits states—Indonesia, Malaysia, and Spain—were purposely excluded. Their work was sent to the committee chair and incorporated into the draft text. As part of the compromise, normal transit and overflight were to be guaranteed through all straits used for international navigation. This included the right of submarines to remain submerged, which was a key demand of the maritime powers. The text never spelled this out, but Tommy Koh, who had a front-row seat throughout the conference, has insisted that none of the negotiators ever seriously argued against it.[21]

A similar regime would apply when transiting sea lanes through archipelagic waters. In exchange for their support on the transit question, the United States and other maritime powers agreed to most of the demands made by the archipelagic states. They would be permitted to connect their outermost islands and reefs with straight baselines and declare everything inside to be archipelagic waters, with certain limitations. One of these was that the ratio of water to land encompassed by the baselines could not exceed nine to one. And importantly, the entire regime applied only to countries composed entirely of archipelagos. Continental states that happened to have offshore archipelagos could not connect those islands with straight baselines.[22] That bargain between maritime and archipelagic states would hold for the remainder of the convention.

On the continental shelf, the delegations were still split into three camps. But those favoring compromise, including the United States, were presenting more sophisticated proposals on revenue sharing and the outer limits of the shelf. By this point, the legal concept of the continental shelf had expanded well beyond its scientific meaning. In geomorphology, the continental shelf is just one of three zones that make up the continental margin—that part of a landmass extending beneath the ocean. Beyond the shelf are the continental slope, where the seabed drops off steeply toward the ocean floor, and the continental rise, an ill-defined area where sediment that has washed off the slope collects. The Margineers wanted rights to all of it. Seeking more clarity, the United States proposed that the legal continental shelf end at 200 miles *or* 60 miles beyond the foot of the continental slope. As the debate over the shelf became more technical, delegates agreed that an international commission would be needed to review claims. This would eventually take the form of the Commission on the Limits of the Continental Shelf.[23]

The work of Committee II accounted for most of the progress made in 1975. But that was ultimately overshadowed by the behavior of its chairman. The committee chairs that year were given unchecked power to draft their sections of the Single Negotiating Text. And Galindo Pohl chose to craft a document that overwhelmingly reflected the interests of those coastal states, like his native El Salvador, seeking the most expansive claims. Other than on straits transit, he made little effort to incorporate the emerging compromises or outstanding disagreements of the previous two months. He also exceeded his mandate by writing articles on marine science and pollution, which rightfully belonged to Committee III. The maritime powers and the LL/GDS were irate, but they had no opportunity to confront the chairman. Pohl quietly left Geneva before the text was shared on the last day of the conference.

Negotiations on dispute settlement became more formal during the 1975 session, with over sixty countries taking part. Some backed taking disputes to the International Court of Justice, others wanted to establish a special tribunal, and still others backed arbitration or conciliation. Since the delegates were divided, an annex to the negotiating text specified that countries should select one or more preferred forms of dispute settlement when they ratified the convention. If a dispute arose, it would be taken to the venue agreed upon by the parties involved. The rules would get more complicated, but this system would remain intact for the rest of the conference.

The anger Pohl had roused in 1975 dogged negotiators when they came together for two sessions in New York the following spring and summer. The U.S. team sought a breakthrough, but election-year politicking and turnover in the negotiating team made progress difficult. One month into the spring session, the U.S. Congress passed the Fishery Conservation and Management Act, which unilaterally established a 200-mile fishing zone. President Ford, seeing it as good domestic politics, signed the bill despite opposition from the State and Defense Departments. The effects on UNCLOS III were mixed. On the one hand, it granted American coastal fishers what they wanted most, which caused them to lose interest in the negotiations. That diminished the domestic constituency pushing for progress. But the move also signaled to other nations that the United States might go it alone if negotiations remained stalled. And that lent some momentum to talks on the deep seabed.

Meanwhile, the two men who had led U.S. law of the sea efforts to that point both stepped down. Ambassador Stevenson retired in December 1975 to reenter private practice. John Norton Moore sought to reunite the power of the Interagency Task Force and the negotiator for the law of the sea under his office. But President Ford appointed former IBM chairman Vincent Learson to lead the negotiating team instead. And when Learson exerted control over the task force as well, Moore followed Stevenson out the door. The new ambassador, however, found himself overshadowed when Kissinger personally intervened in the negotiations. Eager to improve relations with the Group of 77, the secretary saw the law of the sea talks as a plum opportunity.

Kissinger made a major speech at the spring session and then offered several unilateral concessions on seabed mining in the hopes of a breakthrough. The United States had already offered to consider a parallel system for deep seabed mining. Now Kissinger explicitly said that Washington would accept such a system, including setting aside mining sites for eventual direct exploitation by an international authority. He also committed the United States to transfer mining technology, provide financing for this authority, and accept production controls to protect the market share of land-based mineral producers in the developing world. Paul Engo, who chaired Committee I, wrote the parallel system into the draft text released at the end of the spring session. But throughout the summer session, it faced the same withering criticism from the Group of 77 that had killed the Pinto draft a year earlier.[24]

Andres Aguilar resumed the chairmanship of Committee II and spent most of the spring session reviewing and amending the draft that Pohl had forced through in 1975. One area of heated debate remained the status of the new EEZ. About fifty maritime and LL/GDS states favored its being part of the high seas, while an equal number of coastal nations declared the opposite. At stake was whether naval operations, among other things, could be restricted in the zone. Aguilar sought a compromise, writing, "[T]he exclusive economic zone is neither the high seas nor the territorial sea. It is a zone *sui generis* [one of a kind]."[25] But that didn't really answer the question. And Kissinger reiterated that the United States would not accept anything less than explicit high seas freedoms in the new zone aside from select economic rights.

Delegates continued their technical debate on the limits of the continental shelf. The U.S. delegation said that in addition to 200 miles or 60 miles from the foot of the continental slope, it would accept an even more complicated proposal based on the thickness of sediment on the seabed. All these formulae eventually made it into the final convention. The 1976 session also made further progress on dispute settlement. President Amerasinghe drafted a new compromise specifying that should parties to a dispute disagree on the method of resolution, the plaintiff could either choose the one preferred by the defendant or opt for arbitration.[26] From then on, arbitration was to be the default method of dispute settlement under UNCLOS III. Delegates would continue to wrangle over the details, but there was broad consensus on the need for such a system of dispute settlement—so much so, in fact, that it was the first time the Soviet Union had ever supported compulsory arbitration in a treaty.[27] Nearly forty years later, the South China Sea would put this ambitious system to the test.

The 1976 sessions marked the end of the first phase of negotiations in UNCLOS III. At the end of the spring session, the committee chairmen had managed to produce the Revised Single Negotiating Text. It was opposed by many developing coastal states, just as the prior year's draft had been rejected by the maritime powers and LL/GDS. But the conference had reached consensus on the outlines of a new regime for the territorial sea, straits passage, the continental shelf, and the new EEZ. The issues remaining before Committees II and

III were contentious but manageable. Unfortunately, no one wanted to make further concessions in those committees until the logjam in Committee I broke. From 1977 on, negotiations were held hostage by the seabed mining questions. In many ways, the United States still is.

Forging a New Law of the Sea, Phase 2

When the conference reconvened in New York from May to July 1977, its first few weeks were dedicated entirely to deep seabed mining. The session produced yet another draft, this time called an Informal Composite Negotiating Text. After the political transition in the United States, the new U.S. delegation proved far less willing to give ground than they had the year before. Kissinger had gone around the normal consultative process within the U.S. negotiating team to offer his concessions, and that still hadn't gotten the job done. The new Carter administration placed great importance on the law of the sea negotiations, but it was also unhappy with the lack of domestic support and the constrained negotiating positions left by the outgoing government. Carter appointed Elliot Richardson to lead the negotiating team.

To rebuild a domestic constituency in support of the negotiations, Richardson requested two major reviews of law of the sea policy. He tasked the intelligence community to assess how important a new treaty was to U.S. national security. The resulting National Intelligence Estimate concluded that, while a new treaty wouldn't be a silver bullet, it would help restrain excessive maritime claims worldwide. Meanwhile, an interagency review process looked at previous U.S. positions, future negotiating options, and possible domestic legislation on seabed mining. While these played out, Richardson's negotiating team focused on holding the line in New York until they saw some reciprocal movement from the Group of 77.[28]

To change things up, the conference established the Chairman's Working Group of the Whole under Norway's Jens Evensen to seek compromise on seabed mining. On nearly every issue, Evensen split the difference between the positions of the maritime powers and the Group of 77. The resulting text pleased no one, but it had a certain credibility given the inclusive process. It retained the parallel system, with mining rights divided between states and what was now called "the Enterprise." The U.S. delegation didn't accept everything in the draft, but it recognized it as important progress.

Once Committee II reconvened several weeks into the session, there were only a few tricky issues left to debate. One was the legal status of the EEZ. Chairman Aguilar had declared it a zone sui generis, but neither the coastal states nor the maritime powers were happy without further clarity. To break the impasse, Mexico's Jorge Castañeda was asked to lead a negotiating group of fifteen nations representing all sides in the debate. The result was purposely ambiguous and allowed everyone to claim victory, but it carefully enumerated the rights of coastal states while guaranteeing all other freedoms of the high seas. The net effect was to secure within the EEZ most of those freedoms traditionally enjoyed in international waters, including the right to military activities.[29] When this text was forwarded to the full committee, the LL/GDS, among others, were unsatisfied. But they grudgingly consented to its inclusion in the new negotiating text. And that was that.

The continental shelf discussions were still stuck on the outer limits of the zone, with the LL/GDS, Arab, and many African states continuing to insist on 200 miles and no more. As a result, the new text allowed coastal state control over the continental margin but didn't specify how the outer limit should be set. The means of delimiting overlapping EEZ and continental shelf boundaries between states also remained hotly contested. Countries were of two minds. Some wanted a strict use of the median line, or equidistance, principle. This was the default method in the 1958 Convention on the Continental Shelf, so why not keep it? But others, especially the LL/GDS, wanted delimitation based on equitable principles, which expanded on the "special circumstances" allowed by the earlier convention. This was an ill-defined concept but recognized that equidistance could often be unfair. A country with a highly concave coastline—Bangladesh, for example—would find that median lines with its neighbors quickly intersected, leaving it with a very small maritime zone of its own. The conference was equally divided between the two camps, so the best the committee could do was ambiguous language that supported both methods.

In Committees II and III and the plenary discussions on dispute settlement, the 1977 session was basically tying up loose ends. But it was all academic unless Committee I could make progress on seabed mining. The working group under Evensen had finally built some momentum behind compromise, even if it hadn't resolved much. But then Chairman Engo stepped in at the end of the session to reassert his authority. He cloistered himself with a small group of advisors and reworked the Evensen text. This moved it closer to the Group of 77's preferences on almost all points. And Engo kept these changes secret; the delegations only found out when the Informal Composite Negotiating Text was released after the session concluded.[30] A furious Ambassador Richardson announced that the "unfortunate, last minute deviation from what had seemed to be an emerging direction of promise in the deep seabed negotiations" compelled him to recommend that the U.S. government reexamine its participation in the conference.[31]

The United States didn't actually walk away, but the review that followed led to a two-pronged approach. Washington would continue to participate in the conference while also pursuing a smaller treaty with like-minded states and considering unilateral domestic legislation on deep seabed mining. The United States and six other countries met in November 1977 to discuss a fallback treaty on seabed mining should the law of the sea talks fail. But these efforts were primarily a bluff to encourage progress in the conference. Richardson saw a successful law of the sea treaty as the overriding goal.

American negotiators came to the 1978 session in Geneva ready for a fight. They and many others were fed up with the process. First Pohl and then Engo had ignored committee debates and secretly rewritten drafts to reflect their own preferences. To prevent similar incidents, the United States backed Amerasinghe in a bid to take over the ultimate responsibility for revising all texts. Most of the African, Asian, and Western European delegations backed this effort to reduce the power of the committee chairmen. But the Latin American delegations weren't willing to give up the influence they enjoyed in Committee II by virtue of Aguilar's leadership. Instead, they tried to strip Amerasinghe of his position. This led to two weeks of bickering before he was reconfirmed as president of the conference by a wide margin.

Once the theatrics were over, it was agreed that future revision would be made by Amerasinghe and the chairmen working as a team. But everyone knew something more drastic was needed on the most intractable issues. The conference agreed to establish seven new negotiating groups. The first three split up the work of Committee I. Kenya's Frank Njenga led negotiations on how the parallel system for deep seabed mining would work, and Singapore's Koh directed those on financial arrangements for the system. Chairman Engo was left with the less sensitive discussions on the structure and powers of the International Seabed Authority (ISA). The other four negotiating groups tackled access for the LL/GDS to the EEZ, the settlement of disputes over resources in the zone, the outer limit of the continental shelf, and the delimitation of boundaries between states.

These procedural issues took up almost half of the eight-week session in Geneva. The negotiating groups worked feverishly for the rest of the session and then reconvened in New York for another four weeks in the summer. The U.S. delegation was happy enough with the new system that it again began to offer substantial concessions. The group under Njenga produced revised texts on technology transfer, production controls, and the selection of applicants for mining sites. Koh's group wrote a sophisticated paper on financing the ISA and the Enterprise, which relied on a combination of fees, royalties, and profit-sharing by companies. It was all based on a model from the Massachusetts Institute of Technology on the future profitability of seabed mining. (The model was off by several decades, but there was no way to know that at the time.) Engo's group, meanwhile, tweaked the structure of the seabed authority and its subsidiary organs.

The fourth negotiating group produced a text guaranteeing the LL/GDS an appropriate share of surplus fish in their neighbors' EEZs. The LL/GDS were dissatisfied, but their coastal colleagues in the Group of 77 warned that it was the best they were going to get. Negotiating Group 5 settled on a system of compulsory but nonbinding conciliation for disputes involving the resources of the EEZ. The sixth group made no progress on the limit of the continental shelf or how much revenue coastal states should share in the area beyond 200 miles. Consensus was also elusive in Group 7. Delegates remained divided on equidistance versus equitable principles for boundary delimitation. They also disagreed on whether compulsory dispute settlement should be available to de-limit boundaries and whether the median line should be used as a provisional boundary in such cases.

Chairman Aguilar led an article-by-article review of the draft text from Committee II, which gave countries a final chance to raise concerns. A half-dozen straits states again objected to the articles on transit rights. The Soviets tried to reinsert language confirming the EEZ as part of the high seas. And some coastal states attempted the opposite, proposing restrictions on foreign military activity in the zone. But what this process really did was cement consensus by showing the objectors just how little support they enjoyed. Even the United States opposed the Soviet proposal despite agreeing with its substance. The committee was so close to a final deal that most delegations were unwilling to risk it by reopening discussions that had been closed. By the end of the session, many could see the light at the end of the tunnel. The outstanding issues couldn't be wrapped up in the next meeting, but 1980 seemed feasible. And as a sign of this optimism, the conference held its first discussions on the preamble and final articles of the convention.[32]

In 1979, the conference stuck with the pattern established the year before. Delegates traveled to Geneva in the spring and then New York in the summer. They produced a revised version of the Informal Composite Negotiating Text at the end of the spring session. Richardson continued the strategy of using domestic policies to encourage progress at the conference. By that point, the United States was one of just twenty-four countries still formally adhering to a 3-mile territorial sea. Over seventy had already declared a 200-mile EEZ.[33] But despite the consensus on a 12-mile territorial sea and 200-mile EEZ, the United States insisted that such zones wouldn't exist until the convention was signed. Richardson promoted a new policy of regularly objecting to any claims beyond 3 miles. Those objections were backed up by U.S. Navy operations to assert freedom of navigation through such areas. This was the birth of the U.S. Freedom of Navigation Program. Today it is best known for the outrage it provokes from Beijing in the South China Sea. In 1979, the program evoked protests from coastal states in Latin America. And as intended, it encouraged them to wrap up negotiations to make the operations end.

Meanwhile developing nations seeking further progress on seabed mining in the conference pushed through the creation of a Working Group of 21. It was meant to give Njenga, Koh, and Engo a more manageable but still representative forum to test new ideas. Membership was reserved to ten seats for Group of 77 members, seven for the NATO bloc, three for Warsaw Pact members, and a special seat for China. But it quickly ballooned in size as alternate delegates were allowed in. The United States continued to resist the financial arrangements mooted in Koh's negotiating group, though the disagreements were shrinking. But another contentious issue came up in Engo's group, which began debating the composition and voting procedures of the ISA's governing council.

The fourth and fifth negotiating groups wrapped up after the spring session. But Groups 6 and 7 remained stuck on the continental shelf and delimitation issues. Those were the only things keeping Committee II from concluding its work. The options for measuring the outer limits of the continental shelf beyond 200 miles became even more complicated. The revised negotiating text kept the formula of 60 miles from the foot of the slope and the sediment thickness text and added a Soviet proposal that the extended continental shelf be capped at either 350 miles from shore or 100 miles from the 2,500-meter isobath. And the original Nixon proposal for a "trusteeship zone" continued to evolve. States would be required to share a portion of revenue for exploitation of the shelf beyond 200 miles with the international community. Aguilar tweaked this to max out at 7 percent annually after twenty years. Otherwise, the chairman cleverly absented himself from much of the session, making it impossible to reopen settled issues.

In Committee III, final negotiations on environmental issues concluded in the spring session. Discussions on a few U.S. proposals on marine science continued. And the conference's Drafting Committee reviewed the work of the six language groups. The convention was being drafted in English, French, Spanish, Arabic, Russian, and Chinese. Making sure that every technical point matched in each language was no small feat.

The 1980 session continued the split formula, meeting in New York in the spring and Geneva in the summer. After the spring negotiations, the conference produced yet another revision of the Informal Composite Negotiating Text. The U.S. government threw everyone a bit of a curveball during the intersessional break when Congress passed legislation unilaterally authorizing deep seabed mining. Richardson had been supportive of such legislation for the past two years, believing it would be necessary once a treaty was concluded anyway. After delaying congressional action in 1979, he worked with lawmakers to craft the 1980 Deep Seabed Hard Mineral Resources Act, intended to be consistent with the future mining regime emerging in the conference while in the interim encouraging investment in seabed technology and exploration. The law authorized American companies to begin exploring the seabed in 1981 but not exploit it until 1988. And it became the basis for U.S. discussions with other governments considering their own legislation.

It had the effect Richardson intended. After a wave of criticism, developing nations realized that if they didn't want the United States and others to go it alone, they needed to wrap up negotiations. Committee I reached consensus on most outstanding issues. It resolved the tricky question of decision-making in the ISA with a tiered voting system. Procedural questions would need only a simple majority of the thirty-six-member council, but substantive questions would require two-thirds, three-fourths, or a full consensus depending on the issue.[34] As a concession to the United States, a permanent seat on the council would be reserved for the largest consumer of seabed minerals. This would give the United States a veto over the most contentious issues requiring consensus.[35]

Committee II affirmed the complex formulas for the extended continental shelf drafted the year before. And it finally came down on the side of equity rather than strict equidistance for delimiting overlapping boundaries. Committee III reopened and reclosed several issues related to marine science. The plenary continued to finalize language for the preamble and final clauses. And at the end of the summer session, the conference finally produced the Draft Convention on the Law of the Sea.

It was decided the treaty would enter into force one year after sixty states had ratified it. The assembly of the ISA, which included all parties to the treaty, would meet for the first time that day. In the meantime, a preparatory commission would be established to draft regulations for the seabed authority between the signing of the convention and its entry into force. The United States proposed that the commission also be empowered to set aside mining sites for future exploitation by the Enterprise.[36] It looked like the 1981 session would be left with little more than housekeeping and preparatory work.

America Stays Behind

Hamilton Amerasinghe died suddenly in December 1980. He had presided over the UNCLOS III negotiations for seven years and the UN Seabed Committee for five years before that. Few could claim to have had as much impact on the development of maritime law. One of those who came close was Singapore's Tommy Koh, who was elected to take over as president of the conference. Delegates reconvened in March 1981 for what they assumed would be their last session. But they were in for an unpleasant surprise, courtesy of the new

U.S. administration. Ronald Reagan and many of his advisors were suspicious of the proceedings and ideologically opposed to the emerging seabed mining regime. In their opinion, things like technology transfer, revenue sharing, caps on production, and the entire concept of the Enterprise smacked of "socialism." The American delegation had to inform its counterparts that the administration was launching a review of the draft that had been negotiated. Until that was complete, they could not take part in further discussions.

The rest of the international community was forced to wait an entire year. In March 1982, the United States finally announced that it was ready to rejoin the negotiations. The new administration found most of the draft convention acceptable, but demanded changes to Part XI, covering the new regime for deep seabed mining. At the request of the Group of 77, the U.S. delegation compiled a book of proposed amendments which came to be known as the Green Book, for its cover. The changes sought were so extensive that Koh knew developing nations would never accept them as the basis for new negotiations. So he called on a group composed mostly of U.S. allies to prepare compromise proposals. This Group of 12 was made up of Australia, Austria, Canada, Denmark, Finland, Iceland, Ireland, New Zealand, Norway, Sweden, Switzerland, and the Netherlands. The United States rejected all the group's proposed compromises and then demanded a vote on the draft convention.

On April 30, 1982, the conference voted overwhelmingly to adopt the new United Nations Convention on the Law of the Sea, known simply as UNCLOS. The tally was 130 in favor, 17 abstaining, and just 4—the United States, Israel, Turkey, and Venezuela—against. The United States would later argue that it was still entitled to all the rights guaranteed by the convention, except those related to the international seabed regime. Washington would contend that the treaty was a codification of customary international law which had developed through state practice since the 1958 Geneva conventions. But this was not accepted by most other participants. And on issues like archipelagic waters, straits passage, and the details of the EEZ, the conference was clearly establishing new law not codifying existing practices. The chairman of the Group of 77 declared during the final day of the conference that no state that remained outside of the convention should enjoy its benefits. President Koh, among many others, agreed.[37]

Outside of the seabed mining regime, the conference had reached a nearly universal consensus. But that consensus required papering over differences that seemed irreconcilable. Ambiguity had to be maintained and political accommodations made so that states could hold different interpretations of a few key articles. The drafters trusted that state practice or arbitration would eventually settle these matters. Some of them would have considerable impact on the South China Sea disputes.

One of the more difficult issues was whether foreign warships required coastal state permission for innocent passage through the territorial sea. This was hotly debated during the conference but was largely considered settled. Even the Soviets, who had demanded prior authorization in 1958, came to oppose it. The final text answered the question obliquely. Article 17 granted all ships, without distinction, the right of innocent passage. According to Koh, the conference deliberately avoided distinguishing between warships and other vessels. This strongly suggested that coastal states couldn't demand notification. But it was also ambiguous enough that some states could ignore its intended meaning without rejecting the whole convention.

Gabon threatened this delicate consensus by submitting an amendment requiring either prior notification or authorization for innocent passage for warships. It eventually withdrew the motion under considerable pressure from Koh and other conference leaders. A diverse group of twenty-eight states then sponsored an amendment allowing coastal states to regulate innocent passage as it related to security matters. The United States and Soviet Union objected. They argued that such broad authority could be used as an excuse to require prior authorization or otherwise infringe on freedom of navigation. The argument threatened the entire conference and wasn't resolved until its final day. Conference leaders undertook some feverish shuttle diplomacy between the superpowers cloistered in one conference room and representatives of the twenty-eight cosponsors in another. China and the Philippines were among the six countries chosen to represent the cosponsors in these negotiations. President Koh eventually talked them into dropping the amendment in exchange for his reading a statement into the record acknowledging that their decision to pull the amendment was made "without prejudice to the rights of coastal States to adopt measures to safeguard their security interests."[38] So the debate was left unsettled. And though most disagree, a sizable minority of states continue to argue that the convention leaves latitude to restrict the innocent passage of warships.

Another thorny issue concerned the regime of islands under Article 121 of the convention. Many parties, including both archipelagic states and coastal nations with offshore islands, wanted to see all land treated equally. This meant that an island should generate the same maritime entitlements, including a full territorial sea, EEZ, and continental shelf, as the coastline of a continental state. But the LL/GDS and many others objected. They worried about extremely small "islands" with no permanent populations granting rights to vast maritime spaces. This, they argued, would pervert the concept of the EEZ. It would shrink the size of the "common heritage of mankind" for the financial benefit of distant governments that happened to maintain claims to barren rocks.[39] Negotiators never completely agreed on which islands should be entitled to full maritime zones and which shouldn't. The resulting compromise was Article 121.3: "Rocks which cannot sustain human habitation or economic life of their own shall have no exclusive economic zone or continental shelf."[40] What exactly "human habitation" and "economic life of their own" meant was left undefined for the sake of reaching consensus.

These and other unresolved issues were left open to future clarification through negotiation and the extremely ambitious dispute settlement mechanisms written into UNCLOS. In the more than twenty-five years since the convention entered into force, these mechanisms have successfully resolved numerous disputes over interpretation of the treaty, helping to clarify provisions that were by necessity left vague during the original negotiations. But there is still plenty of ambiguity left, and some of the decisions reached by arbitral courts have yet to gain general international acceptance. As Helmut Tuerk, former vice president of the International Tribunal on the Law of the Sea, has described it, "the Convention is a living instrument and its application and interpretation will continue to be shaped by international jurisprudence as well as by State practice."[41]

UNCLOS was opened for signature on December 10, 1982, at Montego Bay, Jamaica. On that first day, 119 countries signed the convention—a record in legal history. In a speech commemorating the occasion, President Koh declared it "a monumental achievement of the international community, second only to the Charter of the United Nations." Addressing the elephant in the room, he lamented the absence of the United States:

> The US is a country that has, throughout its history, supported the progressive development of international law and has fought for the rule of law in the relations between States. The present position of the US government towards this Convention is, therefore, inexplicable in the light of its history, in the light of its specific law of the sea interests and in light of the leading role which it has played in negotiating the many compromises which have made this treaty possible.[42]

Despite widespread anger over the Reagan administration's recalcitrance, most of the international community recognized the importance of keeping the United States and other like-minded maritime states in the law of the sea regime. UN secretary-general Javier Pérez de Cuéllar convened a series of informal consultations that spent the next decade trying to resolve Washington's concerns over deep seabed mining. Fiji's Satya Nandan, who had played an important role during the UNCLOS III negotiations, helped lead these informal efforts.[43] By 1994, Washington was finally satisfied and consensus was reached on an Implementation Agreement for Part XI. In reality, it was a significant amendment to the convention. But "implementation agreement" was more palatable. Most states had agreed to vote on the treaty as a take-it-or-leave-it deal; they accepted this special treatment for the United States and its allies very begrudgingly.[44]

The United States signed the Implementation Agreement in July 1994. President Bill Clinton transferred UNCLOS and the agreement to the Senate for ratification in October. A month later, having secured ratification by the required sixty member-states, UNCLOS finally entered into force. The international bodies it established were soon up and running. The ISA met for the first time in late 1994. Satya Nandan was named secretary-general and would serve for twelve years. In 1996, Indonesia's Hasjim Djalal was elected the first president of the ISA assembly. That year, member-states also elected the first judges to the International Tribunal on the Law of the Sea.[45]

All told, UNCLOS required more than two decades of effort by nearly every country in the world. It was an unprecedented undertaking and arguably the greatest accomplishment of the United Nations to date. By 1996, China and all the Southeast Asian claimants to the South China Sea had ratified the convention.[46] Beijing made a formal declaration to the United Nations at that time reaffirming its claim to the "archipelagoes and islands" of the South China Sea. But it said nothing about the nine-dash line or historic rights over its waters.[47] Taiwan remains ineligible to ratify because it is not a UN member-state, but it has consistently said that it abides by UNCLOS as a matter of customary international law.

And the United States? After all these years, the Senate still hasn't ratified the convention. In fact, the treaty hasn't even come up for a vote. There are virtually no substantive objections left, but successive administrations have feared that ideological opposition to any international governing body, whether the United Nations or the ISA, would lead Republican lawmakers to vote it down. This despite the near universal support for accession by the chairmen of the Joint Chiefs of Staff, chiefs of naval operations, and secretaries of state and defense since 1994.[48] The United States still goes to great pains to assert that it abides by the convention, and U.S. officials continue to frame it as a codification of customary law. In 2012, the International Court of Justice gave their arguments a boost. It ruled that most core provisions of UNCLOS have become customary international law, binding upon all states.[49] So even if that argument was a bit disingenuous in 1982, it has become truer over the years. And it is on this basis that the United States objects to China's expansive claims in the South China Sea.

Staking Claims in the South China Sea

By the end of 1976, the law of the sea negotiations had reached consensus on the general outlines of a new regime. This included a 200-mile EEZ and a continental shelf of at least that much. It would take another six years to wrap up the convention, but countries around the world didn't wait to start staking claims. Among the South China Sea claimants, Vietnam moved first, issuing a statement in May 1977 claiming a 200-mile EEZ and continental shelf.[50] A year later, on the same day he established the Municipality of Kalayaan, President Ferdinand Marcos claimed 200 miles of EEZ and continental shelf for the Philippines.[51] Taiwan followed suit in October 1979. In 1979, Kuala Lumpur issued a new map showing its continental shelf. And in the spring of 1980, Indonesia and Malaysia both claimed a 200-mile EEZ.[52] Only China delayed making formal claims. Though it voiced support for the 200-mile EEZ and continental shelf during the UNCLOS negotiations, Beijing would not officially claim them until it ratified the treaty in 1996.[53]

The hunt for offshore oil and gas created an incentive for these formal claims. They weren't strictly necessary—a country's continental shelf and EEZ would exist whether or not they publicly announced them—but they helped foreign investors feel more confident. For instance, the Philippines now explicitly claimed Reed Bank as part of the continental shelf from its coastline, without any reference to disputed islands. No one else could say the same, which reinforced the conclusion among foreign oil companies that Manila had the strongest claim. Of course, that didn't make Reed Bank any more profitable for its investors. AMOCO told the State Department in October 1979, "The Reed Bank Area was no longer of any interest to American companies because they were now satisfied that there are not any promising exploration areas which have not already been gone over and proven bad."[54]

Interest in oil and gas was growing in parts of the South China Sea, but only in coastal areas far from the disputed Paracel and Spratly Islands. The Philippines had discovered oil at the Nido field off Palawan in 1976 and began commercial production in 1979. That same year it discovered its second commercially viable field, Matinloc, farther north.[55] In late 1979, Indonesia awarded exploration rights in several offshore oil blocks at the southern edge of the South China Sea to American companies. Vietnam objected, arguing that the boundary between their continental shelves in this area was unclear. Jakarta and Hanoi had been negotiating a boundary but broke off talks when Vietnam invaded Cambodia. So Indonesia announced that it would treat the halfway point between the two coastlines as a de facto boundary and explore for oil and gas only on its side. That gave American companies the confidence to invest.[56]

And at the other end of the South China Sea, several U.S. companies seized the opportunity of U.S.-China normalization to win contracts in mid-1979 for oil and gas exploration off the southern coast of China. The U.S. government encouraged this, believing it was good for Sino-American relations. But it was also nervous about the lack of total clarity on Beijing's claims and the existence of disputes with Vietnam and Taiwan. So in July the State Department revised its guidance for American oil companies operating in the South China Sea. It continued to advise against working in disputed waters and said it could not guarantee protection for those who did. This meant that if companies operated in the Gulf of Tonkin or other areas where Vietnam made claims, they did so at their own risk. Elsewhere off the Chinese coast, Washington would not object to American investment but encouraged companies to avoid areas in which Taiwan had already established blocks for oil and gas exploration. It also warned firms to steer clear of any projects near Pratas Island, which was still occupied by ROC forces.[57]

The scramble to formalize maritime claims also played a part in the last new island occupation of this period. When the government of Malaysia issued its new continental shelf map in 1979, it extended one section of the claim line to encompass Commodore Reef. That tiny feature sits at the southeastern edge of the Spratlys. It is almost entirely underwater and of little use to anyone except local fishers and smugglers. The reef is about 100 miles from the Philippines and 110 from Malaysia—close enough for each state to claim fishing and law enforcement rights under the new EEZ concept. Throughout the 1970s, authorities in Manila and Kuala Lumpur both sought to assert jurisdiction over the feature and its surrounding waters.

In early 1980, Malaysia tried to strengthen its claim by planting a sovereignty marker on the reef. The Philippines responded a few months later, sending troops to remove the marker and build a small facility. According to Manila's official histories, this marked the start of Philippine occupation of Commodore.[58] Other sources suggest its presence was intermittent at best for several years.[59] In any case, Malaysia contested the Philippines' claim throughout the 1980s and continued to assert jurisdiction over nearby waters. As late as 1988, Malaysian authorities arrested three Filipino vessels for fishing near the reef without a permit. From that point, there is little doubt that the Philippines kept Commodore permanently garrisoned as its eighth, and most remote, outpost in the Spratlys.[60]

6

Hard Power and People Power

1979–1991

> In our judgement, China's naval operations in the South China Sea and
> construction of permanent bases in the Spratlys are part of a long-term
> Chinese strategy to reassert its sovereignty and get the other parties
> to abandon their claims or negotiate settlements favorable to China.
> Beijing probably chose to act this spring in part because it realized that
> international attention was beginning to focus on finding a Cambodian
> settlement and wished to reinforce its claim to the Spratlys prior to a
> relaxation of ASEAN's tension with Vietnam.
>
> —Report by the CIA Directorate of Intelligence, August 8, 1988[1]

After the fireworks of the late 1970s, the South China Sea quieted for almost a
decade. Tensions persisted and claimants continued jockeying for position, but
the contest didn't factor into the major geopolitical developments in Asia. The
superpowers were focused elsewhere. And the worldwide scramble to extend
new maritime claims was largely replaced by optimism that UNCLOS heralded
a new era of cooperation. This was, unfortunately, premature. By the late 1980s,
the South China Sea was entering a dangerous new cycle of escalation. The violence of 1988 took observers by surprise. Most tried to downplay it as an ab-
erration. But it was soon clear that the South China Sea status quo had been
irrevocably upended.

In the meantime, a political revolution in Manila combined with the end of
the Cold War called into question the future of the U.S.-Philippines alliance.
Taken together, the 1980s saw monumental shifts in the regional balance of
power and the start of a period of deep uncertainty in the U.S. alliance system.
These developments set the stage for a dangerous new era in the South China
Sea, one in which we are still living.

On Dangerous Ground. Gregory B. Poling, Oxford University Press. © Oxford University Press 2022.
DOI: 10.1093/oso/9780197633984.003.0007

Beijing's Maritime Ambitions

After the Battle of the Paracels, officials in Manila and Saigon had worried that Beijing would turn its sights south. But an invasion of the Spratlys never came. American intelligence officials rightly concluded that China lacked the ability to project military force so far from home. The People's Liberation Army-Navy (PLAN) and Air Force were terribly underresourced. China had taken the western Paracels by subterfuge and the element of surprise. That wasn't likely to work again. On top of all that, China had little oceanographic research capacity and didn't understand the geography or ocean conditions in the South China Sea. But under Deng Xiaoping's leadership, a new China was emerging. It was more dynamic and sought a greater role in global affairs. Deng announced a nationwide campaign of "Four Modernizations," one of which was in national defense. That the military needed fixing was painfully obvious after its poor performance during the 1979 invasion of Vietnam. And modernization had to include investments in maritime power.

After decades hugging the coast, subservient to the ground forces, the PLAN wanted the resources and missions of a modern navy. As early as 1975, the brass had presented an "ocean-going navy proposal" that was endorsed by Mao. China's leaders were unnerved by the increasing Soviet presence near their shores. They recognized that a growing merchant marine necessitated the ability to protect sea lanes. And they saw that asserting claims in the South China Sea, including defending the western Paracels they had just seized, required a more capable navy. PLAN submarines sailed into the South China Sea and the Western Pacific for the first time in 1977—a sign that their mandate was expanding beyond coastal defense. Two years later, the PLAN established its first marine brigade. Tellingly, it was placed under the South Sea Fleet with responsibility for the South China Sea.[2]

The wheels of change really started turning in 1982, when Adm. Liu Huaqing became commander-in-chief of the PLAN. He argued that the navy should pursue a strategy variously translated as "active green-water defense" or "off-shore active defense."[3] Liu declared that "the Chinese Navy should exert *effective control* of the seas within the first island chain," which meant the entirety of the East and South China Seas. And it should be able to launch counterattacks and disrupt enemy operations anywhere within the "second island chain," imagined as running across the Western Pacific from Japan's southeast islands through Micronesia, including the U.S. territory of Guam. In June 1985, an enlarged meeting of the Central Military Commission endorsed offshore active defense in a landmark resolution called "Strategic Changes in the Guiding Thoughts on National Defense."[4] Liu served as commander-in-chief until 1987 and was later promoted to vice chairman of the Central Military Commission. In both roles, he spearheaded the modernization of the PLAN and its growing presence in the South China Sea.

In the decade after 1979, the PLAN cut 100,000 personnel from its bloated ranks and began replacing obsolete vessels. Meanwhile it doubled the number of its destroyers and frigates and vastly expanded its fleet of fast-attack boats. In 1988, the PLAN acquired its first *Xia*-class nuclear-powered ballistic missile submarine. The service also overhauled its education and training and began to emphasize joint exercises by submarines, surface ships, and naval air assets. By the end of the decade, the navy had grown from a mere appendage of the ground forces to account for nearly a third of China's official defense budget.[5]

This naval modernization accompanied major advances in oceanography. In December 1977, China's State Oceanic Administration declared three top priories for national marine scientific research: to "thoroughly survey the [South and East] China seas, make advances in the three oceans, and land on Antarctica."[6] This guided state-funded research for the next twenty years, especially in the South and East China Seas. It kicked off a decades-long effort to construct military and civilian survey vessels, invest in research capacity, and conduct ever more frequent marine scientific research and surveys far from shore. In April 1983, Chinese ships began surveying the waters just north of the Spratlys. A month later, two of them made a symbolic visit to James Shoal off Malaysia—the underwater feature erroneously dubbed China's "southernmost territory." China started surveying the Spratlys themselves a year later.[7]

The new oceanographic program was modest, but it brought Beijing a much better understanding of the South China Sea. And the decisions made then continue to pay dividends. China now operates the largest fleet of state-owned civilian survey vessels in the world. It eclipses the U.S. fleet by more than five to one. Forty years ago, the Chinese government was blind to anything more than a few miles from shore. Today it understands global seabed and ocean conditions nearly as well as the established maritime powers. The quality of China's marine scientific research might not be equal to its quantity just yet, but it is one of the top players in the field.[8]

Beijing also took the opportunity to update the official list of 159 "islands" that it claimed in the South China Sea. In 1983, several got more patriotic names, including Scarborough Shoal. This might be the first time any Chinese officials had paid attention to that Philippine-controlled reef in the years since it was placed on the original ROC list. They decided to change its name from Minzhu Jiao (Democracy Reef) to the less politically sensitive Huangyan Dao (Yellow Rock Island). But China still raised no objections when U.S. and Filipino air force pilots spent the next several years using the shoal as an impact range—another sign that Washington continued to see it as uncontested Philippine territory.[9]

Revolution and Distraction

The other longtime claimants to the Spratly Islands entered the 1980s distracted and seemingly content with the status quo. The Philippines, Taiwan, and Vietnam made no effort to occupy new holdings. After Manila's disappointments at Reed Bank, interest in potential oil and gas around the islands had dissipated. The seabed closer to their shores offered better prospects and, as far as foreign investors were concerned, was undisputed. That left fishing by local communities as the only economic activity occurring around the Spratlys.

The Philippine military was consumed with the fight against internal insurgencies. Ferdinand Marcos had hyped the Communist threat as an excuse for martial law in 1972. Over the next decade, anger over his heavy-handed rule helped the growth of the Communist New People's Army. His policies also threw fuel on persistent Moro separatism in the south. By the early 1980s, these twin insurgencies had actually become the national threat that Marcos once pretended they were. With an inward-looking military, no obvious external threat, and few economic incentives around the islands, Philippine interest in the Spratlys waned.

Meanwhile, the 1979 renewal of the Military Bases Agreement and the American election of 1980 heralded a brief period of smooth sailing for the alliance. Ronald Reagan enjoyed a much closer relationship with Marcos than had his predecessor. He was more willing to overlook human rights concerns in the name of the alliance. So long as Marcos brought stability and a dogged anti-Communism, Washington would excuse his excesses. In September 1982, Reagan feted Marcos during a state visit to the White House. Washington and Manila had agreed to review the updated bases agreement every five years. They took up the first review in 1983 and finished in less than two months, signing minor amendments.[10] After the endless arguments of the 1970s, the speedy review must have been a relief for negotiators on both sides.

Reagan embraced Marcos for the sake of his global campaign against Communism, but he had to contend with growing pushback at home. In Congress and the professional bureaucracy, many had already turned against the Philippine leader. His regime was growing ever more autocratic and corrupt. They knew something had to give. They pushed the White House to do more on human rights, and they supported Filipino dissidents at home and abroad. The most prominent of these was Senator Benigno "Ninoy" Aquino Jr. Arrested during the early days of martial law, Aquino had spent seven years in prison. In 1977, Assistant Secretary of State Richard Holbrooke had tried to convince Marcos to release him to exile in the United States. When Marcos instead ordered a court-martial to sentence the former senator to death, Holbrooke warned that President Carter was following the situation and the verdict would have a "devastating effect" on the alliance.[11] Marcos reversed course. After that, Holbrooke and other senior officials continued to push for Aquino's release.

Marcos finally relented in 1980 after Aquino suffered a heart attack. Imelda Marcos convinced her husband that it would be too damaging if his most prominent political opponent died in a Manila hospital. So Marcos extracted a pledge from Aquino to refrain from public activism. Then the president sent him and his family to the United States. After heart surgery in Dallas, the Aquinos settled in Boston. Ninoy quickly chafed at exile, and at being muzzled. By 1983, the former senator was ready to return. Aquino believed he could convince Marcos to make necessary reforms. Otherwise, he feared the country would collapse under the weight of mismanagement. On August 21, 1983, Aquino's plane landed at the Manila airport that now bears his name. A crowd of hundreds had gathered in the terminal to greet the returning senator. Three soldiers came on board to serve as his escort. They separated him from the passengers and press and guided him down the stairs to the tarmac. Gunshots rang out. Moments later, Ninoy Aquino lay dead at the foot of the stairs, a gunshot wound to the back of the head.

The assassination was the beginning of the end for Marcos. It created a martyr and galvanized opposition at home and abroad. Reagan canceled plans to visit Manila in 1983. Fearing instability, wealthy Filipinos began sending money out of the country. The currency plummeted and national debt soared. The Communist insurgency worsened as the economy tanked. In the State and Defense Departments, Congress, and U.S. Pacific Command, those American officials who knew the Philippines best argued that the country had no future with Marcos in power. Assistant Secretary of Defense Richard Armitage revealed that the United States had leased additional land in Guam and the Marianas in case the Philippine bases suddenly needed to be redeployed. But Reagan refused to see it. In a 1984 presidential debate with Democratic candidate Walter Mondale, he insisted that throwing Marcos "to the wolves" would lead to a Communist takeover of the Philippines.[12]

Marcos clung to power for another two and a half years after Aquino's assassination. But he grew so obsessed with maintaining American support that he overlooked the real political threat at home. Ninoy's widow, Corazon "Cory" Aquino, had taken up her husband's mantle. She became a rallying point for those who opposed the dictatorship. In 1985, the Filipino president made a grave miscalculation. He called for snap elections, believing he could rig the results and restore his legitimacy. The U.S. Agency for International Development and the American Embassy bankrolled media campaigns and election-monitoring efforts to make sure the vote would be free and fair. Republic senator Richard Lugar led a delegation of American lawmakers, clergy, and experts to monitor the polls. The vote took place on February 7, 1986. And as expected, Marcos tried to steal it. Both the State Department and Lugar's team reported that fraud was rampant. But although the CIA concluded that Aquino had almost certainly won, Reagan doubted the intelligence. It fell to Ambassador Stephen Bosworth to inform Aquino that the White House was still backing Marcos. He later called it "the single worst day of my life."

Secretary of State George Shultz saw things more clearly. What he needed was time and more evidence to work on the president. He called on Philip Habib. The former undersecretary of state, who had played an important role during the basing renewal talks of the 1970s, had retired after a serious heart attack. He had a well-earned reputation for candor and long experience with Marcos. And he despised him. Now Shultz asked Habib to fly to Manila and "assess the situation." The former diplomat spent a week conducting interviews. He met with Aquino and gave assurances that Washington wasn't abandoning her. Marcos had lost, he concluded, and should be offered asylum if he would step down. As he prepared to fly home, Habib asked an embassy official to relay a warning to Ambassador Bosworth: "Something's going to break."

A group of senior military leaders were planning their own solution. Led by Defense Secretary Juan Ponce Enrile and Philippine Constabulary chief Fidel Ramos, the group had been plotting to oust Marcos for nearly a year. The stolen election finally spurred them to action. They planned to attack the Presidential Palace and kidnap Marcos, forcing him to concede. But the plot was discovered. Fearing arrest, the conspirators holed up in Camp Aguinaldo on February 22. The camp housed the Department of National Defense and the armed forces general headquarters. Enrile called Bosworth to tell him what was happening. After informing Washington, the ambassador repeatedly called Marcos, urging him not to use force. Enrile then held a news conference. He confessed to a litany of crimes ordered by Marcos, including stuffing ballot boxes. He recognized Aquino as the legitimate winner and called for others to do the same. More troops answered the call, swelling the ranks at Camp Aguinaldo. Meanwhile thousands of citizens began to converge on Epifanio de los Santos Avenue, known as EDSA, which runs alongside the camp.

Aquino was in Cebu when the People Power Revolution, also called the EDSA Revolution, started. She assumed that Marcos would crush the rebels. So did the American consul in the city. He offered her refuge on a nearby U.S. Navy vessel, but she refused. Other American officials gave covert assistance to Enrile and Ramos. The commander at Clark Air Base allowed rebel helicopters to refuel and rearm. The U.S. military advisory mission intercepted government communications for the rebels. And the CIA provided a radio transmitter to get their message to the public. In Washington, Shultz organized an emergency meeting of senior State Department leaders. They worried that the Philippines might descend into chaos. This had happened too often when U.S.-backed anti-Communist strongmen inevitably fell. Shultz lamented, "We pay a heavy price for our past." The group agreed that there was only one path forward. Then Shultz met with the national security advisor and senior officials from Defense and CIA. Everyone agreed: Marcos should be urged to step down and offered asylum. The hard part would be convincing Reagan.

The National Security Council met on the afternoon of February 23, a day and a half into the crisis. After a heated debate between Shultz and Habib on one side and Chief of Staff Don Regan on the other, the president finally agreed. Ambassador Bosworth was ordered to tell Marcos his "time was up" and urge him to take the asylum offer. Marcos at first refused. He publicly vowed to "fight to the last breath." But as more troops defected and the crowds on EDSA grew, he wavered. Aquino organized a hasty inauguration on February 24. Reagan approved a public message to Marcos: "Attempts to prolong the life of the present regime by violence are futile. A solution to this crisis can only be achieved through a peaceful transition to a new government." Several hours of shuttle diplomacy later, Marcos gave in. On the afternoon of February 25, an American military chopper flew the Marcoses from the Presidential Palace to Clark Air Base. Then a U.S. Air Force plane carried them to Guam and on to Hawaii. Marcos would die in Honolulu in September 1989, accused of looting billions of dollars from state coffers and facing charges in both countries.[13]

Reagan had finally been convinced to turn on Marcos, but he resented it. That poisoned his relationship with President Aquino. He didn't call to congratulate her for two months after the revolution. When Aquino visited Washington in September 1986, the American president was cordial but distant. By contrast, the U.S. Congress gave her a rapturous welcome. Before a joint session of Congress, Aquino thanked America for its support and pleaded for more assistance. She declared, "You have spent many lives and much treasure to bring freedom to many lands that were reluctant to receive it. And here you have a people who won it by themselves and need only help to preserve it." The subtext was clear: Washington had propped up Marcos while he bankrupted the country; now it should help fix the damage. Clearly moved, the House narrowly approved $200 million in new aid to the Philippines; however, Senate Republicans led by Bob Dole blocked the measure. It was a time of serious budget constraints and Dole accused the House of letting sentiment overrule sound policy. He was also skeptical of Aquino's commitment to the alliance. He noted, for instance, that she never mentioned the U.S. bases in her speech.[14]

Dole had a point. Aquino, like many Filipinos, was conflicted about the alliance. For some on the left, U.S. support for Marcos was reason enough to walk away. Many others appreciated that the United States championed democracy even if it often fell short of its own ideals. But even pro-American Filipinos often worried that the alliance had created an unhealthy dependency. It had certainly disincentivized modernization by the armed forces of the Philippines, which had rarely worried about external defense. Marcos had recognized that and made it a key point during the basing renewal talks a decade earlier. Critics also believed that the alliance prevented Manila from pursuing an independent foreign policy since it always had to worry about aligning with its powerful ally. None of this meant that the alliance was doomed. It still enjoyed strong support among the Filipino public, the armed forces, and most lawmakers. But after Marcos, the Philippines demanded changes to make the relationship more equitable. And as it had a decade earlier, that meant more financial and security assistance. Congressional stinginess fed the naysayers in Manila.

The first order of business for the new government was charter change. Marcos had promulgated the current constitution in 1973 after declaring martial law. Like him, it had to go. One month after her inauguration, President Aquino proclaimed a temporary "Freedom Constitution." It allowed her to reorganize the government and set up a commission to forge a new charter. That body completed its work in October 1986, and the new Philippine constitution was ratified by a plebiscite the following February. It was a progressive document, calling for social justice, women's rights, and public health and education. But it was also a nationalistic document.

The constitutional commission applied the law of the sea selectively, which led to contradictions. It declared, "The State shall protect the nation's marine wealth in its archipelagic waters, territorial sea, and exclusive economic zone, and reserve its use and enjoyment exclusively to Filipino citizens." This reflected the latest developments in maritime law—no other state could claim to have baked the new regime of the EEZ into its constitution. But it also carried over the definition of the national territory used in the 1973 charter. That said nothing about archipelagic waters and instead claimed all the seas within the archipelago as "internal waters"—a position clearly inconsistent with UNCLOS.[15] This would cause tensions with foreign maritime powers and made the Philippines a regular target of the U.S. Freedom of Navigation Program. The constitution's firm call to reserve all marine wealth for Filipinos would also complicate future efforts at joint development in the South China Sea.

That nationalism was threaded throughout the constitution. It sought to promote economic self-sufficiency and limit foreign ownership in key sectors. It explicitly declared, "The State shall pursue an independent foreign policy." And it put the United States on notice: "After the expiration in 1991 of the Agreement between the Republic of the Philippines and the United States of America concerning Military Bases, foreign military bases, troops, or facilities shall not be allowed in the Philippines except under a treaty duly concurred in by the Senate."[16] That meant the next review of the bases agreement would be the last.

When the current pact expired, the two sides would need to negotiate a whole new treaty that could pass muster with the Philippine Congress.

Under the terms of the 1979 deal, the bases agreement needed to be reviewed again in 1988. The two sides started early, in May 1987. And compared to the breezy review of 1983, the negotiations were a slog. Manila made progress conditional on a substantial increase in security and economic assistance. Veterans of the negotiations under Ford and Carter must have been struck by déjà vu. After fifteen months of horse-trading, Shultz and Philippine secretary of foreign affairs Raul Manglapus signed a deal at the U.S. State Department in October 1988. It secured American use of Clark Air Base and Subic Bay Naval Station until the Military Bases Agreement expired in September 1991. In exchange, the United States would provide almost $1 billion in military and economic assistance in 1990 and 1991. That was a 250 percent increase, but still well short of the $1.2 billion annually that Manila sought. To sweeten the deal, the U.S. Overseas Private Investment Corporation and Export-Import Bank would kick in another $500 million in loans and insurance to encourage investment and exports. And Washington would support a $5 billion multilateral aid program for the Philippines.

Despite the deal, neither side was happy. The Philippines had pushed hard to revise the provisions on criminal jurisdiction over American service members. But the United States wouldn't budge, and it remained a sore spot in the alliance. At the signing ceremony, the press asked about U.S. basing beyond 1991. Manglapus said that President Aquino was "keeping her options open." Shultz interjected that both sides were. Back in Manila, House of Representatives Speaker Ramon Mitra said, "1991 is upon us, and I believe that the thinking of the country will depend heavily on how the Americans treated us in this review." Senator Rene Saguisag, an opponent of the bases, insisted that the chances of any new treaty securing ratification were "bleak."[17] They were both right.

New Kids on the Block

Like the Philippines, Vietnam had little attention to spare for the South China Sea. It had become a pariah, facing diplomatic and economic pressure from the United States, China, and the rest of Southeast Asia. That isolation had led Hanoi to open Cam Ranh Bay to Soviet military use in 1979. For Moscow, the access helped boost its naval and air presence in the Pacific. But its goals were to maintain pressure on China and keep up militarily with Washington—a competition that it would soon lose. The Soviets were unlikely to help Vietnam assert its territorial or maritime claims. The Vietnamese military, meanwhile, was preoccupied with Cambodia, where the Khmer Rouge carried on their guerrilla war. And while the 1979 Sino-Vietnamese War had been short, if brutal, its aftershocks continued for years. Chinese forces launched artillery and ground offensives across the border in 1981, 1984, and 1986. On top of all that, the Vietnamese economy was in tatters. After the war with China, reformers in Hanoi began cautiously pushing to decentralize the economy. This eventually led to the Doi Moi (Renovation) policy of 1986 and the transition to a market economy. Facing so many challenges, Vietnam had little incentive to shake things up in the South China Sea. That is, until some new players arrived on the scene.

Malaysia had spent the latter part of the 1970s quietly surveying the waters and seabed off northern Borneo. This included its states of Sabah and Sarawak, along with British-controlled Brunei. Malaysian officials knew that this shallow area of seabed probably contained valuable oil and gas deposits. In 1979, Malaysia had issued a map formally claiming its continental shelf in the area. It declared a 200-nautical-mile EEZ a year later. But Malaysia had no designs on most of the Spratly Islands. The largest features, those its neighbors had occupied and argued over for decades, were well outside its new EEZ and continental shelf.

There was a string of underwater reefs off Sarawak that none of the Southeast Asian claimants considered part of the Spratlys. These features—Luconia Shoals and James Shoal—were on the old lists of "islands" claimed by China and Taiwan, but no one paid those much mind. Malaysia's control over these shoals was taken for granted and would remain so until China began to regularly operate around them in the 2000s. But a dozen rocks and reefs farther north, off Sabah, presented more of a problem. These could reasonably be considered part of the Spratlys. According to UNCLOS, Malaysia could claim the resources of any underwater reefs as parts of its continental shelf. But those above water were trickier. Not only could they be claimed as territory by another state, but they might generate their own EEZs and continental shelves overlapping with Malaysia's. The best hedge against that would be for Malaysia to occupy them first (Figure 6.1).

The largest of these islets, and the farthest from Malaysia, was Amboyna Cay. It was also the only one that had drawn any prior interest. The British had claimed it nearly a century earlier; the French did the same. Both Vietnamese governments had landed troops on the islet but found it too difficult to occupy. Malaysian personnel had landed on the cay in 1977 and 1978. But once it realized what Kuala Lumpur was up to, Hanoi had dispatched its own forces and permanently garrisoned the island. After that missed opportunity, Malaysia next looked to Commodore Reef. It toyed with occupying the feature to keep it out of Filipino hands. But again, it moved too cautiously. Manila occupied the reef, at least part time, in 1980. This put the two most distant islets within Malaysia's claim in foreign hands. Kuala Lumpur couldn't risk the same happening to those closer to shore.

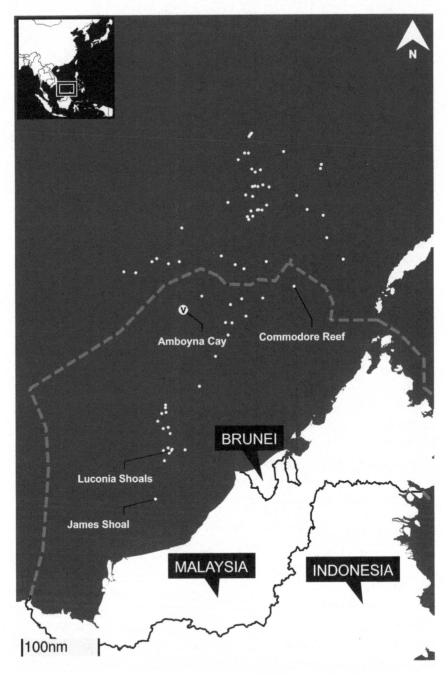

Figure 6.1 Features within Malaysia's continental shelf claim including Vietnam-occupied Amboyna Cay, 1979. Created using Mapcreator and OpenStreetMap.

By 1980, Malaysian troops had erected sovereignty markers on several of these reefs off Sabah. Then in May 1983, Malaysian commandos waded onto the closest, Swallow Reef. A few rocks broke the surface at high tide, but it was otherwise submerged. The government began bringing in sand one barge-load at a time. Over the new few years, Swallow Reef was transformed into a small island. It was only the second time a claimant had artificially expanded one of the Spratlys; the Philippines had done so at Thitu Island in 1979 to build a short runway. But Malaysia's efforts at Swallow were much more ambitious. In 1986, Kuala Lumpur established a permanent naval station on the island. That April, another group of Malaysian commandos landed on Ardasier Reef to the north. That feature is entirely submerged at high tide, so Malaysia anchored a barge to the reef and converted it into a permanent facility. In September, a similar out-post was installed on underwater Mariveles Reef farther north.[18] Then Malaysia took a long break from occupation. Its navy regularly patrolled the other rocks and reefs within its EEZ, and it erected navigational beacons on some of them. It also continued upgrading its outposts, especially Swallow Reef, which would get a civilian diving resort in 1991. But Malaysia wouldn't garrison another feature for more than a decade.

The Malaysian moves finally caught Vietnam's attention. Swallow, Ardasier, and Mariveles Reefs probably didn't arouse much jealousy. They were at a dis-tance from any islands that Vietnam occupied or had shown interest in before. But what if Malaysia wasn't done? There were still half a dozen unoccupied reefs within its claim off Sabah. And one of them was far enough north to be con-cerning. So in March 1987, Vietnamese troops returned to Barque Canada Reef. They had briefly occupied that feature nine years earlier, when they garrisoned Amboyna Cay to keep it out of Malaysian hands. But the conditions were too hazardous and the Barque Canada facility had been quickly abandoned. This time, they stuck it out and built Vietnam's tenth permanent outpost in the Spratly Islands (Figure 6.2).[19]

Around this time, the final claimant to the South China Sea was quietly pla-nning its entry into the disputes. Brunei had gained independence from the United Kingdom at the start of 1984. Sandwiched between Sabah and Sarawak, it shares the same geographical continental shelf as East Malaysia. In 1988, the sultanate quietly issued two maps. One showed the extent of its 200-mile EEZ and the other its continental shelf extending an additional 60 miles. Louisa Reef, the southernmost of the Spratlys, sits in the middle of Brunei's claims. It may have a few rocks that break the surface, and Malaysia had once erected a sovereignty marker on it. It is also technically claimed by China, Taiwan, and Vietnam. But no party has ever tried to permanently occupy it.[20] The extended portion of the continental shelf on Brunei's map also covered Rifleman Bank, where Vietnam would soon build facilities. But Brunei has been cagey about whether it really

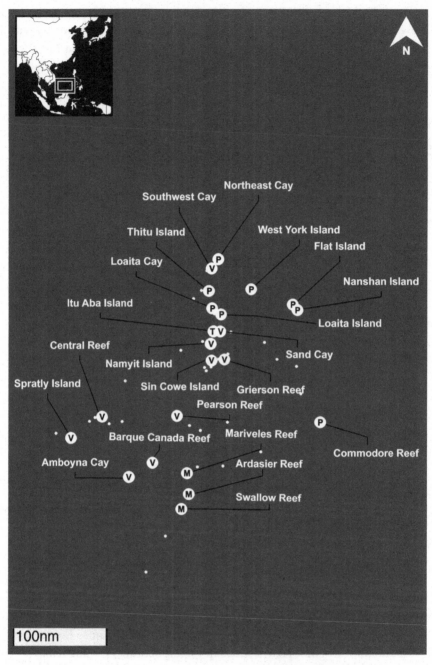

Figure 6.2 Spratly Islands occupied by Malaysia (M), Philippines (P), Taiwan (T), and Vietnam (V), 1987. Created using Mapcreator and OpenStreetMap.

claims that underwater feature. It now downplays that map and says it hasn't set the limits of its continental shelf yet.

China Moves In

China had spent most of a decade quietly surveying the South China Sea and modernizing its naval forces. For the first time, leaders in Beijing believed they could not only establish outposts in the Spratlys but defend them. In early 1987, they decided to give it a shot.[21] The operation would need delicacy and careful planning. To maintain positive relations with the United States and its allies, China would need to target areas occupied mostly by Vietnam. That way, if things turned violent, the damage would be contained. Chinese and Vietnamese forces had been clashing at their land border almost annually since 1979. The international community would probably see a fight in the Spratlys as an extension of that conflict. In July 1986, Soviet leader Mikhail Gorbachev had made a speech in Vladivostok calling for improved relations with China. So robust Soviet support for Vietnam in a confrontation with China seemed increasingly unlikely. Still, Beijing needed a pretext for action.

Chinese diplomats quickly engineered an opportunity. In March 1987, the United Nations Educational, Scientific and Cultural Organization (UNESCO) asked for help setting up a worldwide network of monitoring stations to study ocean conditions. Chinese delegates quietly submitted Fiery Cross Reef, one of the Spratly Islands, as a proposed site. Apparently, no one noticed. Everything in the Spratlys that might be called an island had been occupied for years. Of the reefs that were left, Fiery Cross was better than most: it had a single rock above water at high tide. Even more important was its location. The reef was isolated. Vietnam had bases in three directions, but the closest was 50 miles away; it was twice that far to Taiwan's base on Itu Aba, and Philippine and Malaysian outposts were even farther. An operation at Fiery Cross was unlikely to raise immediate alarms outside of Hanoi.

Over the next two months, the Chinese Academy of Sciences surveyed the reef while the PLAN conducted exercises nearby and deposited a sovereignty marker.[22] In November, Adm. Zhang Lianzhong replaced Liu Huaqing as commander-in-chief of the PLAN. A former submarine officer and subordinate of Liu, he shared his boss's zeal for offshore operations.[23] Both admirals wanted to prove that the navy was ready to assert China's claims. Beijing approved construction of a permanent observation post on Fiery Cross that very month.

Vietnam knew something was up. The flurry of Chinese activity put Hanoi on edge and it started to shore up its defenses near Fiery Cross. The closest features were the London Reefs to the east. These consisted of Central Reef, which housed a Vietnamese base, and East, West, and Cuarteron Reefs, which were unoccupied. Beyond them sat Vietnam's crown jewel, Spratly Island itself. In December, Vietnamese troops set up a new base on West Reef, the last stop before Spratly.

China made its move on January 21, 1988. Four ships arrived at Fiery Cross and began work on the UNESCO-endorsed "observation post." But the blueprints looked an awful lot like a military outpost, with a barracks, wharf, and helipad. A Vietnamese ship showed up the day after construction began. It observed the operation and sailed away. Chinese engineers spent more than a week dredging up coral to create about two acres of artificial land at Fiery Cross. On January 31, two more Vietnamese ships arrived. They planned to force a landing and put a stop to the construction. But bad weather and a larger-than-anticipated Chinese presence forced them to call it off. Beijing had gained its first foothold in the Spratlys.

The Fiery Cross operation was meant as a pilot project, and it worked exactly as planned. China intended to rerun the play at other features, but Vietnam was determined not to let that happen. The result was a race. Over the next few months, the two sides occupied one reef after another. Vietnamese forces landed on Tennent Reef on January 25; they seemed to think it a likely target for China's next occupation and moved in first. Tennent checked most of the same boxes as Fiery Cross. It had a few rocks that kept dry at high tide, and it was just as isolated. The nearest foreign outpost was Philippine-controlled Commodore Reef, which probably wasn't even occupied year-round.

Vietnam then took control of Ladd Reef on February 5. That feature was wholly underwater at high tide. But because it was just 14 miles west of Spratly Island, Hanoi had reason to worry China might try to occupy it. On February 18, Chinese troops instead moved into the London Reefs. They landed on Cuarteron Reef and started building. Hanoi angrily warned that China would bear "all the consequences" unless it abandoned its new outposts. Vietnamese soldiers showed up on East Reef a day later, settling the last of the four London Reefs.

A day after that, Vietnam occupied Discovery Great Reef to the east of Fiery Cross. And on February 27 and 28, it landed troops on Alison and Cornwallis South Reefs. These sat between Vietnam's bases on Pearson and Tennent Reefs.[24] It looked like Hanoi was establishing a firebreak, hoping to keep China from the larger and more densely occupied atolls to the northeast. But Beijing was already committed. Every rock and reef in the southwest was now occupied, except a few near the Malaysian coast. China had nowhere left to go but into the heart of the Spratlys.

The Spratly Islands are spread across a vast area, but most of the best real estate is packed onto five atolls that run along a 100-mile north-south line. Each of these contains numerous islets and reefs, each just a shallow section of the larger atoll. The status quo in this sector hadn't changed since 1978. The Philippines controlled two of the atolls—Thitu Reefs and Loaita Bank—from their namesake islands. Manila and Hanoi maintained an uneasy peace on a third—North Danger Reefs—with their adjacent bases on Northeast and Southwest Cay. On the fourth, Tizard Bank, Taiwan still held Itu Aba, while Vietnam maintained facilities on Namyit Island and Sand Cay. The last atoll, Union Banks, was all Vietnamese, courtesy of bases on Sin Cowe Island and Grierson Reef.

This status quo shattered in mid-March 1988. Vietnam must have known that Chinese forces were mobilizing and expected multiple landings. Hanoi dispatched forces to all the atolls it occupied. Between March 14 and 16, boats tried to offload Vietnamese soldiers and construction material at Collins, Johnson, and Lansdowne Reefs in Union Banks, Petley Reef on Tizard Bank, and South Reef on North Danger Reef.[25] At the same time, a larger and much better equipped PLAN force was rushing to the area. Four of Vietnam's landings went off without a hitch. But the opposing flotillas reached Johnson Reef at nearly the same time. Each side tells a different story about what happened next.

In most versions, the Vietnamese flag was already flying when PLAN sailors waded onto the reef to pull it down. There was a scuffle, shots were fired, and the Chinese withdrew. But the details are murky. Hanoi claims that the Chinese killed a Vietnamese officer and then retreated before the Vietnamese could respond. Beijing maintains that a Vietnamese soldier shot first, and China's troops fell back under fire from the Vietnamese ships. What happened next was also disputed for the next twenty years. But in 2009, the PLAN publicly released footage of the "battle" filmed from one of its ships. The Chinese vessels easily sank Vietnam's three dilapidated ships. Then the video shows what happened to the stranded landing party. As one of the Chinese vessels approached the reef, the Vietnamese troops spread out around their flag and the Chinese machine guns opened fire. Sixty-four Vietnamese were dead in minutes and China had its third outpost in the Spratlys.

Vietnam's already limited navy was hampered by the loss of three ships, and China moved quickly. By April 8, its troops had occupied three more features. First was Hughes Reef, which has often been confused with Kennan Reef right next door. The feature was located at the other end of Union Banks, just a few miles from Vietnamese-held Grierson Reef. Next was Subi Reef, a little more than 12 miles southwest of the Philippine base on Thitu Island. Then came Gaven Reefs, located next to Vietnam's outpost on Namyit and just 13 miles from the Taiwanese forces on Itu Aba.[26] And that was the end of it, at least for a while. Of the reefs that China had occupied, four sported a rock or sandbar that kept dry at high tide. But Hughes and Subi were entirely underwater—a legal distinction that would come back to bite Beijing in a few decades. It is unclear

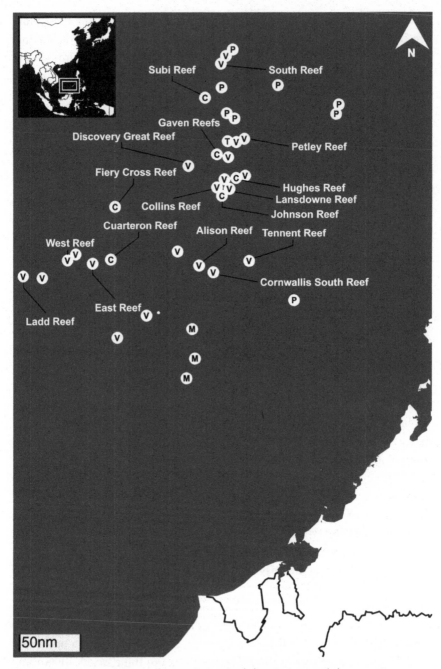

Figure 6.3 Spratly Island occupations by China (C) and Vietnam (V), December 1987–April 1988 (labeled). Existing facilities of Malaysia (M), Philippines (P), Taiwan (T), and Vietnam are also shown. Created using Mapcreator and OpenStreetMap.

whether these six were the only features on Beijing's shopping list. Vietnam may have ruined other plans with its flurry of counteroccupations (Figure 6.3).

China's surveys and naval upgrades had proven their worth. A CIA report written in August 1988 described the operation as "the most extensive ever mounted by the Navy," featuring forty ships from all three of China's fleets. It also noted that the South Sea Fleet "effectively managed the entire operation and rotated its ships to ensure that every major combatant in the fleet saw duty in the Spratlys."[27] The campaign was at once a grand unveiling of China's new navy and a one-of-a-kind training opportunity. And its architects were well rewarded. Liu Huaqing was promoted to full admiral and Zhang Lianzhong to vice admiral. Liu was named vice chairman of the Central Military Commission a year later. He would serve as China's most senior military leader, at the right hand of both Deng Xiaoping and Jiang Zemin, until stepping down in 1997. Zhang would be elevated to admiral in 1993 and continue to lead the PLAN until 1996.

By design, the Spratlys campaign had mostly targeted Vietnamese-held sectors. And China worked hard to frame it as a purely bilateral affair. Chinese media consistently pinned the blame on Hanoi. Its diplomats did the same in the United Nations. Beijing assured Kuala Lumpur, Manila, and Taipei that its operations were not targeting them. Still, the degree to which its neighbors and the international community bought into that narrative was remarkable. The CIA, at least, recognized that China had taken the initiative, seizing on Vietnam's isolation and its own naval modernization. But the agency was also skeptical about Vietnamese claims of being an "innocent victim." And in a classified summary of the Johnson Reef clash, it uncritically reported China's version of events: that Chinese forces had landed first, come under fire from Vietnamese troops, and sunk one ship in response. There was no mention of gunning down stranded troops. And the agency marveled that the Chinese ships "suffered little damage and few casualties."[28]

Senior U.S. officials didn't publicly address the clash. And allies and partners didn't ask. China had accurately judged that it could leverage anti-Vietnam sentiment to get a free pass for its operation. In remarks that Taiwan's government would probably like forgotten, Defense Minister Cheng Wei-yuan of the nationalist Kuomintang party actually suggested that Taipei would help Beijing defend the islands if asked.[29] Officials in the Philippines and Malaysia were a bit more conflicted and urged both sides to negotiate. State-controlled media in Malaysia barely reported on the Johnson Reef clash. On the few occasions that Malaysian officials discussed the issue, they treated it as a purely bilateral matter between China and Vietnam. But they weren't blind. Soon after the clash, Malaysia moved to purchase new offshore patrol vessels and other assets and approved construction of a naval base in Sabah to coordinate South China Sea operations.[30] Prime Minister Mahathir Mohamad even visited Swallow Reef in June 1988 to assess the situation.[31] But in the end, Kuala Lumpur seemed to believe that Beijing would refrain from harassing any of the non-Vietnamese claimants.

Manila was too distracted to do more than take Beijing's assurances at face value. The new post-Marcos regime was consumed by domestic political issues. What time it could dedicate to foreign relations was spent courting foreign trade, investment, and financial assistance, along with the tense basing negotiations with the Reagan administration. Aquino visited Beijing in March, shortly after the Johnson Reef clash, and tried to avoid the issue. Ahead of her trip, a government spokesperson said the Spratlys were "not going to be an issue." The president herself insisted that China and the Philippines maintained "respect and lawful regard" for each other's claims. Chinese officials responded by assuring her that Philippine bases in the Spratlys would not be attacked. And China's state-owned Xinhua news agency reported after her visit that the two governments had agreed "the question of the Nansha Qundao [Spratly Islands] may as well be temporarily shelved."[32] The CIA even reported that Aquino considered pulling out of the islands altogether but was talked down by advisors who still hoped to find valuable energy resources in the area.[33]

After the Johnson Reef clash, Vietnam had little hope of driving China off its new bases. The PLAN had made its naval superiority abundantly clear. So Hanoi focused first on trying to rally international pressure against Beijing. It raised the issue in the United Nations but found little support. It undertook bilateral discussions with Malaysia and the Philippines, which were cordial but mostly fruitless. Even the Soviet Union, Vietnam's closest ally and patron, tried to remain neutral. It backed Vietnam's calls for negotiations to resolve the dispute but refused, when asked, to jointly condemn China's actions. A Soviet interlocutor told American intelligence officials that the Johnson Reef clash had placed it in a difficult position as it was trying to improve ties with Beijing while keeping up the alliance with Hanoi.

While international diplomacy floundered, Vietnam also looked to shore up its position in the islands. And here the Soviets were more helpful. They increased military assistance to Vietnam after the clash, and their base at Cam Ranh Bay provided important logistic support for Vietnamese supply ships heading out to the Spratlys. Those ships busily convoyed troops, weapons, and supplies to Vietnamese bases, especially those that had just been established in response to the Chinese campaign. Hanoi deployed tanks, artillery, radar systems, and surface-to-air missiles to its existing bases. It set up a command headquarters at Cam Ranh Bay, began mobilizing new naval vessels, and deployed fighter-bombers to Phan Rang Air Base, just south of Cam Ranh, to patrol the islands.[34]

Hanoi then thought about securing other unoccupied features that China might covet. Vietnamese governments since the 1950s had returned to the same playbook whenever another claimant expanded its presence in the Spratlys. But this time would be different. Vietnam already controlled twenty-one islands and reefs. Virtually everything in the Spratlys that was even close to the surface had been built on. So in 1989, Vietnam began physically occupying the submerged banks on its continental shelf southwest of the island group. It hoped to someday discover commercially viable oil and gas resources in the area. And it feared China did as well. No government outside of Beijing and Taipei considered these submerged features to be part of the Spratlys. But they had been included among the Nansha Islands for decades, victims of the same cartographic errors as other underwater features, like Macclesfield Bank, Reed Bank, and James Shoal.

Hanoi would eventually build fourteen outposts on these banks. They were dubbed DK1 platforms, short for Dịch vụ-Khoa, or "economic, scientific, and technological service stations."[35] The platforms resembled a fire lookout tower planted in the middle of the ocean. They went up on Prince of Wales, Rifleman, and Vanguard Banks in 1989; Prince Consort Bank in 1990; and Alexandra and Grainger Banks in 1991 (Figure 6.4).[36] Their existence now creates disagreement over how many of the Spratly Islands Vietnam occupies. Chinese sources generally say between twenty-seven and twenty-nine; most others say twenty-one, not considering the DK1 platforms to be in the Spratlys.[37] And legally these underwater banks can't be claimed as territory. Their resources, and the right to

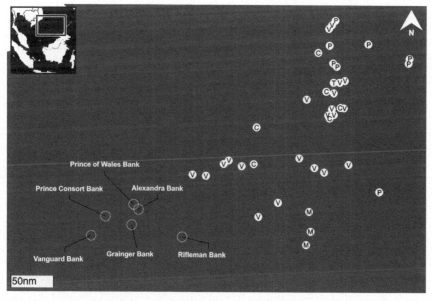

Figure 6.4 Location of Vietnam's DK1 platforms, 1989–91 (labeled). The Spratly bases occupied by China (C), Malaysia (M), Philippines (P), Taiwan (T), and Vietnam (V) are also shown. Created using Mapcreator and OpenStreetMap.

build outposts on them, are governed by the rules of the continental shelf and EEZ under UNCLOS.

Regional and Global Upheaval

At the start of 1988, China found itself embraced by most of the international community. Vietnam's remaining friends were mostly in the Soviet bloc. The United States and the Philippines had just inked another renewal of their basing agreement. And the South China Sea disputes were minor issues which were managed bilaterally by each pair of claimants. Within a year, all of that was in flux.

In April 1989, former Chinese Communist Party general secretary Hu Yaobang died. He had spearheaded many of the reforms of the 1980s before being pushed out of power in 1987. His death sparked protests in Beijing which spread like wildfire. By May, hundreds of thousands were gathering daily in Tiananmen Square to call for democracy. China's leadership decided the movement had become a threat. Liu Huaqing, architect of the Spratlys campaign, now helped crush the demonstrations from his seat on the Central Military Commission. On June 4, People's Liberation Army tanks rolled into the square while troops opened fire on protestors. The death toll was in the hundreds, at least. Publics around the world were appalled. U.S. president George H. W. Bush announced sanctions the very next day, suspending all weapons sales and high-level military visits. Aquino expressed sadness and called on Chinese leaders to "use all available peaceful measures instead of resorting to violence."[38]

Vietnam was moving in the opposite direction, toward reconciliation with the international community. In April 1989, Hanoi announced that it would finally withdraw all forces from Cambodia.[39] This cleared the way for Hun Sen's transitional State of Cambodia and, eventually, the 1991 Paris Peace Agreements. That process was also helped by the turmoil in the Soviet Union, which caused Moscow to reduce aid to both Hanoi and Phnom Penh. The overwhelming victory of Solidarity in Poland's June legislative elections started a domino effect across Eastern Europe. Communist regimes on the continent crumbled, symbolized most vividly by the fall of the Berlin Wall in November. The Soviet Union would continue to shrink for the next two years, until its dissolution at the end of 1991.

The U.S.-Philippine alliance had been on shakier footing ever since the People Power Revolution. Presidents Reagan and Aquino were cordial but never close. And the new government in Manila was less convinced than its predecessor that American basing benefited the Philippines' national security. As a result, the final renewal of the Military Bases Agreement in 1988 was a drawn-out, contentious undertaking. Not for the first time, the discussions hinged on

questions of U.S. financial assistance and criminal jurisdiction over American
service members. Washington and Manila managed to get a deal done, but neither issue was settled satisfactorily.

Relations warmed a bit in 1989. Bush succeeded Reagan as president, which
removed one irritant. In December, Col. Gregorio Honasan led about a thousand Philippine Army troops in an attempted coup against Aquino. It was the
fifth she had faced since 1986, and the second by Honasan. But it was the first that
genuinely threatened her government. Rebel troops seized control of military
bases around Manila, along with the government television station. Then they
attacked the Presidential Palace and other targets with commandeered trainer
aircraft and attack helicopters. As the situation spiraled out of control, officials,
including Fidel Ramos, then serving as defense secretary, urged Aquino to ask
the White House for help. Bush quickly agreed. American F-4 fighter-bombers
took off from Clark Air Base and flew low passes over rebel-held bases in and
around Manila. They never had to fire a shot, but the show of force combined
with government counterattacks helped convince most of the rebels to lay down
their arms.[40]

Aquino appreciated the support. The two sides resumed negotiations later
that month to extend the bases agreement beyond its scheduled expiration
in 1991. The U.S. government now found the Philippine president more supportive, if still frustrating. But the politics were getting increasingly complicated
in Manila. Opinion polls showed that most Filipinos wanted the bases to stay.
Lawmakers, however, were divided. Many saw the bases, and the American alliance overall, as a burden that had kept the Philippines from developing militarily
and economically. Others supported the alliance but thought the United States
was being too tight-fisted. Aquino's government was increasingly fragile and
couldn't afford to ignore the critics. So talks dragged on for a year and a half. And
they grew increasingly bitter, especially on the question of economic assistance.

Nature unexpectedly resolved one point of contention. In June 1991, for the
first time in six hundred years, Mt. Pinatubo erupted. It killed hundreds and
buried Clark Air Base in ash. More than fifteen thousand U.S. Air Force personnel had to be evacuated. The United States had already transferred the last
combat aircraft from Clark to Alaska the previous year—a result of the clock
winding down on the basing agreement. But it had still served as a major logistics center and stopover. Now it would cost more than $500 million to make
usable again. And that decided it—Defense Secretary Dick Cheney announced
that the United States would give up its largest overseas air base.[41]

In July, Philippine foreign secretary Manglapus and U.S. special negotiator
Armitage announced a deal. The United States would retain only Subic Bay
Naval Base. It would hand over four small bases in September, and would clean
up Clark and return it to Philippine control a year later. Washington would

provide Manila $550 million for the bases in 1992, a modest increase over previous years. Then it would pay about $200 million annually to rent Subic for the next nine years.

The deal was immediately controversial. Philippine lawmakers attacked it, some because it didn't kick the Americans out and some because it didn't charge them enough to stay. Several of Aquino's cabinet members resigned to distance themselves from the agreement.[42] Since it was a new treaty, not an extension of the old bases agreement, it required a two-thirds majority in the Philippine Senate. The chamber held a preliminary vote on September 9. The result was twelve for and eleven against, five votes short of ratification. In response, President Bush warned that the United States had "made our best offer." Lugar, a vocal champion of the alliance, called it a "historic tragedy." Cheney agreed, but was more fatalistic. He said, "We'll pack up and leave, that's it."[43] A week later, the Philippine Senate held another vote, but the results were the same.

President Aquino was defiant, at first. She declared that there would be a national referendum. After all, the public overwhelmingly supported the American bases, which pumped hundreds of millions of dollars into the economy.[44] But the move was constitutionally dubious and she eventually backed down. As Bush had promised, Washington refused to adjust its offer. Instead, it tried to buy time by negotiating a three-year withdrawal. But those talks soon hit a wall. In December 1991, the Philippines ordered the United States to leave Subic Bay by the end of the following year. For the first time since the end of World War II, the United States would have no permanent presence in the Philippines, or anywhere else along the South China Sea.

How did this happen? Much of the blame rests with the changing global order. As the Cold War ended, the United States saw less need for Subic and Clark. They were important, but no longer critical. The Bush administration faced considerable domestic pressure to trim military spending. They just weren't willing to make the economic concessions that could have saved the bases. And the perceived threats that forced tough concessions in the 1970s were missing. Moscow's use of Cam Ranh Bay was no longer a compelling threat. And that went for the entire Soviet Pacific Fleet. The Philippine bases offered geographic advantages that couldn't be replaced. But the available alternatives seemed good enough.

Singapore had agreed in 1990 to give American ships and aircraft access to repair and logistics facilities, along with possible deployments. Japan was offering to cover the operating costs for Yokosuka Naval Base to take over Subic's role as a major naval repair facility. Many of the assets from the Philippines would be shifted to Japan, Guam, Hawaii, and Alaska. They would still be in the Pacific theater, if no longer standing ready to uphold the alliance. But voices on both sides wondered whether the alliance was still relevant anyway. The Soviet Union was crumbling, and China had been brought into the international fold, albeit less comfortably since Tiananmen. In rejecting the bases, many lawmakers had argued that the Philippines no longer faced external threats.

That sentiment would last only a few more years.

Diplomacy Disappointed

1992–2008

> The United States has an abiding interest in the maintenance of peace and stability in the South China Sea. The United States calls upon claimants to intensify diplomatic efforts which address issues related to the competing claims, taking into account the interests of all parties, and which contribute to peace and prosperity in the region. The United States is willing to assist in any way that the claimants deem helpful. The United States reaffirms its welcome of the 1992 ASEAN Declaration on the South China Sea.
>
> Maintaining freedom of navigation is a fundamental interest of the United States. Unhindered navigation by all ships and aircraft in the South China Sea is essential for the peace and prosperity of the entire Asia-Pacific region, including the United States.
>
> The United States takes no position on the legal merits of the competing claims to sovereignty over the various islands, reefs, atolls, and cays in the South China Sea. The United States would, however, view with serious concern any maritime claim or restriction on maritime activity in the South China Sea that was not consistent with international law, including the 1982 United Nations Convention on the Law of the Sea.
>
> —U.S. Department of State, Daily Press Briefing, May 10, 1995[1]

The heady optimism that followed the end of the Cold War led a new party to step into the South China Sea morass. The Association of Southeast Asian Nations (ASEAN) decided in 1992 to take upon itself the task of managing tensions in the disputed waterway. Nearly thirty years later, the grouping still struggles under this burden.

What Southeast Asian leaders didn't realize was that a radical shift in the disputes was already underway. For the previous half-century, managing the South China Sea had meant de-escalating the territorial disputes. When no one was trying to occupy new features, the status quo held. When they did, the task was to prevent escalation. Arguments over resources were isolated to the

On Dangerous Ground. Gregory B. Poling, Oxford University Press. © Oxford University Press 2022.
DOI: 10.1093/oso/9780197633984.003.0008

immediate vicinity of disputed islands. The dawn of the EEZ expanded those arguments, but mostly where coastal claims overlapped. By the mid-1990s, however, *everything* would be in dispute: fisheries, oil and gas, marine science, military activities, and more. If it happened anywhere in the South China Sea, it was suddenly provocative. Steering clear of disputed islands wouldn't be enough to keep the peace anymore.

This change was being driven by new thinking in China and Taiwan. For decades, both had doggedly asserted sovereignty over the Nansha and Xisha Islands. They occasionally objected to foreign activities in waters near the islands, such as Philippine oil and gas exploration at Reed Bank in the late 1970s. But that rested on their claims to maritime zones generated by the islands. Any high-tide feature was entitled to a territorial sea and, after UNCLOS I, a continental shelf. UNCLOS III added the caveat that only habitable islands generated a shelf and EEZ. Beijing and Taipei kept their objections within these bounds. They didn't complain about fishing or oil and gas work in the coastal waters of Southeast Asian states. But by the late 1980s, that had started to change. Important voices in China and Taiwan were reinterpreting the old U-shaped line, which had become the nine-dash line in the PRC. All evidence suggests that the line was originally meant as a visual indicator that China claimed all the islands inside it. But now history was being rewritten. On both sides of the Taiwan Strait, the dashes began to take on a new meaning as an ill-defined national boundary. And within that boundary, all rights should belong to China. Some made these arguments out of a sense of nationalism, and some for personal gain.

Enter ASEAN

The end of the Cold War opened space for a new multilateral effort to manage the South China Sea disputes. ASEAN had been born in 1967 as a loose confederation of the five independent, non-Communist states of Southeast Asia: Indonesia, Malaysia, the Philippines, Singapore, and Thailand. In its early years, the grouping's foremost concern had been to give Indonesia a role in regional leadership and thereby blunt its ambitions. This followed the tense era of Konfrontasi (1963–66), during which Jakarta had violently opposed the formation of the Federation of Malaysia. ASEAN's second prime directive was to preserve the autonomy of member-states in the face of great power competition at the height of the Cold War. This had meant a de facto alignment against the Soviet Union and PRC, which had supported Communist insurgencies in all the ASEAN member-states.

After the United States and China had normalized relations, most of the ASEAN states followed suit. That meant ending official recognition of the ROC government on Taiwan, which also boxed Taipei out of all subsequent diplomatic initiatives on the South China Sea. ASEAN had then shifted its focus to Vietnam, whose behavior the members saw as a threat to regional stability. When Vietnamese troops invaded Cambodia in 1978, ASEAN had tacitly endorsed China's retaliatory war. The organization had then helped China and the United States engineer Vietnam's decade of isolation. As a result, ASEAN was not inclined to speak up for Vietnam immediately after the Johnson Reef clash. But China's entry into the Spratlys did raise serious concerns among members. And those concerns deepened after 1989.

By 1991, the end of the Cold War and Vietnam's withdrawal from Cambodia had greatly diminished the perceived threat of Communism in Southeast Asia. So the ASEAN members, which had added Brunei as the sixth of their number in 1984, began to envision a new role for the grouping. It shouldn't just protect against overt threats to their sovereignty; it should actively promote a regional agenda to drive growth and avoid conflict. And a key part of that agenda included extending membership to Cambodia, Laos, Myanmar, and, most important, Vietnam. The ASEAN-6 were convinced that inclusion would give their four neighbors a stake in the peaceful development of the region and help bury the ideological divisions of the Cold War. Vietnam would become an observer to ASEAN in 1993 and a full member in 1995. Laos and Myanmar would follow suit in 1997 and Cambodia in 1999.

The turning point for ASEAN came in June 1992, during its twenty-fifth-anniversary summit in Singapore. Member-states wanted to cement their transition from a loose Cold War coalition to an organization that could claim the mantle of regional leadership. So the six heads of government issued a groundbreaking commitment to "move towards a higher plane of political and economic cooperation to secure regional peace and prosperity." And that meant "[promoting] external dialogues on enhancing security in the region as well as intra-ASEAN dialogues on ASEAN security cooperation."[2]

As if to prove the point, at their annual meeting in Manila that July, the six ASEAN foreign ministers issued the organization's first ever joint statement on the South China Sea. The "Manila Declaration" was short and vague but incorporated several principles that continue to inform ASEAN statements about the South China Sea. These included calls for mutual respect and restraint, peaceful resolution of disputes, and cooperation on less sensitive issues like safety of navigation, marine pollution, and countering piracy.[3] China's foreign minister, who was on hand for the ASEAN Post-Ministerial Conference with the grouping's dialogue partners, was invited to endorse the statement. He declined, arguing that China had no hand in crafting it. But he reportedly said Beijing backed its "principles."[4] Whatever optimism that might have fueled would be short-lived.

Making Mischief

ASEAN organized the first ASEAN Regional Forum (ARF) in 1994. It brought together the foreign ministers of all member-states plus their ten dialogue partners, including China, to discuss the region's most pressing diplomatic and security issues. Today the forum has expanded to include twenty-six countries and the European Union, making it the largest annual ministerial-level gathering in Asia.[5] The early ARFs and accompanying ASEAN-China Post-Ministerial Conferences presented opportunities for senior ministers from all affected countries to discuss the South China Sea. And they largely set the agenda for the flurry of ASEAN-China diplomatic efforts over the next quarter-century. Despite the establishment of higher-level leaders' summits, the ARF and its associated meetings remain the center of the annual geopolitical theater surrounding the South China Sea disputes. The media seizes on each rumored closed-door argument and slight tweak to the language of the chair's statement as a hint of progress or tension. A few months after that first forum, the prospects for peacefully managing the South China Sea disputes dimmed considerably.

The Philippines had recently decided to take another look at oil and gas in the Dangerous Ground. In May 1994, Manila awarded Alcorn Petroleum a contract to study potential resources near Reed Bank. The company, a local subsidiary of U.S.-based Vaalco Energy, was to conduct its assessment entirely on paper, with no new surveys or drilling. The study block overlapped with the one that Salen and AMOCO had explored in the 1970s, but it also covered areas farther south and west. A thin section of the block included the waters around Nanshan and Flat Islands, which were certainly disputed. But the rest covered seabed that most would have considered part of the Philippine continental shelf, outside the disputed Spratlys.[6] Someone leaked word of the contract, and China predictably objected.

A few months later, in January 1995, a Filipino fishing boat came across four suspicious platforms erected on a reef in the middle of Alcorn's study block. The Filipino crew were taken captive and held for a week. They had stumbled across China's newest outpost on the aptly named Mischief Reef.[7] A month later, Manila dispatched a patrol boat and surveillance aircraft to confirm the development. Then it released photographs to the international press.[8] Beijing at first claimed they were just fishermen's shelters, but the wooden structures never came down. And a couple of years later they would be replaced by concrete barracks. China had occupied what was legally a piece of the seabed barely 100 nautical miles from the Philippine coast. For Manila, and ASEAN, it was a wake-up call.

In March, just a few weeks after Manila's announcement to the world, the ASEAN foreign ministers issued their second-ever standalone statement on the

South China Sea. The document called on all sides to observe the Manila declaration of 1992 and "refrain from taking actions that destabilize the region and
further threaten peace and security of the South China Sea." That language, including the refusal to call out China or any other actors by name, would become
a persistent feature, and handicap, of future ASEAN statements. The foreign
ministers continued, "We specifically call for the early resolution of the problems
caused by recent developments in Mischief Reef." And they concluded, "We
encourage all claimants and other countries in Southeast Asia to address the
issue in various fora, including the Indonesia-sponsored Workshop Series on
Managing Potential Conflicts in the South China Sea."[9]

That workshop series was in many ways emblematic of the constant cycle
of hope and disappointment that has plagued diplomatic efforts to manage the
disputes. The first workshop had been held in Bali, Indonesia, in 1990. It brought
together officials and experts from interested parties to discuss concrete paths
forward.[10] It involved only the six ASEAN members. China, Taiwan, Vietnam,
and Laos had joined the second workshop in Bandung in 1991. And from then
on it would be the only regular opportunity for high-level representatives from
all claimants, including both China and Taiwan, to discuss the South China Sea.

The workshops were the brainchild of Hasjim Djalal, Indonesia's foremost
expert on the law of the sea. He had served as ambassador to the United Nations,
was a participant in the UNCLOS III negotiations, and would soon become
president of the ISA. The workshops still exist but in much diminished form.
Sponsored by Indonesia, they were primarily funded during their heyday in
the 1990s and early 2000s by the government of Canada and later Norway.[11]
Participants debated and developed plans for technical cooperation on issues
like marine environmental conservation and safety of navigation, while working
groups were spun off to pursue concrete progress on those opportunities
identified by the larger workshop.

All discussions were premised on a commitment to avoid sensitive areas
of disagreement, particularly the thorny questions of sovereignty. Instead,
participants hoped to make small but measurable progress on managing
tensions and building confidence. But even those limited goals proved too ambitious, despite the dogged efforts of many participants. Sustainable funding
was a major problem, with China reportedly unwilling to participate if anyone
other than Canada and the Scandinavian countries paid for the workshops. It
especially objected to any U.S. or Japanese funding.[12] Numerous opportunities
for cooperation were identified over the years, but none made real progress. For
instance, participants reached consensus on a project to share hydrographic
data funded by Singapore, and another on biodiversity in cooperation with the
UN Environment Programme with funding from the U.S. Department of State.
Both collapsed before they could really start. Ralph Cossa, Brad Glosserman,

and Scott Snyder—all participants in the workshops—blamed this on fears, presumably from China, about internationalizing the disputes. In 2001, they wrote:

> A pattern seems to have emerged. Dialogue is acceptable and discussions about technical cooperation have gained consensus, but when it appears that a project might actually go forward, consensus breaks down—apparently as a result of concerns that actual cooperation efforts might internationalize the issue, or perhaps as part of a deliberate effort to stall any practical cooperation effort in the South China Sea. Yet, non-claimant interest in the South China Sea as a transit-way and global resource for fish and wildlife suggests that international interest is inevitable, as non-claimants are also stakeholders in the maintenance of regional peace and stability.[13]

The workshop series was mentioned positively by nearly every ASEAN Ministerial Meeting joint statement from 1991 until 2004, suggesting that Southeast Asian leaders remained interested in its success.[14] But with China unwilling to move on practical cooperation, their hands were tied. The unrealized potential of the workshop series mirrors the disappointment of official efforts between China and its neighbors after Mischief Reef.

In the wake of the Mischief Reef occupation, China and the Philippines signed a Joint Statement on the South China Sea and on Other Areas of Cooperation. They also undertook a series of confidence-building measures, but those did little to restrain Beijing or reassure Manila. China and ASEAN, meanwhile, held their first dedicated senior officials' meeting on the South China Sea in 1995. This kicked off a long, some might argue endless, series of diplomatic engagements on the issue.[15] Disagreements over the format of negotiations as well as their end goals plagued the process from the beginning. Beijing consistently objected to negotiating with ASEAN as a grouping. It argued that the disputes should be discussed as bilateral matters between China and each of the Southeast Asian claimants. Naturally, Malaysia, the Philippines, and Vietnam preferred to engage through ASEAN, which gave them far more leverage than negotiating individually with their larger neighbor. China also consistently refused to negotiate a legally binding agreement with ASEAN, leading to several false starts in discussions.

In the joint statement following their annual meeting in 1995, the ASEAN foreign ministers "called on [the South China Sea claimants] to refrain from taking actions that could destabilise the region, including possibly undermining the freedom of navigation and aviation in the affected areas."[16] Such language has now become pro forma in virtually every high-level statement on the South China Sea, but it signaled an important shift at the time. It was the first recognition that the disputes were no longer just about contested sovereignty over rocks and islets. The interrelated but distinct set of disagreements over the rules governing waters and airspace had taken center stage. Southeast Asian capitals had recognized that Beijing was in the process of expanding its claims to include vague but far-reaching historic rights over waters and airspace that were clearly inconsistent with international law.

ASEAN's decision to focus more on freedom of navigation and overflight wasn't just a reaction to its own anxieties over Chinese claims. It was an acknowledgment of concerns by outside parties, including the United States. Since the end of World War II, U.S. interests in the South China Sea had been limited to maintaining its credibility as a security guarantor while avoiding picking sides among allies over messy sovereignty debates. But the expansion of Chinese maritime claims in the 1990s changed things. They made the South China Sea disputes about more than just rocks and islands. From then on, the disputes involved critical questions of freedom of the seas and the rule of law, which U.S. leaders had seen as matters of direct national interest for generations.

This was evident in the State Department's response to the Mischief Reef occupation, captured by a statement read during the spokesperson's daily press briefing in May 1995. The statement pulled together the threads of U.S. national interest in the South China Sea that had developed over the decades. The State Department didn't explicitly name China or reference Mischief Reef, but it noted that "a pattern of unilateral actions and reactions in the South China Sea has increased tensions in the region." Despite its misgivings, Washington wasn't ready to elevate the South China Sea to the level of other major irritants in the bilateral relationship, like Taiwan and human rights.

But in a warning against potential aggression, especially toward its ally the Philippines, the State Department declared, "the United States strongly opposes the use or threat of force to resolve competing claims and urges all claimants to exercise restraint and to avoid destabilizing actions." It offered U.S. backing to ASEAN's diplomatic efforts, provided they "[take] into account the interests of all parties." This meant the legal rights of the United States and other outside parties that used the sea. Then came a line that would have sounded familiar to officials launching the Asiatic Fleet a century and a half earlier: "Maintaining freedom of navigation is a fundamental interest of the United States. Unhindered navigation by all ships and aircraft in the South China Sea is essential for the peace and prosperity of the entire Asia-Pacific region, including the United States."[17] Finally, the department described the balance the United States would strike between neutrality on territorial sovereignty and strong support for maritime rights: "The United States takes no position on the legal merits of the competing claims to sovereignty over the various islands, reefs, atolls, and cays in the South China Sea. The United States would, however, view with serious concern any maritime claim or restriction on maritime activity in the South China Sea that was not consistent with international law, including the 1982 United Nations Convention on the Law of the Sea."[18] This remains the U.S. position, and one that tends to irritate all sides. Chinese officials frequently blast the United States for hypocrisy, claiming that Washington violates its stated neutrality by weighing in on maritime rights. Filipino and Vietnamese interlocutors express frustration that the United States will not back their claims to the islands. Both sets of critics tend to ignore the distinction that the United States draws between the disputes over land and water. But this balance has been reached by necessity; it is the only position that allows the United States to remain consistent in its long-standing interests: to uphold freedom of the seas and to remain a credible security partner without picking sides among allies and partners.

The New Historic Rights

The expansion of China's claims started with fish. Chinese and Vietnamese fisherfolk had operated in the Paracel Islands for centuries. They had also worked the Spratlys from time to time. Filipinos had long fished Scarborough Shoal and the reefs of the Dangerous Ground. And boats from Sabah and Sarawak had plied the shoals off Borneo. The upheavals of the early twentieth century interrupted much of that traditional fishing activity. After World War II, Southeast Asian fishers started returning to the reefs. But the boats that once made long seasonal journeys from Hainan to the Spratlys never returned. Instead, more than thirty years later, they were replaced by a modern fleet deployed under orders from the state.

As China built new naval and oceanographic capabilities, it also invented a new Spratly Island fishing fleet. In 1985, Beijing had provided money for five boats from Hainan to outfit themselves for a fishing trip to the Spratlys. Others soon followed. Chinese officials began to urge fishing boats to "maintain conspicuous presence" around the islands and coined a new slogan: "Develop the Spratlys, fisheries go first." The state-owned Guangxi Beihai Fisheries General Company took the lead. Once China had settled onto its first bases in the Spratlys, the company sent four trawlers in early 1989 to investigate the fishing grounds. They ranged well beyond what China might claim as territorial waters or EEZs from the islands. Guangxi Beihai's boats spent the next two years fishing west of the Spratlys, including over the submerged banks where Hanoi was building its DK1 platforms. In 1991, they headed farther south to fish over the Sunda Shelf.[19] The Chinese government started calling this the "southwest fishing grounds." Everyone else called it the EEZs of Indonesia and Malaysia.

In 1994, China's Ministry of Agriculture published the *Atlas of Fishing Grounds in the South China Sea*. It showed ten fishing grounds that were clearly based on the nine-dash line, not the maritime zones defined by UNCLOS.[20] Beijing also began subsidizing fuel costs for boats that fished around the Spratlys that year. Those subsidies would expand considerably in the years ahead. In April 1995, Indonesia admitted for the first time that China was claiming waters within its EEZ.[21]

China's seabed claims followed a trajectory similar to that of its expanding fishing activities. By the early 1980s, claimants had set aside dreams of an oil and gas bonanza under the Spratly Islands. The only commercially viable resources anyone had found were along the coasts, far from disputed territories. In June 1980, Vietnam had signed an agreement with the Soviet Union to jointly explore for offshore oil and gas. China's Foreign Ministry had initially objected, asserting that "the Xisha and Nansha Islands . . . have always been a part of Chinese territory; the natural resources in the above areas belong to China."[22] But it soon became clear that the Soviets were only interested in areas that Western companies had explored off the South Vietnamese coast years before. Those were hundreds of miles south and west of the Spratlys. When a new joint venture, Vietsovpetro, began producing oil from those wells a few years later, China raised no objections.[23]

China continued to promote Deng Xiaoping's idea of "setting aside disputes and pursuing joint development." That proposition was originally meant for the Senkaku Islands in the East China Sea. But in 1986, Deng had told visiting Philippine vice president Salvador Laurel, "We should leave aside the issue of the Nansha Islands for a while." During Cory Aquino's visit shortly after the Johnson Reef clash two years later, Deng told her, "We can set aside this issue for the time being and take the approach of pursuing joint development."[24] Philippine officials responded positively, as did their Malaysian counterparts to similar overtures. But Manila and Kuala Lumpur were interested in joint development in the Spratlys, not what they considered undisputed waters along their coasts. And that soon became a problem.

By the late 1980s, increasing survey activities had piqued Chinese interest in the oil and gas potential around the Spratlys. In 1989, *China Daily* cited official estimates of 25 billion cubic meters of natural gas and 105 billion barrels of oil around the islands, plus another 91 billion barrels in the area of James Shoal. As with fishing, officials were using a very expansive definition of the Spratlys to include areas well beyond the islands themselves. The reference to James Shoal, hundreds of miles from the islands, was especially concerning.

In 1992, an American oilman named Randall Thompson convinced Beijing that he knew the best place to find oil in the South China Sea. More than two decades later, Thompson would tell journalist and author Bill Hayton his version of the story. He was a protégé of Sonny Brinkerhoff, whose company had agreed to drill at Reed Bank in 1976 despite warnings from the U.S. State Department. Thompson was looking for prospects and started poring over the old survey data collected by American companies off South Vietnam. Vietsovpetro had already staked a claim to those basins. And with Washington still sanctioning Hanoi, an American couldn't do business in Vietnam anyway. So instead, Thompson traveled to Hainan to look over China's new survey data. In February 1992, he went to Beijing for a pitch session. He convinced state-owned China National Offshore Oil Corporation to award his tiny company, Crestone, rights to a huge oil and gas block southwest of the Spratlys. The block, called Wan'an Bei 21, covered all six of the underwater banks on which Vietnam had built its DK1 platforms. Much of it was over 200 miles from the nearest island (Figure 7.1). China's claim to the block could be explained only by the nine-dash line, even if Beijing didn't come out and say so.

The Vietnamese government tried to offer Thompson a deal to break the contract with Beijing, but he refused. In the meantime, Hanoi was lining up interest from the Western oil majors in anticipation of improved relations with Washington. In February 1994, the United States lifted its embargo on Vietnam. Mobil, Conoco, and others quickly sought deals for offshore blocks, including some that overlapped with Wan'an Bei 21. Thompson responded by convincing the South China Sea Institute of Oceanography in Hainan to quickly survey

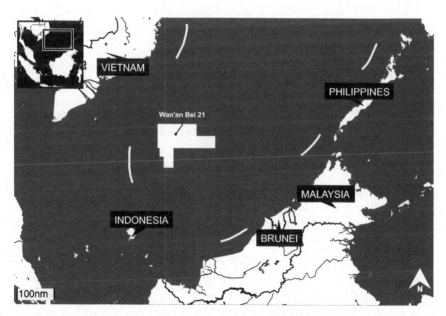

Figure 7.1 Wan'an Bei exploration block and nine-dash line, 1992. Created using Mapcreator and OpenStreetMap.

the block. They tried in April, but three Vietnamese naval ships drove them off. A month later, Vietnam deployed a Vietsovpetro rig to an area within Wan'an Bei 21. Hanoi was closing in on a deal with Conoco for rights to the area and wanted to make a point. China responded by sending two PLAN ships to lay siege to the rig. The standoff continued for weeks until everyone headed home. Two years later, Thompson sold Crestone, and the rights to Wan'an Bei 21, to Benton Oil and Gas for a hefty profit.[25] Singapore's Brightoil would eventually secure those rights at a bargain. But the area remains undeveloped.

By 1994, Beijing was clearly asserting rights to fisheries and seabed resources throughout the entire nine-dash line. And it was willing to take risks to do so. But it hadn't yet offered any justification for those claims. For that, PRC officials would benefit from arguments taking place on the other side of the Taiwan Strait. In 1989, the Ministry of the Interior in Taipei had set up a committee to delimit Taiwan's new territorial sea and EEZ. President Chiang Ching-kuo had died the previous year, leading to splits within the ruling Kuomintang. Two of the three legal scholars on the new boundary committee belonged to a conservative faction that favored reunification with the mainland and saw the new president, Lee Teng-hui, as too confrontational toward Beijing. They came up with a novel idea: why not claim everything within the old U-shaped line as "historic waters"? Fu Kuen-chen was the most vocal of these scholars and championed the idea for years. In April 1993, he found some success. The government approved new policy guidelines which read, "The South China Sea area within the *historic water limit* is the maritime area under the jurisdiction of the Republic of China, in which the Republic of China possesses all rights and interests."[26] The "historic water limit" was, of course, the 1948 U-shaped line.

By contrast, parallel legislation in China was much more constrained. In 1992, Beijing issued the Law on the Territorial Sea and the Contiguous Zone. It didn't claim anything beyond the zones allowed by UNCLOS, and it defined Chinese territory as including the "Diaoyu Islands, Penghu Islands, Dongsha Islands, Xisha Islands, Nansha (Spratly) Islands and other islands that belong to the People's Republic of China."[27] It notably left out the Zhongsha Islands, suggesting that lawyers in Beijing realized it would be absurd to claim maritime zones from the entirely underwater Macclesfield Bank.

But then China began to expand the scope of its official claims. In May 1996, Beijing declared the baselines for measuring its territorial sea. These included lines connecting the outermost Paracel Islands (Figure 7.2).[28] The United States, Vietnam, and others immediately objected. China, as a continental state, was not entitled to claim archipelagic baselines. And even if it could, UNCLOS limited

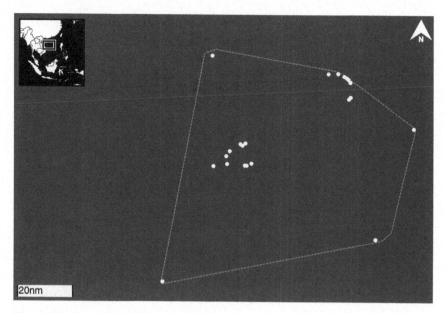

20nm

Figure 7.2 China's Paracel Island straight baselines, 1996. Created using Mapcreator and OpenStreetMap.

the ratio of water to land within such lines to a maximum of nine to one. The ratio within the Paracels baselines was nearly two thousand to one.[29] A month later, China ratified UNCLOS. It made a declaration at that time affirming its rights to an EEZ and continental shelf. And it reiterated its sovereignty over the "archipelagoes and islands" of the South China Sea as listed in 1992. But it claimed no special maritime rights beyond those allowed by the convention.[30]

Fu and other Taiwanese conservatives, meanwhile, called for Taipei and Beijing to synchronize their policy positions on the South China Sea. They frequently engaged with counterparts in the mainland, and that seems to be how the formulation of "historic rights" was introduced to the PRC. Other Taiwanese scholars vigorously opposed Fu's interpretation of the U-shaped line. Many knew that it was inconsistent with UNCLOS and wanted Taiwan to observe international law even if it was formally excluded from the convention. Others objected on policy grounds; they had no interest in greater synchronicity between Beijing and Taipei.

By late 1997, both sides of the Taiwanese political spectrum had reached consensus. Fu and his ilk were sidelined, and all reference to "historic waters" was stripped from Taiwan's 1998 Law on the Territorial Sea and Contiguous Zone.[31] On the other side of the strait, however, Fu's ideas had taken root. That same year, China issued its Exclusive Economic Zone and Continental Shelf Act, which noted, "The provisions of this Act shall not affect the *historical rights* of the People's Republic of China."[32] It was the first time Beijing had admitted it was claiming maritime rights above and beyond those allowed by UNCLOS.

Reviving the Alliance

Mischief Reef didn't just leave Philippine officials outraged; it also left them feeling vulnerable. U.S. forces had barely cleared out of their bases before China had decided to build an outpost in Philippine waters. How could Manila not see a connection between the two? After discovering the Chinese platforms, President Fidel Ramos warned, "While we are hoping for the best, we must prepare for the worst." There wasn't much the Philippines could do about it. The navy was small and obsolete and the air force not much better. In 1995, Manila announced a fifteen-year armed forces modernization program. In the end, less than 10 percent of the $8 billion allocated over the life of the program would be spent.[33] But even if it had worked, it would have been a long-term solution at a time when the Ramos administration needed immediate help.

In the meantime, another crisis reminded Washington of the importance of unimpeded access to the South China Sea. In early 1995, Taiwan's president Lee Teng-hui accepted an invitation to visit his alma mater, Cornell University in New York State. The Clinton administration had refused him a visa just a few months earlier, but this time, the State Department gave in to congressional pressure and granted Lee a visa. Beijing was furious. In response, China conducted missile tests near Taiwan in July and August. A third test followed in March 1996, with missiles landing so close to Taiwanese ports that they disrupted shipping to and from the island.

Taiwan was scheduled to hold its first ever direct presidential election later that month and Beijing wanted to signal that a Lee victory was unacceptable. Instead, it helped boost his campaign and provoked the largest American naval deployment to the region since the Vietnam War. Washington ordered the USS *Independence* carrier battle group from Japan to take up a position near Taiwan. Then it diverted a second carrier group from the Persian Gulf. The USS *Nimitz* and its escorts raced across the Indian Ocean, up through the South China Sea, and then pointedly transited the Taiwan Strait. The show of support convinced Beijing that it was overmatched. It also helped launch the second phase of China's military modernization. One could draw a straight line from the PLAN's humiliation in 1996 to its near-peer status with the U.S. Navy today.

After Mischief Reef and the Taiwan Strait Crisis, Manila and Washington were both distrustful of Beijing's long-term intentions. And they realized that the post–Cold War complacency that led to the withdrawal of American bases from the Philippines had been a mistake. The alliance still held, underpinned by the MDT. But there wasn't much military-to-military interaction since the expiration of the Military Bases Agreement. Without a legal framework to ease the way for troops from each side to visit the other, large-scale exercises and training programs were difficult and time-consuming to organize. To tackle that problem, Manila and Washington launched negotiations on a Visiting Forces Agreement (VFA).

There were sticking points in the negotiations, including the perennial question of criminal jurisdiction over U.S. service members. But the process was relatively quick and easy, at least compared to the fights over the old Military Bases Agreement. U.S. ambassador Thomas Hubbard and Secretary of Foreign Affairs Domingo Siazon Jr. signed the new VFA in February 1998. Newly inaugurated president Joseph Estrada approved it in October, and the Philippine Senate ratified it in May 1999. The U.S. side saw the VFA as an executive agreement, not a new treaty, which raised constitutional questions in the Philippines. But the country's Supreme Court upheld the agreement a year later.[34]

Behind the scenes, the VFA negotiations were also linked to renewed Philippine concerns about the application of the MDT in the South China Sea. Cyrus Vance's 1979 statement had been good enough up to that point. Vance had assured Manila that an attack wouldn't need to occur in the metropolitan Philippines to be covered by Article V. This reflected the internal consensus at the State Department that unprovoked attacks on Philippine vessels or troops at sea should be covered, but incidents on disputed islands might not be. In the wake of the Mischief Reef occupation, Manila began to ask for more specific assurances. In 1997, Arnulfo Acedera, chief of staff of the Armed Forces of the Philippines, announced that he was drawing up contingency plans for a joint response with the United States to an attack in the Philippine EEZ.[35] When China replaced its "fishermen's shelters" on Mischief Reef with a hardened military outpost a year later, Manila grew even more worried.

In August 1998, Secretary of Defense William Cohen visited Manila. The timing was significant: the VFA had just been signed but was still being debated by the Philippine Senate. When pressed on MDT coverage by reporters, Cohen responded that the South China Sea was part of the "Pacific" referred to in Article V. This signaled that any attack on Philippine armed forces, public vessels, or aircraft there would fall within the scope of the treaty.[36] It was a significant public clarification. Cohen knew that it was an important moment to signal American resolve in the South China Sea. A few months later, the VFA was ratified.

By upgrading the facilities on Mischief Reef in 1998, China made clear it wasn't leaving. That was a major problem for the new Estrada government. The reef was barely 100 miles from the Philippine coast and 60 miles from Reed Bank. The closest Philippine base was on Nanshan Island, 50 miles to the north. Mischief Reef was smack in the middle of a strategically important section of the Philippine EEZ, but Manila had no way to keep an eye on it. The Philippine government couldn't let that stand, but it didn't have a lot of options. Its navy consisted of World War II–era rust buckets that couldn't reliably patrol the area. And building its own facility on one of the underwater reefs nearby would be risky and complex. China could easily put a stop to such an operation. So Manila put one of its rust buckets to an unconventional use.

The BRP *Sierra Madre* was first USS LST-821 and then *USS* Harnett County. Built in Evansville, Indiana, in 1944, it saw service in World War II and Vietnam. In 1970, the United States transferred the ship to South Vietnam, which renamed it RVNS *My Tho*. When Saigon fell, it was among the flotilla of Vietnamese Navy ships that Richard Armitage, on special assignment from the Pentagon, escorted across the South China Sea to the safety of Subic Bay. It was transferred to the Philippine Navy and rechristened the *Sierra Madre* in 1976. In 1999, it approached Second Thomas Shoal, about 20 miles from Mischief Reef. The captain steered through the only passable channel into the lagoon, turned around, and intentionally grounded his ship on the reef. The Philippines had its ninth, and most precarious, outpost in the Spratlys.

The *Sierra Madre*'s grounding raised tensions with Beijing, which was irate. When the Chinese government demanded that the ship be removed, President Estrada, feigning ignorance, promised to tow the vessel away as soon as it could be safely floated off the reef. But it was an act. The whole idea had come from senior leadership, particularly Philippine Navy chief Eduardo Santos. A few days after the grounding, he rode a helicopter out to the *Sierra Madre* for a congratulatory briefing with the crew.[37] The episode raised new questions about the U.S. treaty commitment. After all, this was a commissioned Philippine Navy vessel in Philippine waters. What if China decided to take matters into its own hands? When asked, Ambassador Hubbard assured Secretary Siazon that Cohen had meant what he said the year before.[38] Philippine defense secretary Orlando Mercado was given similar assurances when he visited Washington soon after. And in December, in a thinly veiled reference to China, Cohen reiterated American neutrality on territorial disputes but said Washington "[rejected] very strongly any country taking unilateral action to assert sovereignty over the Spratlys."[39]

This period of bilateral tension coincided with Beijing's first real attempts to contest Manila's administration of Scarborough Shoal. The isolated reef, located 120 miles west of Luzon, had been under Philippine control since independence. Chiang Kai-shek's cartographers had originally dubbed it Sikabale—a transliteration of its English name—in 1935. They categorized it as part of the Nansha Islands along with Macclesfield Bank, which sat 200 miles away. That relationship, at least on paper, continued after Macclesfield and its surroundings were renamed the Zhongsha Islands in 1947. But this Chinese claim had gone largely unnoticed even in Beijing. For decades, official Chinese maps affixed the "Zhongsha" label only to Macclesfield Bank, which was invariably given as the English name of the Zhongsha Islands in state media.[40]

China became more aware of Scarborough Shoal during the 1980s as its fishing and survey vessels increased their operations across the South China Sea. In 1985, the Chinese government approved the establishment of a state-sanctioned maritime militia in Tanmen village on Hainan. That militia made its first trip, involving five fishing boats, to Scarborough. They returned frequently in the years after.[41] Then in 1997, a group of nationalistic amateur radio operators from China landed on the reef and set up transmitters. The Philippine Navy drove them off, as it had poachers, smugglers, and many others since the 1960s. The incident proved to be an unexpected turning point. Afterward, the volume of Chinese fishing activity around Scarborough spiked, along with Philippine efforts to stop it. And by 1999, Chinese fishing boats were driving their Filipino counterparts out of the shoal, in one case colliding with a Philippine Navy ship.[42]

Taiwan also showed renewed interest in the shoal at this time. In 1999, Taipei declared territorial baselines from which its maritime zones should be measured. These included one set of straight baselines around Taiwan and its outlying islands, and another around Pratas Reef. For the Zhongsha Islands, the law declared that all maritime zones should be measured from the normal low-water line at Huangyan Dao (Scarborough). The State Department was baffled; it had always equated the Zhongsha Islands with Macclesfield Bank and didn't seem to know what "Huangyan Dao" was referring to. When the department published a legal analysis of Taiwan's claims a few years later, it still thought that Taipei was claiming that Macclesfield itself had a low-water line.[43]

To confront the growing Chinese presence around Scarborough, the Philippine Navy in 1999 decided to rerun the Second Thomas Shoal play and ground another ship. Foreign Secretary Siazon objected. Manila would be hosting a meeting between China's premier Zhu Rongji and ASEAN heads of state in November. He didn't want the navy dashing hopes for diplomatic progress. But Siazon was overruled. Another World War II–era LST, the BRP *Benguet*, sailed to Scarborough with a Philippine Air Force plane serving as escort. It sailed into the lagoon and ran aground in plain view of Chinese fishing boats on the scene. Beijing found out almost immediately, and phones began ringing at the armed forces headquarters and the Department of Foreign Affairs in Manila. Within a month, the government backpedaled and the navy was ordered to remove the ship. They hired a Malaysian tugboat to pull it off the reef and let rumors spread that the *Benguet* had accidentally run aground after colliding with some Chinese fishing boats.[44]

The Philippines wasn't the only one worried about China's intentions at this time. Malaysia was also looking to shore up control of its EEZ. Soon after Beijing

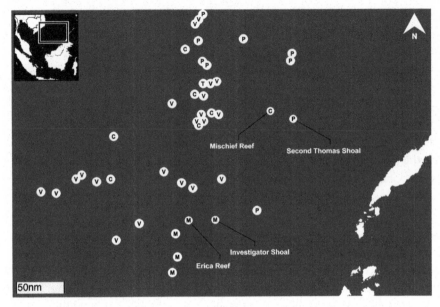

Figure 7.3 Status of occupation by China (C), Malaysia (M), Philippines (P), Taiwan (T), and Vietnam (V) in the Spratly Islands, 1999. Created using Mapcreator and OpenStreetMap.

fortified Mischief Reef, Kuala Lumpur commissioned a local shipbuilder to construct two new barges like those it had installed on Ardasier and Mariveles Reefs a decade earlier. In April 1999, one of the barges was towed under naval escort and installed on Erica Reef, 15 miles northeast of Mariveles. A month later, the other was placed on Investigator Shoal, 25 miles to the east.[45] And that was it. Since 1999, claimants have expanded or upgraded facilities, but no one has added to their count. Vietnam continues to occupy twenty-one of the Spratlys, the Philippines controls nine, China seven, Malaysia five, and Taiwan one (Figure 7.3).

Settling for a Declaration of Conduct

In 1996, ASEAN foreign ministers had called for "a regional code of conduct in the South China Sea which will lay the foundation for long term stability in the area and foster understanding among claimant countries."[46] Three years later, they tasked the Philippines with writing the first draft of that code of conduct (COC). Foreign Secretary Siazon presented it at the ASEAN Ministerial Meeting in July 1999, where it was adopted by his counterparts from across Southeast Asia. They set themselves the goal of quickly reaching a final agreement with

Beijing.[47] ASEAN-China negotiations started a few months later but bogged down almost immediately. More than twenty years later, ASEAN continues to pin its hopes on an effective COC that remains ever out of reach.

Major disagreements on the code's scope and legal status and whether ASEAN was negotiating as a group or individual members plagued talks from the start. When the two sides exchanged drafts in March 2000, they tried to paper over these fundamental issues, with little success. At the behest of Vietnam, ASEAN's draft said the "Disputed Area" included both the Spratlys and Paracels. China's version referred only to the "Nansha [Spratly] Islands." Neither draft was explicitly legally binding or established a dispute settlement mechanism, but ASEAN's was much more detailed and prescriptive. The group sought a commitment to "regular consultations on the observance of this Code of Conduct," which might have led to a formal conciliation mechanism. And ASEAN's stated goal was "to find a comprehensive and durable solution" to the disputes. China's aim was more limited to confidence building and cooperation.

On the details, ASEAN sought to prohibit any new island occupations; China didn't. ASEAN favored a multilateral approach, referring to the obligations of all parties; China stressed bilateral cooperation, especially to manage overlapping sovereignty claims and fisheries. Beijing included "exploration and exploitation of resources" among the cooperative activities that claimants should pursue; ASEAN members avoided mentioning joint development altogether, fearing that China would demand a share in resources not just near the islands but right off their coasts. For the same reason, they rejected China's call to prohibit the arrest of foreign fishing boats in disputed waters. And they had good reason to worry.

By the early 2000s, China's state-owned Guangxi Beihai Fisheries Development Company was being replaced by heavily subsidized private vessels in the "southwest fishing grounds." In 2003, the Ministry of Agriculture would issue new regulations that explicitly defined the Spratly Islands fishery as all waters within the nine-dash line south of 12 degrees latitude. In other words, China claimed its boats could fish the whole southern half of the South China Sea up to a few miles from its neighbors' coasts.[48] And it had subsidized the creation of a whole new fishing industry to assert these historic rights.

Another set of contentious issues in the COC negotiations involved the application of UNCLOS and the rights of outside parties. ASEAN included in its preamble "respect for freedom of navigation and air traffic in the South China Sea, as provided for by international law, including [UNCLOS]." This reflected its own concerns as well as those raised by international partners like the United States. ASEAN concluded its draft by inviting "other countries and organizations . . . to subscribe to the principles contained in this Code of Conduct." China's support for the rights guaranteed by UNCLOS was more circumscribed.

Its proposed language on fisheries effectively denied its neighbors exclusive rights within their own EEZs. And it sought wide-ranging limits on foreign—especially American—military activities. China's draft called on parties to "refrain from conducting any military exercises directed against other countries in the Nansha Islands and their adjacent waters, and from carrying out any dangerous and close-in military reconnaissance." It also sweepingly declared that "military patrol activities in the area shall be restricted." Only then did China say parties should "maintain safety of international navigation in the South China Sea and ensure freedom of navigation of ships and aircraft *in normal passage*" (italics added).[49]

Since "adjacent waters" seemingly included the entire nine-dash line, these proposals would have severely diminished the ability of the United States to engage with its allies and partners in the region. The proposed ban on military reconnaissance targeted long-standing activities by the United States, Australia, and others throughout the South China Sea. This was clearly inconsistent with international law, even to those who thought UNCLOS left some room to restrict foreign military activity in the EEZ. ASEAN found the proposals unacceptable and rejected them out of hand. They would have been unenforceable anyway, as the United States and others doubtless would have *increased* military activity as a sign of noncompliance. But with the benefit of hindsight, it is clear these weren't just bargaining positions. Beijing really did, and still does, seek to limit freedom of navigation in the South China Sea to basic transit while severely restricting other economic and military freedoms.

After another two years of limited progress, ASEAN and China threw in the towel on the COC. Instead, they agreed to sign a nonbinding Declaration on the Conduct of Parties in the South China Sea (DOC). The Southeast Asian parties saw this as an interim step, one that would eventually lead to a binding code. China was vague about whether it agreed. Officials formally adopted the DOC on the sidelines of the November 2002 ASEAN Summit in Phnom Penh. The declaration was never meant to solve the South China Sea disputes. Like all later ASEAN negotiations with China, it was intended to manage tensions. ASEAN hoped that it would calm the waters and "enhance favourable conditions for a peaceful and durable solution," as stated in the preamble.[50] Then the claimants could settle their differences through direct negotiation or arbitration.

The DOC would fall far short of those expectations, first, because it contained only two sections with clear, prescriptive language. In the first, the parties "undertake to resolve their territorial and jurisdictional disputes by peaceful means, without resorting to the threat or use of force, through friendly consultations and negotiations by sovereign states directly concerned." In the second, they "undertake to exercise self-restraint in the conduct of activities that would complicate or escalate disputes and affect peace and stability including, among others, refraining from action of inhabiting on the presently uninhabited islands, reefs, shoals, cays, and other features and to handle their differences in a constructive manner."[51] Neither was a binding pledge; the parties agreed only to "undertake" certain things. In effect, they said they would try their best. Such a voluntary commitment, based on good faith, could and would be set aside if a claimant thought that others were falling short. Years later, the Philippines would successfully argue those points when filing an arbitration case against China.

It might seem that the DOC was doomed because it wasn't binding or enforceable. Indeed, this was a major weakness. But it wasn't necessarily fatal. Breaking commitments still carried real if unquantifiable diplomatic costs. Despite its failures, the parties have continued to pay lip service to the declaration. They have rationalized even their most egregious violations, always arguing that others broke faith first. This normative power explains why none of the parties has built permanent structures on any features that were unoccupied at the time the DOC was signed. That was the only act of "self-restraint" explicitly listed in the document. They have, however, violated the spirit of that proscription.[52]

And that points to the second major weakness of the DOC: it lacked specificity. Other than building on unoccupied features, everything was left open to interpretation. As a result, parties continued to fish, drill for oil and gas, extend new claims, and deploy advanced military platforms wherever they wanted, while insisting that they hadn't violated the declaration. This was amplified by the DOC's refusal to grapple with sensitive issues. The parties agreed to "seek ways . . . to build trust and confidence" and "explore or undertake cooperative activities."[53] But none of the most important issues—fishing, hydrocarbons, law enforcement activities—was listed as a way to do that. Even less sensitive options for cooperation, including marine scientific research, search and rescue, and combating maritime crime, lacked specifics. In the years since the DOC was signed, none has seen real progress. As an example, it was easy for everyone to endorse cooperation on marine conservation *in theory*, but it became much harder to decide who would take the lead or which laws and regulations would apply in disputed waters. These were the same issues that plagued the Indonesia-led Workshop Series on Managing Potential Conflicts in the South China Sea, and they had the same effect.

Finally, the DOC was hamstrung by the inability to agree on geographic scope. Hanoi insisted that the Paracels be included; Beijing refused. China defined the Spratlys as including James Shoal, Vanguard Bank, and other underwater features on the Malaysian and Vietnamese continental shelves. And it claimed all other waters south and west of the Spratlys because of the nine-dash line, which the others refused to acknowledge. Rather than grapple with these issues, the DOC avoided the question altogether. Each party was free to define for itself what areas were covered by the agreement. Predictably, all sides have adopted the view that their own actions have occurred outside the scope of the treaty.

Individually, none of these flaws was fatal. The DOC might still have helped manage tensions if its provisions were vague but supported by an effective dispute resolution mechanism. Conversely, a nonbinding agreement with no dispute resolution provisions could still have led to progress if it outlined detailed plans for practical cooperation. This would have been especially true had the DOC served as an interim step toward a more robust COC, as ASEAN intended. But that never happened. Instead, the DOC's weaknesses combined with China's intransigence to become a millstone around ASEAN's neck. For more than a decade, until Manila decided to break the mold, the DOC provided few benefits while preventing the Southeast Asian claimants from pursuing other diplomatic and legal avenues.

Failure to Launch

From the start, China and the ASEAN were not on the same page when it came to DOC implementation and the goal of a speedy transition to a COC. For the Southeast Asian claimants, the DOC was a means to an end. The declaration had established a framework for practical cooperation which they believed should be pursued immediately. This would, they hoped, create momentum for negotiating a binding COC at an early date. But Beijing saw DOC implementation as an end in itself, and one which would take much longer than the Southeast Asians intended. China continued to signal that the COC was a worthy goal, but it didn't talk about the declaration as a stepping stone the way the Southeast Asians did. ASEAN member-states expected to quickly set up the mechanisms needed under the DOC and then move to practical cooperation. Instead, each step of the process required slow, painful negotiations with Beijing.

At the 2003 ASEAN Ministerial Meeting—the first since the adoption of the DOC—Southeast Asian officials affirmed that the declaration would lead to the early conclusion of a COC.[54] But their enthusiasm was deflated a bit after the ASEAN-China Summit a few months later. Indonesia, as ASEAN chair that year, released a press statement declaring, "ASEAN leaders and Prime Minister Wen [Jiabao] agreed . . . to follow-up the [DOC]. ASEAN Leaders expressed hope that this would lead to the eventual establishment of a code of conduct in the South China Sea."[55] That Prime Minister Wen didn't share those hopes was strongly implied. At their next summit, in 2004, leaders agreed to establish a regular meeting of senior officials to implement the DOC. They also affirmed their "vision" for the "eventual adoption of a code of conduct in the South China Sea."[56] That vision would go unrealized.

Admittedly, the signs that Southeast Asian and Chinese expectations for the DOC and eventual COC were diverging are much clearer in hindsight than they were at the time. Other indicators suggested that the two sides were poised for real progress. The first ASEAN-China Senior Officials Meeting on the implementation of the DOC took place in December 2004. During that meeting, officials agreed to establish a Joint Working Group on the implementation of the DOC. This group was to meet at least twice a year and make recommendations to the Senior Officials Meeting on "guidelines and an action plan for the implementation of the DOC." It was also tasked with planning cooperative activities in five areas: environmental protection, marine scientific research, safety of navigation and communication at sea, search and rescue, and combating transnational crime.[57]

But late 2004 was the highwater mark for the DOC. Afterward, progress slowed to a crawl. At the first Joint Working Group meeting in August 2005, the ASEAN representatives introduced their draft guidelines for the implementation of the DOC. Point 2 of that draft called for the ten ASEAN states to consult before meeting with China.[58] Beijing's representatives objected, as this implied that the DOC was an agreement between China and ASEAN rather than between eleven individual parties. This had been a sticking point since the early days of COC negotiations and had been papered over for the sake of progress. But ignoring it hadn't made the problem go away. As a result, it would take another six years and twenty-one drafts before China and ASEAN finally agreed on guidelines to implement the DOC. That was supposed to be the first, and presumably easiest, task.[59]

As the formal ASEAN-led processes floundered, the Philippines, China, and Vietnam took a shot at practical cooperation outside the DOC. They hoped to jointly explore for oil and gas in disputed waters, which had been deemed too sensitive for inclusion in the declaration. In September 2004, Manila and Beijing agreed to launch the Joint Marine Seismic Undertaking (JMSU). The plan was for their state oil companies—Philippine National Oil Company and China National Offshore Oil Corporation—to conduct a joint seismic survey in waters around Scarborough Shoal and the northern Spratlys. Vietnam objected to the initial agreement, which included areas it might claim around the Spratlys. So Vietnam Oil and Gas Corporation (PetroVietnam) was included as the third member of the agreement in March 2005.[60]

The JMSU was made possible by political change in Manila. Gloria Macapagal Arroyo had ascended to the presidency in 2001 following Estrada's resignation amid mass protests, dubbed EDSA II. In 2004, she was narrowly elected to the office in her own right, though the polls were tainted by irregularities. She hoped to improve ties with Beijing after the rocky years of the Ramos and Estrada administrations. And with a new mandate to govern, along with apparent progress on the DOC, Arroyo saw space to do that. But the JMSU was a political timebomb. It included areas like Reed Bank and the waters around Scarborough that were considered undisputed in Manila. This expectedly drew fire from across the Philippine political arena. Opponents accused the government of selling out the country. A more popular leader might have weathered the storm and kept the JMSU alive; Arroyo, however, was anything but popular. Within months of reelection, her approval ratings were underwater and she spent the rest of her presidency embroiled in scandal.

The JMSU was in some ways unfavorable to the Philippines and Vietnam. For instance, it included confidentiality clauses that barred them from ever sharing the data collected with potential commercial partners. But Manila and Hanoi hadn't surrendered any legal rights over their continental shelves. The undertaking involved only seismic surveys, not actual drilling for oil and gas. It included a proviso that "signing of this Agreement shall not undermine the basic position held by the Government of each Party on the South China Sea." And the Philippine government was careful to independently issue exploration licenses to China National Offshore Oil Corporation and PetroVietnam to signal that it considered the areas in question to be under its jurisdiction.[61] Nonetheless, the agreement fell victim to Arroyo's unpopularity. It was linked in the popular imagination to a series of high-profile corruption cases involving shady Chinese investments in the Philippines. Some of those scandals would land Arroyo in pretrial detention for years after leaving office. When the initial agreement for the JMSU expired in 2008, it wasn't renewed. Challenges to its constitutionality are pending before the Philippine Supreme Court to this day.

Raising the Stakes

2009–2014

The United States, like every nation, has a national interest in freedom of navigation, open access to Asia's maritime commons, and respect for international law in the South China Sea. We share these interests not only with ASEAN members or ASEAN Regional Forum participants, but with other maritime nations and the broader international community. . . .

We oppose the use or threat of force by any claimant. While the United States does not take sides on the competing territorial disputes over land features in the South China Sea, we believe claimants should pursue their territorial claims and accompanying rights to maritime space in accordance with the UN Convention on the Law of the Sea. Consistent with customary international law, legitimate claims to maritime space in the South China Sea should be derived solely from legitimate claims to land features.

— Secretary of State Hillary Clinton, Remarks at Press Availability, ASEAN Regional Forum, Hanoi, July 23, 2010[1]

The South China Sea disputes never reached a stable new equilibrium. But the promise of the DOC helped lower temperatures for a while. Geopolitical shifts also distracted from the South China Sea and gave all parties incentives to keep those waters calm. China and ASEAN entered the new millennium with ties on the upswing. South China Sea negotiations were frustrating, but otherwise Beijing was seen as a positive force in the region. Southeast Asian economies were still recovering from the Asian Financial Crisis of 1997–98. China hadn't played a major role during the crisis, but its neighbors appreciated that it didn't take advantage of the turmoil. And they compared its response favorably with those of Washington and the International Monetary Fund, which were being criticized across the region. China seized this opportunity to launch a "charm offensive," part of which involved more proactively engaging ASEAN and boosting its soft power in Southeast Asia.

On Dangerous Ground. Gregory B. Poling, Oxford University Press. © Oxford University Press 2022. DOI: 10.1093/oso/9780197633984.003.0009

The 9/11 attacks in the United States made everything else secondary in U.S. foreign policy. In early 2002, the first U.S. Special Forces personnel arrived in Mindanao as part of Operation Enduring Freedom—Philippines. They would spend the next thirteen years advising and training the Armed Forces of the Philippines to combat the Abu Sayyaf Group and other Al-Qaeda affiliates. A downsized American presence continues that mission today. The VFA had emerged from the aftermath of Mischief Reef, but it was soon refocused almost entirely on the counterterror mission. Then in October 2002, the Indonesia-based Jemaah Islamiyah group bombed two nightclubs in Bali, killing 202 people. The carnage shocked Southeast Asian publics and put counterterrorism at the center of the regional agenda. President George W. Bush labeled Southeast Asia the "second front in the war against terrorism." And that framing dominated U.S.–Southeast Asia relations for the rest of the decade.

The South China Sea disputes had been shelved, but not solved. And the status quo began to rapidly deteriorate in 2009. It wasn't immediately obvious, but the developments of that year kicked off a cycle of escalation that continues to the present. Part of the blame rests with the global financial crisis that had peaked the year before. The U.S. and European economies were on their knees, while China's had quickly recovered. After three decades of modernization, China was now driving the global economy. And many of its leaders were convinced that the United States was in irreversible decline. On top of that, Chinese citizens had been convinced by twenty years of post-Tiananmen patriotic education that the entire South China Sea was their indisputable patrimony. It was a dangerous mix of hubris and revanchism.

Among other things, the changes that began in 2009 would undermine China's "charm offensive" and complicate its desire for regional leadership. Anxiety about Beijing's intentions would drive Southeast Asian states to seek closer political and security relations with Washington. And the newly inaugurated Obama administration would capitalize on that demand signal. It increased U.S. engagement with Southeast Asia to a level unseen since the end of the Vietnam War. A central component of that engagement was greater U.S. involvement, alongside other parties like Australia and Japan, in the South China Sea disputes. Within a few years, growing Chinese assertiveness would overturn two of Beijing's long-standing goals: it drew the United States deeper into the region and internationalized the South China Sea disputes.

(Re)Enter the Nine-Dash Line

UNCLOS grants coastal states seabed rights over the continental shelf out to 200 nautical miles, and beyond if they can meet certain geological criteria.[2] But claiming an extended continental shelf beyond 200 miles requires extensive surveys of the seabed which must be submitted to the Commission on the Limits of the Continental Shelf (CLCS) for review. The commission can either accept the submission or offer technical advice to improve it. It has no power to delimit overlapping claims, so if any state objects to another's submission, the CLCS simply puts its consideration on hold until the two sides can work things out. UNCLOS originally required states to submit any extended continental shelf claims within ten years of ratification.[3] But negotiators badly underestimated the cost and time needed for surveys, which can take anywhere from three to ten years.[4] As a result, very few countries could meet the original ten-year deadline to submit to the CLCS.

The parties to UNCLOS eventually recognized the problem and, in 2001, agreed to extend the deadline for submissions. They pointed out that the CLCS hadn't even adopted the scientific and technical guidelines by which submissions would be evaluated until 1999. Countries couldn't be expected to start their surveys without those. So any state that had ratified the convention before May 1999 would be given ten years from that date to submit.[5] This unintentionally created a time bomb in the South China Sea—one that few were aware of until it blew up in May 2009.

Russia made the first submission to the CLCS in 2001. Over the next six years, only eight more states claimed an extended continental shelf. But in the year leading up to the May 2009 deadline, the commission was flooded with forty-one submissions. More than half of those came rushing in during the last two weeks.[6] Among these procrastinators were Malaysia and Vietnam. Recognizing that their extended continental shelves would necessarily overlap in the southern portion of the South China Sea, the two countries decided to submit a joint claim. In effect, they asked the commission to confirm that geography gave them both a valid claim to what they called the "Defined Area," stretching from the outer limits of Malaysia's EEZ to those of Vietnam's (Figure 8.1). Once the commission confirmed that they both had a valid claim to the area, they would negotiate a boundary themselves.[7] Vietnam also submitted a separate claim in the northern part of the South China Sea, which covered part of the Paracel Islands.[8]

China had already been apprised of these plans and responded in less than a day. On May 7, Beijing transmitted two nearly identical notes to the UN secretary-general objecting to the Malaysian and Vietnamese submissions. They read, "China has indisputable sovereignty over the islands in the South China Sea and the adjacent waters, and enjoys sovereign rights and jurisdiction over the relevant waters as well as the seabed and subsoil thereof (see attached map)." Affixed to both notes was a copy of the nine-dash line.[9] It was the first time Beijing had ever used the line to represent its claim in an official international

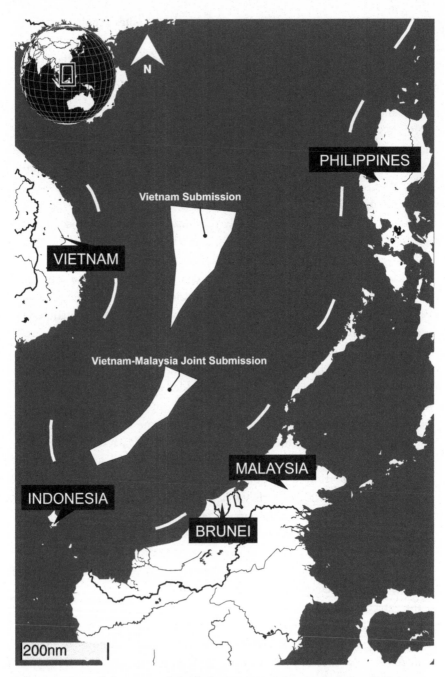

Figure 8.1 Extended continental shelf submissions and the nine-dash line, 2009.
Created using Mapcreator and OpenStreetMap.

setting. And the note made clear that China wasn't just claiming the islands and maritime entitlements they generated; it was demanding rights to all "relevant waters" within the dashes regardless of what UNCLOS had to say about it. This was where the historic rights discussions of the 1990s had finally led.

The notes kicked off a diplomatic back-and-forth lasting two years. Vietnam responded the very next day with a letter to the secretary-general reaffirming its claim to the Spratlys and Paracels and charging that the nine-dash line "has no legal, historical or factual basis, therefore is null and void."[10] Malaysia needed another twelve days to form a more tactful response. It made no reference to the nine-dash line but insisted that the joint submission was in accordance with UNCLOS, without prejudice to future delimitations, and noted that China had been informed of Malaysia's position prior to the submission.[11] The Philippines weighed in twice. First, in August, it submitted twin notes objecting to the Malaysian and Vietnamese submissions because they overlapped with potential maritime entitlements from the islands it claimed. The letter responding to the joint submission in the south also referenced the Philippines' long-standing but deeply problematic claim to North Borneo, which constitutes the Malaysian state of Sabah. Malaysia and Vietnam replied that their submissions had been made without prejudice to future delimitations. Malaysia also quoted a 2001 International Court of Justice opinion that labeled Philippine claims to North Borneo "mere relics of another international legal era, one that ended with the setting of the sun on the age of colonial imperium."[12]

Nearly a year later, a more thorough objection came from an unexpected source: Indonesia. Jakarta had been rudely reminded that the nine-dash line overlapped with its own EEZ from the Natuna Islands. Its letter began by reiterating that Indonesia was not a claimant to any disputed territory in the South China Sea. Then it turned to a thoughtful attack on the nine-dash line, of which it said, "[T]here is no clear explanation as to the legal basis, the method of drawing, and the status of those separated dotted-lines." Indonesia speculated that perhaps China hoped to claim all the waters within the line as entitlements from the disputed islands. But then it quoted Beijing's own delegations to recent ISA and UNCLOS meetings, which had argued that "uninhabited, remote or very small islands" could not generate EEZs and continental shelves under the convention. It also previewed the concern that would lead outside parties, including the United States, to get more involved—that such an excessive claim "concerns the fundamental principles of the Convention and encroaches the legitimate interest of the global community." The letter concluded that "the so called 'nine-dotted-lines map' ... clearly lacks international legal basis and is tantamount to upset the UNCLOS 1982."[13]

The next year, the Philippines sent another letter, this time with its own objections to the nine-dash line. It reiterated Manila's claim to the Kalayaan

Islands Group and asserted that the only "adjacent" waters to those disputed features were those permitted by Article 121 of UNCLOS, which defined the maritime entitlements of islands. The note repeated Vietnam's assertion that China's claim to "relevant waters" throughout the nine-dash line "would have no basis under international law."[14] Barely a week later Beijing sent its response, reiterating all the claims made in its first letter and accusing Manila of having "invaded" the Spratlys in the 1970s. Then, without referring directly to Indonesia's note, it asserted that the Spratlys were fully entitled to an EEZ and continental shelf.[15] The hail of diplomatic missiles ended on May 3 when Vietnam sent a final letter reiterating its claims to the Spratlys and Paracels.[16]

Taiwan was absent from these debates because it had no seat at the UN table, and Brunei's silence reflected its extreme wariness to reveal the extent of its claims. In June 2008, the parties to UNCLOS had been compelled to give another reprieve to those who were clearly not going to make the May 2009 deadline for CLCS submissions. They decided that those countries unable to complete the necessary surveys in time could make a partial submission outlining their intent and timeline for doing so.[17] Forty-five states took this option over the next year, including Brunei.[18] A week after Malaysia and Vietnam claimed their extended continental shelves, Brunei sent a partial submission to the CLCS declaring its intention to do the same. It said the government expected to make a full submission within twelve months.[19] But that was before it saw the diplomatic storm that Vietnam and Malaysia had set off. At the time of writing, Brunei has missed its expected delivery date by 134 months.

New President, New Problems

Barack Obama had entered office in 2009 determined to repair America's global image after what he saw as severe missteps since 9/11. Much of that early focus was on improving relations with the Middle East, but the administration also looked to bolster ties in Asia. Relationships in Southeast Asia had come to be seen almost entirely through the lens of counterterror cooperation. And many were strained by perceived anti-Muslim bias in U.S. policy. Obama, who had spent several years in Indonesia as a child, looked to reverse those trends. Secretary of State Hillary Clinton shared that mission. In February 2009, she took her first trip as secretary to Tokyo, Jakarta, Seoul, and Beijing. Later that month, the administration launched a review of U.S. policy toward Myanmar (Burma), whose diplomatic isolation had become a drag on American engagement with the rest of ASEAN. In July, the United States acceded to the Treaty of Amity and Cooperation, ASEAN's founding document.[20] And in November, President Obama met with his counterparts for the first-ever U.S.-ASEAN

Leaders Meeting on the sidelines of the Asia-Pacific Economic Cooperation (APEC) Summit in Singapore.[21]

If the George W. Bush administration had paid too little attention to Southeast Asia beyond counterterrorism, it had done a much better job prioritizing Northeast Asia. The Obama team looked to build on that progress, especially with China. Presidents Obama and Hu Jintao met for the first time in April 2009. They announced the establishment of a Strategic and Economic Dialogue, which merged and elevated two forums established by Hu and Bush. And at the highest levels, both capitals pushed the message that a new era of cooperation was dawning. But beneath those headlines, trouble was brewing. And the South China Sea was already emerging as a major source of tension for the new administration.

In March 2009, the USNS *Impeccable*, an unarmed navy surveillance ship, was surveying waters 75 miles south of Hainan when it was surrounded by five Chinese vessels. The *Impeccable* and its sister ship, the *Victorious*, operating in the Yellow Sea, had been tailed by Chinese ships and planes for days. But this was different. Three of the ships belonged to Chinese military and law enforcement agencies—the PLAN, Fisheries Law Enforcement Command, and China Marine Surveillance. The other two appeared to be civilian fishing boats. They were part of a state-sanctioned militia force operating out of Sanya City in Hainan. But the *Impeccable* didn't know that.[22]

The government vessels hung back while the trawlers approached the *Impeccable*. It was towing a sonar array, and one of the fishing boats crossed its wake to try to damage the equipment. When that failed, the Chinese crew tried using boat hooks to grab the array. The *Impeccable* turned a high-pressure water hose on the fishermen, temporarily driving them off. Then it radioed the Chinese ships and asked them to clear a path so it could leave before the situation escalated further. Instead, the Chinese trawlers cut their engines in front of the *Impeccable* and began dropping pieces of wood in its way. Then the China Marine Surveillance ship moved into its path as well, while the PLAN loitered on its port side. The *Impeccable* was forced to order an emergency all-stop to avoid a collision before finally being allowed to leave.[23]

It wasn't the first time U.S. surveillance operations had led to tensions with Beijing. China was among a minority of states, but a sizable one, that argued UNCLOS allowed restrictions on foreign military activities in the EEZ. It had fought unsuccessfully to bake those restrictions into an agreement with ASEAN. In April 2001, just months into Bush's presidency, a Chinese fighter jet had collided with a U.S. EP-3 surveillance aircraft about 70 miles from Hainan. The Chinese pilot was killed and the Americans made an emergency landing in China, sparking a diplomatic crisis. There were obvious parallels with the *Impeccable* harassment. Both involved unsafe behavior meant to intimidate

American operators. And both fueled speculation that Beijing was testing the new president. But the EP-3 collision had ultimately been caused by pilot error; the danger presented to the *Impeccable* was brazen and intentional.

The Pentagon responded the next day, criticizing the "unprofessional maneuvers by Chinese vessels and violations under international law."[24] Criticisms flew back and forth until March, when Foreign Minister Yang Jiechi met with Obama, Clinton, and other senior officials in Washington. Both sides wanted to keep the episode from poisoning the bilateral relationship and agreed to "work to ensure that such incidents do not happen again." But the United States also wanted to be clear that it wasn't going to back down. While Yang was in Washington, the guided missile destroyer USS *Chung-Hoon* was sent to the South China Sea to "keep an eye" on the *Impeccable*. Together, the two ships returned to the site of the incident and completed the survey.[25]

James Steinberg, the deputy secretary of state, and Jeffrey Bader, senior director for Asian affairs on the National Security Council, visited Beijing in March 2010. During one meeting, they were walked through a list of issues, including the South China Sea, on which China hoped for deference from the administration. The *New York Times* reported that Steinberg and Bader were told the South China Sea was one of Beijing's "core interests"—a label previously reserved for Taiwan and the restive provinces of Tibet and Xinjiang.[26] Two months later, Clinton reported that she was told the same thing by State Councilor Dai Bingguo, China's senior-most foreign policy official.[27] Chinese leaders didn't publicly label the South China Sea a "core interest" at this time, and there is debate about the exact words used in these meetings.[28] But either way, it was clear the maritime disputes had rocketed up China's list of priorities.

Beijing wasn't just harassing foreign survey ships and launching diplomatic salvos at the United Nations. It was upping the ante across the board. Southeast Asian governments complained that China was increasingly harassing and arresting their fishing vessels.[29] And pressure on oil and gas operations was reaching a breaking point, especially for Vietnam. BP had started pumping natural gas from Block 06-1 at the southern edge of the nine-dash line back in 2002. Chinese officials had complained, but the company moved forward anyway. In 2007, BP announced plans to drill in an adjacent block. This time Fu Ying, China's incoming ambassador to the United Kingdom, delivered a blunt warning. If BP continued, Beijing would reconsider all its contracts in China and couldn't guarantee the safety of its workers on the drilling project. The company caved. And so did its partner in the project, ConocoPhillips. They returned their stakes to PetroVietnam at a loss. Chevron came under similar pressure and suspended exploration in Block 122, which wasn't even in the nine-dash line. The same went for a Japanese consortium led by Idemitsu, which had planned to explore a block next to BP's.

By 2010, there were only two major players left in Vietnam's offshore energy industry. The first was ExxonMobil, which was apparently big enough to
ignore China's threats. It had signed a deal to explore three blocks off the central Vietnamese coast in early 2009. But it was receiving plenty of threats from
Beijing. And then there were the Russians, to whom China seemed to give a pass
(for the time being). Vietsovpetro still had the wells it drilled in the 1980s. And
BP was preparing to offload Block 06-1 to its Russian joint venture, TNK-BP.[30]
On the other side of the South China Sea, the Philippines was taking another
look at Reed Bank. Forum Energy, which was majority-owned by Philippine-
based PXP Energy, had acquired rights to explore the area in 2005 and conducted
some seismic surveys. But the government wouldn't approve further work while
the JMSU was underway. In early 2010, Forum received a new service contract
and started planning where to drill test wells, despite opposition from Beijing.

Hanoi was scheduled to host the annual ASEAN Regional Forum in July
2010. It was a big moment for Vietnam, which had chaired ASEAN only once
before, in 1998. And Vietnamese leaders wanted to make the most of it. As far
as they were concerned, the South China Sea was the most important issue on
the regional agenda. Ahead of the summit, Southeast Asian leaders approached
the United States to voice their concerns over China's tougher approach to the
disputes. In the wake of the *Impeccable* incident and the tough talk they were
hearing from Chinese counterparts, U.S. officials were sympathetic. They agreed
that Secretary Clinton would address the issue at the forum, but only if the
ASEAN members did so first. Washington wanted it to be clear that the United
States was responding to regional concerns, not stirring up trouble.

On July 13, senior officials from twenty-six countries plus the European
Union gathered in Hanoi. As the chair, Vietnamese foreign minister Pham Gia
Khiem rose first and expressed his country's concerns about the South China
Sea. One by one, his counterparts from the other nine ASEAN member-states
did the same. Then Clinton spoke. In remarks she would later repeat to the press,
the secretary said the United States had a "national interest in freedom of navigation, open access to Asia's maritime commons, and respect for international
law in the South China Sea." It opposed the "use or threat of force" and offered to
facilitate cooperation under the framework of the DOC. And while Washington
remained neutral on sovereignty disputes, it insisted that maritime claims be
consistent with international law. In a none too subtle jab at the nine-dash line,
Clinton said that "legitimate claims to maritime space in the South China Sea
should be derived solely from legitimate claims to land features."[31]

Yang Jiechi was blindsided. Normally known as a cool-headed and affable
diplomat, he now lost his cool, stood up, and stormed out of the room. An
hour later he marched back in and harangued the assembled ministers for thirty
minutes. He accused the United States of plotting against China. He mocked his

Vietnamese hosts. And, while staring down Singapore's George Yeo, he bluntly declared, "China is a big country and other countries are small countries, and that's just a fact."[32] The line continues to haunt Chinese diplomats across the region.

China's Pressure and America's Pivot

If the Southeast Asian claimants hoped that international attention would restrain China, they quickly learned otherwise. Tension continued to build over fisheries, and a series of incidents introduced a new level of risk to oil and gas operations. The Philippines was the first target. Benigno "Noynoy" Aquino III—son of Ninoy and Cory Aquino—was inaugurated president at the end of June 2010. He entered office hoping to balance relations between the United States and China, but almost immediately walked into a crisis. In August, a disgraced former police officer hijacked a tourist bus in downtown Manila. Most of the passengers were from Hong Kong. The police badly bungled the operation, which left eight hostages dead. China's government and public were outraged. Over the next few months, Aquino bent over backward to try to improve relations. He ordered Philippine officials to boycott the Nobel Peace Prize ceremony for Chinese dissident Liu Xiaobo, dispatched Vice President Jejomar Binay to Beijing to plead for the lives of Filipino drug offenders on death row, and deported fifteen Taiwanese criminals to China for punishment. But none of it helped much.

In February 2010, Manila gave Forum Energy permission to identify promising drill sites around Reed Bank. On March 2, the survey ship M/V *Veritas Voyager* was doing just that when it was aggressively approached by two Chinese law enforcement vessels. The Armed Forces of the Philippines responded by deploying an Islander observation plane and an OV-10 light attack aircraft to the area, but the Chinese boats were already gone. The Philippine Coast Guard dispatched two of its ships to escort the *Veritas Voyager* for the rest of its survey. Then the Philippine government lodged a formal complaint with Beijing. The Ministry of Foreign Affairs was unapologetic: "China owns indisputable sovereignty over the Nansha Islands and their adjacent waters. Oil and gas exploration activities by any country or company in the waters under China's jurisdiction without permission of the Chinese government constitutes violation of China's sovereignty, rights and interests, and thus are illegal and invalid." Aquino responded by postponing his first visit to Beijing, which had been planned for May.[33]

The Philippine response was resolute, but it showed how far the country's capabilities had degraded. If China's ships had returned to harass the *Veritas*

Voyager again, the Philippine Coast Guard boats would have been badly outmatched. And dispatching the Islander and OV-10 only served to highlight that the Philippine Air Force had no real maritime patrol aircraft or fighter jets; its last American-built F-5s had been retired in 2005. The armed forces modernization program launched by the Ramos government in 1995 had been an abject failure. After the Reed Bank incident, Aquino pledged to allocate hundreds of millions of additional dollars to the armed forces under a new modernization plan. That would lead to progress, though not as much as hoped.

The United States also sped up efforts to lend a hand. The Pentagon had already outlined plans to boost maritime capacity-building support to the Philippines. For instance, it helped Manila set up an interagency National Coast Watch System to improve maritime domain awareness. But its most visible effort was the transfer of the BRP *Gregorio del Pilar*, formerly the USCGC *Hamilton*.[34] This 1960s-era U.S. Coast Guard cutter was transferred to the Philippines in May 2011 and steamed into Manila Bay in August as the Philippine Navy's new flagship. Two more cutters of the same class would follow in 2012 and 2016. They couldn't do much against China's modern naval ships, but they at least had the endurance to patrol the Spratlys.

Next it was Vietnam's turn. At the end of May 2011, PetroVietnam dispatched the *Binh Minh 02* to survey four oil and gas blocks off the country's central coast. The ship was operating 120 miles offshore when three Chinese law enforcement vessels appeared. The ships exchanged bridge-to-bridge warnings, and then one of the Chinese ships intentionally ran across the exploration cables the *Binh Minh 02* was towing, severing them. The standoff continued for a few hours before the Chinese left. The *Binh Minh 02* managed to repair its cables and finish its work.[35]

The Norwegian-flagged *Viking 2* ran into trouble a day later. It was surveying Block 05.1 under contract with PetroVietnam and Japan's Idemitsu. Tokyo had convinced the company to suspend work in the area a few years earlier. But the relationship with Beijing had recently soured, especially after a run-in between the Japan Coast Guard and a Chinese fishing boat captain near the Senkakus the previous autumn. The *Viking 2* was operating 150 miles from the Vietnamese coast when an unidentified Chinese ship ran into the instruments it was towing. The survey vessel radioed for help from two security ships, which played cat and mouse with the aggressor for a couple hours. Two days later, the *Viking* was again harassed by two Chinese fishing boats. They tried to damage its cables but were stopped by the escort ships.[36] The fishing boats were later reported to be members of the maritime militia, just like those that harassed the *Impeccable*.[37]

China's bullying helped facilitate the Obama administration's engagement strategy in Southeast Asia. Washington was finding a receptive audience in the region and South China Sea concerns were laced throughout its efforts. In 2010, the United States appointed a resident ambassador to ASEAN—the first of the organization's dialogue partners to do so—and established a new comprehensive partnership with Indonesia. A year later, the new U.S. Mission to ASEAN got its first liaison officer from Pacific Command.[38] In June 2011, Secretary of Defense Robert Gates outlined plans for greater U.S. engagement in the region, including with more port calls, naval exercises, and cooperation with partners. He also announced that the United States would deploy up to four of its new class of Littoral Combat Ships to Singapore. And then he enumerated four principles that Washington saw as paramount for regional stability: free and open commerce, adherence to the rule of law, open access to the global commons, and peaceful dispute resolution. The connection to the South China Sea was unmistakable, especially to his audience of Asian security experts and officials.[39]

Clinton kept up a relentless diplomatic pace, becoming the most well-traveled secretary of state in American history. She was backed up by an equally peripatetic assistant secretary for Asia, Kurt Campbell. The two made sure that the Obama administration's focus on Asia was unmistakable. And in October 2011, Clinton gave it a name. Writing in Foreign Policy, she said the United States was at a "pivot point" after ten years of distraction in Afghanistan and Iraq. It was time to "pivot to new global realities"—that the Asia Pacific was the most important region for U.S. national interests. And the South China Sea was a major part of this turn toward the region. Clinton wrote that the United States must "protect unfettered access to and passage through the South China Sea" and "uphold the key international rules" governing maritime claims. But she underestimated the scale of the challenge. The secretary boasted that the administration had already "been instrumental in efforts to address disputes in the South China Sea" and, since her 2010 ARF appearance, had "made strides in protecting our vital interests in stability and freedom of navigation and [had] paved the way for sustained multilateral diplomacy."[40]

A month later, President Obama flew to Honolulu to host the APEC Leaders Meeting. He warned that a rising China must "play by the rules" and declared major progress on a free trade deal called the Trans-Pacific Partnership, involving Australia, Brunei, Chile, Malaysia, New Zealand, Peru, Singapore, Vietnam, and the United States.[41] Then the president headed to Canberra, where he made a historic speech to the Australian Parliament and announced that hundreds of U.S. marines would be rotationally deployed to Darwin, in northern Australia.[42] While Obama was speaking to one ally in Canberra, Clinton was addressing another. Standing on board the guided missile cruiser USS Fitzgerald in Manila Bay, she committed to ensure the U.S.-Philippines alliance could "[deter] provocations from the full spectrum of state and nonstate actors."[43] Then the secretary and president met up in Bali, where Obama became the first American president to attend the East Asia Summit. That meeting involved the leaders of all ten ASEAN members and their eight most important dialogue partners.[44]

In hindsight, the trip was probably the high-water mark for the "pivot to Asia." The administration had made impressive strides in Southeast Asia. Every American initiative seemed to be welcomed with open arms. But that had as much to do with the region's growing fear of Beijing as it did with anything Washington was doing. And as those fears grew, particularly in the South China Sea, the administration would be criticized for not following through on its promises.

Confusion at Scarborough

A Philippine Navy patrol plane was flying over Scarborough Shoal on April 8, 2012, when it spotted eight Chinese fishing boats at the reef. Manila dispatched the newly acquired *Gregorio del Pilar* to have a look. In hindsight, Philippine officials probably wish they had sent the coast guard. Having the country's naval flagship on station only helped escalate the crisis that followed. The *Gregorio del Pilar* arrived two days later and sent a boarding team into the lagoon to inspect the fishing boats. They found that the ships were not only fishing without permission but had been poaching endangered clams, sharks, and other species. Before they could be arrested, the Chinese fishers sent out a distress call. Two Chinese law enforcement vessels soon arrived and took up position between the *Gregorio del Pilar* and the only channel into the lagoon, where the fishing boats remained.[45]

Over the next few days, the two sides traded accusations while insisting they were open to a diplomatic solution. The Philippine government replaced the *Gregorio del Pilar* with a coast guard vessel, while China beefed up its presence with a third law enforcement ship. On April 13, Philippine secretary of foreign affairs Albert del Rosario met with China's ambassador to Manila, Ma Keqing. Del Rosario described the meeting as "very friendly" and said, "We both want to have this resolved ASAP and we have agreed that both sides will not do anything to escalate the situation there any further."[46] The next day, two of the Chinese law enforcement vessels escorted the fishing boats out of the shoal and departed. The two sides were down to one ship apiece. But talks broke down within twenty-four hours and a second Chinese vessel was sent back to Scarborough.[47]

Up to that point, Manila had tried to avoid internationalizing the standoff. Del Rosario told the press after his initial meeting with Ambassador Ma that the question of American involvement didn't even come up.[48] But with talks at a standstill, the Philippine government changed tack. Del Rosario called on support from ASEAN and told the press that China's actions threatened the freedom of navigation of all nations that used the South China Sea.[49] Then he proposed submitting the dispute to international arbitration, which Beijing angrily rejected.[50] Over the next week, China made some efforts to de-escalate, including pulling its ships back from the shoal for brief periods. But talks went nowhere. The Philippines sent a second ship from its fisheries bureau to Scarborough. And on April 26, del Rosario said that the Philippines would seek to "maximize the benefits" of the U.S.-Philippines MDT to resolve the standoff.[51]

Del Rosario and Defense Secretary Voltaire Gazmin flew to Washington on April 30 to meet with their American counterparts, Clinton and Leon Panetta. It was the first official "2+2 meeting" in the history of the alliance. The worsening standoff at Scarborough dominated the news coverage, and undoubtedly the discussions. It was an open secret that Manila was pushing for a public guarantee that any aggression by China would trigger MDT obligations. Doing so would have been in keeping with the treaty clarifications offered by Cyrus Vance in 1979 and William Cohen in 1998. But the Obama administration wasn't prepared to take that step. U.S. officials were frustrated by what they saw as Philippine mismanagement of the standoff.[52] Clinton and Panetta reaffirmed the U.S. "commitment and obligations under the mutual defense treaty" but didn't say what those were. In wrapping up their joint press conference after the meeting, Gazmin asked for U.S. support to "bring the case to international legal bodies."[53]

Washington pledged further capacity-building support to help the Philippines reach what del Rosario dubbed a "minimum credible defense posture."[54] The goal was to make sure the Philippines, like its counterparts in Vietnam, could at least monitor Chinese activities and, if necessary, give the PLAN a bloody nose. That would hopefully be enough to deter a fight in the first place. But it was a long-term, and arguably long-shot, solution. Manila needed an immediate fix to the deteriorating situation at Scarborough. China's presence around the shoal was steadily growing. Beijing would eventually deploy eight law enforcement vessels and dozens of fishing boats to the scene.[55] The latter proved to be more than commercial fishers; they belonged to China's maritime militia and were serving under orders from the state.[56] The Philippines had two law enforcement vessels outside the reef and a couple of fishing boats loitering inside the lagoon. They were badly outmatched.

The stalemate continued through May as the two sides alternated between diplomatic overtures and nationalistic posturing. Del Rosario believed that Beijing was not negotiating in good faith and favored a hard line. He insisted that only international pressure could bring China around to compromise. But President Aquino was unsure. While publicly backing his foreign secretary's efforts, Aquino also reached out to Senator Antonio Trillanes as a backchannel to Beijing. Trillanes made frequent trips to China over the next two months, meeting more than a dozen times in private with Fu Ying, now vice foreign minister, and another official. These two diplomatic channels often worked at cross purposes, and later del Rosario and Trillanes would each accuse the other of sabotaging his efforts.

On June 6, Aquino and del Rosario flew to Washington. They briefed President Obama on the situation at Scarborough and received more promises of security assistance. If they hoped a face-to-face meeting between the presidents would lead to more clarity on the MDT, they were disappointed. Instead, they got another boilerplate statement of American commitment to the alliance. Around the same time, Kurt Campbell met with Fu Ying in a hotel in southern Virginia in the hopes of finding a diplomatic solution. Campbell proposed that both sides simultaneously withdraw all their ships from the shoal. If Beijing agreed to this return to the status quo ante, he would convince Manila. What happened next is still a matter of dispute.[57]

Most American accounts of the meeting hold that Fu agreed to the plan. Campbell thought so, and the U.S. government proceeded accordingly. But Chinese accounts disagree. They argue that Fu agreed only to relay the proposal to Beijing. In her memoir, Fu claims to have told Campbell she couldn't make promises but thought "there would be no need" for the Chinese vessels to stay if the Filipinos withdrew.[58] Some of the other Americans left the room unsure whether a deal had been struck. Either way, the Philippines took the chance.

Manila ordered its fishing boats out of the lagoon and then, on June 15, told its two law enforcement ships to head home. At first, Filipino officials blamed the withdrawal on an approaching typhoon. But two days later, the Department of Foreign Affairs announced that China was expected to pull out too as part of an "arrangement."[59] Apparently Manila believed the storm would offer both sides a convenient excuse to withdraw while saving face. Jake Sullivan, one of Clinton's top advisors, forwarded the secretary an email that same day quoting Campbell on the issue. The assistant secretary said China had made "commitments to 'de-escalate' over Scarborough" and acknowledged that the State Department had "put a lot of pressure on the [Philippines] to step back."[60]

The next day, the Chinese Foreign Ministry denied any agreement but indicated that its fishing boats might leave anyway due to the bad weather. Over the next week, Philippine officials, including President Aquino, decried China's bad faith and threatened to send their ships back to the shoal. Some reports indicated that the Chinese briefly left during the storm, at least for a day or two. Fu claims "only 1–2 law enforcement ships" stayed behind. But when a Philippine Air Force plane flew over Scarborough on June 26, it spotted five Chinese government vessels and more than twenty fishing boats. Trillanes later claimed to be blindsided when Aquino called and asked him why China had broken the agreement, which he knew nothing about. The senator said he was negotiating a separate deal with the Chinese for a staged withdrawal from the shoal, which

Beijing called off after Manila's public criticism. The Philippines decided not to send its ships back even though they had been resupplied and put on standby. China has been in uncontested control of Scarborough ever since.[61]

A lot of unanswered questions remain about the messy diplomacy of June 2012. Opinion pieces in Philippine papers still argue about who "lost" Scarborough. Was it del Rosario? Trillanes? Or were the Americans to blame? Did the Chinese government break faith, or was there no agreement to break? It seems entirely plausible that del Rosario and Trillanes were both accurately reporting what they thought they were hearing from Chinese interlocutors. The same goes for Campbell and the other U.S. officials in that Virginia hotel. But there was no overlap in the negotiating teams; no one with firsthand knowledge could identify discrepancies. That was especially important when Chinese negotiators were vague or noncommittal. The only person involved in all the discussions who might have the answers is Fu Ying, whose memoir is incomplete and far from evenhanded on the subject.

Trillanes claims that he made one last attempt to influence events. He attended a cabinet meeting on July 5 at which Philippine officials were debating their next moves. The senator told Aquino that China had indicated through his backchannel that it might still withdraw from Scarborough, but only if Manila agreed not to "internationalize the dispute" at the upcoming ASEAN Ministerial Meeting and ARF.[62] Whether true or not, it was too late. The previous two months had erased whatever hesitation Aquino had about del Rosario's hardnosed approach to China. From that point on, he was committed to rallying international pressure against Beijing.

ASEAN Consensus Collapses

The South China Sea is the most difficult problem facing ASEAN. It is the only regional security issue that directly involves China and the interests of major outside players. And so it invites exactly the type of interference that ASEAN was established to mitigate. This creates a strong incentive, especially among the original five members, to assert "ASEAN centrality" in managing the disputes. They fear that doing otherwise would encourage China to ride roughshod over individual claimants. And some worry that too much involvement by the United States and other outsiders would turn the region into an arena of great power conflict. But the nonclaimants within ASEAN also face strong incentives to do nothing. The South China Sea disputes don't directly involve them. Cambodia, Laos, and Myanmar are particularly reliant on China as their major economic benefactor and have no desire to upset Beijing. These competing interests had for years made ASEAN's approach to the South China Sea a frequent source of disagreement among members. But no one was ready for how Cambodia would handle the issue as ASEAN chair in 2012.

Control of Scarborough Shoal had become the most visible flashpoint in the South China Sea, but it wasn't the only one. The standoff brought greater attention to the annual fishing ban that Beijing had declared over the northern half of the South China Sea every year since 1999. The ban started in mid-May and ended in early August, covering waters north of 12 degrees latitude. That included the Paracels and, in theory, Scarborough. Each year, Hanoi objected and run-ins between Vietnamese fishers and Chinese law enforcement spiked around the Paracels. Now Filipinos were in the crosshairs for the first time. Early in the standoff, Manila had tried to defuse tensions by announcing its own fishing ban over waters including Scarborough.[63] But by July it was the Chinese coast guard driving Philippine fishing boats away from the reef.

Oil and gas disputes were also heating up again. At the end of February, Manila had put out a call for bids on fifteen oil and gas blocks around the country. Two of them were off the coast of Palawan and fell just inside the nine-dash line. They were only 60 miles from the Philippine coast and nearly 150 miles from the nearest disputed islands, Flat and Nanshan. But that didn't stop China from lodging a protest over the "unlawful" violation of its "indisputable sovereignty." Taiwan also got in on the act, reiterating its claim to Reed Bank—which the blocks didn't include—and its "surrounding waters."[64]

Then, barely a week after the Philippines withdrew its vessels from Scarborough, Reed Bank itself was back in the news. Manuel Pangilinan, who had a controlling stake in Forum Energy and therefore the Reed Bank project, announced in late June that he had traveled to China for discussions with state-owned China National Offshore Oil Corporation (CNOOC). Pangilinan insisted that Beijing was open to a commercial deal in which both sides would set aside sovereignty and develop seabed resources. The plan was flawed from the start: it lacked official approval and would have been illegal in Manila unless the Chinese agreed to a contract under Philippine law. Beijing certainly wasn't going to do that. Pangilinan's own partner in the Reed Bank project criticized his private diplomacy and disavowed any concessions to Beijing.[65] The effort went nowhere and only served to stoke more anger in the Philippines against China.

A few days later, Beijing poured fuel on the fire. CNOOC announced it was opening nine offshore oil and gas blocks for foreign bidding. But they weren't off China's shores. The blocks were all within 200 miles of Vietnam and as much as 600 miles from Hainan. They overlapped with several concessions already awarded by Hanoi, including to Australia's Talisman Energy and India's Oil and Natural Gas Corporation. Chinese officials and CNOOC executives defended the blocks as falling within the "adjacent waters" of the Paracels and Spratlys. But there was no way to draw maritime zones from the islands that would cover all of them. The only possible explanation was the nine-dash line.[66] It was further evidence that Beijing's claim had evolved far beyond "islands and adjacent waters." No foreign company ever bid on the blocks, which were egregious even by South China Sea standards. But the episode ensured that Manila wasn't the only one ready to air grievances against Beijing at the upcoming ASEAN meetings.

The ten Southeast Asian foreign ministers met in Phnom Penh for the annual ASEAN Ministerial Meeting and related events on July 8. These included the ARF, which brought together the foreign ministers of China, the United States, and all of ASEAN's other dialogue partners. Since the first ministerial meeting in 1968, the ASEAN meeting had always been capped by the release of a joint communiqué summarizing the ministers' discussions. In this case, Cambodia's foreign minister Hor Namhong as chair tasked his counterparts from Indonesia, Malaysia, the Philippines, and Vietnam to draft the communiqué. They drew up 132 paragraphs summarizing the ministers' deliberations. Three of those covered the South China Sea. During the meeting, the Philippines had raised China's occupation of Scarborough Shoal and Vietnam had complained of CNOOC's recent issuance of oil and gas blocks off its coast. The discussions were reflected in seemingly uncontroversial language in the draft communiqué: "In this context, we discussed in-depth recent developments in the South China Sea, including the situation in the affected Shoal/disputed area, exclusive economic zones and continental shelves of coastal states, particularly those contrary to the provisions of the 1982 UNCLOS."[67] As diplomatic as it was, this language outraged Hor Namhong. He declared that there was no consensus and demanded that all the sections referencing the South China Sea be struck out. This provoked exchanges with each of the four foreign ministers who helped draft the language, during which Hor Namhong refused to budge. He insisted that it was unnecessary and provocative to mention the words "shoal," "exclusive economic zones," and "continental shelves," and that doing so inappropriately dragged ASEAN into bilateral matters between each claimant and China.[68] The discussions continued over the weekend, with Hor Namhong's counterparts suggesting compromises and the Cambodian foreign minister rejecting them out of hand.

Del Rosario tried, without success, to sway his Cambodian counterpart with references to ASEAN centrality: "We are also ignoring the fact that there are gross violations of the DOC in the EEZs in the Philippines and Vietnam. It is a challenge to ASEAN's leadership, centrality and solidarity."[69] Afterward it became widely rumored that Hor Namhong repeatedly left the room to share the draft language and receive instructions from Chinese officials.[70] In the end, the chair reportedly "picked up his papers and stormed out of the room."[71] On the morning of July 13, ASEAN was forced to admit that for the first time in its history, it couldn't agree on language for a joint communiqué.

The press had a field day as regional diplomats eagerly but anonymously voiced their frustrations with Phnom Penh. They blasted Hor Namhong and accused Cambodia of having sacrificed ASEAN centrality in favor of Chinese interests. One unnamed source told the *New York Times,* "China bought the chair, simple as that." Yang Jiechi didn't help matters by publicly thanking Cambodian prime minister Hun Sen for defending Beijing's "core interests."[72] Hor Namhong hit back by accusing the Philippines and Vietnam of seeking to "hijack" ASEAN for their own narrow interests.[73] And Cambodian diplomats penned a series of op-eds in the regional press defending Phnom Penh's behavior and pointing the finger at Hanoi and Manila.[74]

Indonesia's foreign minister Marty Natalegawa took it upon himself to try to salvage ASEAN consensus after the debacle at the ministerial meeting. In the space of two days he flew to Manila, Hanoi, Bangkok, Phnom Penh, and Singapore to mend fences. He started by getting del Rosario to sign off on a six-point consensus that echoed long-standing ASEAN talking points on the South China Sea. Once all the others had agreed, he left it to Hor Namhong as the ASEAN chair to officially announce the "Six Principles on the South China Sea." They called for full implementation of the 2002 DOC and the 2011 guidelines for its implementation; the early conclusion of a COC; respect for international law, including UNCLOS; self-restraint and nonuse of force; and peaceful resolution of disputes.[75] It was the bare minimum and certainly didn't repair the damage that had been done in Phnom Penh. The whole episode suggested that ASEAN, while important on many fronts, was too hamstrung by its consensus-based decision-making to effectively manage the South China Sea disputes. The Philippines was left particularly disillusioned and looking for other avenues to defend its interests.

A Widening Credibility Gap

The war of words between China, the Philippines, and Vietnam continued for the rest of 2012, but international attention soon shifted north. That was because a new, potentially explosive crisis was brewing around the Senkaku Islands in the East China Sea. Three of those disputed rocks were owned by a private Japanese citizen who had been leasing them to the government for years. In late 2011, the governor of Tokyo had launched an effort to buy them outright. When the plan became public in April, the Chinese and Japanese governments entered talks to avoid a crisis. Beijing believed Japanese leaders would restrain the wayward governor. But by July, Prime Minister Yoshihiko Noda decided that the only way to do that would be to nationalize the islands. The Chinese and Taiwanese governments were both furious. When U.S. officials were briefed, they expressed concern about escalation and urged Japan to explore alternatives. Japan formally nationalized the islands in September, declaring that doing so would ensure "peaceful and stable management" and was preferable to letting nationalistic elements in the Tokyo governor's office take control.[76]

The Noda government underestimated how China would respond. PRC authorities unleashed anti-Japan protests across the country and encouraged a boycott of Japanese goods. Chinese law enforcement vessels were dispatched to patrol around the islands, often entering their 12-mile territorial sea. Japan was forced to deploy half of its coast guard fleet to keep up. The United States urged calm while reaffirming that its obligations under the U.S.-Japan MDT extended to the Senkakus. The situation remained perilous for an entire year until China started decreasing the pace of its patrols.[77] But it would maintain a regular presence around the islands from that point on. The U.S. show of support was credited with helping dissuade outright aggression.

The episode only heightened Filipino frustrations over Scarborough. One ally had received a clear defense commitment and kept control of its claimed territory; the other had gotten ambiguous statements of support and lost control. Of course, there was much more to it than that, including that Japan boasted a world-class coast guard and considerable military capabilities of its own. But there was no denying that the two allies had received different treatment. And for many in the Philippines, that renewed serious doubts about American reliability.

Washington was also facing a problem when it came to declaratory policy. U.S. officials kept standing at podiums and decrying Chinese violations of international law, especially UNCLOS. But Chinese officials threw their words back at them, pointing out that the United States still wasn't a party to the convention. That didn't nullify China's obligations under the treaty, and U.S. government lawyers argued that the United States abided by the convention as a matter of customary law, but the charges of hypocrisy had an effect. Whatever the legal realities, they undercut U.S. credibility and gave China an easy way to deflect criticism. The Obama administration knew this and kept promising ratification. But it was never really a top legislative priority.

Before Obama was even inaugurated, UNCLOS ratification had been on the agenda. It had featured prominently in Clinton's January 2009 confirmation hearing before the Senate Foreign Relations Committee. When Senator Lisa Murkowski of Alaska asked whether UNCLOS would be a priority, Clinton answered, "Yes, it will be, and it will be because it is long overdue, Senator. The Law of the Sea Treaty is supported by the Joint Chiefs of Staff, environmental, energy, and business interests. I have spoken with some of our—our naval leaders, and they consider themselves to be somewhat disadvantaged by our not having become a party to the Law of the Sea."[78] Senator John Kerry, as chair, had affirmed that the committee would take up the treaty, saying, "[T]he key here is just timing."[79] Four months later, the administration had included UNCLOS in a list of priority treaties it wanted the Senate to pass.[80] After her showdown with Yang at the ARF in 2010, Clinton told the press, "[The Law of the Sea Convention] has strong bipartisan support in the United States, and one of our diplomatic priorities over the course of the next year is to secure its ratification in the Senate."[81] Democrats held a majority of between fifty-seven and sixty seats over the course of the 111th Congress, offering the best chance the treaty has ever had for ratification. But the global financial crisis and the bruising fight over the Affordable Care Act ate up most of the legislative calendar. And what political capital the White House had left over for treaty fights it spent on getting the New START arms control pact ratified in late 2010.

The Senate Foreign Relations Committee finally took up the convention in 2012. It had last received a hearing in 2007, when Senator Joe Biden was committee chair. At that time, it passed out of committee with support from the Bush administration but languished in the Democratic-controlled Senate without getting a vote. This time Kerry wanted to make sure that when the convention reached the Senate floor, everyone would understand the stakes. He organized three well-publicized hearings in May and June. Democratic control of the Senate had by then shrunk to just fifty-three seats, but with White House support and Scarborough Shoal giving the issue global attention, ratification still seemed possible.

Senators heard first from administration witnesses on the strategic imperatives for ratification. Then a "24-star panel" of admirals and generals testified to why the military supported the convention. Afterward, industry had its say; witnesses from the Chamber of Commerce, National Association of Manufacturers, American Petroleum Institute, and Verizon argued for ratification. Dozens of other corporations, labor unions, and environmental organizations submitted letters of support. Just two opponents testified: Donald Rumsfeld, the only secretary of defense to oppose ratification, and Steven Groves of the Heritage Foundation. In a blast from the past, their only arguments concerned the International Seabed Authority.[82]

The level of support was impressive. There was no other issue on which military brass, industry, organized labor, and environmental activists agreed. But it was also election season, and politics overrode policy. Heritage Action for America and other conservative lobbyists launched a campaign urging Republican lawmakers to oppose the treaty. Barely two weeks after the last committee hearing, thirty-four senators announced they would block ratification— exactly enough to prevent a two-thirds majority. Rob Portman and Kelly Ayotte, both members of the Armed Services Committee, were the last to do so. Their stated reason: "No international organization owns the seas." Kerry insisted that he would still pass the treaty out of committee, but not until after the November elections.[83]

Obama won reelection. A month later, there was another reminder of how lawless the South China Sea was becoming. The *Binh Minh 02*, which had been harassed by Chinese law enforcement ships in 2011, was conducting a survey about 40 miles off the Vietnamese coast. Two Chinese fishing vessels, later identified as members of the maritime militia, intentionally severed its exploration cables again.[84] The East and South China Seas were only getting more unstable, which should have lent urgency to the push for UNCLOS ratification. It would have been difficult but not impossible—Democrats had increased their majority in the Senate to fifty-five seats. The leadership, however, had moved on. Kerry replaced Clinton as secretary of state in January 2013. The Senate Foreign Relations Committee never turned back to UNCLOS and the White House didn't ask it to.

Taking China to Court

On January 22, 2013, Ambassador Ma Keqing was summoned to the Department of Foreign Affairs in Manila. He was handed an official Notification and Statement of Claim initiating arbitral proceedings under Article 287 and Annex VII of UNCLOS.[85] The Philippine government was following through with the threats made by del Rosario and Gazmin after Scarborough. Solicitor General Francis Jardeleza was to be the Philippines' legal representative in the case. He would soon be appointed to the country's Supreme Court and replaced as solicitor general by Florin Hilbay. American lawyer Paul Reichler had been hired as lead counsel. Reichler had earned a reputation as a giant slayer after representing Nicaragua in a successful International Court of Justice case against the United States during the Reagan years. The legal team also included Bernard Oxman, who had played a key role in U.S. preparations for the UNCLOS III conference; British jurists Philippe Sands and Alan Boyle; and Reichler's partners at FoleyHoag, Lawrence Martin and Andrew Loewenstein. Other important proponents of the case included Henry Bensurto, a lawyer and head of the West Philippine Sea bureau in the Department of Foreign Affairs, and Antonio Carpio, a justice on the Philippine Supreme Court.

UNCLOS includes multiple venues for compulsory and binding dispute settlement, including the International Court of Justice and International Tribunal on the Law of the Sea. But if the parties to a dispute disagree on which to use or haven't identified a preference, the default is an ad hoc arbitral tribunal established according to rules laid out in Annex VII of the convention. That is where this case was headed. The Philippines had thought long and hard about its substance. There was no way to arbitrate sovereignty over the islands without China's participation. And such matters were beyond the scope of UNCLOS. So the Philippines could only seek arbitration on maritime rights. Even then, UNCLOS allows states to exempt certain kinds of disputes from arbitration. China had taken all the available exemptions. It couldn't be forced to delimit overlapping boundaries or to settle disputes related to military activities, among others.[86]

The Philippines crafted its case to avoid these issues. It didn't ask who owned Scarborough Shoal or the Spratly Islands. And it didn't request the tribunal draw EEZ or continental shelf boundaries. Instead, it attacked the very foundations of China's claims. It pointed out that the nine-dash line was not a territorial sea, EEZ, or continental shelf boundary and therefore not a legal claim at all. Then it argued that Scarborough and three of China's Spratly outposts—Johnson, Cuarteron, and Fiery Cross Reefs—were "rocks which cannot sustain human habitation or economic life of their own" under Article 121.3 of UNCLOS. That entitled them to 12-mile territorial seas but not EEZs or continental shelves. And regardless of ownership, the Philippines asked the tribunal to recognize that China had illegally blocked its fishing rights around Scarborough and Johnson. As for China's bases on Gaven, Mischief, Subi, and Hughes Reefs (the last of which Manila incorrectly identified as neighboring McKennan Reef), the Philippines asserted that they were entirely underwater at high tide. Not only did they generate no maritime zones, but China couldn't legally occupy them in the first place. Mischief and Hughes/McKennan belonged to the Philippine continental shelf, while the status of the other two was undetermined. And finally, since the nine-dash line was illegal and none of the islands could generate more than a territorial sea, Manila argued that there were no overlapping claims within the Philippine EEZ. Any Chinese effort to exploit resources within 200 miles of the Philippine coast, including at Reed Bank, was therefore illegal.[87]

China was predictably angry. A month after the notification, the Ministry of Foreign Affairs said the document was "historically and legally incorrect and included unacceptable accusations."[88] It insisted China wouldn't participate and would ignore any ruling. But UNCLOS is very clear that nonparticipation by one party doesn't stop the dispute settlement process. The next step was the appointment of a five-judge panel. The Philippines had nominated Germany's Rudiger Wolfrum. China was given thirty days to make its own nomination. When that didn't happen, the president of the International Tribunal on the Law of the Sea, Shunji Yanai, stepped in as required by UNCLOS. He named Poland's Stanislav Polack. China continued to ignore requests to help fill out the tribunal, so again Yanai was forced to do so. Jean-Pierre Cot of France, Alfred Soons of the Netherlands, and Christopher Pinto from Sri Lanka were appointed, and Pinto was named president. In May, Pinto resigned to avoid any appearance of bias;

his wife happened to be Filipina. So Yanai tapped Ghana's Thomas Mensah to replace him.[89]

In July, the arbitrators met for the first time at the Peace Palace in The Hague. They decided that the Permanent Court of Arbitration, located in the palace, would serve as the registry for the case. Beijing was again invited to join but refused. In August, the tribunal adopted its rules of procedure. The Philippines was asked to submit its memorial, which would lay out the formal arguments in the case, on March 30, 2014.[90]

During the early stages of the arbitral process, tensions continued to build at sea. The Philippines accused Chinese ships of using water cannons to drive away fishing boats at Scarborough in January and February 2013. A few months later, it formally protested the growing presence of Chinese law enforcement vessels near Second Thomas Shoal, where a small contingent of Filipino marines still manned the rusting *Sierra Madre*.[91] Both incidents would make their way into the memorial. The case was growing in scope as Reichler and his legal team realized they had to plug holes in the initial statement of claim and preemptively respond to arguments that China would make were it to participate.

The Philippines' friends and neighbors seemed unsure how to respond to the arbitration. There were no cheers from within ASEAN. It was understood that some in the group were angry that they weren't consulted. There was no official outpouring of support from Europe, Australia, or Japan, where the Liberal Democratic Party under Prime Minister Shinzo Abe had retaken power at the end of 2012. The Obama administration was focused on finding ways to work with Beijing on North Korea and the deteriorating situation in Syria. The issue didn't even come up in the State Department daily press briefing until almost a month after the Philippines filed its Statement of Claim. When asked on February 19 if the department was disappointed by China's refusal to participate, spokeswoman Victoria Nuland was measured in her response: "The United States supports the use of diplomatic and other peaceful means to manage and resolve these kinds of disagreements, including the use of arbitration or other international legal mechanisms."[92] So the United States was supportive, but not effusively so. It has been suggested that the Obama administration privately discouraged the arbitration, seeing it as too escalatory. It is hard to say for sure given publicly available data. But if so, the administration soon changed its mind.

While the Philippines was pursuing legal remedies, China was taking what would prove to be monumental steps toward eventually controlling the South China Sea. In July 2012, it had established a new provincial-level "city," Sansha, on Woody Island in the Paracels.[93] It was tasked with administering everything within the nine-dash line. At the National Congress of the Chinese Communist Party that November, Hu Jintao had introduced a new goal of becoming a "maritime power." And key to that would be "[safeguarding] maritime rights and interests." The congress also saw Xi Jinping succeed Hu as party general secretary. He would prove much more aggressive than his predecessors, especially in pursuing China's territorial and maritime claims. Xi became president of China and chairman of the Central Military Commission in March 2013. In July, he reiterated Hu's "maritime power" objective and linked it to his signature vision, alternately called the "rejuvenation of the Chinese nation" or the "China Dream." Henceforth, the South China Sea would be inseparably bound up with Xi's legacy. That same month, Beijing officially inaugurated the new China Coast Guard (CCG), integrating four previously separate law enforcement agencies.[94] It would soon become the largest coast guard in the world in both number of ships and overall tonnage.

China also continued to push the margin in the East China Sea. Its ships were still patrolling around the Senkakus, though not as aggressively as the year before. In May 2013, the People's Liberation Army submitted a proposal to the government to establish an Air Defense Identification Zone (ADIZ) over the East China Sea. The leadership quickly signed off, and in November the Ministry of Defense announced the new zone, which overlapped those of Japan, South Korea, and Taiwan. Washington was given less than an hour's notice. The ADIZ was particularly egregious not only because of its size but for requiring all aircraft flying through it, not just those planning to enter Chinese airspace, to report flight plans and follow other rules. This was wildly out of step with international norms regarding such identification zones.

U.S. officials immediately derided the announcement. Kerry said it would "increase tensions in the region and create risks of an incident." He also reiterated that "freedom of overflight and other internationally lawful uses of sea and airspace are essential to prosperity, stability, and security in the Pacific."[95] Defense Secretary Chuck Hagel echoed those concerns and added a reaffirmation that Article V of the U.S.-Japan MDT applied to the Senkakus, which were covered by the identification zone.[96] Three days after China's announcement, the United States flew two B-52 bombers through the ADIZ near the Senkakus without informing Beijing. Japan and South Korea also sent military aircraft through. All three continue to do so, making the zone an enduring point of contention.[97]

Elsewhere, the United States looked to build on the gains made during Obama's first term. The "pivot," which State tried to rebrand the "rebalance to Asia," remained especially popular in Southeast Asia. But questions were being raised about whether Washington was up to the challenge posed by Beijing. Scarborough had damaged U.S. credibility. Secretary Kerry spent less time in the region than Clinton had and seemed more focused on the Middle East—the exact thing the "pivot" had promised to change. And most U.S. trade and security initiatives were proving easy to launch but difficult to implement.

The place where the administration was probably making the most progress was Vietnam. The former enemies had made major strides on diplomatic, economic, and even security cooperation. That was thanks in large part to Vietnam's worries about China. In July 2013, President Truong Tan Sang made a rare visit to Washington, where he and Obama announced a new comprehensive partnership. And in December, Kerry traveled to Hanoi and announced a slate of initiatives, including $18 million for capacity-building assistance to the Vietnam Coast Guard.[98] Two months earlier, Kerry had led the U.S. delegations to the annual APEC and East Asia Summits, held in Indonesia and Brunei. Obama had canceled his appearance because the U.S. government was shut down over a budget fight in Congress. These two trips really encapsulated the later Obama years in Asia. The United States was actively boosting ties, especially in the security space, and providing tangible benefits, but it was also distracted and, many feared, unreliable.[99]

Alliance Ups and Downs

Typhoon Haiyan, called "Yolanda" in the Philippines, made landfall in the Visayas on November 7, 2013. It was by some measures the strongest typhoon ever recorded. It left more than six thousand dead and millions homeless before moving out into the South China Sea. The devastation, especially in the city of Tacloban, was beyond belief. It took days for Philippine military personnel to gain access and conduct initial assessments. The United States rushed C-130s to the scene, providing airlift capabilities that the Armed Forces of the Philippines lacked. They began delivering emergency supplies and evacuating survivors— eventually more than twenty-one thousand—from remote areas. The USS *George Washington* carrier strike group and 31st Marine Expeditionary Unit soon arrived from Japan. U.S. Pacific Command established a joint task force for what was dubbed Operation Damayan, meaning "help in a time of need." More than 13,400 U.S. military personnel, 66 aircraft, and 12 ships took part over the next month. After his trip to Vietnam, Kerry flew to the Philippines and visited Tacloban, announcing $86 million in humanitarian aid.[100]

The disaster relief operation was a reminder that the United States could marshal resources and provide public goods that no other partner could match. It was facilitated by the VFA inked fifteen years earlier. And that knowledge added momentum to ongoing negotiations for a new military pact. Originally called the Increased Rotational Presence Framework Agreement, the idea was to increase U.S. access to Philippine military bases and permit the United States to build facilities on them for the use of both countries. It sought to supercharge the VFA, facilitate modernization of the Philippine military, and create a regular, rotational U.S. security presence beyond the Special Forces still doing counterterror operations in the south. Everyone involved knew that the impetus was China's aggressive behavior at sea—preparatory discussions had started soon after Scarborough. American and Filipino officials ironed out the details over eight negotiating rounds between August 2013 and April 2014. The document that emerged, renamed the Enhanced Defense Cooperation Agreement, was still focused on maritime security and capacity building, but its value for future disaster relief operations was a major selling point, which officials actively promoted.[101]

China, meanwhile, continued to increase pressure on the Philippines. Chinese law enforcement vessels had been consistently patrolling near Second Thomas Shoal, home to the *Sierra Madre*, since May 2013. They started sailing menacingly close to the wreck in July. Beijing insisted that it was monitoring Philippine resupply missions to make sure they weren't sneaking in construction materials. It was no secret that Manila hoped to turn the rusting ship into a more sustainable outpost. Hoping to "avoid confrontation," the Philippine Navy began contracting its supply runs to civilian vessels, which made trips to Second Thomas in June and November 2013. It probably helped that U.S. patrol aircraft began flying over the reef so the Chinese knew they were being watched. The situation temporarily de-escalated after Typhoon Haiyan, which forced the Chinese ships to return to port. In January 2014, Beijing offered a deal: it would withdraw from Scarborough Shoal and increase its investments in the Philippines if Manila would drop the arbitration case. But while the Philippine government was considering the offer, Chinese patrols returned to Second Thomas. This probably helped convince President Aquino and his cabinet, who were already skeptical after the Scarborough experience, that Beijing couldn't be trusted. They rejected the offer, which was leaked to the press, and confirmed that the Philippines would submit its memorial to the tribunal in March as scheduled.[102] Solicitor-General Jardeleza even called on other claimants to join the case or file their own.[103]

On March 9, two civilian ships were en route to Second Thomas to resupply and relieve the marines aboard the *Sierra Madre*. The boats were intercepted by CCG cutters, which blocked their path and scared them off using sirens and megaphones. Beijing defended its actions, alleging that the ships were carrying building materials and insisting that Manila remove the *Sierra Madre* altogether.[104] Filipino officials later confirmed plans to repair the ship, but it is unclear if the resupply boats were involved.[105] The Philippine government protested on March 11 and the U.S. Embassy did the same a day later. Chargé d'Affaires Brian Goldbeck said Washington was "troubled" by the incident and insisted, "Pending resolution of competing claims . . . there should be no interference with efforts of claimants to maintain the status quo." He reiterated the

U.S. position that "safe and unimpeded lawful commerce, freedom of navigation, stability, and respect for international law must be maintained."[106]

A couple days later, Manila for the first time admitted that the *Sierra Madre* was a "permanent Philippine government installation" intentionally placed on the reef.[107] Prior to that, Filipino officials had maintained the fiction that the ship accidentally ran aground in 1999 and they hadn't gotten around to removing it yet. Over the next two weeks, the Philippine Navy conducted two airdrops to get basic supplies to the trapped marines. But that couldn't sustain them for long. The USS *Blue Ridge* pulled into Manila Bay for a visit on March 18 and Vice Adm. Robert Thomas told the press, "Without going into hypotheticals, the Seventh Fleet is going to support this alliance, period." It was enough for the Department of Foreign Affairs to declare that the Americans would abide by their MDT commitments. A week later, on the sidelines of the Nuclear Security Summit in The Hague, Obama privately warned Xi not to use force at Second Thomas Shoal.[108]

The Philippine Navy decided to run the blockade on March 28. Two ships—a civilian boat and a government survey vessel, the BRP *Fort San Antonio*—were loaded with food, water, and a fresh rotation of marines. Filipino and Western journalists were invited onto the ships to "publicize and internationalize" the Chinese response. When the civilian boat ran into engine trouble, everyone piled onto the *Fort San Antonio*. The operation had been planned with great secrecy; those involved were forbidden from discussing it over the phone or by email. But as the resupply ship approached Second Thomas, it was clear the mission had been compromised.[109] A Chinese military patrol aircraft circled overhead, as did a Philippine Navy plane and a U.S. P-8A Poseidon. They all flew low enough to be identified by those on board the ship. Two CCG vessels approached, while at least two others loitered farther off. One began blaring its horn and crossing just 70 yards from the bow of the *Fort San Antonio*. It commanded the Filipinos to "stop immediately, stop all illegal activities, and leave." That went on for an hour, until the survey ship made a run for the shallow water over the reef, where the larger CCG vessel couldn't follow. The Chinese didn't give chase, and the supply ship reached the *Sierra Madre*. After unloading its provisions and relieving the marines, the *Fort San Antonio* was allowed to depart Second Thomas in peace.[110] A Philippine military source later speculated to one of the journalists, "Had the U.S. Navy planes not made low passes over your ship and the *Sierra Madre*, the China Coast Guard could have been more aggressive in blocking you."[111] The CCG has maintained a constant patrol around the reef ever since. It has occasionally harassed other resupply missions to the *Sierra Madre*, but never as aggressively as in 2014.

On the same day that the *Fort San Antonio* sailed away from Second Thomas Shoal, the Philippines' legal team submitted its memorial to the arbitral tribunal in The Hague. The arguments on jurisdiction and the merits of the case took up 272 pages. The annexes, including maps, letters, news clippings, and legal precedents, filled a dizzying ten volumes and roughly four thousand pages.[112] The Philippines had reordered its case into fifteen separate submissions, largely matching those in the original statement of claim. But there were a few additions and adjustments. For one, the case now included Second Thomas Shoal. The Philippines asked the tribunal to rule that, like Mischief and Subi Reefs, it was a low-tide elevation not "capable of appropriation by occupation or otherwise." And since they were both within 200 miles of the coast, Manila asked for confirmation that Mischief and Second Thomas were part of the Philippine EEZ and continental shelf. The Philippines also charged that China's blockade had illegally interfered with its navigational rights and endangered the "health and well-being" of the soldiers stationed on board the *Sierra Madre.*

Then there were the legal fixes. Reichler's team realized that the original submission had mixed up Hughes and unoccupied McKennan Reef next door. They fixed that by conflating the two: "McKennan Reef (including Hughes Reef)." And they dropped the request to recognize that low-tide elevation as part of the Philippine EEZ and shelf. Instead, the lawyers admitted that it was within 12 miles of Vietnamese-held Sin Cowe Island and so might be used as a basepoint for measuring that feature's territorial sea. The same went for Gaven Reef, which was within 12 miles of Namyit Island. The memorial also clarified the claims about Chinese harassment of Filipino fishing. It dropped that charge regarding Johnson Reef. And it specified that according to UNCLOS, Filipinos were entitled to "traditional fishing activities" at Scarborough regardless of who owned it. Manila also accused the CCG of operating "in a dangerous manner causing serious risk of collision" around Scarborough. And finally, the Philippines asserted that China's actions at Scarborough and Second Thomas violated its legal obligations to protect the marine environment.[113]

The next month, Obama made a four-country tour of allies and partners in Asia. He started in Japan, where he declared, "Our commitment to Japan's security is absolute and Article V covers all territories under Japan's administration, including the Senkaku Islands." It wasn't a new position, but it was the first time the president himself had said it. He went on to elaborate the U.S. position on both the East and South China Seas: "We don't take a position on this piece of land or this piece of rock but we do take a position on the peaceful resolution of these disputes. . . . [A]ll of us have responsibility to maintain the rule of law— large and small countries have to abide by what is considered just and fair and resolve disputes in a peaceful fashion."[114] The latter point was a clear nod to the Philippines and its arbitration effort. After stops in Seoul and Kuala Lumpur, Obama landed in Manila, where expectations were running high. The day before, U.S. ambassador Philip Goldberg and Defense Secretary Gazmin had publicly

signed the Enhanced Defense Cooperation Agreement.[115] In a packed audito-
rium, Obama said the new agreement was evidence that his administration really was "rebalancing" to Asia. He hailed the coordinated response to Typhoon
Haiyan as proof that the alliance was strong. And turning to the South China Sea
and the recent blockade of Second Thomas Shoal, he declared, "International
law must be upheld. Freedom of navigation must be preserved. Disputes must
be resolved peacefully and not by intimidation or by force."[116]

But the only line most would remember was this: "Our commitment to defend the Philippines is ironclad and the United States will keep that commitment because allies never stand alone."[117] Nothing about the South China Sea,
the Spratly Islands, or Scarborough Shoal. No clarification of Article V. In any
other context, it would have been a welcome statement of U.S. support, but after
the events of the previous two years, it had the opposite effect. There were several reasons the administration wanted to remain ambiguous. The Armed Forces
of the Philippines weren't as capable as their counterparts in Japan and didn't
coordinate as closely with the Americans. That led many in the Pentagon to fear
an Article V clarification might embolden Manila to pick a fight it couldn't win.
There were also historical and legal differences between the two treaties.[118] In
any case, the bottom line was the U.S. commitment to the Philippines wasn't as
"ironclad" as the one to Japan.

Cyrus Vance, William Cohen, and Thomas Hubbard had all intimated that
the U.S.-Philippine MDT obligated the United States to respond to an attack
on Filipino troops in disputed waters, if not on disputed islands. But the United
States had been cagier about that commitment since the Scarborough Shoal
standoff. Manila worried that Washington was moving the goal posts. That
seemed especially galling at Scarborough, which had once been considered
U.S. territory. For the next four and a half years after Obama's visit, American
officials would repeat the "ironclad" line but never directly answer questions
about the MDT. And that would seriously undermine confidence in the alliance. No matter how much effort Washington put into capacity building, joint
training, increased presence, and support for the arbitration, doubts about its
credibility lingered. And they would do considerable harm to both U.S. and
Philippine interests in the South China Sea.

Arbitration and Artificial Islands

2014–2016

> We discussed the need for tangible steps in the South China Sea to lower tensions, including a halt to further reclamation, new construction and militarization of disputed areas. Freedom of navigation must be upheld and lawful commerce should not be impeded. I reiterated that the United States will continue to fly, sail, and operate wherever international law allows, and we will support the right of all countries to do the same. We will continue to help our allies and partners strengthen their maritime capabilities. And we discussed how any disputes between claimants in the region must be resolved peacefully, through legal means, such as the upcoming arbitration ruling under the U.N. Convention of the Law of the Seas, which the parties are obligated to respect and abide by.
>
> —President Barack Obama, Remarks at U.S.-ASEAN Press Conference, Sunnylands, California, February 16, 2016[1]

The Philippines had decided to move forward with its arbitral case no matter what. And China responded by growing even more assertive. Two crises erupted in May 2014. One would last a few months, while the other would permanently alter the balance of power in the South China Sea. First was the deployment of a deep-water drilling rig in waters claimed by Vietnam. That prompted a high-stakes game of chicken between dozens of Chinese and Vietnamese vessels. And in the middle of that crisis, the world learned that China had launched the most impressive, and escalatory, dredging project in history. The international community, and especially the United States, struggled to articulate an effective response. Short on ideas, interested parties looked to the arbitral proceedings in The Hague as the best chance to leverage China into a more responsible course. But political change in Manila and Washington would soon dash those hopes.

On Dangerous Ground. Gregory B. Poling, Oxford University Press. © Oxford University Press 2022.
DOI: 10.1093/oso/9780197633984.003.0010

China's Mobile Territory

On May 1, Vietnam detected the *Haiyang Shiyou* 981 (HYSY 981) oil rig and three service ships sailing past the Paracel Islands.[2] The rig was CNOOC's crown jewel—a $1 billion deep-water drilling platform launched in 2012. At that time, the company's chairman had declared it "mobile national territory" and a "strategic weapon" to assert Beijing's claims.[3] The rig parked in waters 120 nautical miles east of Vietnam's Ly Son Island and 180 miles south of Hainan. The closest disputed feature was barren Triton Island, 17 miles to the north. Under any equitable arrangement, the area belonged to Vietnam's EEZ and continental shelf. At the very least, Beijing had to recognize that it was legally disputed.[4]

Nonetheless, China's Maritime Safety Administration announced that the HYSY 981 would conduct exploratory drilling in the area until August 15.[5] Vietnam immediately dispatched half a dozen law enforcement vessels as a "show of force" to prevent the rig from operating.[6] In response, Beijing deployed a mixed force of forty CCG, PLAN, and militia vessels to protect it. They formed up in concentric rings, with the PLAN closest to the HYSY 981 and the militia farthest out where it would have the most contact with the Vietnamese. No shots were fired, but things quickly turned violent. China released video of a Vietnamese ship ramming two CCG vessels. Vietnam published photos of Chinese ships using high-pressure water hoses and intentionally colliding with Vietnamese boats, in one case rupturing a vessel's hull.[7]

Vietnam actively internationalized the issue. Its embassies around the world held press conferences and released evidence of the violence. Japan and the European Union issued statements of support.[8] Even the ASEAN foreign ministers, meeting in Myanmar, managed to express "serious concerns over the on-going developments" without naming China.[9] The U.S. State Department criticized Beijing's "provocative and unhelpful" behavior.[10] And Assistant Secretary for East Asia Daniel Russel suggested Vietnamese leaders might "avail themselves of international legal mechanisms"—a sign of how much Washington had come around on the Philippine arbitration case.[11]

Both sides continued to pour more forces into the standoff. By the middle of May, Hanoi claimed that China had deployed 130 vessels to the scene; Beijing said Vietnam had 60 ships involved. The Vietnamese were not only outnumbered but outmatched. The CCG ships were larger and better-armed than Vietnam's law enforcement vessels. And once Hanoi started deploying its own fishing militia to the scene, the wooden boats found themselves dwarfed by their larger steel-hulled Chinese counterparts. Soon enough a Vietnamese fishing boat was rammed and sunk, though the crew was rescued safely.

Authorities in Hanoi also did something unusual in Vietnam: they encouraged popular protests. Hundreds of citizens marched outside the Chinese embassy in Hanoi and its consulate in Ho Chi Minh City. State television eagerly reported on the demonstrations, which was an obvious sign of government support. But the movement soon got out of hand. Fueled, at least in some cases, by frustrations over workplace conditions as much as geopolitical anger, crowds across Vietnam began vandalizing factories believed to be owned by Chinese companies. (Many were actually Taiwanese or Korean.) At least six Chinese citizens were killed, and police struggled to get the violence under control.[12] Hanoi had clearly underestimated the depth of anti-China sentiment among the populace. Vietnamese authorities have kept a tight lid on popular demonstrations against Beijing ever since.

China must have known that deploying the HYSY 981 would carry some risk, but it seemed surprised by Vietnam's determined response. The longer the standoff continued, the more likely it became that there would be a loss of life at sea, whether by design or mishap. On May 27, China moved the rig about 20 miles to the east.[13] It was still much closer to Vietnam than to China, and well outside the territorial sea of any disputed islands. On June 18, China's top diplomat, Yang Jiechi, paid a visit to Hanoi. Afterward, several of China's vessels headed home and the rig visibly retracted its drilling equipment.[14] It stayed in that location until July 15, when CNOOC announced it was withdrawing a month ahead of schedule in the face of an approaching typhoon.[15] Chinese officials insisted the rig had finished its work early, but Vietnamese officials celebrated what they saw as a victory. Most outsiders agreed with them.[16] In the years since, the HYSY 981 has repeatedly redeployed to waters near the Paracels but always closer to China's coast than Vietnam's.

Dredging Up Trouble

The next crisis started on the internet. At the beginning of May 2014, members of an online forum in China published a dozen photos showing Chinese ships and construction vehicles working on a large patch of reclaimed land at Johnson Reef, where only a few rocks normally broke the surface. The pictures also showed PLAN vessels guarding the construction site and several Vietnamese ships near enough to observe. Why the Vietnamese kept quiet until the news broke is unclear. In any case, the photos quickly went viral. China's state-owned *Global Times* was the first to respond, dismissing the work as "merely a renovation."[17] At the ASEAN Summit in Myanmar a week later, the Philippines revealed that it had been monitoring Chinese dredging and landfill work at Johnson for over two months. It had even filed a diplomatic protest with Beijing in early

April but was rebuffed.[18] Four days after the summit, Manila took the story to
the press and released its own aerial surveillance photos to prove the work was
far more than "renovation."[19]

In retrospect, it is possible to identify the exact start of China's island-building
campaign by tracking publicly available transponder signals from the first ship involved. The *Tianjing* was at that time the largest dredging vessel in Asia and third-
largest in the world. Operated by Tianjin Dredging, a subsidiary of state-owned
China Communications Construction Company, it cost $130 million to build
between 2008 and 2010. Known as a cutter suction dredger, the ship grinds up
the seabed in waters up to 100 feet deep and spews the resulting sand and gravel
onto shore at a rate of 160,000 cubic feet per hour. After touring Cuarteron and
Fiery Cross Reefs, presumably gauging their suitability for dredging, it got to
work at Johnson on December 17, 2013.

The *Tianjing* spent two and a half months grinding up the reef at Johnson.
It dug out a new harbor and created twenty-seven acres of land. Then it moved
on while support vessels and construction vehicles took over, smoothing and
shaping the new island. That was the work that could be seen in the photos posted
online a few months later. In the meantime, the *Tianjing* repeated the process in
fits and starts at Hughes and Cuarteron Reefs. By late May it had created nine-
teen acres of land at the former and fifty-six at the latter, though the Philippines
didn't seem aware of that at the time.[20] Later analysis of satellite imagery showed
that in each case, the *Tianjing* was preceded by a fleet of clam-harvesting boats
from Hainan. These vessels would anchor over shallow reef surfaces and use
custom-made brass propellors to pulverize the coral. That allowed them to more
easily scoop up the endangered giant clams embedded in the coral. They tossed
the meat and transported the shells back to Hainan for use in overpriced jewelry
and statuary. Everything about the operation was illegal under both Chinese and
international law. But the *Tianjing* helped destroy the evidence, and the scale of
their poaching, which soon extended to dozens of reefs across the Spratlys and
Paracels, wouldn't be known for years (Figures 9.1 and 9.2).[21]

After breaking news of the island building at Johnson, Philippine officials
went on the offensive. They blasted China's "hypocrisy" in complaining about
repairs to the *Sierra Madre* while building whole new islands. The Presidential
Palace declared the revelations proof that Manila had been right to pursue arbitration. And Aquino said such wanton violations of the DOC showed that
ASEAN needed to push for a legally binding COC immediately. But Beijing was
anything but chastened. The Ministry of Foreign Affairs confirmed the reports
about Johnson and said China was well within its rights. Then on May 22, the
Tianjing along with two other dredgers moved from Cuarteron to Gaven Reef
and started work on a fourth artificial island. By mid-June, the reef was home to
thirty-four acres of new land.[22]

Figure 9.1 The overfished but otherwise healthy reef around Philippine-occupied Thitu Island, February 2016. Photograph by John McManus, 2016.

Figure 9.2 An unoccupied reef east of Thitu Island after being visited by China's clam harvesting fleet, February 2016. Photograph by John McManus, 2016.

The United States addressed the island-building campaign for the first time on May 31, when Defense Secretary Hagel spoke at the annual Shangri-La Dialogue in Singapore. He criticized China's "destabilizing, unilateral actions," including the East China Sea ADIZ, Second Thomas Shoal blockade, HYSY 981 deployment, and new dredging work. And then he summed up why Washington cared:

The United States has been clear and consistent. We take no position on competing territorial claims. But we firmly oppose any nation's use of intimidation, coercion, or the threat of force to assert those claims. We also oppose any effort—by any nation—to restrict overflight or freedom of navigation—whether from military or civilian vessels, from countries big or small. The United States will not look the other way when fundamental principles of the international order are being challenged.[23]

In June, the Philippine government publicized the dredging and landfill work at Hughes, Cuarteron, and Johnson Reefs. Chinese experts then told the press that a much larger artificial island was being planned at Fiery Cross Reef, complete with an airstrip and deep-water port (Figure 9.3). Sketches of these facilities had begun circulating in the Chinese press. They originally came from China State Shipbuilding Corporation, a large state-owned enterprise, which had published the plans online in 2012 before quickly pulling them down.[24] That

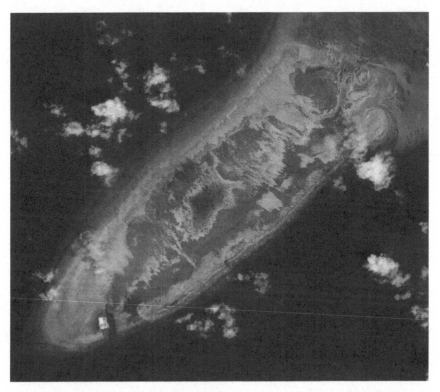

Figure 9.3 Fiery Cross Reef in its natural state, March 29, 2009. The small Chinese facility on the southwestern end of the reef sits atop the only rock that remains dry at high-tide. Photograph by CSIS Asia Maritime Transparency Initiative/Maxar, 2022.

suggested the island-building campaign had been planned years in advance, just waiting for the go-ahead from a more aggressive leader like Xi Jinping. It also indicated that the four initial islands were test runs. The next three would be much more ambitious.

On June 16, Albert del Rosario tried to get ahead of the problem, calling for a moratorium on any new construction and reclamation in the South China Sea.[25] The Vietnamese Foreign Ministry weighed in the same day, blasting China without endorsing a construction freeze. Manila and Hanoi were increasingly coordinating their approaches to the disputes. A week earlier, they had even played a symbolic soccer match on Southwest Cay, which South Vietnam had seized from the Philippines back in 1974.[26] But they weren't totally on the same page. When it came to a moratorium, the problem was Hanoi's own quiet upgrades. It had been reclaiming land at a few islands for the past year or two, using barges and backhoes instead of modern dredging ships. Vietnam would argue there was a qualitative difference between expanding natural islands and creating whole new ones. But setting aside the question of moral high ground, Hanoi wasn't going to stop in the face of Beijing's recent activity. By 2016, Vietnam would add 120 acres of sand to its eight largest islets. Over the same period, China would create 3,200 acres at its seven reefs.[27] In hindsight, maybe Vietnam wishes it had joined the calls for a moratorium. But there is no reason to think that would have made a difference to China.

In July, the United States endorsed del Rosario's call for a moratorium. Deputy Assistant Secretary of State Michael Fuchs suggested it should also cover interference in "longstanding economic activities . . . in disputed areas." Washington and Manila both lobbied ASEAN members to endorse the idea. And at the start of August, the Philippine Department of Foreign Affairs went a step further, issuing the "Triple Action Plan." The moratorium should be the first step, it argued, followed by the rapid negotiation of a COC and then resolution of the disputes through arbitration. The Philippines claimed the support of some of its neighbors, but none said so publicly. At the ASEAN Ministerial Meeting and ARF in Myanmar a week later, Secretaries Kerry and del Rosario pushed these proposals but found little support. Many of the members liked the idea but preferred to work through existing ASEAN-China mechanisms, especially the DOC working groups.[28] It was a mistake they would make repeatedly in the years ahead.

On the sidelines of the ARF, Foreign Minister Wang Yi suggested China could agree to halt its island building if the Philippines dropped the arbitration case.[29] But again Manila refused, convinced that Beijing wouldn't follow through on any voluntary commitment. The skepticism seemed warranted. Even as Wang was speaking, a dredger was at work on Fiery Cross Reef. There would be three dredgers at the reef by September and six by November.[30] As expected, the project was much more ambitious than the first four. China would eventually dump almost seven hundred acres of sand on Fiery Cross Reef and dredge a harbor large enough to host naval combatants.[31] When photos of the work began circulating widely in November, a Pentagon spokesperson confirmed that the island was apparently designed to host a 3,000-meter airstrip—long enough to accommodate any plane in the People's Liberation Army arsenal (Figures 9.4 and 9.5).[32]

Dredgers showed up at China's last two outposts, Subi and Mischief Reefs, in January 2015. The artificial islands there would be even larger than at Fiery Cross. And dozens of dredging ships were involved at each of those underwater reefs. By the fall of 2015, Subi would be home to almost one thousand acres of land and Mischief to nearly fourteen hundred (Figures 9.6 and 9.7). The entire lagoon at each reef would become a massive port. And each would sport a 3,000-meter airstrip of its own.[33]

Figure 9.4 Dredgers digging out Fiery Cross Reef's new harbor during the latter stages of island building, January 15, 2015. Photograph by CSIS Asia Maritime Transparency Initiative/Maxar, 2022.

Figure 9.5 Fiery Cross Reef in its current state, March 27, 2020. It is covered with almost seven hundred acres of dry land. Photograph by CSIS Asia Maritime Transparency Initiative/Maxar, 2022.

Law and Failed Diplomacy

The best chance to de-escalate before it was too late might have been November 2014, when Xi hosted the APEC Leaders Meeting in Beijing. Heads of state from across the Pacific, including President Obama, flew to China. It accorded Xi his first opportunities to meet with Prime Minister Abe and President Aquino. Playing the gracious host, the Chinese president played down the tensions in the East and South China Seas. Aquino told the press afterward that the meeting offered a "new beginning" and a chance to "develop areas of cooperation."[34] But that new beginning was forgotten in about a month.

The arbitral tribunal in The Hague had given China until December 15 to submit its countermemorial responding to the Philippines. China had again insisted it would neither recognize nor participate in the proceedings.[35] But as the deadline approached, the international community held out hope that

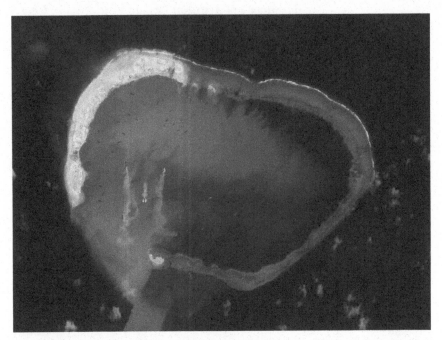

Figure 9.6 Dozens of dredgers at work digging out the lagoon and dumping sand atop Mischief Reef, April 13, 2015. Prior to their arrival, the reef had no dry land at all. Photograph by CSIS Asia Maritime Transparency Initiative/Maxar, 2022.

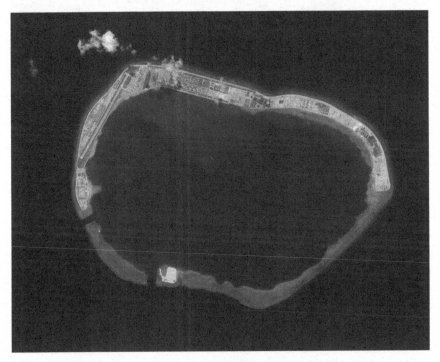

Figure 9.7 Mischief Reef in its current state, May 4, 2020. It is covered with nearly fourteen hundred acres of dry land. Photograph by CSIS Asia Maritime Transparency Initiative/Maxar, 2022.

Beijing might change its mind. It was well-known that some jurists in China disagreed with the decision to sit out the proceedings. They believed that China would be better served by defending itself, at least during the early stages when it might still convince the arbitrators that they lacked jurisdiction. Then, in the first week of December, China was one of three parties that weighed in on the case.

The United States was the first, albeit indirectly. The State Department on December 5 released an analysis of Beijing's South China Sea claims. It was part of a series of reports called *Limits in the Sea* which had been published since 1970. It gave department lawyers a way to publicly analyze foreign maritime claims for consistency with international law. The report focused on three possible interpretations of the nine-dash line. If it was merely a claim to islands—as originally intended—that was fine. Washington was neutral on sovereignty, and maritime entitlements from each feature could be determined based on their status under UNCLOS. That was exactly what the Philippines was asking the tribunal to do. But if the line was meant as a national boundary, then it was illegal. It was too far from anything to be an EEZ or continental shelf boundary, and those were the only options allowed by international law. Finally, the study tackled the notion of historic rights. That took up most of the report since it was the only interpretation that accorded with China's recent behavior. The department concluded that UNCLOS left no room for such rights. And if China had claimed them prior to the advent of UNCLOS, "the Convention's provisions prevail over any such historic claims."[36]

Vietnam delivered a statement to the arbitral tribunal that same day. Hanoi asked the arbitrators to pay "due regard" to how their decision might affect Vietnam's claims. But it also recognized the tribunal's jurisdiction. And it agreed with the Philippines that the nine-dash line was illegal and none of the features occupied by China qualified for EEZs or continental shelves.[37]

Two days later, the Chinese government sent a "position paper" to the tribunal, press, and foreign governments. It offered three arguments. First, Beijing maintained that no matter how Manila framed it, the case ultimately affected territorial sovereignty, which was beyond the scope of UNCLOS. Second, it argued that the Philippines had no right to bring a case of any sort because it had agreed in the 2002 DOC to settle disputes only through negotiation. Third, if the arbitrators didn't buy those arguments, China insisted they lacked jurisdiction because the case amounted to the delimitation of maritime boundaries. And China had exempted itself from compulsory arbitration on such matters, as allowed by the convention.[38]

The position paper seemed like an internal compromise for the Chinese government. It allowed Beijing to participate in the proceedings without admitting it. Chinese officials knew that the tribunal would have to consider their points and hopefully throw out the case. In response, the arbitrators asked the Philippines to provide a supplemental submission by March 2015 responding to China's arguments along with several questions from the tribunal.[39] Manila's lawyers did so, furnishing the judges with over two hundred pages of answers, along with eleven volumes of supporting materials and expert reports.

That submission introduced two important new arguments. The tribunal had asked the Philippine legal team to consider whether the Spratlys might be treated as an archipelago and enclosed by straight baselines. If so, then they might generate maritime entitlements as a group rather than separately. Manila argued that UNCLOS wouldn't allow it for several reasons, not least being that China wasn't an archipelagic state. The judges also requested more information on some of the larger islands not mentioned in the original memorial: Itu Aba, Thitu, and West York.[40] If any of those could generate EEZs, then they would overlap with the areas discussed in the case. And that would involve boundary delimitation, from which Beijing was exempt. The status of Itu Aba, as the largest natural feature in the Spratlys, would be a major point of debate from then on.

ASEAN, meanwhile, was increasingly irrelevant in the changing state of play. At the group's Foreign Ministers' Retreat in January, several members voiced concern about China's island building. But according to the host, Malaysian foreign minister Anifah Aman, they could agree only to "intensify efforts" to implement the DOC and reach a COC. The group had issued that same statement dozens of times without effect. Del Rosario lamented, "Our inaction on this would undermine the principle of centrality, since we are unable to address in a unified and collective way such a critical issue in our own backyard."[41] He was right—the clearer it became that ASEAN couldn't or wouldn't deal with the South China Sea, the more member-states and outside powers would look beyond the organization.

Pressure was also growing on the Obama administration, which had made speeches but taken little direct action in response to China's island building. Adm. Jonathan Greenert, who served as chief of naval operations from 2011 to 2015, believed that a more forceful response might have caused Chinese leaders to "recalibrate." His PLAN counterpart, Adm. Wu Shengli, made clear in private meetings that Beijing had been expecting a stronger reaction from Washington. Greenert would later write, "When there was no such response, the island-building campaign continued apace."[42]

In March, the top Democrats and Republicans on the Senate Armed Services Committee sent a letter to Kerry and Secretary of Defense Ashton Carter. They called for "a formal policy and clearly articulated strategy . . . to slow down or stop China's reclamation activities." The senators recognized that China's reliance on "non-military methods of coercion," including the CCG and militia, required a multifaceted response alongside partners and allies. They suggested limiting security cooperation with the People's Liberation Army, increasing capacity-building support for other claimants, releasing more intelligence on China's activities, and increasing diplomatic pressure in as many forums as possible.[43]

The administration would pursue some of these, particularly capacity-building support and public naming and shaming, but it never formulated a coherent strategy. During a speech in Canberra at the end of March, Pacific Fleet commander Adm. Harry Harris blasted China for building a "Great Wall of Sand" in the Spratly Islands.[44] He would soon be elevated to commander-in-chief of U.S. Pacific Command, where he remained the administration's most vocal proponent for a tough approach to China. In May, reports indicated that Secretary Carter had ordered a review of how the military might conduct close-in patrols around the artificial islands under the Freedom of Navigation Program.[45] But as the senators had pointed out, China was relying on nonmilitary coercion to destabilize the South China Sea. The Pentagon couldn't confront it alone. And that was a problem—the president and senior White House aides wouldn't embrace a hard line on China. The conventional wisdom was that the administration was afraid to push back too hard in the South China Sea lest it undermine cooperation with Beijing on global priorities like climate change and Iran's nuclear ambitions. Carter would later remark:

> I fear that China, and the South China Sea in particular, may have been one area in which the president's analysis misled him. He believed that traditional Washington foreign policy thinkers were prone to reach for confrontation and containment as strategies when a less forceful approach was called for. So he viewed recommendations from me and others to more aggressively challenge China's excessive maritime claims and other counterproductive behaviors as suspect. When I would travel to Asia, his direction to me was succinct: "Don't go banging pots and pans over there." I was not to make trouble.[46]

In late May, the U.S. Navy invited a CNN crew to fly along on a P-8A surveillance flight near the Spratlys. Taking off from the Philippines, the journalists listened in as the plane was hailed eight times by PLAN personnel yelling that they were "approaching our military alert zone" and needed to "leave immediately!"[47] Chinese diplomats had spent the past few months trying to argue that the artificial islands were just civilian facilities for search-and-rescue assistance, weather forecasting, and so on. The CNN footage didn't help their case. Neither did the Pentagon's announcement a week later that it had observed a pair of mobile artillery pieces on one of the islands.[48] During the Shangri-La Dialogue at the end of the month, Carter again called for a halt to all construction and island building. During a one-on-one meeting he tried, and failed, to convince his Vietnamese counterpart to embrace a moratorium.[49]

China tried to deflect the mounting criticism, accusing the United States of being the one "militarizing" the South China Sea with its surveillance operations, joint exercises, and network of alliances. When Kerry again demanded a halt to new construction during the ARF in August, Foreign Minister Wang insisted that China already *had* stopped. He accused the Vietnamese of being the only ones still expanding their bases. In reality, China had completed landfill at Fiery Cross, but the dredgers kept working at Subi and Mischief into the fall.[50] China was also quietly reclaiming hundreds of acres of land at Woody Island and other bases in the Paracels, which would continue until mid-2017.[51]

Chinese vessels were also making their presence felt elsewhere in the South China Sea. And that was forcing other governments to respond even when they would rather have ignored the issue. PLAN ships had occasionally made patriotic cruises by James Shoal—the so-called southernmost territory of China—for years. But in September 2013, China had established a more regular presence in Malaysian waters. A CCG vessel had traveled to Luconia Shoals and dropped anchor near Luconia Breakers, which contains the only sandbar on those vast reefs. The Malaysian government led by Prime Minister Najib Razak had little interest in playing up the issue. Kuala Lumpur had long championed its "special relationship" with Beijing; Malaysia was the first ASEAN member to normalize relations with China. And the Najib government was increasingly reliant on Chinese capital to cover the debts its 1MDB fund was racking up through plunder and fraud, though that wasn't fully known at the time.

Still, Malaysia couldn't entirely ignore foreign law enforcement vessels parked in its waters. Shahidan Kassim, a minister in the prime minister's office, had first raised the CCG presence at Luconia in Parliament in March 2014. Malaysian naval and law enforcement vessels began patrolling the area more frequently. But the Chinese didn't back off. In June 2015, Shahidan got so frustrated that he released aerial photos of a CCG vessel at Luconia on Facebook. It was a break from the government's usual attempts to downplay tensions with Beijing and caused a small uproar in Parliament and the state-controlled press. As ASEAN chair for the year, Malaysia was already facing pressure to adopt a tougher line on China; now it had to worry about domestic critics accusing the government of not adequately defending its sovereign rights. But just before the ASEAN and East Asia summits kicked off in November, the CCG left Luconia Shoals. It was an olive branch from Beijing which allowed the Malaysian government to save face.[52] Najib managed to balance the competing voices at the summits and released a chair's statement that didn't differ from previous ASEAN language in any appreciable way. The CCG was back by January 2016 and has been at Luconia almost every day since.[53] But Malaysian officials have been loath to admit that.

Fixating on FONOPs

In December 2015, Obama hosted Xi in the Oval Office. The two discussed economic tensions, including intellectual property theft, and reached a tentative agreement on cyber espionage. They hailed progress on the Paris climate agreement signed a few months earlier. And they had "candid discussions on the East and South China Sea." In a joint press conference in the White House Rose Garden, Obama reiterated the U.S. commitment to "sail, fly and operate anywhere that international law allows" and warned against reclamation and "militarization of disputed areas." Then, in what might have been an unscripted moment, Xi said the construction activities "do not target or impact any country, and China does not intend to pursue militarization."[54] For years afterward, American and Southeast Asian officials would hold up those words as proof of Beijing's dishonesty.[55]

Obama's line that the United States would "sail, fly and operate" was becoming a mantra. Carter had been the first to use it during a speech in May. He repeated it almost every time the South China Sea came up.[56] That was no accident—it coincided with a growing fixation on one tool of U.S. policy in the South China Sea: freedom of navigation operations (FONOPs). These operations involve a U.S. Navy or Air Force platform intentionally disregarding a foreign maritime claim that Washington considers illegal. They are just one part of the Freedom of Navigation Program established back in 1979.[57] The program starts with State and Defense Department lawyers who analyze foreign claims. Those deemed excessive are flagged for U.S. diplomats to protest. If diplomatic channels fail, the Department of Defense is called on to operationally challenge the claim. This is meant to pressure foreign governments and establish a record of U.S. noncompliance, which would be useful in future arbitration or negotiation. FONOPs happen all over the world. They target both adversaries and allies.[58] But in the South China Sea, they would take on a symbolic importance wildly out of proportion to their original intent.

In September, Admiral Harris and Assistant Secretary of Defense for Asia David Shear testified before the Senate Armed Services Committee. Chairman John McCain and several others grilled them about whether the United States was backing up its rhetoric by conducting FONOPs around China's artificial islands. They were particularly interested in whether the U.S. Navy was operating within 12 miles of those naturally underwater features, like Mischief Reef, that weren't entitled to a territorial sea at all. Shear replied that the navy was conducting other kinds of FONOPs in the South China Sea but hadn't sailed within 12 miles of one of the reefs since 2012. Harris added that Pacific Command wasn't flying over the submerged features even though they should have no territorial airspace.

This was the first time that most journalists and analysts had ever heard of the sleepy Freedom of Navigation Program. And that led to misunderstandings. Reports began to equate FONOPs only with operations inside 12 miles of a disputed feature. The navy was challenging other Chinese claims, like the baselines around the Paracels, but that point was lost. There were also different kinds of FONOPs within 12 miles. The committee wanted the Pentagon to assert that underwater features didn't have a territorial sea. But most FONOPs within the 12-mile limit, including around the Spratlys and Paracels, were meant to assert the right of innocent passage without prior notification. Despite debates on that topic dating back to UNCLOS I, the issue had never been fully settled. And China, Taiwan, and Vietnam all demanded that foreign warships get permission before transiting their territorial seas.

The pressure built until late October, when the United States finally undertook a FONOP within 12 miles of one of China's artificial islands. To appear evenhanded, the USS *Lassen* first passed through the territorial seas of Northeast and Southwest Cays, held by the Philippines and Vietnam, respectively. It did so in innocent passage, ignoring Hanoi's requirements for prior permission. Then it passed within 12 miles of Subi Reef. In a first for the Freedom of Navigation Program, the Pentagon quickly leaked the story to the press. And many observers cheered the operation for signaling that Subi, as a low-tide elevation, had no territorial sea.[59] That was, after all, what the Philippines was arguing in the arbitration case. But then things got weird.

Navy sources began admitting that the *Lassen* hadn't sailed past Subi in its normal mode of operations; it had done so in innocent passage. That seemed like an admission that China could claim a territorial sea around the reef. Stories popped up all over the place accusing the Pentagon of having screwed up.[60] Two analysts, Bonnie Glaser and Peter Dutton, figured out what really happened more than a week later, but by then it was too late to change the media narrative. The nearest occupied feature to Subi was Thitu Island, nearly 13 miles away. But between the two was a tiny sandbar, generously labeled "Sandy Cay."[61] Ironically, that sandbar has grown in recent years and at least two more have appeared due to the accumulation of reclaimed sand washing off Subi. Since it was above water at high tide, Sandy Cay was entitled to its own territorial sea. And since Subi Reef was within 12 miles of it, the low-tide elevation could arguably be used as a basepoint to extend the sandbar's territorial sea.[62] Given these hypotheticals, any U.S. Navy ship sailing near Subi engages in innocent passage to cover its bases. The Pentagon wouldn't clarify any of this for two months. In January

2016, Carter finally responded to questions from Senator McCain, writing, "Given the factual uncertainty, we conducted the FONOP in a manner that is lawful under all possible scenarios to preserve U.S. options. . . . The specific excessive maritime claims challenged in this case are less important than the need to demonstrate that countries cannot restrict navigational rights and freedoms around islands and reclaimed features contrary to international law as reflected in [UNCLOS]."[63] It was all needlessly complicated. If the Pentagon wanted to challenge China's demand for prior permission before innocent passage, it could have sailed past Cuarteron, Johnson, or Fiery Cross Reefs. Everyone agreed those were above water and had territorial seas. If it wanted to silence the critics on Capitol Hill and assert that underwater features weren't entitled to any maritime zones, it had to do so at isolated Mischief Reef. FONOPs near the other three—Hughes, Gaven, and especially Subi—accomplished nothing because of their unclear legal status.

Maybe the Defense Department rushed the *Lassen* FONOP because of political pressure. But the real problem was the messaging failure. Whoever leaked the operation to the press clearly thought it was cause for celebration. When the criticisms began rolling in, the Pentagon didn't have answers ready and lost control of the story. The whole episode did more harm than good. It strengthened an emerging linkage between American credibility and FONOPs, and it reinforced the idea that the only operations that really counted would be those conducted within 12 miles and *not* in innocent passage. In other words, it had to be Mischief Reef or bust.

A few days after the *Lassen* operation, a Pentagon official said the administration would undertake FONOPs in the South China Sea "about twice a quarter or a little more than that."[64] But the storm of criticism seemed to wreck that plan. In its final year, the Obama administration launched just three more FONOPs in the South China Sea. Two challenged China's demand for prior notification for innocent passage and one targeted the illegal baselines around the Paracels.[65] Each FONOP was much clearer than the *Lassen*'s and accompanied by more disciplined messaging. But they didn't quiet the critics. At home and abroad, it was said the White House was slow-walking FONOP approvals. That the navy still hadn't launched an operation within 12 miles of Mischief fed into that narrative. The net effect was that FONOPs raised more questions about U.S. credibility than they answered. But neither the Obama administration nor its successor could stop the operations once they had started. That would be even more damaging.

Other U.S. efforts had more effect than FONOPs, but often received less attention. The United States and ASEAN signed a strategic partnership agreement in November 2015.[66] It wasn't clear what exactly that meant—strategic partnerships were usually reserved for bilateral relationships—but it signaled

U.S. commitment to the organization. Obama followed that by hosting the ten leaders of ASEAN at a landmark summit in Sunnylands, California, in February 2016. The resulting "Sunnylands Declaration" included the strongest language ASEAN as a grouping has ever endorsed on the South China Sea, though it didn't directly reference China or the arbitration. The eleven leaders affirmed the following:

> Shared commitment to peaceful resolution of disputes, including *full respect for legal and diplomatic processes*, without resorting to the threat or use of force in accordance with universally recognized principles of international law and [UNCLOS]. Shared commitment to maintain peace, security and stability in the region, ensuring maritime security and safety, including the rights of freedom of navigation and overflight *and other lawful uses of the seas*, and unimpeded lawful maritime commerce as described in [UNCLOS] *as well as non-militarization* and self-restraint in the conduct of activities. (italics added)[67]

The inclusion of "other lawful uses of the seas" was significant. The United States was being criticized for a perceived fixation on naval freedom of navigation in the South China Sea, which was only heightened by the new debate around FONOPs. Partners in the region worried that when Washington talked about "freedom of navigation and overflight" it meant only for warships and commercial traffic. Most of what China restricted in the South China Sea were fishing, oil and gas operations, and the other lawful rights of coastal states. The new language at Sunnylands was an effort to show that Washington considered all maritime rights important, not just its own. That became muddled when most U.S. statements afterward reverted to the "sail, fly and operate" mantra. The Pentagon and State Department wouldn't get the message about the more expansive "other lawful uses of the sea" or "freedom of the seas" until 2019. But Sunnylands was a start.

The U.S.-Philippine alliance was also growing steadily closer. The Enhanced Defense Cooperation Agreement had been tied up in litigation since the day it was signed. But the Supreme Court of the Philippines finally affirmed its constitutionality in January 2016. The justices agreed with the Aquino administration that the pact was necessary under Article II of the U.S.-Philippines MDT, which says the parties "by self-help and mutual aid will maintain and develop their individual and collective capacity to resist armed attack."[68] Two months later, Washington and Manila reached agreement on the first five "agreed locations" to which U.S. forces would gain access and be able to construct facilities. One was Fort Magsaysay, the country's largest army base. The other four were airbases, including Basa in central Luzon and Antonio Bautista in Palawan. They offered the closest access to Scarborough and the Spratlys, respectively.[69]

In March 2016, Chief of Naval Operations John Richardson announced that the United States was monitoring Chinese surveys at Scarborough Shoal which suggested the reef was "a next possible area of reclamation."[70] Later than month, Obama hosted Xi and other world leaders at the Nuclear Security Summit in Washington. Scarborough didn't come up during a joint press conference the two held.[71] But according to later reports, Obama privately warned Xi that Scarborough was a red line for the United States.[72] Any attempt to build a permanent facility would have serious repercussions for the overall Sino-American relationship. Soon after, 5,000 American troops joined 3,500 Filipino counterparts for their largest annual joint exercises, called Balikatan (shoulder-to-shoulder).[73] A contingent of U.S. Air Force A-10 Thunderbolts stuck around after the exercises. They took off from Clark Air Base on April 21 and conducted what U.S. Pacific Command called an "air and maritime domain awareness mission" around Scarborough. But A-10s, nicknamed "Warthogs," are built for close air support and ground attack, not patrol.[74]

A few days later, an unnamed People's Liberation Army source seemed to confirm that China was preparing to build an artificial island on Scarborough.[75] Then China reportedly withdrew the vessels that were worrying U.S. officials. Analysts and former officials declared it a tactical victory for the United States—one of the few it could claim in the South China Sea. But the Pentagon wouldn't confirm the operation.[76] This led to charges that the White House had "muzzled" Pacific Command, and it lent credence to a widely held belief that the National Security Council was blocking a more forceful U.S. strategy.[77] The details of what happened at Scarborough in the spring of 2016 remain murky. Philippine defense secretary Delfin Lorenzana would later claim that China had barges of sand heading for the shoal as late as June but turned back after firm warnings from the United States.[78] What seems clear is that Beijing was at least considering building another artificial island at the shoal. And the Obama administration knew that the alliance, and American credibility as a regional security provider, couldn't afford another failure at Scarborough.

In April, the administration also released the first tranche of funds in a new five-year, $425 million effort dubbed the Southeast Asia Maritime Security Initiative. The idea had originated with John McCain and the Senate Armed Services Committee. Congress authorized it as the "South China Sea Initiative" in the 2016 National Defense Authorization Act. The program set aside a pot of money for training and equipment to boost the maritime domain awareness and maritime security capabilities of five partners: Indonesia, Malaysia, the Philippines, Thailand, and Vietnam. Brunei, Singapore, and Taiwan could also join activities held through the program, but they wouldn't get funding.[79] The

Philippines received the lion's share of the money that first year, and in most years since. The initiative soon gained considerable traction in the region even if it didn't improve maritime security overnight, as some critics seemed to expect. Congress later extended the program through 2023 and renamed it the "Indo-Pacific Maritime Security Initiative." They added Bangladesh and Sri Lanka to the list of eligible partners but didn't authorize any increase in funding.[80]

The focus on maritime domain awareness helped expand interest beyond the loudest claimants: the Philippines and Vietnam. Indonesia, for instance, had grown much more vocal about Chinese fishing in its waters. Joko Widodo, known as "Jokowi," had won election as Indonesia's president in 2014. He had tapped businesswoman Susi Pudjiastuti as fisheries minister and empowered her to launch a wide-ranging crackdown on illegal fishing. Susi proved even more effective than Jokowi could have expected. Soon after taking office, she instituted a controversial but wildly popular policy of blowing up foreign fishing boats caught illegally in Indonesian waters.[81] Eventually she stopped blowing them up out of environmental concern and began just sinking them. Less visible, but probably more important, policies under Susi involved strengthening Indonesian law enforcement and surveillance capabilities, banning transshipment of catch, and revoking foreign fishing licenses. From the start, the biggest question was whether Indonesia would enforce these new rules against Chinese vessels, which had been fishing without permission in its EEZ since the 1980s.

For the first two years, Indonesia seemed to be applying the rules unevenly. Vietnamese, Malaysian, and Thai vessels were caught and sunk by the dozens. Chinese ships were noticeably absent from the list of those sent to the deep. Some of that was just because they were harder to arrest. China's boats were larger, operated in large groups farther from shore, and were often escorted by the CCG. But politics was also at play. Jokowi had named infrastructure his top priority and was actively courting Beijing. Susi was the most popular member of his cabinet but caused major headaches for those tasked with attracting Chinese financing. A series of incidents involving illegal fishing gave her the upper hand, but only for a while.

On March 20, 2016, an Indonesian law enforcement vessel interdicted a Chinese trawler less than 50 miles from Indonesia's Natuna Islands. Before his ship was boarded, the captain sent a call for help to the CCG—a benefit of the subsidy program that put a Beidou satellite positioning and communication system on every Chinese fishing boat. Hours later, as the Indonesians were towing the trawler back to Natuna Besar (Greater Natuna) for impoundment, a CCG vessel appeared on the horizon. In a shocking violation of law and safe conduct, it intentionally rammed the trawler, apparently trying to shut down its engine so it couldn't be towed. Then a second, better-armed

CCG ship turned up and ordered the Indonesians to release the fishing boat. Outnumbered and outgunned, Indonesian law enforcement had no choice but to comply, though they kept the eight crew members in custody. Susi later alleged that the ramming occurred less than 2.5 miles from one of the Natunas—well within Indonesia's territorial sea. Jakarta was outraged and filed a formal protest. The Ministry of Foreign Affairs in Beijing insisted that the trawler, captured at the southern edge of the nine-dash line, was operating in "traditional Chinese fishing grounds."[82]

Tensions continued to build for the next several months. Jakarta announced plans to upgrade its military facilities on Natuna Besar and increased patrols. In May, an Indonesian Navy frigate was forced to fire shots at a Chinese trawler before arresting its crew and towing it back to port. A CCG ship was serving as escort nearby but decided not to intervene. But Beijing did issue a protest of its own.[83] Another arrest occurred a month later, again with shots fired. This time a Chinese fisherman was injured and had to be flown back to Hainan for treatment. The Chinese Ministry of Foreign Affairs "lodged a strong protest" and insisted that "China and Indonesia have overlapping claims" in the area.[84] Indonesia, as it had consistently since the 1990s, denied any overlap. Susi continued to speak out against Chinese illegal fishing, but the issue slowly faded from the headlines.[85] Jakarta and Beijing tried to focus attention instead on their positive economic relations. Of course, sweeping it under the rug didn't make the problem go away, and Chinese fishing would reemerge as a major flashpoint in the relationship in 2019.

The Road to Judgment Day

The first hearings in the Philippines' case against China were held on July 7, 2015. They involved only jurisdictional matters. The judges heard two rounds of arguments over the next weeks. China had been invited to submit any final written arguments by June but refused. And as expected, it didn't appear for the proceedings. Indonesia, Malaysia, Vietnam, Thailand, and Japan, however, sent observers to The Hague.[86] Del Rosario gave the Philippines' opening statement, declaring:

> This is a matter that is most important not only to the Philippines, but also to all coastal States that border the South China Sea, and even to all the States Parties to UNCLOS. It is a dispute that goes to the very heart of UNCLOS itself. . . . If China can defy the limits placed by the Convention on its maritime entitlements in the South China Sea, and disregard the entitlements of the Philippines under the Convention,

then what value is there in the Convention for small States Parties as regards their bigger, more powerful and better armed neighbors?[87]

On October 29, the tribunal issued a 151-page decision on jurisdiction. It reiterated that China's refusal to participate would not prevent the case from moving forward. The decision also rejected Beijing's argument that the DOC prevented Manila from bringing a case. As for the fifteen claims the Philippines made against China, the tribunal found that it clearly had jurisdiction over seven of them. These involved the legal status of each feature, charges of endangering Philippine vessels, and engaging in destructive fishing practices. On seven others, the arbitrators said they would have to decide on jurisdiction when they considered the merits of the case. At issue, mostly, was the status of Itu Aba. If it was an island entitled to an EEZ, then the tribunal wouldn't have jurisdiction over several of the Philippine claims because they would require first delimiting maritime boundaries. On the final claim, requesting Beijing be ordered to "desist from further unlawful claims and activities," the judges asked for more specifics.[88]

China's Foreign Ministry released a statement the next day. It declared that the ruling on jurisdiction was "null and void, and has no binding effect on China."[89] And that was the last time it would engage with the proceedings until the tribunal's final award. The Philippine legal team returned to the Peace Palace a month later to argue the merits of the case. This time, Australia and Singapore joined the other "interested States Parties" in the gallery. The United States tried to attend, but its request was rejected; as a nonparty to UNCLOS, it had no standing. China of course refused to take part. It was provided a transcript of the hearings and given until January 1, 2016, to submit any comments.[90] It didn't.

If China wasn't going to defend itself, another party was determined to have a say. Taiwan had asked to be recognized as an interested party in the case, like Vietnam, but was refused. Not only was the ROC the originator of China's claims, but its forces had been occupying Itu Aba continuously since 1956— longer than any other claimant in the Spratlys. That island was the largest naturally formed land feature in the group, at just under one hundred acres. It had a small supply of naturally potable water. And Taiwan had been quietly upgrading its infrastructure for years, completing a 1,200-meter runway on the island in 2007. As a presidential candidate in 2008, Ma Ying-jeou had proposed making the island a marine peace park.[91] And as president, he oversaw the dredging of a new harbor and creation of eight acres of reclaimed land on the island.[92] Ma had graduated from New York University and Harvard Law, writing his thesis on the Senkaku Islands dispute in the East China Sea.

He was personally invested in having Itu Aba recognized as a fully entitled island under UNCLOS.

The Ma government decided that if it couldn't take part in the arbitration, it would affect the proceedings from afar. In late January, Taiwan's ministers of foreign affairs, mainland affairs, and environmental protection led a delegation to Itu Aba. The group included two foreigners: José Abeto Zaide, a former Philippine ambassador turned journalist, and this author.[93] They were accompanied by a camera crew producing a documentary on the island for the government in Taipei. Two days later, President Ma visited the island himself and then held a press conference laying out Taiwan's arguments. At the end of March, Taiwan released a position paper on its South China Sea policy. And two days later, the Chinese (Taiwan) Society of International Law submitted an amicus curiae brief to the tribunal detailing historical and legal evidence that Itu Aba could support human habitation.[94] To ensure these arguments received appropriate publicity, authorities took another delegation to the island, this time consisting of foreign journalists.[95]

Taipei's efforts worked, at least in drawing the tribunal's attention. The judges asked the Philippines to respond to all the evidence presented. It did so in two supplemental submissions in March and April 2016. The arbitrators also had to act as Beijing's advocates, considering all possible arguments in China's defense. They asked Paul Reichler's team to respond to materials dug out of archives in London and Paris. In the end, the Philippines compiled data on China's outposts, Itu Aba, the other features named in the memorial and supplemental submissions, and, for good measure, every other rock and reef in the Spratlys.[96]

There was also a diplomatic tussle playing out in embassies and international forums across the world. After the tribunal's ruling on jurisdiction, China had given up on trying to influence the case itself. Instead, it focused on undermining the legitimacy of the process. Beijing railed in bilateral and multilateral meetings that the tribunal lacked jurisdiction, that compulsory dispute settlement was a violation of state sovereignty, and even accused the judges of being bought and paid for by Washington and Tokyo. In response, Philippine diplomats called on nations around the world to publicly back the tribunal and insist that whatever the judges ruled would be legally binding. The United States lent considerable support to these efforts, as did Japan.

At the Sunnylands summit in February, Obama declared that China and the Philippines would be "obligated to respect and abide by" the arbitration ruling.[97] In March, the European Union expressed concerns about militarization of the artificial islands and urged claimants to resolve disputes "in accordance with international law including UNCLOS and its arbitration procedures." All twenty-seven

EU members along with five nonmembers in Europe endorsed the statement.[98] And in April, the foreign ministers of Canada, France, Germany, Italy, Japan, the United Kingdom, and the United States issued a special "Statement on Maritime Security" during a Group of 7 meeting in Hiroshima. It called on states to "fully implement any decisions rendered by the relevant courts and tribunals which are binding on them, including as provided under UNCLOS."[99] Their heads of state endorsed the statement a month later.[100] Similar endorsements came in from Australia, Botswana, New Zealand, and Vietnam. Tellingly, no other member of ASEAN followed suit. But the Philippines managed to get forty countries on the record publicly calling for compliance with the ruling.[101]

China was working hard to build its own competing coalition. By June, the Ministry of Foreign Affairs in Beijing was publicly claiming to have the support of more than sixty countries.[102] In reality, only thirty-one publicly agreed that the tribunal lacked jurisdiction or that compulsory dispute settlement was invalid, and twenty-two of those did so through a single line tucked into a dense China–Arab League joint declaration in May. Another thirty-six countries refused to comment when Chinese officials claimed their support, and four—Cambodia, Fiji, Poland, and Slovenia—publicly rebutted such claims.[103] When the tribunal announced at the end of June that it would issue its final award on July 12, it seemed the Philippines was in the driver's seat. It clearly had more support. And while everyone expected China to reject the ruling, it also seemed there would be a considerable diplomatic price to pay.

But something else happened in the meantime: Rodrigo Duterte was inaugurated the new president of the Philippines. The longtime mayor of Davao City in Mindanao, Duterte was an unapologetic populist. He billed himself as the solution to all the country's problems, which he laid at the feet of corrupt Manila elites. Two of those elites—Senator Grace Poe and Interior Secretary Manuel "Mar" Roxas—had tried to claim Aquino's legacy. Instead, they divided the vote and Duterte won in a landslide with 39 percent. The only thing the new president railed against as much as Manila was Washington. He had been a vocal opponent of the alliance for decades and an ardent admirer of Beijing. He also evinced very little interest in the South China Sea.

When the award was issued twelve days after Duterte's inauguration, it was an overwhelming victory for the Philippines. Manila won fourteen of its fifteen claims, the judges ruling that they lacked jurisdiction only on the question of interference at Second Thomas Shoal, which touched on military activities which Beijing had exempted from arbitration. Most important, the tribunal agreed that the nine-dash line and any claim to historic rights within it were invalid. And most controversial, the judges found that none of the Spratlys, including Itu Aba, was entitled to an EEZ or a continental shelf. They used a fairly simple test for habitability: the fact that the islands had never hosted a permanent population. The islands had been known to seafarers for centuries; if people could have settled on them, they would have. That meant Cuarteron, Fiery Cross, and Johnson were rocks entitled to 12-mile territorial seas. So was Gaven Reef, despite the Philippine assertion to the contrary.

Hughes, Subi, and Mischief Reefs were all deemed low-tide elevations that generated no maritime zones of their own. The former two could be used as basepoints to extend the territorial sea of nearby islands. But Mischief Reef belonged to the continental shelf and EEZ of the Philippines and was illegally occupied by China. Second Thomas Shoal was also a piece of the Philippines' shelf and EEZ. Scarborough Shoal was ruled a rock with a 12-mile territorial sea. But the court agreed that Filipino fishers, along with those from China and Vietnam, enjoyed traditional fishing rights at that reef regardless of who owned it (Figure 9.8).

The judges agreed that China had illegally destroyed the marine environment through clam harvesting, intentionally created the risk of collision to foreign ships, and prevented the Philippines from accessing the resources of its EEZ and continental shelf. And they berated China for building artificial islands while the arbitration was underway. It had effectively destroyed evidence, along with the marine environment, while having no bearing on the legal merits of the case.[104]

Australia, Canada, Japan, New Zealand, and the United States immediately called on China to comply with the ruling. Vietnam issued a somewhat tortured statement reiterating its earlier support for the process. Just three ASEAN members—Malaysia, Myanmar, and Singapore—positively acknowledged the ruling but stopped short of calling for compliance. Indonesia, where officials had previously said they would endorse the outcome, issued a neutral statement instead. Brunei, Cambodia, Laos, and Thailand did the same. China—and Taiwan—rejected it entirely.[105] Beijing even had a white paper ready to release the very next day reiterating that it claimed internal waters, territorial seas, EEZs, and continental shelves from all features in the Nansha, Zhongsha, and Xisha Islands, *and* historic rights beyond that.[106]

And how did the new Philippine government react to its own victory? By saying it had to study the matter. That ambivalence from Manila made it easy for other countries to walk back their previous support in the face of pressure from Beijing. Three days after the ruling, the European Union issued a statement acknowledging the award but not calling for compliance. It was a significant shift away from its advocacy just four months earlier.[107] Montenegro, one of the nonmembers who had endorsed the March statement, had even switched sides and was now backing China.[108] When the ASEAN Ministerial Meeting and ARF gathered in Laos a month later, newly installed Philippine foreign secretary

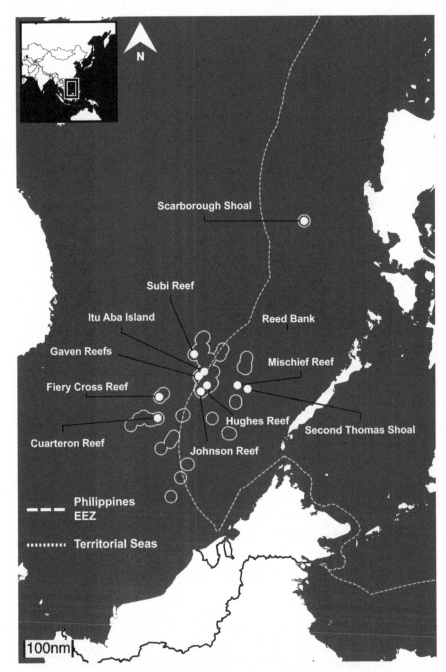

Figure 9.8 Outcomes of the South China Sea Arbitration Award, July 12, 2016. Created using Mapcreator and OpenStreetMap.

Perfecto Yasay didn't advocate for the ruling. It wasn't even mentioned in the foreign minsters' communiqué.[109] Under domestic pressure, Philippine officials, starting with the energy minister, finally endorsed the ruling in the fall. But they remained unenthusiastic. And in December, Duterte pledged to "set aside" the award after receiving pledges of aid and investment from China.[110] That promised windfall would never come, but the damage was done. Manila would never again have the world's attention focused on the South China Sea the way it did in July 2016.

A Course to Steer

2016–2021

> Like President Obama, we believe China can and should play a con-
> structive role in the region. We also acknowledge that the costs of
> seeking to shape China's behavior in the maritime commons may affect
> other elements of our bilateral relationship. But if China continues to
> pursue a coercive and escalatory approach to the resolution of mari-
> time disputes, the cost to regional security and prosperity, as well as to
> American interests, will only grow. For the international community to
> continue benefiting from the rules-based international order that has
> brought stability and prosperity to the Indo-Pacific region for the last
> seven decades, the United States must work together with like-minded
> partners and allies to develop and employ a strategy that aims to shape
> China's coercive peacetime behavior.
> —Senators John McCain, Jack Reed, Bob Corker, and Bob Menendez,
> letter to Secretary of Defense Ashton Carter and Secretary of State John
> Kerry, March 19, 2015[1]

In hindsight, it is easy to call out watershed moments in recent South China Sea history. Critics can point to each and lament that things should have been dif-ferent. Washington and Manila were outplayed at Scarborough, with long-lasting consequences for the alliance. The United States failed to impose sufficient costs for China's artificial island building, which only encouraged more militarization. The international community, egged on by the new Philippine president, aban-doned principle after the arbitral award. And so Beijing continued to throw its weight around, squeezing its neighbors out of their own waters while paying al-most no price.

These weren't isolated crises. They were part of a long-term strategy with which China radically altered the status quo and expanded its physical control over disputed waters. They fit an even older pattern of creeping expansion in Beijing's definition of rights and interests. Faced with these trends, Washington struggled to articulate a strategy or properly communicate why the maritime

On Dangerous Ground. Gregory B. Poling, Oxford University Press. © Oxford University Press 2022.
DOI: 10.1093/oso/9780197633984.003.0011

disputes mattered at all. U.S. policymakers most often approached the South China Sea tactically rather than strategically. They treated each crisis as an isolated incident to be managed and then minimized. Nowhere was this more evident than at Scarborough. But it applied to most U.S. responses over the history of the disputes.

The most coherent effort to forge a South China Sea strategy came during the last two years of the Obama administration. That was led mostly by the Defense Department with uneven support from State. It was never embraced by those, including in the White House, who viewed the disputes as something to be managed rather than fixed. It was overly militarized—a result of the Pentagon and Pacific Command having to lead by default. And the diplomatic planks of the strategy rested too much on activating ASEAN and rallying international support behind the Philippines. When those failed—the first predictably and the second very unexpectedly—China was free to advance its interests while U.S. policy drifted aimlessly.

From Bad to Worse

After Rodrigo Duterte decided to shelve the arbitral award, the Obama administration considered its hands tied. It kept talking about the ruling when asked, but it didn't lobby others. Few states were going to upset Beijing and risk their access to Chinese capital when the Philippines was no longer asking for their help. And suddenly it seemed like the U.S.-Philippine alliance faced more immediate threats. The famously anti-American Duterte entered office vowing to cancel joint exercises with the United States, stop buying U.S. arms, and scrap the Enhanced Defense Cooperation Agreement (EDCA).[2] In October 2016 he declared his "separation" from the United States during a speech in Beijing, raising fears that he would abrogate the MDT itself.[3] And as justification, Duterte often cited the U.S. failure at Scarborough and argued that the United States wouldn't fulfill its alliance obligations.[4] It didn't help that his relationships with President Obama and Ambassador Philip Goldberg were toxic from the start, as both men criticized his signature war on drugs and the thousands of extrajudicial killings involved.[5]

Then the U.S. presidential elections delivered a surprise of their own, lifting Donald Trump to victory over Hillary Clinton. Most Asia watchers had been anticipating a renewed focus on the region under a Clinton presidency. That might have included a more coherent South China Sea strategy. But no one knew what the Trump administration would mean for the region beyond an increase in trade fights. As president-elect, Trump mentioned the South China Sea only once. A PLAN vessel illegally seized a U.S. Navy unmanned underwater vehicle off the Philippines in December 2016. The craft was eventually returned, presumably after every component was examined and photographed. Trump pointed to the episode as evidence of Obama administration weakness.[6]

That was the last time the president publicly addressed the issue. For most of the Trump administration, the Pentagon was wholly responsible for South China Sea policy. The president's first secretary of state, Rex Tillerson, spent his tenure fighting his own bureaucracy. There was no assistant secretary of state for Asia for two and a half years until David Stilwell was confirmed in June 2019. Ambassadorships across Asia remained empty for much of the Trump presidency. Some, like Singapore, were never filled. In late 2017, Trump addressed the APEC Leaders Meeting in Danang, Vietnam, unveiling his administration's vision of a "free and open Indo-Pacific." But while free sea lanes were often mentioned as part of that goal, there was no clear policy to secure them.[7]

In this strategic vacuum, the Department of Defense did what it could. In March 2017, Secretary of Defense James Mattis decided that he would not send FONOP requests to the White House on a case-by-case basis, as the Obama administration had. Instead, he demanded a schedule of operations for the entire year to ensure they would be conducted regularly and without political interference. He reportedly passed that schedule to Trump in April, and it was approved without delay.[8] On May 24, the USS *Dewey* finally undertook the operation many had been waiting for. It sailed within 12 nautical miles of Mischief Reef in what was clearly not innocent passage and then performed a "man overboard" drill to drive home that it was in international waters.[9] The navy undertook FONOPs roughly every six weeks for the remainder of the administration, usually alternating between the Spratlys and Paracels. And as intended, the operations slowly lost the overblown symbolism they had accumulated during the last year of the Obama administration. Beyond FONOPs, the Department of Defense continued to provide capacity-building support through the Maritime Security Initiative and other programs. And in April 2018, Mattis disinvited China from the biannual Rim of the Pacific naval exercises in Hawaii as punishment for its coercion in the South China Sea.[10] But the department was just treading water. FONOPs, capacity building, strengthening deterrence—it was all necessary but insufficient. Ultimately the United States couldn't secure its interests in the South China Sea with military tools alone.

The U.S.-Philippine alliance survived one crisis after another. When Islamic State–linked militants occupied much of the southern Philippine city of Marawi in mid-2017, U.S. support was crucial in shortening the siege. That gave the Armed Forces of the Philippines some leverage to get Duterte to back off his threats against the alliance, for a while. The pace of joint exercises and equipment transfers returned to normal. EDCA was saved from the chopping block, but implementation slowed to a snail's pace.[11] In December 2018, Secretary of National Defense Delfin Lorenzana, long a proponent of the alliance, suddenly announced that the Philippines would undertake a review of the MDT due to U.S. ambivalence on the South China Sea. In remarkably quick time, Washington recognized the danger a cleavage would present for U.S. interests in the region. Following President Trump's February 2019 summit with Kim Jong Un in Hanoi, Secretary of State Mike Pompeo made a detour to Manila. He met with Duterte and top officials at the airport. And then he announced to the press, "As the South China Sea is part of the Pacific, any armed attack on Philippine forces, aircraft or public vessels will trigger mutual defense obligations [under the MDT]."[12] It was an unambiguous clarification of the Vance-Cohen-Hubbard positions: Article V applies to all Filipino forces whether at sea or on land, including on disputed islands.

There was still one crisis to go. In February 2020, Duterte announced he was abrogating the VFA, effective in six months. The immediate cause was the State Department's decision to revoke former police chief and current senator Ronald "Bato" dela Rosa's visa to the United States. Dela Rosa was Duterte's right-hand man in the drug war. Ending the VFA would effectively kill EDCA and neuter the MDT. After months of closed-door diplomacy, Secretary of Foreign Affairs Teodoro Locsin Jr. announced that Duterte had "suspended" his decision for six months.[13] De la Rosa had gotten his visa, China had grown even more aggressive at sea, and the COVID-19 pandemic had turned the world upside down. Duterte was convinced to hit the pause button again in November 2020 and in June 2021. He finally agreed to cancel the abrogation threat in July 2021 after a meeting with newly-installed Secretary of Defense Lloyd Austin.

What was China doing while the United States treaded water? After building its artificial islands, Beijing covered them in military infrastructure. By the end of 2017, it had completed airstrips, helipads, hangars, harbor facilities, fuel and ammunition storage, and radar and sensor networks across both the Paracel and Spratly Islands.[14] That facilitated new deployments. Between 2017 and 2018, the first military patrol and transport aircraft landed on Subi and Mischief Reefs (that milestone had already happened on Fiery Cross); surface-to-air and antiship missile platforms were deployed to all three of the large bases in the Spratlys; two of them got advanced jamming equipment; J-11 fighter jets rotated through Woody Island more frequently; and an H-6K bomber landed on the island for the first time. Virtually every modern class of PLAN and CCG ship began regularly calling at the major bases in the Spratlys. And the number of maritime militia vessels anchored at the islands exploded, reaching more than three hundred per day by late 2018.[15] China held off on deploying fighter jets to the Spratlys but built seventy-two hangars for them. All the other claimants understood they could appear anytime.

The most significant change wrought by China's new island bases was the way they increased nonmilitary pressure on the neighbors. The new radar and sensor arrays meant China could see everything that moved on or above the South China Sea. Not even the United States could make that claim. And the ability to forward-deploy CCG and militia boats to the Spratlys rather than 800 miles away on Hainan was a game-changer. Chinese militia and law enforcement ships began loitering for months at a time near other claimants' outposts. China's actual fishers, not just the militia, grew bolder. Dozens of boats under CCG escort spent weeks fishing off Malaysia and Indonesia at the end of 2019. After a two-year break, the clam harvesting fleets from Hainan started tearing up coral reefs again. CCG ships began showing up every time someone attempted to drill a new oil and gas well, even if it was in a block that had been developed for decades. They played chicken with the civilian boats that service oil rigs, purposely creating a risk of collision. In 2017 and again in 2018, Chinese threats forced Hanoi to break contracts with Spain's Repsol to drill near Vanguard Bank. In late 2019, more than a hundred Chinese and Vietnamese ships engaged in a four-month standoff over a new well Russia's Rosneft drilled in Block 06.1. China deployed its own survey vessel to operate in Vietnam's waters in retaliation. And just months later, a nearly identical standoff occurred over drilling by Malaysia's Petronas. That one lasted five months.[16]

While pressure built at sea, it disappeared from the diplomatic arena. China seized the opportunity offered by Duterte's ascendance to deflect international criticism. Shortly after his inauguration, Beijing offered to restart talks on the long-mooted COC. In 2018, Wang Yi even unilaterally declared that a code should be signed by 2021. The first draft the parties produced was no better, and arguably worse, than the DOC. It didn't even try to tackle the sensitive issues that sank previous attempts.[17] It became painfully clear that China was just buying time; it had no intention of signing a COC unless it was so watered-down as to be meaningless. Still, after the bruising years of 2009–16, most ASEAN members were willing to play along if it bought the group a measure of peace. Most often, the Vietnamese were the only ones openly airing grievances.[18] But without Philippine support they couldn't move the organization in any appreciable way. All the process did was further weaken ASEAN and give China more leeway to strengthen its grip on the South China Sea.

With David Stillwell's appointment in 2019, the State Department's Asia hands found their voice for the first time in the Trump administration. And Pompeo, who had replaced Tillerson a year earlier, was eager to push back on China at every opportunity. The department began seeking a greater role in South China Sea policy. It finally released a long-promised vision document on the Free and Open Indo-Pacific. It was more fact sheet than strategy paper, but it showed a commitment to the region that State had been missing for the previous two years. The paper helpfully used "freedom of the seas" rather than "freedom of navigation" and included the administration's strongest condemnation yet of Beijing's "unfounded, unlawful, and unreasonable" claims in the South China Sea. It also specifically called out interference with Vietnam's offshore oil and gas operations and highlighted ongoing capacity-building support for partners.[19]

In December 2019, Malaysia made a surprise submission to the Commission on the Limits of the Continental Shelf, outlining the northern portion of its extended continental shelf in the South China Sea. In a redux of 2009, it set off a flurry of diplomatic notes to the commission. China objected the very next day, recycling its usual language about indisputable sovereignty and historic rights. The Philippines jumped in a few months later to attack both the Malaysian claim and China's response. Beijing hit back, followed by Vietnam, then Indonesia, and so on. Unlike 2009, outside parties also weighed in, with the United States, Australia, France, Germany, and the United Kingdom all deriding China's claims.[20] In July 2020, Pompeo issued a statement clarifying the U.S. position on maritime claims in the South China Sea. For the first time, Washington explicitly endorsed the merits (not just the process) of the 2016 arbitral award and declared it would side with Southeast Asian claimants whenever China violated their EEZ and continental shelf rights.[21]

That opened new avenues for the United States to impose costs on China, including potential economic sanctions. But the Treasury Department wasn't ready to back that kind of escalation yet. As a half-measure, the Commerce Department in August 2020 placed twenty-four Chinese companies that "played a significant role" in the artificial island building on the Entity List.[22] That restricted their ability to source certain goods in the United States. At the same time, State announced that it would not issue visas to Chinese nationals "responsible for, or complicit in, either the large-scale reclamation, construction, or militarization of disputed outposts in the South China Sea, or the PRC's use of coercion against Southeast Asian claimants to inhibit their access to offshore resources."[23] Neither move had much impact on those targeted, but they showed that Washington was at least cracking open the economic toolkit.

The U.S. position in the South China Sea, along with those of its partners, steadily eroded for most of the Trump administration. Disinterest in Washington and Manila accelerated the negative trends already evident in 2016. And the positive legacies of the Obama and Aquino administrations—especially the arbitral award—were squandered. A combination of factors—new State Department advocacy, continued military engagement, a nascent turnaround in the alliance, and global distrust of China—may have stopped the strategic bleeding by late 2020. But America's hand was much weaker heading into the U.S. elections than it had been four years earlier.

Joe Biden's victory opened new avenues for international cooperation on the South China Sea. Vowing to rebuild American credibility abroad, the Biden White House has moved quickly to rebuild relations with allies and partners. It has focused particularly on Europe and fellow members of the "Quad": Australia, India, and Japan. Strengthening those partnerships and bringing them to bear on the South China Sea could be decisive in convincing Beijing to alter course. But the Philippines remains the critical missing piece. For at least the remainder of the Duterte presidency, scheduled to end on June 30, 2022, Manila will remain on the fence. In both capitals, supporters of the alliance will be stuck fighting to save, rather than strengthen, it. And that will waste more time—something that is running short for the Philippines, the United States, and like-minded partners in the South China Sea.

The Stakes

As the strategic environment deteriorates, commentators are right to lament that the United States is "losing" the South China Sea. But what exactly is being "lost"? What metrics should be used to judge success and failure? Understanding how the United States historically approached the South China Sea, and the oceans at large, can help define these terms and inform strategy. The past doesn't offer a clear blueprint for "winning," but it gives hints. It shows which national interests have been most abiding. It reveals the prices paid to secure them and the costs when they have been ignored. It helps show where the United States should hold the line in the South China Sea, and where compromise would better serve its interests.

China's claims, especially to historic rights throughout the nine-dash line, threaten a centuries-old U.S. commitment to freedom of the seas. That commitment helped underwrite American prosperity and security. Today it stabilizes international commerce, mitigates naval tensions, and guarantees equitable access to resources. When everyone plays by an agreed set of rules, conflict is less likely. States can pursue their interests and arbitrate grievances in legal rather than military spheres. If they lose one battle, they can respect the outcome knowing they might win the next. And since they helped write the rules, they are invested in upholding the system. It is clear what happens without those rules. The early American republic spent more time fighting wars over maritime rights than nearly any other issue.

UNCLOS is one of the most ambitious and widely adopted treaties in history. It represents more than the outcome of the Third UN Conference on the Law of the Sea—it is the work of decades spent negotiating and codifying maritime law. And it has unmatched legitimacy as a truly global effort. China had as much say in its creation as any state. And the same goes for most of its neighbors, which is why they cling to it so fiercely. In the United States, a small but vocal minority stands in the way of ratification. But for every American involved in maritime affairs, whether naval, commercial, or scientific, UNCLOS is effectively the law of the land. China's claims are so antithetical to the convention that it could not long survive their acceptance. If Beijing could claim 1,000 miles of ocean and seabed, why shouldn't others? And as the aftermath of the Truman Proclamations showed, the spread of new maritime claims is nearly impossible to stop once it begins. The effects of an unraveling UNCLOS would threaten American interests from the Arctic to the Persian Gulf. Russia already toys with the idea of historic rights in the former, and Iran would seize on any opportunity to legitimize its efforts to control the latter.

China's claims undermine more than just one convention. They strike at the most basic principle of international law: the equality of states. As Yang Jiechi said, "China is a big country and other countries are small countries, and that's just a fact." But that fact shouldn't change China's legal rights or obligations. Of course, large powers seek to bend rules and institutions to accommodate their interests. The United States does. But there is a difference between bending and breaking. China's leadership would treat international law the way it does domestic law: as a tool of power but never a constraint on it. Allowing UNCLOS to be undermined without significant cost would only confirm that. Beijing would rightly conclude that if it can dispense with something as widely respected as the law of the sea, then more-contested norms are fair game. And that would inform its approach to competition across the board, from economics to space and everything in between.

The United States' other most abiding interest in the South China Sea has been its commitment to allies, balanced against neutrality on territorial disputes. American leaders have been loath to take sides in historical arguments. But they have consistently recognized the damage that could be done if the disputes turned violent and the U.S. response was found wanting. That balancing act is less complicated now that the United States has only one treaty ally left in the disputes. But the alliance with the Philippines is more strained than it has been in decades, while the likelihood of major conflict in the South China Sea is higher than at any time since the late 1930s. The Philippines might not provide the access it once did, and it is not the force multiplier that Australia, Japan, or South Korea are. But the alliance is still an important, and often underappreciated, aspect of American power in the region.

The strategic consensus in the United States since the end of World War II has been that national security is best served by actively maintaining stability in Asia. And that has been made possible by a robust network of alliances enabling U.S. presence. None of those alliances exists in a vacuum. Any perceived failure to uphold treaty obligations to the Philippines would weaken faith in U.S. commitment across the region. That is especially true because of the unique ties that bind the two countries. No other country in the region has as much cultural, interpersonal, and historical connection to the United States. The Philippines was an American colony for more than forty years. The U.S.-Philippine MDT was the first security treaty the United States signed in Asia. Filipinos and Americans fought together in every major conflict of the twentieth century. That history gives the Philippines a special claim to U.S. support in times of need.

Without a credible commitment to help defend its forces against aggression in disputed areas, Manila can't be expected to stand up to Beijing or allow increased American access. And without both of those, the United States will find it much more difficult—perhaps impossible—to dissuade further Chinese revisionism. That makes the alliance vital to securing other U.S. interests. Secretary Pompeo's clarification of the Article V commitment was an important step. It paved the way for closer coordination on South China Sea contingencies and could strengthen deterrence against China. But it also raised the stakes. Pompeo tied the United States' credibility in the Philippines even more clearly to its ability to deter and respond to Chinese aggression in disputed waters. Should Beijing test that commitment, the United States would have no ambiguity left to hide behind; any failure to respond would be condemned as abandonment of an ally in need. And Beijing would gladly drum up that failure as proof that the United States had become a paper tiger.

Since the 1980s, the PLAN has sought primacy within the first island chain and the ability to contest U.S. control of the second.[24] China hasn't yet accomplished that goal. But it is much closer in the South China Sea than Washington cares to admit. China's island building and militarization, paired with a massive naval and air force modernization program, raise serious questions about U.S. military primacy in the area. Adm. Phil Davidson, commander of U.S. Indo-Pacific Command, testified before the Senate in 2018 that China "is now capable of controlling the South China Sea in all scenarios short of war with the United States."[25] In reality, the balance has shifted even more than that.

The United States probably *could* neutralize China's artificial island bases and establish dominance over the sea and airspace of the South China Sea. But the effort would be costly, time-consuming, and uncertain. In the absence of rotational access to the Philippines, U.S. forces are too far from the theater. The closest U.S. combat aircraft are based in Okinawa and Guam, at distances of 1,300 and 1,500 miles from the Spratlys, respectively. China has four airbases in the South China Sea, not counting those along its coast. It could deploy combat aircraft to the islands for short tours of duty at the drop of a hat. Given current force structure, China would have control over the airspace above the South China Sea during the early stages of any conflict. And its considerable advantage in missile forces would turn the South China Sea into a shooting gallery. It would quickly become clear that the United States couldn't protect surface combatants operating in the area.

China's radar and signals intelligence capabilities in the islands are extensive and, most important, redundant. They couldn't be easily blinded; China would see U.S. forces coming. And thanks to their surface-to-air, antiship, jamming, and point defense systems, the islands are more defensible than often believed. Sheer size also presents complications—Pearl Harbor Naval Base could fit inside the lagoon at Subi, and Mischief Reef is roughly the size of the I-495 Beltway around Washington, DC. Plus, much of their military infrastructure has been buried or hardened against attack. Neutralizing the bases could require hundreds of missiles. And Pacific Command doesn't have the magazine capacity to spare, especially when any Sino-U.S. conflict is unlikely to be limited to the South China Sea. Anything thrown against the Spratlys would have to be taken away from the defense of Tokyo or Taipei. The math is brutal and getting worse. It increasingly looks like the United States would have little choice but to cede the South China Sea in the opening stages of a conflict.[26]

But all of that might be beside the point. The PLAN isn't looking for a fight with the U.S. Navy. Even if it won, the costs would outweigh the benefits. Instead, Beijing hopes to convince the rest of Asia that the fight is already over. The greatest danger for U.S. military power is China's peacetime activities. By using the CCG and militia to steadily erode its neighbors' access to their own waters, China hollows out the value of the United States as a regional security provider. U.S. forward presence rests on the access provided by partners. Along the South China Sea, that means Singapore and the Philippines, though U.S. surveillance flights also quietly operate out of Malaysia. Those partners increasingly wonder what they're getting in exchange for that access. The U.S. Navy might be free to sail the South China Sea, but Southeast Asians are being excluded from their own waters. The more Chinese pressure builds, the more support for the United States seems like a bad bet—one that disproportionately benefits America but not its partners.

The most vital and abiding U.S. interests in the South China Sea are freedom of the seas and America's alliance commitment to the Philippines, both of which support its ability to operate in the region. Pacific Command can't project power in the Indo-Pacific without free seas and willing allies. Those allies won't stick around if the United States defends its freedom but not theirs. And acceptance of Chinese claims would unravel both. There are of course other issues at play, but they need to be put into proper context.

Complicating Factors, Not Easy Answers

The most frequent lede in articles about the South China Sea is that it is the world's busiest shipping route. And that is true. Roughly one-third of global shipping, valued at nearly $3.4 trillion in 2016, passes through the waterway. And most of that is heading to or from the Strait of Malacca, the artery connecting East Asia to the Indian Ocean, the Middle East, Africa, and, ultimately, Europe. But the value of the South China Sea is not evenly distributed. The waterway carried just under 6 percent of total U.S. trade in goods in 2016—over $200 billion worth—and nearly 40 percent of China's, valued at almost $1.5 trillion. It is also carries almost one-fifth of Japan's trade in goods, one-quarter of Brazil's, and one-third of India's. That makes the South China Sea extremely important to worldwide commercial traffic, but not necessarily indispensable.

Should the Malacca Strait ever be closed, by disaster or hostile intent, it would be devastating to a few countries and moderately inconvenient to the rest. Shippers would in almost all cases find ways to divert. Rerouting tankers through Indonesia's Lombok and Sunda Straits would cost the world an estimated $65 million in additional shipping costs. That is less than 0.1 percent of the value of trade passing through the South China Sea each week in 2016. The numbers get worse in a scenario in which all sea lanes through the South China Sea are closed. Most trade would be diverted all the way around Australia at an added cost of about $650 million a week, or 1.0 percent of the total trade normally passing through the South China Sea.[27] The ones who would feel the impact most would be Southeast Asian states; there is no way to ship goods to or from Vietnam, for instance, without transiting the South China Sea.

Setting aside arguments about cost, it is difficult to envision a scenario in which the South China Sea is actually closed to trade. Chinese strategists have long worried about the "Malacca Dilemma"—the idea that U.S. forces might close the strait to deprive China of needed resources in a conflict. That would be damaging, but effective in the long run only if the United States also shut multiple straits throughout Indonesia, the Philippines, and Japan. And given China's growing naval, air, and missile capabilities, that seems a very tall order. It is also a choice that would have considerable negative consequences for the Philippines, Singapore, Japan, Taiwan, and South Korea—the partners and allies the United States would hope to stand with in this hypothetical conflict. An argument for China closing the sea to commercial traffic is even harder to make given its own dependence on those sea lanes. The only scenario that holds up to scrutiny is one in which neither power intentionally closed sea lanes but shippers willingly diverted around the South China Sea as much as possible during a conflict. That wouldn't be a complete closure, and goods would still flow to and from Singapore, Thailand, or Vietnam, albeit with much higher insurance premiums.

Seabed resources have also been painted as the prime driver of the disputes from time to time. Chinese government documents frequently assert that Southeast Asian parties began to contest Chinese claims only after the discovery of oil and gas basins in the 1970s. The history of the disputes shows that to be false. Others reverse the argument, claiming that it was the potential to develop hydrocarbons that drove China to expand its presence in the Paracels in 1974 and enter the Spratlys in 1988. But again, this ignores the consistency of postwar Chinese claims *on paper,* even if Beijing lacked the ability to physically assert them.

Tensions over the South China Sea predate the discovery of offshore oil and gas by decades. The first resource disputes in the islands were over guano, not hydrocarbons. And if the hunt for energy didn't spark the disputes, then fixating on it won't solve them. Unlike in 1968, now all the claimants know that there is no commercially viable oil and gas around the islands themselves. The exploitable basins are along the coasts and on a handful of underwater features like Reed Bank and Vanguard Bank. A desire to access such resources can't explain the rush to occupy, and more recently to militarize, isolated islets and reefs hundreds of miles away. Nor does it explain the other demands China makes within the nine-dash line, from fishing rights to restrictions on foreign military activities.

Oil sells for the same price on the global spot market regardless of where it is extracted. That makes drilling in disputed waters risky and much less attractive than other investments. A resource nationalism argument—that China in particular wants to secure oil for domestic use—doesn't hold up very well, either. The U.S. Geological Survey in 2012 estimated there might be 12 billion barrels of undiscovered oil beneath the South China Sea. China consumed 12.8 billion barrels in 2018 alone.[28] That leaves natural gas, which is by far the more plentiful resource in the area. The only commercially viable way to extract it is to transport it by pipeline for use or processing on shore. That means China would need to lay an undersea pipeline across nearly 1,000 miles of difficult geography and contested waters to access gas in the southern portion of the South China Sea. On-site liquefaction is the only other option. But even if a company wanted to try, it is hard to see how it could compete with liquefied natural gas (LNG) produced more cheaply from the United States and elsewhere. And it would be difficult to convince any buyer to trust in the long-term security of a natural gas contract from such a highly contested area. So the only viable use of most natural gas in the South China Sea is for electricity generation by the nearest coastal state. Gas from Reed Bank is no good to anyone outside the Philippines; Vanguard Bank's gas can help only Vietnam.

The hunt for energy resources has at times escalated the disputes. Marcos ordered the physical occupation of the Kalayaan Islands in part to secure suspected oil and gas resources. Protecting its continental shelf was clearly the driver for Malaysia's occupations in the 1980s. Mischief Reef was occupied with an eye to Reed Bank, and the *Sierra Madre* was run aground on Second Thomas as a counter. Players within the oil and gas industry—or officials close to it—have repeatedly used governments' desires to assert claims as a means of furthering their own interests. CNOOC has been particularly active in this space, but it isn't the only one. And the same is true of stakeholders in other areas—fisheries, tourism, construction, and militaries. Individual actors have been incentivized, and often heavily subsidized, to pursue their parochial interests in the South China Sea so long as it furthered the national goal of asserting claims. Those actors have often triggered or escalated tensions. But the primary drivers of the disputes remain political and strategic, not economic.

The other major concern in the South China Sea involves fisheries. For centuries, before anyone thought to claim or occupy the scattered reefs, fisherfolk had been making their living in the South China Sea. It is among the most biodiverse marine habitats on the planet. The waterway accounts for an estimated 12 percent of global fish catch and may employ more than half of the world's fishing vessels. Around 3.7 million people make their livelihoods from the area's fishing industry. The 2016 arbitral award concluded that Chinese, Vietnamese, and Filipino fishers could all claim traditional rights at Scarborough Shoal. The same should be true for Chinese and Vietnamese boats in the Paracels. In the Spratlys and waters farther south, Southeast Asian fishers continue to operate commercially while China heavily subsidizes its fleets to show the flag where they otherwise wouldn't operate.[29]

All this activity puts the South China Sea fishery under desperate threat. Fish stocks have been depleted by between 70 and 95 percent since the 1950s. Catch rates declined as much as 75 percent over the past two decades.[30] And the area's coral reefs were declining by 16 percent per decade *before* China's clam harvesters and dredgers showed up. Since 2015, the clam diggers have severely damaged or destroyed about twenty-five thousand acres of reef and the dredgers have torn up another fifteen thousand.[31] If something doesn't change soon, the region will see a cascade of fish stock collapses. That will devastate coastal communities, especially in the Philippines and Vietnam, and threaten food security across the region. Of course, no one knows exactly how close that day is. The disputes make it impossible to complete regionwide stock assessments. But it is thought to be a matter of years, not decades.

Possible Futures

There are three likely futures for the South China Sea. The first is the one Beijing seeks and toward which the region is drifting. China's peacetime coercion will continue to raise the risks to its neighbors for undertaking normal activities in their own waters. It will become impossible to attract foreign investment in off-shore oil and gas exploration or other commercial activity. Fishers will lose their livelihoods, either because the Chinese militia and coast guard make life too difficult or gross overfishing and reef destruction wipes out stocks. Most other claimants will eventually hold their noses and take whatever deal Beijing is still putting on the table. The only alternative would be to watch China finish taking what it wants. The U.S.-Philippines alliance will likely end as Manila concludes that it only irritates Beijing. U.S. ability to project power into the South China Sea will steadily decline as China's grows. Other states will more aggressively assert their own excessive maritime claims, further undermining UNCLOS. This will start with bad actors, but eventually spread as rule-abiding states see themselves disadvantaged by the excessive claims of their neighbors. And China, confident in America's inexorable decline, will challenge other rules and institutions, especially in Asia. The net effect will be a regional and global order that is less stable and much more threatening to the interests of the United States and its remaining allies.

The second option is conflict. Neither side wants a fight, but that doesn't make one impossible. A PLAN ship came within 45 yards of hitting the USS *Decatur* during a FONOP in 2018.[32] Militia boats have behaved even more aggressively. Miscalculations are plausible. And while there are mechanisms to prevent incidents and de-escalate those that occur, Chinese ships rarely follow the bridge-to-bridge protocols and hotlines often go unanswered.[33] Even more likely is that something goes wrong during one of the many occasions when Chinese boats play chicken with their counterparts from Southeast Asia. A CCG vessel rammed and sank a Vietnamese fishing boat in the Paracels in April 2020.[34] A likely militia ship did the same to a Filipino fishing boat in October 2019.[35] Then it left the crew to their fate; luckily, a passing Vietnamese boat rescued them. In many other cases, especially during the harassment of oil and gas activities, collisions have been avoided by the narrowest margins. Given how many actors China has deployed to its neighbors' waters, and how aggressively they are encouraged to behave, a loss of life seems inevitable. Were that to involve the Philippines, the United States might be called upon to respond under the MDT. Failure to do so would only accelerate Chinese control over the South China Sea. But armed intervention would probably require the United States to jump several rungs up the escalation ladder.[36] And if both sides felt compelled to posture rather than de-escalate, things could get out of hand. No matter how such a conflict ended, each would lose more than it gained.

The third option—the only one that would secure American interests at an acceptable cost—would be leveraging China toward a compromise its neighbors and the international community could live with. Before exploring how that might happen, it is important to set the parameters. What end-state should be acceptable to the United States and its partners? As U.S. officials have been saying since the 1990s, any agreement between the claimants must be consistent with UNCLOS. That means it must recognize all the freedoms of the seas: unimpeded navigation for commercial traffic, access for foreign navies, and resource rights for coastal states. And it must be reached without force or coercion. Luckily, the convention provides plenty of opportunities for compromise if all sides are serious about it.

There is no shortage of ideas about how to equitably manage the South China Sea disputes. Unfortunately, none of them is going to be included in the China-ASEAN COC. The organization has invested too much energy to just abandon the code, but it is past time to accept its limitations. The COC, if completed, will lay out broad principles for cooperation. Those could be helpful, but they will be insufficient. There will need to be separate and much more detailed negotiations on fisheries, marine conservation, oil and gas exploration, law enforcement cooperation, and more. And those discussions should include only the claimants—other ASEAN states don't need to be there and generally don't want to be. The most helpful thing the COC could do is endorse those parallel negotiations and establish a mechanism to mediate disputes over their interpretation. Those talks shouldn't wait for the completion of the COC. By the time ASEAN and China finish the code, there won't be any fish left to manage.

Forging a network of agreements to manage the South China Sea will be difficult and drawn out. But it is the only way forward. And if all parties negotiate in good faith, there are sufficient loopholes in both UNCLOS and their domestic laws to make it work. For instance, the South China Sea is a semi-enclosed sea. Under Article 123 of the convention, the states around it are obligated to cooperate on marine environmental protection and conservation of fish stocks. Similar obligations are woven throughout the treaty. And since China has never clearly defined the nine-dash line or historic rights, Beijing could get quite creative in what those "rights" entail. It could decide that helping manage stocks and enforce mutually agreed rules is enough; it doesn't need to fish without permission in its neighbors' waters. A deal on oil and gas resources would be more complicated, but not impossible.[37] And it might be made easier by global shifts in energy markets. The boom in renewables and LNG exports could negate the value of most offshore exploitation in the South China Sea. That is probably already true of Reed Bank, for instance. The Philippines is facing an energy crunch

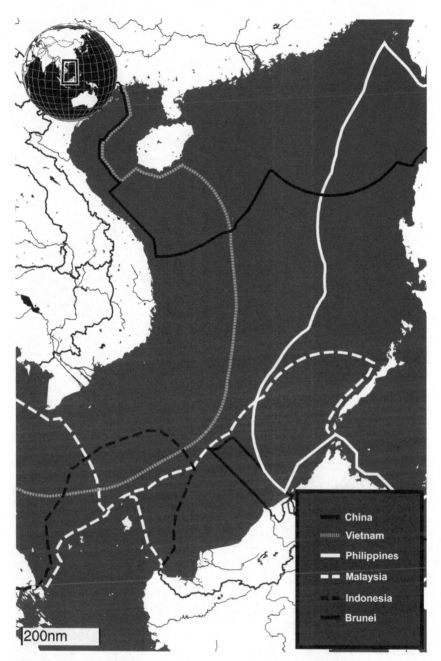

China

Vietnam

Philippines

Malaysia

Indonesia

Brunei

200nm

Figure 10.1 EEZ claims in the South China Sea, 2021. Created using Mapcreator and OpenStreetMap.

Note: Figures 10.1 and 10.2 show only those EEZs and continental shelves explicitly claimed in accordance with international law. For readability, Taiwan's claims are not displayed but would overlap with the eastern two-thirds of those shown for China.

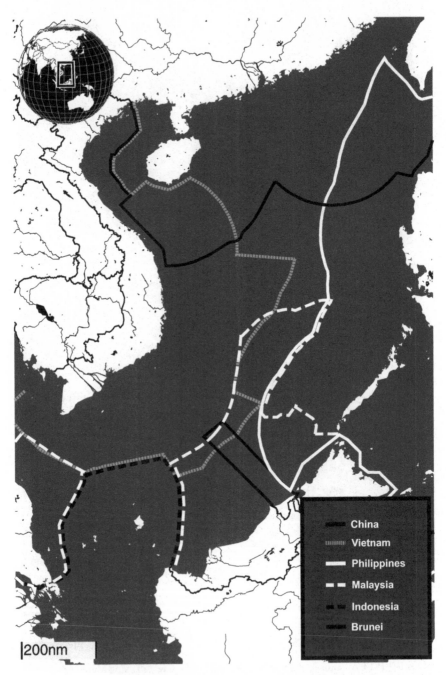

Figure 10.2 Continental shelf claims in the South China Sea, 2021. Created using Mapcreator and OpenStreetMap.

that will require a turn toward either coal or LNG. By the time a project could be brought online at Reed Bank, its gas might no longer be in demand.

As for the islands themselves, the sovereignty disputes are irreconcilable, at least for a while. The only way to divide them up would be arbitration before the International Court of Justice, which none of the parties has endorsed. The most likely endgame in the Spratlys is recognition of the current status quo. Southwest Cay is the only island to ever change hands between two of the modern claimants. In all other cases, the one who got there first (excepting Japan and France, which publicly ceded or quietly abandoned their claims, respectively) is still in control. Scarborough is best left unoccupied, as it has always been, with a cooperative management scheme for traditional fishing. The Paracels are the toughest nut to crack. Vietnam's claim is probably older, but China has administered the entire group for nearly fifty years; it won't leave. Both sides should enjoy traditional fishing rights around the islands. But otherwise, as Deng Xiaoping said, "It is not an urgent issue and can wait. . . . [T]he next generation will have more wisdom."[38]

Charting a Course

The details of the arrangements between China and its neighbors shouldn't matter to the United States. The goal of American policy should be to cajole China into seeking compromise and then support the claimants in whatever they decide, so long as it is legal and peaceable. Doing so will require a years-long effort to impose costs and shape incentives. And the United States can't do it alone; it must involve a coalition of Asian and European partners. That coalition must impose diplomatic and economic costs, as well as strengthen Southeast Asian capabilities and help deter outright aggression from China. Since 2016, Beijing has been running away with the game and has little reason to want a deal. But that could change if a critical mass of states began treating China the way they do other bad actors—Russia, for instance, after its annexation of Crimea and support for paramilitaries in eastern Ukraine. That would make it apparent that Beijing's policies in the South China Sea undermine its larger goals. It would signal that China can be a global leader or a regional bully, but not both.

Building that international coalition will require persistent, multifaceted lobbying from U.S. officials. The South China Sea and the 2016 arbitral award should be raised at every opportunity: ASEAN meetings, the Group of Seven, the United Nations General Assembly, and so on. And Washington should be clear with Manila and Hanoi that they must speak up for themselves if they expect continued international support. The Philippine government will need to start advocating for itself after Duterte leaves office in 2022, if not sooner.

And Vietnam will need to get more consistent in its public diplomacy. All of Vietnam's top leaders are either over the mandatory retirement age or will be before the next Party Congress in 2026. A new generation of leadership will take over sooner rather than later, and they might be more willing to rock the boat. The United States, Japan, Australia, Europe, and eventually India should help amplify these messages, but they need claimants to line up behind.

The United States should also recognize that there are limits to how far Southeast Asian states can go. They are too economically exposed to China and lack the geopolitical heft to impose serious costs themselves. That is where foreign partners come in. They must play the bad cops, imposing costs so Philippine and Vietnamese offers of compromise are more attractive. Public naming and shaming has an important role in this. The United States and other parties should document and publish Chinese illegal and aggressive behavior more consistently, as they do for Russia, Iran, and North Korea. And those campaigns should be linked to targeted economic punishments. The Trump administration's decision to add dredging and construction companies to the Entity List was symbolic but didn't hurt anyone's bottom line. To do that, the United States will need to impose financial sanctions on companies and individuals engaged in specific, well-documented illegal activity. That could include fishing, tourism, telecommunications, and energy companies, among others. Washington and Brussels have been quick to engage in such targeted punishments against Russian and North Korean illicit actors. It is time to treat China's criminal networks the same way.

The United States should stay far away from the historical arguments over sovereignty, as it has for the past century. None of the claims is as strong as their proponents suggest. And there is no way for Washington to support one partner or ally without alienating others. That would only weaken U.S. influence and sow discord among the Southeast Asian claimants. The one exception is Scarborough Shoal. But any decision to recognize Philippine sovereignty or administration now would be dangerous. It would raise questions about whether the MDT requires the United States to help eject Chinese forces at the shoal, and it could provoke Beijing to build a permanent facility. Either scenario would precipitate a crisis. Instead, the United States should publicly champion Philippine rights to fish at the shoal and encourage a lasting agreement between Manila and Beijing to that effect. It should reiterate that the United States would respond in consultation with the Philippines to any attack on Filipino ships or personnel at Scarborough. And U.S. officials should reiterate President Obama's warning that any effort to permanently build on the reef would precipitate a crisis in U.S.-China relations.

On the legal front, the most important thing the United States could do is ratify UNCLOS. The substantive arguments against the convention were laid to rest in 1994. An ideological minority has held the convention hostage in the

Senate for too long. The failure to ratify excludes American companies from the deep seabed concessions on which opponents are so fixated. It prevents the United States from documenting the limits of its extended continental shelf, which is especially worrying in the Arctic. It robs the United States of a voice in new rulemaking in the oceans. And it undermines U.S. credibility in defending freedom of the seas. Accusing Washington of hypocrisy is one of Beijing's best shields against criticism. It is time to take it away.

It is also time for Washington to crack open the door to discussions with Beijing on some of their differing legal interpretations. China's claims to historic rights, EEZs and continental shelves from small rocks, claims to underwater features, and baselines between islands all contradict settled law. But the two issues that most often provoke tensions between Beijing and Washington are more contested. First are the rules concerning innocent passage of warships through the territorial sea. China demands prior authorization; the United States refuses. This is the most common target for U.S. FONOPs, both in the South China Sea and worldwide. UNCLOS *implies* that the United States is right, but the issue has never been settled. It nearly sank the entire convention at the eleventh hour. If the Soviets had been willing to endorse a requirement for prior notification rather than prior authorization back in 1958, it would have become part of the Convention on the Territorial Sea and Contiguous Zone. That remains the obvious compromise, and perhaps the only one that might someday garner an international consensus.

The second disagreement is over the right of coastal states to restrict foreign military activity in the EEZ. UNCLOS is more settled on this. The language of the convention is convoluted, but the negotiators' intent is clear: foreign military vessels have largely unrestricted rights in the EEZ. But the convention is not meant to be the final word on every maritime issue. And just because a state has a legal right to do something doesn't mean it has to. Washington and Moscow negotiated the Incidents at Sea Agreement in 1972 in which both sides agreed to refrain from certain actions at sea that were otherwise legal. At the 2014 Western Pacific Naval Symposium, twenty-one countries, including China and the United States, agreed to the Code for Unplanned Encounters at Sea. That agreement sets out a list of things naval forces voluntarily agree to do, or not do, to avoid escalations at sea. These are not perfect parallels and China often doesn't abide by its commitments under the Code for Unplanned Encounters at Sea. But they suggest that China and the United States could, with enough political will, negotiate voluntary restrictions on certain military activities. That might include specific kinds of surveillance at a certain distance from shore. And the gulf between the two sides on these issues should shrink as the PLAN expands its global reach, which increasingly involves its own surveillance activities near foreign shores.

Any bilateral negotiations on these issues should be predicated on progress between China and the other claimants. Beijing insists that its disagreements with Washington have nothing to do with those involving Manila or Hanoi. But that isn't true. The most important of America's interests in the disputes involve its commitment to allies and freedom of the seas, not just naval freedoms. A deal over innocent passage or military surveillance wouldn't address either. Talks on bilateral issues should be offered as a concession once China shows good faith with its neighbors, not before. Negotiating a U.S.-China agreement first would only reinforce the narrative that the United States doesn't care about Southeast Asian maritime rights and undermine any effort to steer Beijing toward a broad compromise.

There are no military solutions in the South China Sea—at least, none that wouldn't cost all sides more than they gained. But American hard power will play an indispensable role in any successful strategy. A multilateral campaign to change Beijing's calculus through diplomatic, economic, and legal pressure will take years. And in the meantime, China's military power will continue to grow. Pressure on its neighbors will build. The only thing that will buy them the space and time they need to see through a long-term strategy is U.S. military support. The United States and other security partners must continue to provide capacity-building support to the region. Southeast Asian navies and coast guards will never stand toe-to-toe with the PLAN and CCG. But they can maintain a degree of access to their own waters. They can continue to monitor and report on Chinese activities. They can keep their outposts resupplied in the face of Chinese intimidation. And, as Vietnam has, they can develop the ability to hit back. Vietnam's modest fleet of submarines and its fourth-generation fighter jets wouldn't last long against the People's Liberation Army. But they would exact a toll, and China knows it. That raises the costs for aggression and helps incentivize Beijing to play the long game rather than resorting to force.

The most important role the U.S. military can play in the region is direct deterrence on behalf of the Philippines. The presence of a U.S. P8 overhead affected China's calculations at Second Thomas Shoal in 2014. The flyover by A-10s and Obama's warning to Xi probably averted a second crisis at Scarborough in 2016. But as Chinese strength grows, it will test the seams of the alliance more often. And in the absence of rotational access to the Philippines, the United States will find it increasingly difficult to credibly respond to provocations. If China opts to remove the *Sierra Madre* by force, for instance, U.S. power in Okinawa and Guam won't matter. The United States needs a small but capable force of air and missile assets in the Philippines, close enough to hold Chinese surface ships at risk and respond to small provocations before they escalate.

Without EDCA, or something like it, the alliance is dangerously brittle. Mike Pompeo stood on the Manila tarmac and made a promise—one that was overdue.

But it will be increasingly hard to keep. The U.S. and Philippine militaries should have spent the years since 2016 building up the EDCA sites and investing in joint capabilities. Instead, they have been fighting a rearguard action just to save the foundations of the alliance. After 2022, there will need to be a concerted effort to assess damage and build back. In the meantime, U.S. diplomats and military officials should be honest with their Filipino counterparts. The Philippine Supreme Court was right in 2016: if the allies are going to maintain their "collective capacity to resist armed attack," then the United States needs greater access.

China's control over disputed waters is steadily growing. The other claimants are running out of time. So is the United States if it hopes to secure its national interests, some of which are as old as the South China Sea disputes themselves. There are some who insist that the South China Sea is already lost. That isn't true, at least not yet. No other government has endorsed China's interpretation of maritime law. No country has accepted the nine-dash line. The United States is still the preferred security partner for most of the region. And the U.S.-Philippines alliance is still alive and overwhelmingly popular. There are also those who say that China will never compromise, no matter what. But there is no evidence that Beijing would sacrifice its global ambitions for the sake of historic fishing rights off Indonesia or to keep Vietnam from drilling at Vanguard Bank. The international community has never imposed enough cost on Beijing to test the proposition.

There is still a path to secure U.S. national interests at an acceptable cost. It is narrower and more uncertain than it was a few years ago, but that should be cause for urgency, not resignation. The United States and its allies are "losing" the South China Sea. They haven't yet "lost."

NOTES

Introduction

1. Harry B. Harris Jr., remarks at the Australian Strategic Policy Institute, March 31, 2015.
2. For simplicity, this book uses "nautical mile" on first reference in each chapter and thereafter uses "miles" to signify nautical miles.
3. Tommy Koh, *Building a New Legal Order for the Oceans* (Singapore: National University of Singapore Press, 2020), 174.
4. Ibid., 176.
5. Ann L. Hollick, *U.S. Foreign Policy and the Law of the Sea* (Princeton, NJ: Princeton University Press, 1981), 5.
6. Koh, *Building a New Legal Order*, 181.
7. Michael Green, *By More Than Providence: Grand Strategy and American Power in the Asia Pacific Since 1783* (New York: Columbia University Press, 2017).
8. U.S. Department of State, Office of the Historian, "Barbary Wars, 1801–1805 and 1815–1816," accessed June 7, 2020, https://history.state.gov/milestones/1801-1829/barbary-wars.
9. Ibid.
10. Hunter Stires, "'They Were Playing Chicken'—The U.S. Asiatic Fleet's Gray-Zone Deterrence Campaign against Japan, 1937–40," *Naval War College Review* 72, no. 3 (Summer 2019): 142, https://digital-commons.usnwc.edu/cgi/viewcontent.cgi?article=8046&context=nwc-review.
11. Ibid.
12. Hillary Rodham Clinton, "Remarks at Press Availability," July 23, 2010, https://2009-2017.state.gov/secretary/20092013clinton/rm/2010/07/145095.htm.

Chapter 1

1. Quoted in Jay L. Batongbacal and Efren P. Carandang, eds., *Bajo de Masinloc: Scarborough Shoal Maps and Documents* (Taguig City, Philippines: National Mapping and Resource Information Authority, 2014), 59–62.
2. François-Xavier Bonnet, *Geopolitics of Scarborough Shoal*, IRASEC Discussion Paper 14 (Bangkok: Research Institute on Contemporary Southeast Asia, November 2012), 8–9.
3. Raul (Pete) Pedrozo, *China versus Vietnam: An Analysis of the Competing Claims in the South China Sea*, CNA Occasional Paper (Arlington, VA: CNA, August 2014), 39.
4. The islands were the site of frequent shipwrecks. Most famously, in 1698 the French vessel *Amphitrite* wrecked on the eastern group of islands which still bears its name. See Monique Chemillier-Gendreau, *Sovereignty over the Paracel and Spratly Islands* (The Hague: Kluwer Law International, 2000), 35.
5. Ibid., 36.

6. François-Xavier Bonnet, "The Spratlys: A Past Revisited," *World Bulletin* 23 (July–December 2004): 15.

7. Stein Tønnesson, "The South China Sea in the Age of European Decline," *Modern Asian Studies* 40, no. 1 (February 2006): 6.

8. Bill Hayton, "The Modern Origins of China's South China Sea Claims: Maps, Misunderstandings, and the Maritime Geobody," *Modern China* 45, no. 2 (2019): 7.

9. Chemillier-Gendreau, *Sovereignty over the Paracel and Spratlys Islands*, 36–37.

10. Pratas Island is a small sandy cay on the much larger Pratas Reef. But the two names are often used interchangeably.

11. Ulises Granados, "Japanese Expansion into the South China Sea: Colonization and Conflict, 1902–1939," *Journal of Asian History* 42, no. 2 (2008): 123.

12. "Japan and the Island of Pratas," *Hong Kong Daily Press*, December 7, 1907, cited in Hayton, "Modern Origins," 8.

13. Hayton, "Modern Origins," 11–12; Granados, "Japanese Expansion," 123.

14. Hayton, "Modern Origins," 11–12.

15. Pedrozo, *China versus Vietnam*, 88.

16. U.S. Navy Hydrographic Office, *Asiatic Pilot* (Washington, DC: Government Printing Office, 1915), 4:119.

17. Granados, "Japanese Expansion," 124, 129.

18. Pedrozo, *China versus Vietnam*, 27.

19. Granados, "Japanese Expansion," 125–26.

20. Ibid., 129.

21. Pedrozo, *China versus Vietnam*, 15.

22. Ibid., 19.

23. Hayton, "Modern Origins," 18–19.

24. Pedrozo, *China versus Vietnam*, 50.

25. Contemporary reports in China claimed that France had annexed nine islands rather than seven. This seems to be because Chinese observers were making their own count based on the coordinates claimed in 1930 rather than the formal list of islands annexed in 1933. Of course, the actual number could be seven, nine, or even more depending on how Paris chose to interpret the "dependent islets" clause of its annexation notice.

26. Tønnesson, "The South China Sea in the Age of European Decline," 5–8.

27. *China Press*, August 4, 1933, quoted in Bonnet, "The Spratlys," 16.

28. Hayton, "Modern Origins," 20–21.

29. Bonnet, "The Spratlys," 17.

30. H. Chiu and C. H. Park, "Legal Status of the Paracel and Spratly Islands," *Ocean Development and International Law* 3 (1975): 12, quoted in Bill Hayton, "When Good Lawyers Write Bad History: Unreliable Evidence and the South China Sea Territorial Dispute," *Ocean Development and International Law* 48, no. 1 (2017): 26.

31. Hayton, "Modern Origins," 24–25.

32. Bonnet, *Geopolitics of Scarborough Shoal*, 17.

33. Hayton, "Modern Origins," 28–29.

34. Pedrozo, *China versus Vietnam*, 16.

35. Bill Hayton, *The South China Sea: The Struggle for Power in Asia* (New Haven, CT: Yale University Press, 2014), 55–56.

36. Bonnet, "The Spratlys," 20.

37. Hayton, "Modern Origins," 32–34.

38. Granados, "Japanese Expansion," 133.

39. Bonnet, "The Spratlys," 18.

40. *Philippine Tribune*, August 23, 1933, quoted in ibid.

41. Aileen S. P. Baviera and Jay Batongbacal, *The West Philippine Sea: The Territorial and Maritime Jurisdiction Disputes from a Filipino Perspective: A Primer*, monograph, University of the Philippines, Manila, 2013, 21, https://ac.upd.edu.ph/index.php/resources/books-and-monographs/1352-the-west-philippine-sea-the-territorial-and-maritime-jurisdiction-disputes-from-a-filipino-perspective.

42. Bonnet, "The Spratlys," 18.

43. Letter from W. Carr to the Secretary of War, October 9, 1933, quoted in ibid., 19.

44. Bonnet, "The Spratlys," 19.

45. Tønnesson, "The South China Sea in the Age of European Decline," 21.

46. See Batongbacal and Carandang, *Bajo de Masinloc*, 13, 18–20.

47. U.S. Bureau of the Census, *Census of the Philippine Islands*, vol. 1 (1918), 595, quoted in ibid., 51.

48. Batongbacal and Carandang, *Bajo de Masinloc*, 59–62.

49. Granados, "Japanese Expansion," 135.

50. Stires, " 'They Were Playing Chicken,' " 147.

51. Ibid., 148–50.

52. Tønnesson, "The South China Sea in the Age of European Decline," 9–10.

53. Granados, "Japanese Expansion," 135–36.

54. Tønnesson, "The South China Sea in the Age of European Decline," 13.

55. Ibid., 10.

56. Granados, "Japanese Expansion," 135–36.

57. Tønnesson, "The South China Sea in the Age of European Decline," 11–12.

58. Granados, "Japanese Expansion," 135–36.

59. Ibid., 137.

60. Ibid., 138.

61. Tønnesson, "The South China Sea in the Age of European Decline," 15.

62. Granados, "Japanese Expansion," 138–39.

63. Bonnet, "The Spratlys," 19–20.

64. Letter from the American Consulate of Java to the Secretary of State, July 10, 1939, quoted in ibid., 20.

65. Bonnet, "The Spratlys," 21.

66. U.S. Department of State, Office of Intelligence Research, "Islands of the South China Sea," Intelligence Report 7283, August 17, 1956, 3–4, https://www.cia.gov/readingroom/docum ent/cia-rdp08c01297r000300180019-2.

67. Reminiscences of Thomas C. Hart [Adm., USN (Ret.)], Columbia University Oral History Research Office (New York), microfiche, accessed at Naval Historical Collection, Naval War College, Newport, RI, quoted in Stires, " 'They Were Playing Chicken,' " 154.

68. Eric Morris, *Corregidor: The American Alamo of World War II* (New York: Cooper Square Press, 1981), 52–54.

69. Ibid., 209, 470.

70. Ibid., 61–63, 109–14.

71. Ibid., 448.

72. "Darter (SS 227)," U.S. Naval History and Heritage Command, January 30, 2017, https:// www.history.navy.mil/research/library/online-reading-room/title-list-alphabetically/u/uni ted-states-submarine-losses/darter-ss-227.html.

73. Hayton, *The South China Sea*, 57.

74. A. B. Feuer, *Commando: The M/Z Unit's Secret War against Japan* (Westport, CT: Praeger, 1996), 70–76.

75. Cairo Declaration, November 26, 1943, Wilson Center Digital Archive, https://digitalarch ive.wilsoncenter.org/document/122101.

76. Potsdam Declaration, July 26, 1945, National Diet Library, para. 8, https://www.ndl.go.jp/ constitution/e/etc/c06.html.

77. Hayton, *The South China Sea*, 57.

78. U.S. Department of State, "Islands of the South China Sea," 9.

79. Chemillier-Gendreau, *Sovereignty over the Paracel and Spratlys Islands*, 39.

80. Letter from General Juin, Chief of Staff of National Defense, to the Chairman of the Committee on Indochina, October 7, 1946, quoted in Pedrozo, *China versus Vietnam*, 49.

81. Tønnesson, "The South China Sea in the Age of European Decline," 25.

82. Ibid., 24.

83. Hayton, *The South China Sea*, 58.

84. Ibid., 63.

85. Tønnesson, "The South China Sea in the Age of European Decline," 26–27.

86. Pedrozo, *China versus Vietnam*, 20–21.
87. Chris P. C. Chung, "Drawing the U-Shaped Line: China's Claim in the South China Sea, 1946–1974," *Modern China* 42, no. 1 (January 2016): 43, cited in Hayton, "Modern Origins," 34.
88. Hayton, "Modern Origins," 34–35.
89. To avoid confusion, this book uses the pinyin romanization of Chinese words and place names in most cases, though that system was not formally adopted until 1958 and then only in the PRC.
90. Hayton, *The South China Sea*, 59.
91. Tønnesson, "The South China Sea in the Age of European Decline," 21–22.
92. Feliciano Belmonte Jr., "P.I. Claim to Spratly Islands in 1946 Bared," *Manila Chronicle*, June 14, 1956.
93. Tønnesson, "The South China Sea in the Age of European Decline," 21–22.
94. Ibid.
95. An exact date is hard to pin down, but the French meteorology service in Indochina reported that weather reports from the ROC outposts on Woody Island and Itu Aba ceased on May 4 and 5. See ibid., 33.
96. Pedrozo, *China versus Vietnam*, 32.
97. "Nanwei" is the name of Spratly Island itself. The PRC wouldn't follow the ROC in officially adopting the name "Nansha" for the entire island group until 1952. "Hsisha" would become standardized as "Xisha" with the adoption of pinyin in 1958. Jerome Alan Cohen and Hungdah Chiuh, *People's China and International Law: A Documentary Study* (Princeton, NJ: Princeton University Press, 1974), 345.
98. Pedrozo, *China versus Vietnam*, 32.
99. Ibid., 96.
100. Adrian David, "How Malaysia's Five Naval Stations at Spratlys Were Built," *New Straits Times*, March 4, 2019, https://www.nst.com.my/news/nation/2019/03/465854/how-malaysias-five-naval-stations-spratlys-were-built.

Chapter 2

1. Hollick, *U.S. Foreign Policy and the Law of the Sea*, 112.
2. Ibid., 19.
3. Koh, *Building a New Legal Order*, 113–14.
4. Hollick, *U.S. Foreign Policy and Law of the Sea*, 20–23.
5. Ibid., 28–30.
6. Ibid., 34–61.
7. Ibid., 68–79.
8. Ibid., 72.
9. See Northwest Atlantic Fisheries Organization, "International Commission for the Northwest Atlantic Fisheries (ICNAF)," accessed June 20, 2020, https://www.nafo.int/About-us/ICNAF/icnaf-convention#convention.
10. See North Pacific Anadromous Fish Commission, "International North Pacific Fisheries Commission (1952–1992)," accessed June 20, 2020, https://npafc.org/inpfc/.
11. Hollick, *U.S. Foreign Policy and Law of the Sea*, 99–101.
12. Ibid., 83–89, 100–101.
13. Ibid., 118.
14. Ibid., 111–12.
15. Ibid., 115–16.
16. Ibid., 94.
17. International Law Commission, Report of the International Law Commission to the General Assembly, Document A/3159, July 1956, Art. 3, in *Yearbook of the International Law Commission 1956 Volume II: Documents of the Eighth Sessions, Including the Report of the Commission to the General Assembly*, A/CN.4/SER.A/1956/Add.1 (New York: United Nations, 1957), 256, https://legal.un.org/ilc/publications/yearbooks/english/ilc_1956_v2.pdf.
18. Koh, *Building a New Legal Order*, 48.

19. Hollick, *U.S. Foreign Policy and the Law of the Sea*, 127–40.
20. Nugroho Wisnumurti, "Legal Regimes of Archipelagic States," *Jakarta Post*, March 27, 2014, https://www.thejakartapost.com/news/2014/03/27/legal-regimes-archipelagic-states.html.
21. Hollick, *U.S. Foreign Policy and the Law of the Sea*, 136–38.
22. United Nations Convention on the Territorial Sea and the Contiguous Zone, Geneva, Switzerland, April 29, 1958, https://treaties.un.org/doc/Treaties/1964/11/19641122%2002-14%20AM/Ch_XXI_01_2_3_4_5p.pdf.
23. Hollick, *U.S. Foreign Policy and the Law of the Sea*, 141–42.
24. United Nations Convention on the Territorial Sea and the Contiguous Zone.
25. International Law Commission, Report of the International Law Commission, Art. 24.
26. Hollick, *U.S. Foreign Policy and the Law of the Sea*, 144.
27. United Nations Convention on the High Seas, Geneva, Switzerland, April 29, 1958, https://treaties.un.org/doc/Treaties/1964/11/19641122%2002-14%20AM/Ch_XXI_01_2_3_4_5p.pdf.
28. Hollick, *U.S. Foreign Policy and the Law of the Sea*, 145–46.
29. Convention on Fishing and Conservation of the Living Resources of the High Seas, Geneva, Switzerland, April 29, 1958, https://treaties.un.org/doc/Treaties/1964/11/19641122%2002-14%20AM/Ch_XXI_01_2_3_4_5p.pdf.
30. Hollick, *U.S. Foreign Policy and the Law of the Sea*, 150–51.
31. United Nations Convention on the Continental Shelf, Geneva, Switzerland, April 29, 1958, https://treaties.un.org/doc/Treaties/1964/11/19641122%2002-14%20AM/Ch_XXI_01_2_3_4_5p.pdf.
32. CIA, *Law of the Sea Country Study: Philippines*, May 1974, 5, https://www.cia.gov/readingroom/docs/CIA-RDP79-01054A000100100001-9.pdf.
33. Epsey Cooke Farrell, *The Socialist Republic of Vietnam and the Law of the Sea: An Analysis of Vietnamese Behavior within the Emerging International Oceans Regime* (The Hague: Martinus Nijhoff, 1998), 113.
34. United Nations Treaty Collection, Depositary, Status of Treaties, Chapter 21: Law of the Sea, accessed July 5, 2020, https://treaties.un.org/pages/ViewDetails.aspx?src=TREATY&mtdsg_no=XXI-1&chapter=21&clang=_en.
35. Koh, *Building a New Legal Order for the Oceans*, 48.
36. Hollick, *U.S. Foreign Policy and the Law of the Sea*, 157–58.
37. Arthur H. Dean, "The Second Geneva Conference on the Law of the Sea: The Fight for Freedom of the Seas," *American Journal of International Law* 54, no. 4 (October 1960): 779–82.
38. United Nations Treaty Collection, Chapter 21: Law of the Sea.
39. Declaration of the Government of the People's Republic of China on China's Territorial Sea, September 4, 1958, https://www.documentcloud.org/documents/1341822-declaration-of-the-government-of-the-prc-on.html. For a discussion of North Vietnamese premier Pham Van Dong's response to China's declaration, see Chapter 3.
40. For more on these Chinese naming conventions, see Chapter 1.
41. Nugroho Wisnumurti, "Legal Regimes of Archipelagic States."
42. *Yearbook of the International Law Commission 1955*, Vol. 2, A/CN.4/Ser.A/1955/Add.1 (New York: United Nations, 1960), 52–53, https://legal.un.org/ilc/publications/yearbooks/english/ilc_1955_v2.pdf.
43. CIA, *Law of the Sea Country Study: Philippines*, 5–6.
44. Hanns Jürgen Buchholz, *Law of the Sea Zones in the Pacific Ocean* (Singapore: Institute of Southeast Asian Studies, 1987), 34.
45. John G. Butcher and R. E. Elson, *Sovereignty and the Sea: How Indonesia Became an Archipelagic State* (Singapore: NUS Press, 2017), 143.

Chapter 3

1. Minutes of Washington Special Actions Group Meeting [Washington, January 25, 1974], *Foreign Relations of the United States, 1969–1976*, vol. 10, *Vietnam, January 1973–July 1975*, Document 122, https://history.state.gov/historicaldocuments/frus1969-76v10/d122.

2. Thailand has no bilateral defense treaty with the United States. But in a 1962 communiqué between Thai foreign minister Thanat Khoman and U.S. secretary of state Dean Rusk, Washington pledged to defend Thailand against aggression. Both countries publicly cite this communiqué, along with the otherwise defunct Manila Pact, which established the Southeast Asia Treaty Organization, as the basis of the alliance.

3. Republic of Vietnam Ministry of Foreign Affairs, White Paper on the Hoang Sa (Paracel) and Truong Sa (Spratly) Islands, 1975, 18, https://huongduongtxd.com/tshs_whitepaper.pdf.

4. Ibid., 7.

5. Chemillier-Gendreau, Sovereignty over the Paracel and Spratlys Islands, 42.

6. Pedrozo, China versus Vietnam, 20, 23.

7. Ibid., 42.

8. Ibid., 55.

9. Ibid., 52.

10. U.S. Department of State, "Islands of the South China Sea," 2.

11. Marwyn Samuels, Contest for the South China Sea (New York: Methuen, 1982), 168–71.

12. A. V. H. Hartendorp, History of Industry and Trade of the Philippines: The Magsaysay Administration (Manila: Philippine Education Company, 1961), 209–10.

13. Ibid., 210–11.

14. Ibid., 211.

15. The description of the note is vague, but it was presumably sent to the Philippine Ministry of Foreign Affairs, which suggests it was intended as a warning to the Philippine government, not just Meads.

16. U.S. Department of State, "Islands of the South China Sea," 4.

17. Hayton, The South China Sea, 64–65.

18. Pedrozo, China versus Vietnam, 19.

19. Hayton, The South China Sea, 65.

20. Pedrozo, China versus Vietnam, 19.

21. Baviera and Batongbacal, The West Philippine Sea, 21.

22. Hartendorp, History of Industry and Trade, 213.

23. Hayton, The South China Sea, 67; U.S. Department of State, "Islands of the South China Sea," 5.

24. Pedrozo, China versus Vietnam, 22.

25. U.S. Department of State, "Islands of the South China Sea," 4.

26. Hartendorp, History of Industry and Trade, 216, 226; U.S. Department of State, "Islands of the South China Sea," 4.

27. Hayton, The South China Sea, 67.

28. Hartendorp, History of Industry and Trade, 222.

29. Hayton, The South China Sea, 67.

30. Chemillier-Gendreau, Sovereignty over the Paracel and Spratlys Islands, 43.

31. Hartendorp, History of Industry and Trade, 226–27.

32. Ibid., 230.

33. Ibid., 232.

34. U.S. Department of State, "Islands of the South China Sea," iii.

35. Ibid., 1.

36. Ibid., 2.

37. Letter from the Chargé d'Affaires of the Permanent Mission of China to the United Nations Addressed to the Secretary-General, March 28, 1988, A/43/259-S/19694, 2, https://digital library.un.org/record/159645?ln=en.

38. For more on this declaration, see Chapter 2.

39. Declaration of the Government of the People's Republic of China on China's Territorial Sea, September 4, 1958.

40. Letter from Pham Van Dong to Zhou Enlai, September 14, 1958, quoted in Letter from the Chargé d'Affaires of the Permanent Mission of China to the United Nations Addressed to the Secretary-General, June 9, 2014, A/68/907, https://undocs.org/pdf?symbol=en/a/68/907.

41. Todd C. Kelly, "Vietnamese Claims to the Truong Sa Archipelago," *Explorations in Southeast Asian Studies* 3 (Fall 1999): 39.

42. The United States had mutual defense treaties with both the Philippines and the Republic of China; it had no such treaty with South Vietnam but considered the country a beneficiary of the Southeast Asia Treaty Organization's promise of protection to any Southeast Asian state threatened by a Communist attack.

43. Republic of Vietnam Ministry of Foreign Affairs, White Paper on the Hoang Sa (Paracel) and Truong Sa (Spratly) Islands, 1975.

44. Baviera and Batongbacal, *The West Philippine Sea*, 33.

45. Ibid., 21.

46. Ibid., 22.

47. Hayton, *The South China Sea*, 69.

48. Samuels, *Contest for the South China Sea*, 168.

49. Ibid., 169–71.

50. U.S. Department of State, Bureau of Intelligence and Research, "Sovereignty Claims in the South China Sea," Report No. 672, January 6, 1977, 30, https://www.cia.gov/readingr oom/docs/CIA-RDP08C01297R000300180010-1.pdf; Baviera and Batongbacal, *The West Philippine Sea*, 23;

51. Pedrozo, *China versus Vietnam*, 57–58.

52. Hayton, *The South China Sea*, 71.

53. Ibid., 69.

54. Ibid.

55. Juan Arreglado, *Kalayaan: Historical, Legal, Political Background* (Manila: Foreign Service Institute, 1982), 83–84.

56. U.S. Department of State, Bureau of Intelligence and Research, "Sovereignty Claims in the South China Sea," 4.

57. Hayton, *The South China Sea*, 72.

58. Ibid.

59. Andrew Chubb, "PRC Assertiveness in the South China Sea: Measuring Continuity and Change, 1970–2015," *International Security* 45, no. 3 (Winter 2020–21): 100; Toshi Yoshihara, "The 1974 Paracels Sea Battle: A Campaign Appraisal," *U.S. Naval War College Review* 69, no. 2 (Spring 2016): 46–47.

60. Chubb, "PRC Assertiveness in the South China Sea," 100.

61. Hayton, *The South China Sea*, 72.

62. Ibid.; Yoshihara, "The 1974 Paracels Sea Battle," 47nn13, 14.

63. Journalist and author Bill Hayton first brought this report to light in his 2014 book *The South China Sea: The Struggle for Power in Asia*.

64. Hayton, *The South China Sea*, 76–77; Yoshihara, "The 1974 Paracels Sea Battle," 47n14.

65. Hayton, *The South China Sea*, 76–77; Yoshihara, "The 1974 Paracels Sea Battle," 48, 50.

66. CIA, The President's Daily Brief, January 18, 1974, accessed via CIA Freedom of Information Act Electronic Reading Room, https://www.cia.gov/readingroom/.

67. CIA, The President's Daily Brief, January 19, 1974, accessed via CIA Freedom of Information Act Electronic Reading Room.

68. CIA, The President's Daily Brief, January 21, 1974, accessed via CIA Freedom of Information Act Electronic Reading Room.

69. Hayton, *The South China Sea*, 76–77.

70. Ibid.

71. Reuters, "U.S. Cautioned 7th Fleet to Shun Paracels Clash," *New York Times*, January 21, 1974.

72. Minutes of Washington Special Actions Group Meeting [January 25, 1974].

73. Pedrozo, *China versus Vietnam*, 56.

74. Memorandum of Conversation [Washington, January 23, 1974], *Foreign Relations of the United States, 1969–1976*, vol. 18, *China, 1973–1976*, Document 66, https://history.state. gov/historicaldocuments/frus1969-76v18/d66.

75. Ibid.

76. Minutes of Washington Special Actions Group Meeting [January 25, 1974].

77. Ibid.

78. Ibid.
79. Telegram from Ambassador William Sullivan (Manila) to State Department, No. 0998, "Philippine Position with Respect to Spratley [sic] Islands," January 26, 1974, accessed via U.S. Department of State, Central Foreign Policy Files, July 1, 1973—December 31, 1979, National Archives, https://aad.archives.gov/aad/series-description.jsp?s=4073&cat=all&bc=sl/.
80. CIA, The President's Daily Brief, January 29, 1974, accessed via CIA Freedom of Information Act Electronic Reading Room.
81. CIA, The President's Daily Brief, January 22, 1974, accessed via CIA Freedom of Information Act Electronic Reading Room; CIA, The President's Daily Brief, January 30, 1974, accessed via CIA Freedom of Information Act Electronic Reading Room.
82. CIA, The President's Daily Brief, January 31, 1974, accessed via CIA Freedom of Information Act Electronic Reading Room.
83. Ibid.
84. CIA, The President's Daily Brief, February 1, 1974, accessed via CIA Freedom of Information Act Electronic Reading Room.
85. CIA, "Wrap-Up on Spratlys," February 5, 1974, accessed via CIA Freedom of Information Act Electronic Reading Room.
86. CIA, The President's Daily Brief, February 7, 1974, accessed via CIA Freedom of Information Act Electronic Reading Room; CIA, Central Intelligence Bulletin, February 7, 1974, 11, accessed via CIA Freedom of Information Act Electronic Reading Room.
87. CIA, The President's Daily Brief, February 1, 1974.
88. The 1954 Mutual Defense Treaty between the United States and the Republic of China covered only Taiwan and the Pescadores but could be expanded to other territories by mutual agreement. The scope of the U.S.-Philippines defense treaty is more ambiguous and is discussed in greater detail in Chapter 4.

Chapter 4

1. Memo from National Security Advisor Brent Scowcroft to President Gerald Ford, No. 4286, "Key Issues in Our Base Negotiations with the Philippines," October 1976, accessed via U.S. Department of State, Central Foreign Policy Files.
2. Hayton, The South China Sea, 102.
3. Telegram from Ambassador William Sullivan (Manila) to State Department, No. 5250, "GOP Concern over NVN Incursion into Spratley [sic] Area," April 24, 1975, accessed via U.S. Department of State, Central Foreign Policy Files.
4. Nhung Anh Hung, Dac Cong Hai Quan Lu Doan 126 [Heroes of the Maritime Special Forces Brigade 126] (Hanoi: Nha xuat ban chinh tri quoc gia, 2016), 25–28.
5. From unpublished research by Alexander Vuving, Asia Pacific Center for Strategic Studies, interview with author, April 14, 2020.
6. Bureau of Intelligence and Research, "Sovereignty Claims in the South China Sea," 15.
7. Pedrozo, China versus Vietnam, 59; At that time, Dong Nai included the city of Vung Tau and the coastline closest to the Spratlys.
8. See Gregory Winger, "Be Careful What You Wish For: A Historical Retrospective on the Philippines-US Mutual Defense Treaty," Asia Pacific Pathways to Progress Foundation, February 25, 2019, https://appfi.ph/resources/commentaries/2530-be-careful-what-you-wish-for-a-historical-retrospective-on-the-philippines-us-mutual-defense-treaty.
9. Security Treaty between the United States, Australia, and New Zealand (ANZUS), September 1, 1951, http://avalon.law.yale.edu/20th_century/usmu002.asp.
10. Mutual Defense Treaty between the United States and the Republic of the Philippines, August 30, 1951, Art. IV–V, http://avalon.law.yale.edu/20th_century/phil001.asp.
11. Treaty of Mutual Cooperation and Security between Japan and the United States of America, January 19, 1960, Art. V, https://www.mofa.go.jp/region/n-america/us/q&a/ref/1.html.
12. Telegram from Ambassador William Sullivan (Manila) to State Department, No. 4777, "Disputed Territories in South China Sea," April 16, 1975, accessed via U.S. Department of State, Central Foreign Policy Files.

13. Telegram from Ambassador William Sullivan (Manila) to State Department, No. 5250, "GOP Concern over NVN Incursion into Spratly Area," April 24, 1975, accessed via U.S. Department of State, Central Foreign Policy Files.

14. Ibid.

15. Telegram from Secretary of State Henry Kissinger to Embassy in the Philippines, No. 116037, "Disputed Territories in South China Sea," May 15, 1975, accessed via U.S. Department of State, Central Foreign Policy Files.

16. Telegram from Ambassador William Sullivan (Manila) to State Department, No. 6840, "Disputed Territories in South China Sea," May 20, 1975, accessed via U.S. Department of State, Central Foreign Policy Files.

17. Telegram from Secretary of State Henry Kissinger to U.S. Embassy Manila, No. 133765, "U.S. MDT Commitment and Spratlys," June 9, 1975, accessed via U.S. Department of State, Central Foreign Policy Files.

18. Telegram from Ambassador William Sullivan (Manila) to State Department, No. 7196, "Spratley [sic] Islands," May 27, 1975, accessed via U.S. Department of State, Central Foreign Policy Files; telegram from Ambassador William Sullivan (Manila) to State Department, No. 11980, "GOP Action in Spratly Island Area," August 27, 1975, accessed via U.S. Department of State, Central Foreign Policy Files.

19. See Chapter 3.

20. Telegram from Ambassador William Sullivan (Manila) to State Department, No. 12464, "Petroleum Concessions in the Spratly Areas," September 5, 1975, accessed via U.S. Department of State, Central Foreign Policy Files; telegram from Secretary of State Henry Kissinger to U.S. Embassy Manila, No. 215761, "Petroleum Concessions in the Spratly Areas," September 11, 1975, accessed via U.S. Department of State, Central Foreign Policy Files.

21. Micah S. Muscolino, "Past and Present Resource Disputes in the South China Sea: The Case of Reed Bank," *Cross-Currents: East Asian History and Culture Review* 8 (September 2013): 84–85, https://cross-currents.berkeley.edu/sites/default/files/e-journal/articles/muscolino.pdf.

22. Memo from Thomas J. Barnes to National Security Advisor Brent Scowcroft, No. 2998, "Philippines-Vietnam Incident in the Spratly Islands," May 21, 1976, accessed via U.S. Department of State, Central Foreign Policy Files.

23. Muscolino, "Past and Present Resource Disputes," 86–87.

24. Telegram from Ambassador William Sullivan (Manila) to State Department, No. 07149, "Philippine Involvement in Spratly Islands," May 24, 1976, accessed via U.S. Department of State, Central Foreign Policy Files.

25. See, for instance, Department of State, Memorandum of Conversation, "Secretary's Meeting with Philippines Foreign Secretary Romulo," Waldorf Towers, New York, October 6, 1976, accessed via U.S. Department of State, Central Foreign Policy Files.

26. See Comptroller General of the United States, "Report to Congress: Military Assistance and Commitments in the Philippines," April 12, 1973, 10, https://www.gao.gov/assets/210/203866.pdf.

27. Telegram from Secretary of State Henry Kissinger to U.S. Embassy Manila, No. 287342, "Philippine Base Negotiations: November 23 Aide Memoire," November 23, 1976, accessed via U.S. Department of State, Central Foreign Policy Files.

28. Telegram from Sullivan, No. 07149.

29. Telegram from Ambassador William Sullivan (Manila) to State Department, No. 11504, "Marcos Announces Gas Discovery in Reed Bank," August 4, 1976, accessed via U.S. Department of State, Central Foreign Policy Files.

30. Muscolino, "Past and Present Resource Disputes," 86.

31. Telegram from Ambassador William Sullivan (Manila) to State Department, No. 10545, "AMOCO Interest in Reed Bank," July 19, 1976, accessed via U.S. Department of State, Central Foreign Policy Files.

32. Telegram from Ambassador William Sullivan (Manila) to State Department, No. 14158, "AMOCO Participation in Reed Bank Exploration," September 15, 1976, accessed via U.S. Department of State, Central Foreign Policy Files.

33. Telegram from Ambassador William Sullivan (Manila) to State Department, No. 11734, "Text of Aide Memoire Presented to DepSec 8/6," August 6, 1976, accessed via U.S. Department of State, Central Foreign Policy Files.

34. Ibid.

35. Memo from Thomas J. Barnes to National Security Advisor Brent Scowcroft, No. 4510, "Marcos-Robinson Meeting August 6, 1976 and Philippine Negotiating Strategy," August 6, 1976, accessed via U.S. Department of State, Central Foreign Policy Files.

36. Memo from National Security Advisor Brent Scowcroft to President Gerald Ford, No. 4286.

37. Minutes of the Secretary of State's Staff Meeting [Washington, October 16, 1976] in *Foreign Relations of the United States, 1969–1976*, vol. E-12, *Documents on East and Southeast Asia, 1973–1976*, edited by Bradley Lynn Coleman, David Goldman, and David Nickles (Washington, DC: United States Government Printing Office, 2010), Document 350, https://history.state.gov/historicaldocuments/frus1969-76ve12/d350.

38. Ibid.

39. Memo from William Gleysteen to National Security Advisor Brent Scowcroft, No. 4942, "Next Steps in the Philippine Base Negotiations," September 2, 1976, accessed via U.S. Department of State, Central Foreign Policy Files.

40. Memo from National Security Advisor Brent Scowcroft to President Gerald Ford, No. 4286.

41. Memo from Secretary of Defense Donald Rumsfeld to President Gerald Ford, No. 2763, "Philippine Base Negotiations," September 27, 1976, accessed via U.S. Department of State, Central Foreign Policy Files.

42. Memo from National Security Advisor Brent Scowcroft to President Gerald Ford, No. 4286.

43. Department of State, Memorandum of Conversation, "Secretary's Meeting with Philippines Foreign Secretary Romulo," Waldorf Towers, New York, October 6, 1976, accessed via U.S. Department of State, Central Foreign Policy Files; telegram from Under Secretary of State Charles Robinson to U.S. Embassy Manila, No. 250861, "Secretary's Meeting with Philippine Foreign Secretary," October 8, 1976, accessed via U.S. Department of State, Central Foreign Policy Files.

44. Department of State, Memorandum of Conversation, "Secretary's Meeting with Philippines Foreign Secretary Romulo"; telegram from Under Secretary of State Charles Robinson to U.S. Embassy Manila, No. 250861.

45. Telegram from Secretary of State Henry Kissinger to Commander in Chief, U.S. Pacific Command, No. 268153, "Mutual Defense Treaty: Aide-Memoire," November 9, 1976, accessed via U.S. Department of State, Central Foreign Policy Files.

46. Telegram from Secretary of State Henry Kissinger to U.S. Embassy Manila, No. 267580, "Philippine Base Negotiations: Secretary's Luncheon with Romulo," October 30, 1976, accessed via U.S. Department of State, Central Foreign Policy Files.

47. Telegram from Secretary of State Henry Kissinger to U.S. Embassy Manila, No. 287342, "Philippine Base Negotiations: November 23 Aide Memoire," November 23, 1976, accessed via U.S. Department of State, Central Foreign Policy Files.

48. Telegram from Secretary of State Henry Kissinger to U.S. Embassy Manila, No. 287549, "Philippine Base Negotiations: Secretary's November 23 Meeting with Romulo," November 24, 1976, accessed via U.S. Department of State, Central Foreign Policy Files.

49. Telegram from Ambassador William Sullivan (Manila) to State Department, No. 18586, "Philippine Base Negotiations," November 29, 1976, accessed via U.S. Department of State, Central Foreign Policy Files.

50. Telegram from Secretary of State Henry Kissinger to U.S. Embassy Manila, No. 300727, "Philippine Base Negotiations," December 10, 1976, accessed via U.S. Department of State, Central Foreign Policy Files.

51. Ibid.

52. Telegram from Secretary of State Henry Kissinger to U.S. Embassy Manila, No. 296271, "New York Times Article on Philippine Base Negotiations," December 5, 1976, accessed via U.S. Department of State, Central Foreign Policy Files.

53. Telegram from Ambassador William Sullivan (Manila) to State Department, No. 18879, "Philippine Base Negotiations," December 6, 1976, accessed via U.S. Department of State, Central Foreign Policy Files.

54. Telegram from Kissinger to Sullivan, No. 300727.

55. Telegram from Secretary of State Cyrus Vance to U.S. Embassy Manila, No. 016551, "Philippine Base Negotiations," January 25, 1977, accessed via U.S. Department of State, Central Foreign Policy Files.

56. Telegram from Chargé d'Affaires Lee Stull (Manila) to State Department, No. 8102, "Discussion with Marcos on New Arms Transfer Policy," May 26, 1977, accessed via U.S. Department of State, Central Foreign Policy Files.

57. Telegram from Secretary of State Cyrus Vance to U.S. Embassy Manila, No. 248525, "Consultations on Philippine Defense Relationship," October 16, 1977, accessed via U.S. Department of State, Central Foreign Policy Files.

58. Telegram from Chargé d'Affaires Lee Stull (Manila) to State Department, No. 16038, "Background Study for Philippine Base Negotiations," October 7, 1977, accessed via U.S. Department of State, Central Foreign Policy Files.

59. Telegram from Ambassador William Sullivan (Manila) to State Department, No. 4258, "Drill Ship Glomar Tasman for Reed Bank," March 23, 1977, accessed via U.S. Department of State, Central Foreign Policy Files; telegram from Chargé d'Affaires Lee Stull (Manila) to State Department, No. 8143, "AMOCO Drilling at Reed Bank," May 27, 1977, accessed via U.S. Department of State, Central Foreign Policy Files.

60. Telegram from Chargé d'Affaires Lee Stull (Manila) to State Department, No. 11736, "AMOCO Drilling at Reed Bank," July 29, 1977, accessed via U.S. Department of State, Central Foreign Policy Files.

61. Telegram from Ambassador David Newsom (Manila) to State Department, No. 18316, "1978 Oil Exploration Work on Reed Bank," November 18, 1977, accessed via U.S. Department of State, Central Foreign Policy Files.

62. Muscolino, "Past and Present Resource Disputes," 97–98.

63. Bureau of Intelligence and Research, "Sovereignty Claims in the South China Sea," 31.

64. Marites Dañguilan Vitug, *Rock Solid: How the Philippines Won Its Maritime Case against China* (Quezon City: Ateneo de Manila University Press, 2018), 13.

65. Telegram from Secretary of State Cyrus Vance to U.S. Embassy Kuala Lumpur, No. 255574, "Claims to Spratly Islands," October 26, 1977, accessed via U.S. Department of State, Central Foreign Policy Files; telegram from Ambassador Robert Miller (Kuala Lumpur) to State Department, 8314, "Claims to Spratly Islands," November 1, 1977, accessed via U.S. Department of State, Central Foreign Policy Files; telegram from Ambassador Robert Miller (Kuala Lumpur) to State Department, No. 9715, "Claims to Spratly Islands," December 23, 1977, accessed via U.S. Department of State, Central Foreign Policy Files; telegram from Deputy Secretary of State Warren Christopher to U.S. Embassy Kuala Lumpur, No. 000939, "Claims to Spratly Island," January 4, 1978, accessed via U.S. Department of State, Central Foreign Policy Files.

66. Bureau of Intelligence and Research, "Sovereignty Claims in the South China Sea," 2–6.

67. Telegram from Vance, No. 255574.

68. Adrian David, "How Malaysia's Five Naval Stations at Spratlys Were Built," *New Straits Times*, March 4, 2019.

69. Vitug, *Rock Solid*, 13.

70. See Alexander L. Vuving, "South China Sea: Who Occupies What in the Spratlys?," *The Diplomat*, May 6, 2016, https://thediplomat.com/2016/05/south-china-sea-who-claims-what-in-the-spratlys/; Asia Maritime Transparency Initiative, "Philippines Island Tracker," accessed April 11, 2020, https://amti.csis.org/island-tracker/philippines/.

71. The error even cropped up during arbitral proceedings that the Philippines initiated against China in 2013. Manila enlisted foreign experts to analyze the geography of occupied islands in the Spratlys based on satellite imagery but didn't warn them about the mislabeling of Panata. As a result, the evidence presented includes a detailed but irrelevant analysis of the water-line at Lankiam Cay (alongside satellite imagery of the unoccupied reef) and says nothing about the Philippines' actual outpost on Loaita Cay. See Clive Schofield, J. R. V. Prescott, and Robert van de Poll, "An Appraisal of the Geographical Characteristics and Status of Certain Features in the South China Sea, Annex 513 in South China Sea Arbitration (Philippines v. China)," *Supplemental Written Submission of the Philippines* 9, March 16, 2015, https://files.

pca-cpa.org/pcadocs/The%20Philippines%27%20Supplemental%20Written%20Submiss
ion%20-%20Volume%20IX%20%28Annexes%20500-521%29.pdf, 66.

72. Mai Thanh Hai, "Giữ Trường Sa trước tham vọng bá quyền—Kỳ 5: Quyết tử" [Holding the
    Spratly Islands before Hegemony—Episode 5: Fatal Decision], *Thanh Nien*, October 25,
    2014, https://urldefense.com/v3/__https://thanhnien.vn/thoi-su/giu-truong-sa-truoc-
    tham-vong-ba-quyen-ky-5-quyet-tu-505025.html__;!!KRhing!KFRdyDsnicNHEXfSM_
    uPzHr_58bv5dXJ9ztqdIIsME9P8kyNaa73WIX4zvfdBA$.

73. From unpublished research by Alexander Vuving, Asia Pacific Center for Strategic Studies,
    interview with author, April 14, 2020.

74. Baviera and Batongbacal, *The West Philippine Sea*, 21.

75. Government of the Philippines, Presidential Decree No. 1596, Declaring Certain Area Part
    of the Philippine Territory and Providing for Their Government and Administration, June
    11, 1978, https://www.officialgazette.gov.ph/1978/06/11/presidential-decree-no-1596-s-
    1978/.

76. Later Philippine government documents freely admit that the cay was first occupied in 1978.

77. Chi-kin Lo, *China's Policy toward Territorial Disputes: The Case of the Spratly Islands*
    (London: Routledge, 1989; digital printing 2005); telegram from Ambassador David
    Newsom (Manila) to State Department, No. 4382, "Spratly Islands: Visit to Manila of PRC
    Vice Premier," March 17, 1978, accessed via U.S. Department of State, Central Foreign
    Policy Files.

78. Telegram from Ambassador David Newsom (Manila) to State Department, No. 4537, "PRC
    Vice Premier's Visit to Philippines," March 21, 1978, accessed via U.S. Department of State,
    Central Foreign Policy Files.

79. Telegram from Newsom, No. 4382.

80. Telegram from Ambassador David Newsom (Manila) to State Department, No. 16906,
    "Pham Van Dong's Visit to Philippines—The Acting ForMin's Observations," September 26,
    1978, accessed via U.S. Department of State, Central Foreign Policy Files.

81. Ministry of Foreign Affairs of China, "Set Aside Dispute and Pursue Joint Development,"
    accessed May 17, 2020, https://www.fmprc.gov.cn/mfa_eng/ziliao_665539/3602_665
    543/3604_665547/t18023.shtml.

82. Ibid.

83. Government of the United States, Taiwan Relations Act, Public Law 96-8, 22 U.S.C. 3301,
    January 1, 1979, https://www.congress.gov/96/statute/STATUTE-93/STATUTE-93-
    Pg14.pdf.

84. Telegram from Deputy Secretary of State Warren Christopher to U.S. Embassy Manila, No.
    322026, "Reply to Marcos," December 2, 1978, accessed via U.S. Department of State, Central
    Foreign Policy Files.

85. Telegram from Ambassador Richard Murphy (Manila) to State Department, No. 103, "Base
    Negotiations: Final Steps," January 3, 1979, accessed via U.S. Department of State, Central
    Foreign Policy Files.

86. Telegram from Ambassador Richard Murphy (Manila) to State Department, No. 459,
    "Amendment to Military Bases Agreement—Letter from President Carter to President
    Marcos," January 8, 1979, accessed via U.S. Department of State, Central Foreign Policy Files.

87. Telegram from Ambassador Richard Murphy (Manila) to State Department, No. 461,
    "Amendment to Military Bases Agreement—Letter from Secretary Vance to Foreign Minister
    Romulo," January 8, 1979, accessed via U.S. Department of State, Central Foreign Policy Files.

88. Telegram from Ambassador Richard Murphy (Manila) to State Department, No. 2594,
    "FonMin Romulo on Amendment of MBA," February 6, 1979, accessed via U.S. Department
    of State, Central Foreign Policy Files.

89. Telegram from Ambassador Richard Murphy (Manila) to State Department, No. 550, "Base
    Negotiations—Why Did Marcos Sign?," January 9, 1979, accessed via U.S. Department of
    State, Central Foreign Policy Files.

90. Ibid.

91. Telegram from Secretary of State Cyrus Vance to American Embassy Paris, No. 48677,
    "Soviet Naval Presence Near China," February 28, 1979, accessed via U.S. Department of
    State, Central Foreign Policy Files.

92. Ibid.; telegram from Deputy Secretary of State Warren Christopher, No. 88397, "U.S. Policy on Indochina," April 9, 1979, accessed via U.S. Department of State, Central Foreign Policy Files.

93. Telegram from Deputy Secretary of State Warren Christopher, No. 88397.

94. Richard Burt, "Soviet Ships Arrive at Cam Ranh Bay," New York Times, March 29, 1979, https://www.nytimes.com/1979/03/29/archives/soviet-ships-arrive-at-cam-ranh-bay-us-is-concerned-over-russians.html.

95. Telegram from Deputy Secretary of State Warren Christopher, No. 95597, "April 16 EA Press Summary," April 16, 1979, accessed via U.S. Department of State, Central Foreign Policy Files.

96. Leszek Buszynski, Soviet Foreign Policy and Southeast Asia (London: Routledge, 1986).

97. Telegram from Ambassador Richard Murphy (Manila) to State Department, No. 11764, "Marcos Opposes ASEAN Supply of Military Assistance to Thailand," June 14, 1979, accessed via U.S. Department of State, Central Foreign Policy Files.

98. Telegram from Ambassador Richard Murphy (Manila) to State Department, No. 20780, "Marcos/Holbrooke Meeting October 25: Spratly Islands," October 29, 1979, accessed via U.S. Department of State, Central Foreign Policy Files.

99. CIA Directorate of Intelligence, "The Soviet Air and Naval Presence at Cam Ranh Bay, Vietnam: An Intelligence Assessment," June 1984, accessed via Central Intelligence Agency Freedom of Information Act Electronic Reading Room, https://www.cia.gov/readingroom/docs/CIA-RDP91T01115R000100190003-2.pdf.

100. Telegram from Secretary of State Cyrus Vance to Secretary of Defense Harold Brown, No. 206994, "Refugee Push-Offs and Sea Rescues," August 9, 1979, accessed via U.S. Department of State, Central Foreign Policy Files.

101. Telegram from Chargé d'Affaires Paul Gardner (Jakarta) to State Department, No. 9669, "Oil Companies Warned against Accepting Refugees on Their South China Sea Facilities," June 18, 1979, accessed via U.S. Department of State, Central Foreign Policy Files; telegram from Secretary of State Cyrus Vance to American Consulate Hong Kong, No. 232643, "Exxon Oil Exploration in South China Sea," September 5, 1979, accessed via U.S. Department of State, Central Foreign Policy Files.

102. Telegram from Vance, No 206994.

103. Telegram from Secretary of State Cyrus Vance, No. 274516, "Holbrooke Discussion with Phan Hien," October 20, 1979, accessed via U.S. Department of State, Central Foreign Policy Files.

Chapter 5

1. Richard Nixon, "United States Foreign Policy for the 1970's: A New Strategy for Peace," First Annual Report to the Congress on United States Foreign Policy, February 18, 1970, reported in "Nixon's Report to Congress on Foreign Policy," New York Times, February 19, 1970, https://www.nytimes.com/1970/02/19/archives/nixons-report-to-congress-on-foreign-policy-introduction-genuine.html.

2. Hollick, U.S. Foreign Policy and the Law of the Sea, 161–63, 174–78.

3. Ibid., 209.

4. Helmut Tuerk, "The 25th Anniversary of the Entry into Force of the United Nations Convention on the Law of the Sea," paper presented at the Diplomatic Academy of Vietnam's 11th South China Sea International Conference, Hanoi, November 6, 2019.

5. Hollick, U.S. Foreign Policy and Law of the Sea, 198–99, 210–11.

6. U.S. National Commission on Marine Science, Engineering and Resources, Our Nation and the Sea, 144, quoted in ibid., 188.

7. Hollick, U.S. Foreign Policy and Law of the Sea, 222–29.

8. Nixon, "United States Foreign Policy for the 1970's."

9. Ibid., 231–34, 241–42.

10. UN General Assembly Resolution 2881 (XXVI), December 21, 1971, https://undocs.org/en/A/RES/2881(XXVI).

11. Hollick, U.S. Foreign Policy and the Law of the Sea, 245–48, 257–58.

12. UN Resolution 3067 (XXVIII), November 16, 1973, https://undocs.org/en/A/RES/3067(xxviii).
13. Hollick, *U.S. Foreign Policy and the Law of the Sea*, 24.
14. Koh, *Building a New Legal Order*, 132–33.
15. Hollick, *U.S. Foreign Policy and the Law of the Sea*, 281–85.
16. Tuerk, "The 25th Anniversary of the Entry into Force of the United Nations Convention on the Law of the Sea."
17. Koh, *Building a New Legal Order*, 4–5.
18. Hollick, *U.S. Foreign Policy and the Law of the Sea*, 288–96.
19. A/CONF.62/C.2/L.85, August 28, 1974, quoted in ibid., 296.
20. Hollick, *U.S. Foreign Policy and the Law of the Sea*, 297–305.
21. Koh, *Building a New Legal Order*, 15.
22. Ibid., 17, 96.
23. Ibid., 33–35.
24. Hollick, *U.S. Foreign Policy and the Law of the Sea*, 307–16, 354–56.
25. United Nations, Introductory Note, Revised Single Negotiating Text (Part II), A/Conf.62/WP.8/Rev.1/PartII, May 6, 1976, https://legal.un.org/docs/?path=../diplomaticconferences/1973_los/docs/english/vol_5/a_conf62_wp8_rev1_part2.pdf&lang=E.
26. Hollick, *U.S. Foreign Policy and the Law of the Sea*, 318, 321–23.
27. Koh, *Building a New Legal Order*, 42.
28. Ibid., 361–62.
29. Ibid., 32–33.
30. Hollick, *U.S. Foreign Policy and the Law of the Sea*, 326–28.
31. Richard G. Darman, "The Law of the Sea: Rethinking U.S. Interests," *Foreign Affairs*, January 1978, https://www.foreignaffairs.com/articles/oceans-seas/1978-01-01/law-sea-rethinking-us-interests?cid=rss-letter_from_newdelhi-the_law_of_the_sea_rethinking-000000.
32. Hollick, *U.S. Foreign Policy and the Law of the Sea*, 333–40.
33. Koh, *Building a New Legal Order*, 5.
34. Hollick, *U.S. Foreign Policy and the Law of the Sea*, 341–49, 363–72.
35. Koh, *Building a New Legal Order*, 62–63.
36. Hollick, *U.S. Foreign Policy and the Law of the Sea*, 344–46.
37. Koh, *Building a New Legal Order*, 9, 19, 53–55, 88.
38. Ibid., 10–13, 220–21.
39. Tuerk, "The 25th Anniversary of the Entry into Force of the United Nations Convention on the Law of the Sea."
40. United Nations Convention on the Law of the Sea (UNCLOS), 1982, Art. 121.3, https://www.un.org/Depts/los/convention_agreements/texts/unclos/closindx.htm.
41. Tuerk, "The 25th Anniversary of the Entry into Force of the United Nations Convention on the Law of the Sea."
42. Koh, *Building a New Legal Order*, 85–89.
43. Ibid., 138.
44. Tuerk, "The 25th Anniversary of the Entry into Force of the United Nations Convention on the Law of the Sea."
45. Koh, *Building a New Legal Order*, 138.
46. The Philippines ratified in 1984; Indonesia in 1986; Vietnam in 1994; Brunei, Malaysia, and China in 1996.
47. See "Declarations and Reservations: China," United Nations Treaty Collection, 1996, https://treaties.un.org/Pages/ViewDetailsIII.aspx?src=TREATY&mtdsg_no=XXI-6&chapter=21&Temp=mtdsg3&clang=_en#EndDec.
48. Donald Rumsfeld is the only post-1994 secretary of defense to publicly oppose ratification, though the Department of Defense during his time in office pushed for it. Former secretary of defense James Mattis and former secretary of state Mike Pompeo have not taken public positions. Neither have Secretary of Defense Lloyd Austin or Chairman of the Joint Chiefs of Staff Mark Milley, but they likely will considering President Joe Biden's previous support for ratification as vice president and as chairman of the Senate Foreign Relations Committee. Former secretary of defense Mark Esper and former secretary of state Rex Tillerson publicly

supported ratification before they served in those roles. For references to support from other senior officials, see transcript of The Law of the Sea Convention, Hearings before the Committee on Foreign Relations, United States Senate, May 23, June 14, and June 28, 2012, https://www.govinfo.gov/content/pkg/CHRG-112shrg77375/pdf/CHRG-112shrg77 375.pdf.

49. International Court of Justice, Territorial and Maritime Dispute (Nicaragua v. Colombia), Judgment, November 19, 2012, https://www.icj-cij.org/public/files/case-related/124/124-20121119-JUD-01-00-EN.pdf, 666, 673, 674, 690, 693.

50. Government of the Socialist Republic of Viet Nam, Statement on the Territorial Sea, the Contiguous Zone, the Exclusive Economic Zone and the Continental Shelf, May 12, 1977, https://www.un.org/Depts/los/LEGISLATIONANDTREATIES/PDFFILES/VNM_197 7_Statement.pdf.

51. Government of the Philippines, Presidential Decree No. 1599, Establishing an Exclusive Economic Zone and for Other Purposes, June 11, 1978, https://www.officialgazette.gov.ph/ 1978/06/11/presidential-decree-no-1599-s-1978/.

52. See Yann-huei Song, "The PRC's Peacetime Military Activities in Taiwan's EEZ: A Question of Legality," paper presented at Peace Forum, Taiwan Security in the Year 2000: Retrospect and Prospects, Taipei, December 15, 2000; Government of Indonesia, Declaration by the Government of Indonesia concerning the Exclusive Economic Zone of Indonesia, March 21, 1980, https://www.un.org/depts/los/LEGISLATIONANDTREATIES/PDFFILES/ IDN_1980_DeclarationEEZ.pdf; Government of Malaysia, Proclamation of the Exclusive Economic Zone, April 25, 1980, http://extwprlegs1.fao.org/docs/pdf/mal4799.pdf.

53. Guifang Xue, "China and the Law of the Sea: An Update," in International Law and Military Operations, International Law Studies 84, ed. Michael D. Carsten (Providence, RI: U.S. Naval War College, 1984), 104.

54. Telegram from Secretary of State Cyrus Vance to American Embassy Manila, No. 273669, "Assessment of Philippine Domestic Oil Production." accessed via U.S. Department of State, Central Foreign Policy Files.

55. Ibid.

56. Telegram from Ambassador Edward Masters (Jakarta) to State Department, No. 14422, "Pertamina to Award New Exploratory Blocs in South China Sea," September 11, 1979, accessed via U.S. Department of State, Central Foreign Policy Files; telegram from Ambassador Edward Masters (Jakarta) to State Department, No. 19560, "Indonesian FonDept Reacts to Vietnamese Criticism of Indonesian Oil Drilling in South China Sea," December 10, 1979, accessed via U.S. Department of State, Central Foreign Policy Files; telegram from Ambassador Edward Masters (Jakarta) to State Department, No. 19810, "Pertamina Signs Five New Oil Exploration Contracts," December 14, 1979, accessed via U.S. Department of State, Central Foreign Policy Files.

57. Telegram from Deputy Secretary of State Warren Christopher to American Embassy Beijing, No. 181636, "US Oil Company Operations in South China Sea," July 14, 1979, accessed via U.S. Department of State, Central Foreign Policy Files.

58. Vitug, Rock Solid, 10, 14.

59. Vuving, "South China Sea."

60. Baviera and Batongbacal, The West Philippine Sea, 37.

Chapter 6

1. CIA Directorate of Intelligence, "Sino-Vietnamese Confrontation in the Spratlys Unlikely for Now," August 8, 1988, 1, accessed via Central Intelligence Agency, Freedom of Information Act Electronic Reading Room, https://www.cia.gov/readingroom/docs/DOC_0000789 471.pdf.

2. Alexander Chieh-cheng Huang, "The Chinese Navy's Offshore Active Defense Strategy," Naval War College Review 47, no. 3 (Summer 1994): 9, 16.

3. You Ji, "The Evolution of China's Maritime Combat Doctrines and Models: 1949–2001," IDSS Working Papers 22 (May 2002): 7, https://dr.ntu.edu.sg/bitstream/10356/90547/1/ RSIS-WORKPAPER_30.pdf.

4. Swaran Singh, "Continuity and Change in China's Maritime Strategy," *Strategic Analysis* 23, no. 9 (December 1999), https://ciaotest.cc.columbia.edu/olj/sa/sa_99sis01.html.

5. Huang, "The Chinese Navy's Offshore Active Defense Strategy," 9, 16–18, 24–25.

6. Ryan D. Martinson and Peter A. Dutton, *China Maritime Report No. 3: China's Distant Ocean Survey Activities: Implications for U.S. National Security*, U.S. Naval War College, November 2018, https://digital-commons.usnwc.edu/cgi/viewcontent.cgi?article=1002&context=cmsi-maritime-reports, note 11.

7. Hayton, *The South China Sea*, 80.

8. Martinson and Dutton, *China's Distant Ocean Survey Activities*, 15–16.

9. Baviera and Batongbacal, *The West Philippine Sea*, 33.

10. James A. Gregor, "The Key Role of U.S. Bases in the Philippines," Heritage Foundation, January 10, 1984, https://www.heritage.org/report/the-key-role-us-bases-the-philippines.

11. Stanley Karnow, *In Our Image: America's Empire in the Philippines* (New York: Ballantine Books, 1989), Kindle edition, Loc. 10485.

12. Ibid., Loc. 10717–49.

13. Ibid., Loc. 10851—1087.

14. Ibid., Loc. 145–244.

15. The Constitution of the Republic of the Philippines, February 2, 1987, Art. I; Art. XII, Sec. 2, https://www.officialgazette.gov.ph/constitutions/1987-constitution/.

16. Ibid., Art. XVIII, Sec. 25.

17. Elaine Sciolino, "U.S. and Philippines Sign Pact on Bases," *New York Times*, October 18, 1988, https://www.nytimes.com/1988/10/18/world/us-and-philippines-sign-pact-on-bases.html?auth=login-email&login=email.

18. David, "Malaysia's Five Naval Stations."

19. See Jianming Shen, "International Law Rules and Historical Evidence Supporting China's Title to the South China Sea Islands," *Hastings International and Comparative Law Review* 21, no. 1 (Fall 1997): 56, https://repository.uchastings.edu/cgi/viewcontent.cgi?article=1467&context=hastings_international_comparative_law_review; unpublished research by Alexander Vuving, Asia Pacific Center for Strategic Studies, interview with author, April 14, 2020.

20. See Renate Haller-Trost, "The Brunei-Malaysia Dispute over Territorial and Maritime Claims in International Law," *Maritime Briefings* 1, no. 3 (1994): 48–49, 55, https://www.durham.ac.uk/media/durham-university/research-/research-centres/ibru-centre-for-borders-research/maps-and-databases/publications-database/Maritime-Briefings-(Vol.-1-no.-3).pdf.

21. M. Taylor Fravel, *Strong Borders, Secure Nation: Cooperation and Conflict in China's Territorial Disputes* (Princeton, NJ: Princeton University Press, 2008), 292.

22. Hayton, *The South China Sea*, 81.

23. Huang, "The Chinese Navy's Offshore Active Defense Strategy," 16–17.

24. Hayton, *The South China Sea*, 82–83; Vuving, interview with author.

25. Vuving, interview with author.

26. Hayton, *The South China Sea*, 83.

27. CIA Directorate of Intelligence, "Sino-Vietnamese Confrontation," 2.

28. Ibid., 4.

29. Cheng-yi Lin, "Taiwan's South China Sea Policy," *Asian Survey* 37, no. 4 (April 1997): 332; CIA Directorate of Intelligence, "Sino-Vietnamese Confrontation," 6.

30. Peter Kreuzer, *Facing China: Crises or Peaceful Coexistence in the South China Sea*, PRIF Report 134 (Frankfurt: Peace Research Institute Frankfurt, 2015), 10.

31. CIA Directorate of Intelligence, "Sino-Vietnamese Confrontation," 6.

32. Kreuzer, *Facing China*, 12.

33. CIA Directorate of Intelligence, "Sino-Vietnamese Confrontation," 6.

34. Ibid., 7.

35. For more on the DK1 platforms, see Asia Maritime Transparency Initiative, "Slow and Steady: Vietnam's Spratly Upgrades," April 8, 2019, https://amti.csis.org/slow-and-steady-vietnams-spratly-upgrades/.

36. See Shen, "International Law Rules and Historical Evidence," 56; Asia Maritime Transparency Initiative, "South China Sea Features," accessed November 22, 2019, https://amti.csis.org/scs-features-map/.

37. The disagreement among Chinese sources stems from some counting Rifleman Bank as a single unit while others divide it into constituent parts. Two of those, Kingston Shoal and Orleana Shoal, currently host DK1 platforms, while a third, Bombay Castle, did in the past.

38. "World Leaders Outraged by Army Action," *New Straits Times*, June 6, 1989.

39. Steven Erlanger, "Vietnam Promises Troops Will Leave Cambodia by Fall," *New York Times*, April 6, 1989, https://www.nytimes.com/1989/04/06/world/vietnam-promises-tro ops-will-leave-cambodia-by-fall.html#:~:text=Ten%20years%20and%20three%20mon ths,by%20the%20end%20of%20September.

40. Criselda Yabes, "Manila Turns Back Coup Bid with Help of U.S. Air Power," *Washington Post*, December 2, 1989, https://www.washingtonpost.com/archive/politics/1989/12/02/manila-turns-back-coup-bid-with-help-of-us-air-power/62895eef-23e2-4311-bf1b-4da4a 63267f0/.

41. John M. Broder, "U.S. Reaches Accord with Manila, Will Leave Clark Air Base: Philippines: Volcano Causes Abandonment of Field; But Americans Will Keep Subic Naval Base for 10 Years," *Los Angeles Times*, July 18, 1991, https://www.latimes.com/archi ves/la-xpm-1991-07-18-mn-3381-story.html.

42. Ibid.

43. Don Oberdorfer, "U.S. Base Rejected in Philippines," *Washington Post*, September 10, 1991, https://www.washingtonpost.com/archive/politics/1991/09/10/us-base-rejected-in-phil ippines/d580e52d-5060-4cf8-9443-48e689593149/.

44. Philip Shenon, "Philippine Senate Votes to Reject U.S. Base Renewal," *New York Times*, September 16, 1991, https://www.nytimes.com/1991/09/16/world/philippine-senate-votes-to-reject-us-base-renewal.html.

Chapter 7

1. U.S. Department of State, Daily Press Briefing, May 10, 1995, quoted in Michael McDevitt, *The South China Sea: Assessing U.S. Policy and Options for the Future*, CNA Occasional Paper (Arlington, VA: CNA, November 2014), 1, https://www.cna.org/cna_files/pdf/IOP-2014-U-009109.pdf.

2. Singapore Declaration of 1992, Singapore, January 28, 1992, ASEAN, https://asean.org/?stat ic_post=singapore-declaration-of-1992-singapore-28-january-1992.

3. 1992 ASEAN Declaration on the South China Sea, Manila, July 22, 1992, Centre for International Law, National University of Singapore, https://cil.nus.edu.sg/wp-content/uplo ads/2017/07/1992-ASEAN-Declaration-on-the-South-China-Sea.pdf.

4. Rodolfo C. Severino, "The Philippines and the South China Sea," in *Entering Uncharted Waters? ASEAN and the South China Sea*, ed. Pavin Chachavalpongpun (Singapore: Institute of Southeast Asian Studies, 2014), 187.

5. The first ARF included ministers from the ten current ASEAN members plus Australia, Canada, China, the European Union, India, Japan, New Zealand, Russia, South Korea, and the United States. The organization has since expanded to include Bangladesh, Mongolia, North Korea, Pakistan, Papua New Guinea, Sri Lanka, and Timor-Leste. The United Kingdom is soon ex- pected to join as ASEAN's newest dialogue partner. Department of Foreign Affairs and Trade of Australia, "ASEAN Regional Forum," accessed August 27, 2019, https://www.dfat.gov.au/international-relations/regional-architecture/asean-regional-forum-arf.

6. See Lisolotte Odgaard, "Between Deterrence and Cooperation: Eastern Asian Security after the Cold War," *IRBU Boundary and Security Bulletin* (Summer 1998): 73, https://www.dur ham.ac.uk/media/durham-university/research-/research-centres/ibru-centre-for-borders-research/maps-and-databases/publications-database/boundary-amp-security-bulletins/bsb6-2_odgaard.pdf.

7. Hayton, *The South China Sea*, 85.

8. Philip Shenon, "Manila Sees China Threat on Coral Reef," *New York Times*, February 19, 1995, https://www.nytimes.com/1995/02/19/world/manila-sees-china-threat-on-coral-reef.html.

9. Quoted in Severino, "The Philippines and the South China Sea," 188.
10. Scott Snyder, Brad Glosserman, and Ralph A. Cossa, "Confidence Building Measures in the South China Sea," *Issues and Insights* 2-01, Pacific Forum, 2001, F-1, https://pacforum.org/wp-content/uploads/2019/02/issuesinsightsv01n02.pdf.
11. For example, see David Scott, "Conflict Irresolution in the South China Sea," *Asian Survey* 52, no. 6 (2012): 1024.
12. Snyder, Glosserman, and Cossa, "Confidence Building Measures," 14.
13. Ibid., 12–13.
14. See "Documents on ASEAN and the South China Sea," Centre for International Law, National University of Singapore, June 2011, https://cil.nus.edu.sg/wp-content/uploads/2011/06/Documents-on-ASEAN-and-South-China-Sea-as-of-June-2011-pdf.pdf.
15. Kavi Chongkittavorn, "ASEAN-China Tussles: COC Endgame," presentation at 9th Annual CSIS South China Sea Conference, Center for Strategic and International Studies, Washington, DC, July 24, 2019.
16. Joint Communique of the 28th ASEAN Ministerial Meeting, July 30, 1995, in "Documents on ASEAN and the South China Sea."
17. U.S. Department of State, Daily Press Briefing, May 10, 1995.
18. Ibid.
19. Ryan Martinson, "Catching Sovereignty Fish: Chinese Fishers in the Southern Spratlys," *Marine Policy* 125 (March 2021): 2–6.
20. Ministry of Agriculture, South China Sea Fisheries Law Enforcement Department, *Atlas of Fishing Grounds in the South China Sea* (Guangzhou: Guangdong Map Press, 1994), cited in ibid., 5.
21. Hayton, *South China Sea*, 87.
22. Shen, "International Law Rules and Historical Evidence," 68.
23. See CIA Directorate of Intelligence, "Vietnam: Is There Oil in Its Future? An Intelligence Assessment," February 1986, accessed via CIA Fredom of Information Act Electronic Reading Room, https://www.cia.gov/library/readingroom/docs/CIA-RDP04T00794R000100610001-1.pdf.
24. Ministry of Foreign Affairs of China, "Set Aside Dispute and Pursue Joint Development," accessed May 17, 2020, https://www.fmprc.gov.cn/mfa_eng/ziliao_665539/3602_665543/3604_665547/t18023.shtml.
25. Hayton, *The South China Sea*, 129–30.
26. Kuan-Ming Sun, "1995 Policy of the Republic of China towards the South China Sea," *Marine Policy* 19, no. 5 (September 1995): 401, quoted in Bill Hayton, "The Modern Creation of China's Historic Rights Claim in the South China Sea," *Asian Affairs* 49, no. 3 (2018): 8.
27. People's Republic of China, Law on the Territorial Sea and the Contiguous Zone, February 25, 1992, https://www.un.org/depts/los/LEGISLATIONANDTREATIES/PDFFILES/CHN_1992_Law.pdf.
28. Declaration of the Government of the People's Republic of China on the Baselines of the Territorial Sea, May 15, 1996, https://www.un.org/Depts/los/LEGISLATIONANDTREATIES/PDFFILES/CHN_1996_Declaration.pdf.
29. Asia Maritime Transparency Initiative, "Reading between the Lines: The Next Spratly Legal Dispute," March 21, 2019, https://amti.csis.org/reading-between-lines-next-spratly-dispute/.
30. United Nations Treaty Collection, "Declarations and Reservations: China," 1996, https://treaties.un.org/pages/ViewDetailsIII.aspx?src=TREATY&mtdsg_no=XXI-6&chapter=21&Temp=mtdsg3&clang=_en#EndDec.
31. Hayton, "The Modern Creation of China's Historic Rights," 9–10.
32. People's Republic of China, Exclusive Economic Zone and Continental Shelf Act, June 26, 1998, https://www.un.org/Depts/los/LEGISLATIONANDTREATIES/PDFFILES/chn_1998_eez_act.pdf.
33. Scott W. Harold, Derek Grossman, Brian Harding, Jeffrey W. Hornung, Gregory Poling, Jeffrey Smith, and Meagan L. Smith, *The Thickening Web of Asian Security Cooperation: Deepening Defense Ties among U.S. Allies and Partners in the Indo-Pacific* (Washington, DC: RAND, 2019), 298.

34. Larry Niksch, "Philippine-U.S. Security Relations," CRS Report for Congress, October 10, 2000, https://www.everycrsreport.com/files/20001010_RS20697_8fcdb8a5e8c9b131e9cd85f17e0c53ee2d56ccb0.pdf.

35. Greg Austin, "Unwanted Entanglement: The Philippines' Spratly Policy as a Case Study in Conflict Enhancement?," *Security Dialogue* 34, no. 1 (March 2003): 49–50.

36. "DFA Chief Clarifies US Support under Mutual Defense Treaty," *Philippine Star*, May 10, 2012, https://www.philstar.com/headlines/2012/05/10/805080/dfa-chief-clarifies-us-support-under-mutual-defense-treaty.

37. Vitug, *Rock Solid*, 15–16.

38. "DFA Chief Clarifies US Support under Mutual Defense Treaty."

39. Austin, "Unwanted Entanglement," 51.

40. See Zou Keyuan, "Scarborough Reef: A New Flashpoint in Sino-Philippines Relations?," *IBRU Boundary and Security Bulletin* (Summer 1999): 71.

41. Conor M. Kennedy and Andrew S. Erickson, "Model Maritime Militia: Tanmen's Leading Role in the April 2012 Scarborough Shoal Incident," Center for International Maritime Security, April 21, 2016, http://cimsec.org/model-maritime-militia-tanmens-leading-role-april-2012-scarborough-shoal-incident/24573.

42. Baviera and Batongbacal, *The West Philippine Sea*, 33.

43. U.S. Department of State, *Taiwan's Maritime Claims*, Limits in the Sea No. 127, November 15, 2005, 14, 25, https://2009-2017.state.gov/documents/organization/57674.pdf.

44. Vitug, *Rock Solid*, 16–17; Baviera and Batongbacal, *The West Philippine Sea*, 33.

45. David, "Malaysia's Five Naval Stations."

46. Joint Communique of the 29th ASEAN Ministerial Meeting, July 21, 1996, in "Documents on ASEAN and the South China Sea."

47. Joint Communique of the 32nd ASEAN Ministerial Meeting, July 24, 1999, in "Documents on ASEAN and the South China Sea."

48. Martinson, "Catching Sovereignty Fish," 4–5.

49. Carlyle A. Thayer, "South China Sea: Background to ASEAN-China Code of Conduct," Thayer Consultancy Background Brief, Canberra, April 26, 2017, https://seasresearch.wordpress.com/2017/04/27/draft-asean-china-codes-of-conduct-text-and-analysis/.

50. Declaration on the Conduct of Parties in the South China Sea, November 4, 2002, ASEAN, posted October, 17, 2012, https://asean.org/?static_post=declaration-on-the-conduct-of-parties-in-the-south-china-sea-2.

51. Ibid.

52. For instance, China seized effective control of Scarborough Shoal from the Philippines in 2012 but has so far refrained from constructing permanent facilities on it. China also reportedly erected sovereignty markers on Boxall Reef and Amy Douglass Bank in 2011, which were removed by Filipino forces. And it has constructed small facilities on previously unoccupied features in the Paracel Islands, though Beijing has always contended that the Paracels are outside the scope of the DOC. Vietnam in 2015 attempted to construct two new outposts on Cornwallis South Reef, other parts of which it already occupied, but abandoned the attempt after its work was washed out by a storm. And in 2017, China prevented Philippine forces from constructing shelters on unoccupied sandbars near Thitu Island. Philippine officials later admitted that the construction would have violated the DOC. See Dona Z. Pazzibugan, "Philippines Pulls Spratlys 'Foreign' Posts," *Philippine Daily Inquirer*, June 16, 2011, https://newsinfo.inquirer.net/15230/philippines-pulls-spratlys-foreign-posts; Asia Maritime Transparency Initiative, "China Quietly Upgrades a Remote Reef," November 20, 2018, https://amti.csis.org/china-quietly-upgrades-bombay-reef/; Asia Maritime Transparency Initiative, "Washed Away," Center for Strategic and International Studies, February 17, 2016, https://amti.csis.org/typhoon-spotlights-island-building/; Carmela Fonbuena, "PH Aborts Construction on Pag-asa Sandbar after China Protest," *Rappler*, November 8, 2017, https://www.rappler.com/nation/187690-ph-china-pagasa-standoff-lorenzana.

53. Declaration on the Conduct of Parties in the South China Sea, November 4, 2002.

54. Joint Communique of the 36th ASEAN Ministerial Meeting, June 17, 2003, in "Documents on ASEAN and the South China Sea."

55. Press Statement of the Chairperson of the ASEAN+China Summit, ASEAN+Japan Summit, ASEAN+Republic of Korea Summit and ASEAN+India Summit, October 3, 2003, in "Documents on ASEAN and the South China Sea."

56. Plan of Action to Implement the Joint Declaration on ASEAN-China Strategic Partnership for Peace and Prosperity, November 29, 2004, ASEAN, posted June 18, 2012, https://asean. org/?static_post=plan-of-action-to-implement-the-joint-declaration-on-asean-china-strate gic-partnership-for-peace-and-prosperity.

57. Terms of Reference of the ASEAN-China Joint Working Group on the Implementation of the Declaration on the Conduct of Parties in the South China Sea, December 7, 2004, ASEAN, posted May 14, 2012, https://asean.org/?static_post=terms-of-reference-of-the-asean-china-joint-working-group-on-the-implementation-of-the-declaration-on-the-conduct-of-parties-in-the-south-china-sea.

58. Tran Truong Thuy, "Recent Developments in the South China Sea: From Declaration to Code of Conduct," in *The South China Sea: Towards a Region of Peace, Security and Cooperation*, ed. Tran Truong Thuy (Hanoi: Gioi, 2011), 104, cited in Carlyle Thayer, "ASEAN'S Code of Conduct in the South China Sea: A Litmus Test for Community-Building?," *Asia-Pacific Journal Japan Focus* 10, no. 4 (August 19, 2012), https://apjjf.org/2012/10/34/Carlyle-A.-Thayer/3813/article.html.

59. Thayer, "ASEAN's Code of Conduct in the South China Sea."

60. Baviera and Batongbacal, *The West Philippine Sea*, 39.

61. Ibid.

Chapter 8

1. Hillary Rodham Clinton, "Remarks at Press Availability," July 23, 2010, https://2009-2017. state.gov/secretary/20092013clinton/rm/2010/07/145095.htm.

2. See Chapter 6.

3. UNCLOS, Annex II, Art. 4, https://www.un.org/Depts/los/convention_agreements/texts/ unclos/closindx.htm.

4. Tuerk, "The 25th Anniversary of the Entry into Force of the United Nations Convention on the Law of the Sea."

5. SPLOS/72, Decision regarding the date of commencement of the ten-year period for making submissions to the Commission on the Limits of the Continental Shelf set out in article 4 of Annex II to the United Nations Convention on the Law of the Sea, May 29, 2001, https:// documents-dds-ny.un.org/doc/UNDOC/GEN/N01/387/64/PDF/N0138764.pdf?Open Element.

6. UN Division for Ocean Affairs and Law of the Sea, "Submissions, through the Secretary-General of the United Nations, to the Commission on the Limits of the Continental Shelf, pursuant to article 76, paragraph 8, of the United Nations Convention on the Law of the Sea of 10 December 1982," updated November 21, 2019, https://www.un.org/Depts/los/clcs_ new/commission_submissions.htm.

7. Malaysia and the Socialist Republic of Vietnam, Joint Submission to the Commission on the Limits of the Continental Shelf: Executive Summary, May 6, 2009, https://www.un.org/ Depts/los/clcs_new/submissions_files/mysvnm33_09/mys_vnm2009excutivesumm ary.pdf.

8. Socialist Republic of Vietnam, Submission to the Commission on the Limits of the Continental Shelf: Executive Summary, May 7, 2009, https://www.un.org/Depts/los/clcs_ new/submissions_files/vnm37_09/vnm2009n_executivesummary.pdf.

9. Permanent Mission of the People's Republic of China to the United Nations, Note Verbale CML/17/2009, May 7, 2009, https://www.un.org/Depts/los/clcs_new/submissions_files/ mysvnm33_09/chn_2009re_mys_vnm_e.pdf; Permanent Mission of the People's Republic of China to the United Nations, Note Verbale CML/18/2009, May 7, 2009, https://www. un.org/Depts/los/clcs_new/submissions_files/vnm37_09/chn_2009re_vnm.pdf.

10. Permanent Mission of the Socialist Republic of Viet Nam to the United Nations, Note Verbale No. 86/HC-2009, May 8, 2009, https://www.un.org/Depts/los/clcs_new/submissions_fi les/mysvnm33_09/vnm_chn_2009re_mys_vnm_e.pdf.

11. Permanent Mission of Malaysia to the United Nations, Note Verbale HA 24/09, May 20, 2009, https://www.un.org/Depts/los/clcs_new/submissions_files/mysvnm33_09/mys_re_chn_2009re_mys_vnm_e.pdf.

12. Permanent Mission of Malaysia to the United Nations, Note Verbale HA 41/09, August 21, 2009, https://www.un.org/Depts/los/clcs_new/submissions_files/mysvnm33_09/mys_re_phl_2009re_mys_vnm_e.pdf; Permanent Mission of the Socialist Republic of Viet Nam to the United Nations, Note Verbale No. 240/HC-2009, August 18, 2009, https://www.un.org/Depts/los/clcs_new/submissions_files/submission_mysvnm_33_2009.htm;

13. Permanent Mission of the Republic of Indonesia, Note Verbale No. 480/POL-703/VII/10, July 8, 2010, https://www.un.org/Depts/los/clcs_new/submissions_files/mysvnm33_09/idn_2010re_mys_vnm_e.pdf.

14. Permanent Mission of the Philippines to the United Nations, Note Verbale No. 000228, April 5, 2011, https://www.un.org/Depts/los/clcs_new/submissions_files/mysvnm33_09/phl_re_chn_2011.pdf.

15. Permanent Mission of the People's Republic of China to the United Nations, Note Verbale CML/8/2011, April 14, 2011, https://www.un.org/Depts/los/clcs_new/submissions_fi les/mysvnm33_09/chn_2011_re_phl_e.pdf.

16. Permanent Mission of the Social Republic of Viet Nam to the United Nations, Note Verbale No. 77/HC-2011, May 3, 2011, https://www.un.org/Depts/los/clcs_new/submissions_fi les/vnm37_09/vnm_2011_re_phlchn.pdf.

17. SPLOS 183, Decision regarding the workload of the Commission on the Limits of the Continental Shelf and the ability of States, particularly developing States, to fulfil the requirements of article 4 of annex II to the United Nations Convention on the Law of the Sea, as well as the decision contained in SPLOS/72, paragraph (a), June 20, 2018, https://documents-dds-ny.un.org/doc/UNDOC/GEN/N08/398/76/PDF/N0839876.pdf?Open Element.

18. UN Division for Ocean Affairs and Law of the Sea, "Preliminary Information Indicative of the Outer Limits of the Continental Shelf Beyond 200 Miles," updated August 15, 2019, https://www.un.org/depts/los/clcs_new/commission_preliminary.htm.

19. Brunei Darussalam, Preliminary Submission Concerning the Outer Limits of its Continental Shelf, May 12, 2009, https://www.un.org/depts/los/clcs_new/submissions_files/prelimin ary/brn2009preliminaryinformation.pdf.

20. Instrument of Accession to the Treaty of Amity and Cooperation in Southeast Asia by the United States of American, July 22, 2009, https://www.asean.org/storage/images/archive/DOC-TAC-USA.pdf.

21. Ernest Z. Bower, "U.S.-ASEAN Summit: President Obama Engages Southeast Asia," CSIS Critical Questions, November 9, 2009, https://www.csis.org/analysis/us-asean-summit-president-obama-engages-southeast-asia.

22. Andrew S. Erickson and Conor M. Kennedy, "China's Daring Vanguard: Introducing Sanya City's Maritime Militia," Center for International Maritime Security, November 5, 2015, http://cimsec.org/chinas-daring-vanguard-introducing-sanya-citys-maritime-militia/19753.

23. Michael Green, Kathleen Hicks, Zack Cooper, John Schaus, and Jake Douglas, Countering Coercion in Maritime Asia: The Theory and Practice of Gray Zone Deterrence (Washington, DC: Center for Strategic and International Studies, May 2017), 57–59, https://www.csis.org/analysis/countering-coercion-maritime-asia.

24. Jim Garamone, "Chinese Vessels Shadow, Harass Unarmed U.S. Survey Ship," American Forces Press Service, March 9, 2009, https://archive.defense.gov/news/newsarticle.aspx?id=53401.

25. Green et al., Countering Coercion, 63.

26. Edward Wong, "Chinese Military Seeks to Extend Its Naval Power," New York Times, April 23, 2010, https://www.nytimes.com/2010/04/24/world/asia/24navy.html?login=email&auth=login-email.

27. Hillary Rodham Clinton, "Interview with Greg Sheridan of The Australian," November 8, 2010, https://2009-2017.state.gov/secretary/20092013clinton/rm/2010/11/150671.htm.

278   NOTES TO PAGES 184-190

28. See, for example, Michael D. Swaine, "China's Assertive Behavior—Part One: On 'Core Interests,'" *China Leadership Monitor* 34 (November 15, 2010): 8–10, https://carnegieen dowment.org/files/CLM34MS_FINAL.pdf.

29. John Pomfret, "U.S. Takes a Tougher Tone with China," *Washington Post*, July 30, 2010, https://www.washingtonpost.com/wp-dyn/content/article/2010/07/29/AR2010072906 416.html?sid=ST2010072906761.

30. Cable from U.S. Embassy Hanoi to State Department, "2008 Recap of the Sino-Vietnam South China Sea Territorial Disputes," Wikileaks, quoted in International Crisis Group, *Stirring Up the South China Sea (IV): Oil in Troubled Waters*, Asia Report No. 275 (Brussels: International Crisis Group, 2016), 12; Hayton, *South China Sea*, 136–43.

31. Clinton, Remarks at Press Availability, July 23, 2010.

32. Pomfret, "U.S. Takes a Tougher Tone."

33. Ian Storey, "China and the Philippines: Implications of the Reed Bank Incident," *China Brief* 11, no. 8 (May 6, 2011), https://jamestown.org/program/china-and-the-philippines-impli cations-of-the-reed-bank-incident/.

34. Ibid.

35. Vietnam News Agency, "Chinese Marine Surveillance Ships Violate VN's Sovereignty," Vietnamese Embassy in the United States, May 27, 2011, http://vietnamembassy-usa. org/news/2011/05/chinese-marine-surveillance-ships-violate-vns-sovereignty; "Vietnam Accuses China in Seas Dispute," BBC, May 30, 2011, https://www.bbc.com/news/world-asia-pacific-13592508.

36. "Another Vietnamese Ship Disturbed in Territorial Waters: Report," *Thanh Nien News*, June 1, 2011, http://www.thanhniennews.com/politics/another-vietnamese-ship-disturbed-in-terr itorial-waters-report-12055.html.

37. See Andrew S. Erickson, "Exposed: Pentagon Report Spotlights China's Maritime Militia," *National Interest*, August 20, 2018, https://nationalinterest.org/feature/exposed-pentagon-report-spotlights-china%E2%80%99s-maritime-militia-29282.

38. See White House, "The U.S.-Indonesia Comprehensive Partnership," Press Release, June 27, 2010, https://obamawhitehouse.archives.gov/the-press-office/us-indonesia-compre hensive-partnership; U.S. Embassy in Indonesia, "Fact Sheet: U.S. Institutional Support for ASEAN," September 2011, https://id.usembassy.gov/our-relationship/policy-history/emba ssy-fact-sheets/fact-sheet-u-s-institutional-support-for-asean/.

39. Damien Tomkins, "US Reaffirms Asia Role," *The Diplomat*, June 8, 2011, https://thediplo mat.com/2011/06/us-reaffirms-asia-role/.

40. Hillary Clinton, "America's Pacific Century," *Foreign Policy*, October 11, 2011, https://foreig npolicy.com/2011/10/11/americas-pacific-century/.

41. David Nakamura, "Obama at APEC Summit: China Must 'Play by the Rules,'" *Washington Post*, November 12, 2011, https://www.washingtonpost.com/world/obama-at-apec-sum mit-china-must-play-by-the-rules/2011/11/12/gIQALRu2FN_story.html.

42. White House, Remarks by President Obama to the Australian Parliament, November 17, 2011, https://obamawhitehouse.archives.gov/the-press-office/2011/11/17/remarks-president-obama-australian-parliament.

43. Floyd Whaley, "Clinton Reaffirms Military Ties with the Philippines," *New York Times*, November 16, 2011, https://www.nytimes.com/2011/11/17/world/asia/clinton-reaffirms-military-ties-with-the-philippines.html.

44. Australia, China, India, Japan, New Zealand, Russia, South Korea, and the United States.

45. "Scarborough Shoal Standoff: A Timeline," *Philippine Daily Inquirer*, May 9, 2012, https://globalnation.inquirer.net/36003/scarborough-shoal-standoff-a-historicaltimeline.

46. Kimberly Jane Tan, "DFA: 1 of 3 Chinese Vessels in Panatag Shoal Standoff Leaves; Diplomatic Talks Resume," *GMA News*, April 13, 2012, https://www.gmanetwork.com/news/news/nat ion/254783/dfa-1-of-3-chinese-vessels-in-panatag-shoal-standoff-leaves-diplomatic-talks-resume/story/.

47. Green et al., *Countering Coercion*, 103.

48. Tan, "DFA: 1 of 3 Chinse Vessels."

49. AFP, "Other Nations Must Take Stand on China: PH," *ABS-CBN News*, updated April 23, 2012, https://news.abs-cbn.com/nation/04/22/12/other-nations-must-take-stand-china-ph.

50. Zhang Yunbi and Qiu Quanlin, "Manila's Attempt to Internationalize Dispute Rejected," *China Daily*, April 19, 2012, http://www.chinadaily.com.cn/china/2012-04/19/content_1 5084608.htm.

51. Jerry E. Esplanada, "Philippines to Seek US Help in Dealing with China over Spratlys Issue—DFA," *Philippine Daily Inquirer*, April 26, 2012, http://globalnation.inquirer.net/34857/phil ippines-to-seek-us-help-in-dealing-with-china-over-spratlys-issue-dfa.

52. Green et al., *Countering Coercion*, 110.

53. Hillary Rodham Clinton, "Remarks with Secretary of Defense Leon Panetta, Philippines Foreign Secretary Albert del Rosario, and Philippines Defense Secretary Voltaire Gazmin after Their Meeting," U.S. State Department, April 30, 2012, https://2009-2017.state.gov/ secretary/20092013clinton/rm/2012/04/188982.htm.

54. Ibid.

55. For a chart of deployments over time, see Michael Green, Kathleen Hicks, Zack Cooper, John Schaus, and Jake Douglas, "Counter-Coercion Series: Scarborough Shoal Standoff," *Asia Maritime Transparency Initiative*, May 22, 2017, https://amti.csis.org/counter-co-scarboro ugh-standoff/.

56. Kennedy and Erickson, "Model Maritime Militia."

57. Green et al., *Countering Coercion*, 116–18.

58. Fu Ying, "Huangyan Dao, and What Happened in 2012: A Witness Account," in *Kan Shi Jie* 2 [*Watching the World* 2] (Beijing: CITIC Publishing Group, 2021). Thanks to Swee Lean Collin Koh for a translated version of this chapter, which was shared with attendees at a conference of the National Institute for South China Sea Studies in Hainan.

59. "Palace: China Expected to Pull Ships Out of Shoal after Exit of PHL Boats," *GMA News*, June 17, 2012, https://www.gmanetwork.com/news/news/nation/262228/palace-china-expec ted-to-pull-ships-out-of-shoal-after-exit-of-phl-boats/story/.

60. Email from Jacob J. Sullivan to Hillary Clinton, "Subject: Dai," June 17, 2012, available at http://graphics.wsj.com/hillary-clinton-email-documents/.

61. Green et al., *Countering Coercion*, 117–19; Fu, "Huangyan Dao."

62. Green et al., *Countering Coercion*, 120.

63. "PHL Won't Recognize China Fishing Ban in West Philippine Sea," *GMA News*, May 14, 2012, https://www.gmanetwork.com/news/news/nation/258155/phl-won-t-recognize-china-fishing-ban-in-west-philippine-sea/story/.

64. Gregory B. Poling, "Arguing over Blocks: Do China and the Philippines Both Have a Claim," Center for Strategic and International Studies, April 16, 2012, https://www.csis.org/analy sis/arguing-over-blocks-do-china-and-the-philippines-both-have-claim.

65. Doris C. Dumlao, "Pangilinan Brings in Chinese to Disputed Recto Bank Oil Exploration Group," *Philippine Daily Inquirer*, June 24, 2012, https://business.inquirer.net/67089/pangili nan-brings-in-chinese-to-disputed-recto-bank-oil-exploration-group.

66. Gregory B. Poling, "CNOOC Pulls Back the Curtain," Center for Strategic and International Studies, August 17, 2012, https://www.csis.org/analysis/cnooc-pulls-back-curtain.

67. Carlyle Thayer, "ASEAN'S Code of Conduct in the South China Sea: A Litmus Test for Community-Building?," *Asia-Pacific Journal Japan Focus* 10, no. 4 (August 19, 2012), https:// apjjf.org/2012/10/34/Carlyle-A.-Thayer/3813/article.html.

68. Ibid.

69. Ibid.

70. Ernest Z. Bower, "China Reveals Its Hand on ASEAN in Phnom Penh," *CSIS Commentary*, July 19, 2012, https://www.csis.org/analysis/china-reveals-its-hand-asean-phnom-penh.

71. Jane Perlez, "Asian Leaders Fail to Resolve Disputes over South China Sea," *New York Times*, July 12, 2012, https://www.nytimes.com/2012/07/13/world/asia/asian-leaders-fail-to-resolve-disputes-on-south-china-sea-during-asean-summit.html.

72. Ibid.

73. Zsombor Peter and Kuch Naren, "Cambodia Criticized for Asean Meeting Failure," Reuters, July 13, 2012, quoted in Thayer, "ASEAN's Code of Conduct in the South China Sea."

74. Thayer, "ASEAN's Code of Conduct in the South China Sea."

75. Ibid.

76. Green et al., *Countering Coercion*, 142.

77. Ibid., 142–46.
78. Duncan B. Hollis, "Treaty Tips from the SFRC Clinton Hearing," *OpinioJuris*, January 15, 2009, http://opiniojuris.org/2009/01/15/treaty-tips-from-the-sfrc-clinton-hearing/.
79. Ibid.
80. U.S. Department of State, "Treaty Priority List for the 111th Congress," May 11, 2009, https://www.gc.noaa.gov/documents/gcil_bd_2009TreatyPriorityList.pdf.
81. Clinton, Remarks at Press Availability, July 23, 2010.
82. Transcript of The Law of the Sea Convention, Hearings before the Committee on Foreign Relations, United States Senate, May 23, June 14, and June 28, 2012, https://www.govinfo.gov/content/pkg/CHRG-112shrg77375/pdf/CHRG-112shrg77375.pdf; Senate Foreign Relations Committee, "'24 Star' Military Witnesses Voice Strong Support for Law of the Sea Treaty" (Press Release), June 14, 2012, https://www.foreign.senate.gov/press/chair/rele ase/24-star-military-witnesses-voice-strong-support-for-law-of-the-sea-treaty.
83. Austin Wright, "Law of the Sea Treaty Sinks in Senate," *Politico*, July 16, 2012, https://www.politico.com/story/2012/07/law-of-the-sea-treaty-sinks-in-senate-078568.
84. Jeremy Page, "Vietnam Accuses Chinese Ships," *Wall Street Journal*, December 3, 2012, https://www.wsj.com/articles/SB10001424127887323717004578157033857113510; Erickson, "Exposed."
85. Albert del Rosario, "Statement: The Secretary of Foreign Affairs on the UNCLOS Arbitral Proceedings against China," *Government of the Philippines Official Gazette*, January 22, 2013, https://www.officialgazette.gov.ph/2013/01/22/statement-the-secretary-of-foreign-affairs-on-the-unclos-arbitral-proceedings-against-china-january-22-2013/.
86. See UNCLOS, Articles 287 and 298.
87. Republic of the Philippines Department of Foreign Affairs, Note Verbale No. 13-0211, "Notification and Statement of Claim," January 22, 2013, https://dfa.gov.ph/images/UNC LOS/Notification%20and%20Statement%20of%20Claim%20on%20West%20Philipp ine%20Sea.pdf.
88. AP, "China Rejects U.S. Arbitration of Maritime Dispute," *New York Times*, February 19, 2013, https://www.nytimes.com/2013/02/20/world/asia/china-rejects-un-arbitration-of-maritime-dispute.html.
89. Jay Batongbacal, "Arbitration 101: Philippines v. China," Asia Maritime Transparency Initiative, January 21, 2015, https://amti.csis.org/arbitration-101-philippines-v-china/.
90. Permanent Court of Arbitration, "Arbitration between the Republic of the Philippines and the People's Republic of China: Arbitral Tribunal Establishes Rules of Procedures and Initial Timetable" (Press Release), August 2, 2013, https://pcacases.com/web/sendAttach/227.
91. Batongbacal, "Arbitration 101."
92. U.S. Department of State, Daily Press Briefing, February 19, 2013, https://2009-2017.state.gov/r/pa/prs/dpb/2013/02/204955.htm.
93. Austin Ramzy, "China's Newest City Raises Threat of Conflict in South China Sea," *Time*, July 24, 2012, https://world.time.com/2012/07/24/chinas-newest-city-raises-threat-of-confl ict-in-the-south-china-sea/.
94. See Ryan D. Martinson, "From Words to Actions: The Creation of the China Coast Guard," paper presented at China as a Maritime Power Conference, CNA, Arlington, Virginia, July 28–19, 2015, 1–4, https://www.cna.org/cna_files/pdf/creation-china-coast-guard.pdf.
95. U.S. Department of State, "Statement by Secretary of State John Kerry on the East China Sea Air Defense Identification Zone," November 23, 2013, https://www.andrewerickson.com/2013/11/statements-by-secretary-of-state-john-kerry-and-secretary-of-defense-chuck-hagel-on-the-east-china-sea-air-defense-identification-zone/.
96. U.S. Department of Defense, "Statement by Secretary of Defense Chuck Hagel on the East China Sea Air Defense Identification Zone," November 23, 2013, https://archive.defense.gov/releases/release.aspx?releaseid=16392.
97. Green et al., *Countering Coercion*, 152–66.
98. U.S. Department of State, "U.S.-Vietnam Comprehensive Partnership," December 16, 2013, https://2009-2017.state.gov/r/pa/prs/ps/2013/218734.htm.

99. Sean Mirski, "American Paralysis and Troubles in the South China Sea: A Primer on the Philippines-China Arbitration," *Lawfare*, October 13, 2013, https://www.lawfareblog.com/american-paralysis-and-troubles-south-china-sea-primer-philippines-china-arbitration.

100. U.S. Embassy Manila, "JTF 505 Disestablished," December 1, 2013, https://web.archive.org/web/20140125090056/http://manila.usembassy.gov/jtf-505-disestablished.html; Matthew Lee, "Secretary of State John Kerry Announces $25M in New Aid for Typhoon-Ravaged Philippines," AP, December 18, 2013, https://globalnews.ca/news/1037251/secretary-of-state-john-kerry-announces-25m-in-new-aid-for-typhoon-ravaged-philippine-city/.

101. See Department of Foreign Affairs of the Philippines, "Frequently Asked Questions (FAQs) on the Enhanced Defense Cooperation Agreement," April 28, 2014, https://www.dfa.gov.ph/dfa-releases/2693-frequently-asked-questions-faqs-on-the-enhanced-defense-cooperation-agreement; Carl Thayer, "Analyzing the US-Philippines Enhanced Defense Cooperation Agreement," *The Diplomat*, May 2, 2014, https://thediplomat.com/2014/05/analyzing-the-us-philippines-enhanced-defense-cooperation-agreement/.

102. Green et al., *Countering Coercion*, 173–83.

103. Jim Gomez, "Philippines Asks Neighbors to Join Case vs China," *Philippine Star*, February 28, 2014, https://www.philstar.com/headlines/2014/02/28/1295521/philippines-asks-neighbors-join-case-vs-china.

104. Ministry of Foreign Affairs of the People's Republic of China, "Foreign Ministry Spokesperson Qin Gang's Regular Press Conference," March 10, 2014, https://www.fmprc.gov.cn/mfa_eng/xwfw_665399/s2510_665401/2511_665403/t1136288.shtml.

105. Francisco Tuyay, "BRP Sierra Madre Set to Be Repaired," *Manila Standard*, March 23, 2014, https://manilastandard.net/news/-main-stories/143480/brp-sierra-madre-set-to-be-repaired.html.

106. Tarra Quismundo, "US Troubled by Ayungin Shoal Incident," *Philippine Daily Inquirer*, March 12, 2014, https://globalnation.inquirer.net/100211/us-troubled-by-ayungin-shoal-incident.

107. Department of Foreign Affairs of the Philippines, "DFA Statement on China's Allegation That the Philippines Agreed to Pull-out of the Ayungin Shoal," March 14, 2014, https://dfa.gov.ph/index.php/2013-06-27-21-50-36/dfa-releases/2333-dfa-statement-on-china-s-allegation-that-philippines-agreed-to-pull-out-of-the-ayungin-shoal.

108. Green et al., *Countering Coercion*, 186–88.

109. Nikko Dizon, "AFP Uses Couriers to Foil China Spies," *Philippine Daily Inquirer*, April 29, 2014, https://globalnation.inquirer.net/103076/afp-uses-couriers-to-foil-china-spies.

110. Green et al., *Countering Coercion*, 192–93.

111. Dizon, "AFP Uses Couriers."

112. See Permanent Court of Arbitration, *The South China Sea Arbitration (The Republic of Philippines v. The People's Republic of China)*, The Philippines' Memorial, vols. 1–11, March 30, 2014, https://pca-cpa.org/en/cases/7/.

113. Ibid., vol. 1, 271–72.

114. Justin McCurry and Tania Branigan, "Obama Says US Will Defend Japan in Island Dispute with China," *Guardian*, April 24, 2014, https://www.theguardian.com/world/2014/apr/24/obama-in-japan-backs-status-quo-in-island-dispute-with-china.

115. U.S. Embassy Manila, "Signing of Enhanced Defense Cooperation Agreement," April 28, 2014, https://ph.usembassy.gov/signing-enhanced-defense-cooperation-agreement/.

116. Mark Felsenthal, "Obama Says U.S. Commitment to Defend Philippines 'Ironclad,'" Reuters, April 29, 2014, https://www.reuters.com/article/us-philippines-usa-obama-idUSBREA3S02T20140429.

117. Ibid.

118. For more on this, see Chapter 5.

Chapter 9

1. White House, "Remarks by President Obama at U.S.-ASEAN Press Conference," February 16, 2016, https://obamawhitehouse.archives.gov/the-press-office/2016/02/16/remarks-president-obama-us-asean-press-conference.
2. Vietnamese Embassy in Germany, "Viet Nam's International Press Conference," May 7, 2014, http://www.vietnambotschaft.org/viet-nams-international-press-conference-on-7th-may-2014/.
3. Green et al., *Countering Coercion*, 204.
4. Gregory B. Poling, "China-Vietnam Tensions High over Drilling Rig in Disputed Waters," Center for Strategic and International Studies, May 7, 2014, https://www.csis.org/analysis/china-vietnam-tensions-high-over-drilling-rig-disputed-waters.
5. Green et al., *Countering Coercion*, 207.
6. Chris Brummit, "Vietnam Tries to Stop China Oil Rig Deployment," *USA Today*, May 7, 2014, https://www.usatoday.com/story/news/world/2014/05/07/vietnam-china-oil-rig/8797007/; Xinhua, "China Requires Vietnam to Stop Any Form of Disruptions of Chinese Company's Operations," *People's Daily*, May 9, 2014, http://en.people.cn/90883/8621898.html.
7. Green et al., *Countering Coercion*, 209.
8. Ministry of Foreign Affairs of Japan, "Press Conference by Foreign Minister Fumio Kishida," May 9, 2014, https://www.mofa.go.jp/press/kaiken/kaiken4e_000068.html; U.K. Foreign and Commonwealth Office, "UK Speaks in Support of EU Statement on Tensions in South China Sea," press release, May 10, 2014, https://www.gov.uk/government/news/uk-speaks-in-support-of-eu-statement-on-tensions-in-south-china-sea.
9. ASEAN Foreign Ministers' Statement on the Current Developments in the South China Sea, May 10, 2014, https://asean.org/wp-content/uploads/2012/05/24th-AFMs-Statement-on-SCS.pdf.
10. U.S. Department of State, "Daily Press Briefing," May 6, 2014, https://2009-2017.state.gov/r/pa/prs/dpb/2014/05/225687.htm.
11. U.S. Embassy Hanoi, "Press Roundtable with Assistant Secretary Daniel Russel," May 8, 2014, https://vn.usembassy.gov/press-roundtable-with-assistant-secretary-daniel-russel/.
12. Green et al., *Countering Coercion*, 214–20.
13. "China Moves Illegal Oil Rig to New Area, Still in Vietnam's Waters," *Tuoi Tre News*, May 27, 2014, https://tuoitrenews.vn/society/19907/china-moves-illegal-oil-rig-to-new-area-still-in-vietnams-waters.
14. Green et al., *Countering Coercion*, 221–22.
15. "CNPC Ends Drilling Off Xisha Islands," Xinhua, July 16, 2014, http://www.china.org.cn/business/2014-07/16/content_32963102.htm.
16. See Green et al., *Countering Coercion*, 222–23.
17. "Alleged South China Sea Reef Construction Is 'Renovation,'" *Global Times*, May 4, 2014, http://english.sina.com/china/2014/0503/697230.html.
18. Marlon Ramos and Tarra Quismundo, "China Building Airstrip on Reef in Philippine Waters," *Philippine Daily Inquirer*, May 15, 2014, https://globalnation.inquirer.net/104333/manila-says-china-reclaiming-land-in-disputed-sea.
19. Department of Foreign Affairs of the Philippines, "China's Reclamation on Mabini Reef," May 15, 2014, https://www.dfa.gov.ph/index.php/2013-06-27-21-50-36/dfa-releases/2871-china-s-reclamation-on-mabini-reef.
20. Green et al., *Countering Coercion*, 240–41; Asia Maritime Transparency Initiative, "China Island Tracker," accessed October 1, 2020, https://amti.csis.org/island-tracker/china/.
21. Victor Robert Lee, "Satellite Imagery Shows Ecocide in the South China Sea," *The Diplomat*, January 15, 2016, https://thediplomat.com/2016/01/satellite-images-show-ecocide-in-the-south-china-sea/; John W. McManus, "Offshore Coral Reef Damage, Overfishing, and Paths to Peace in the South China Sea," *International Journal of Marine and Coastal Law* 32 (2017): 199–237.
22. Green et al., *Countering Coercion*, 242–43; Asia Maritime Transparency Initiative, "China Island Tracker."

23. U.S. Department of Defense, "Remarks by Secretary Hagel at Plenary Session at International Institute for Strategic Studies Shangri-La Dialogue," May 31, 2014, https://archive.defense. gov/transcripts/transcript.aspx?transcriptid=5442.

24. Edward Wong and Jonathan Ansfield, "To Bolster Its Claims, China Plants Islands in Disputed Waters," *New York Times*, June 16, 2014, https://www.nytimes.com/2014/06/17/world/ asia/spratly-archipelago-china-trying-to-bolster-its-claims-plants-islands-in-disputed-wat ers.html.

25. "Philippines Calls for Construction Freeze in South China Sea," Reuters, June 16, 2014, https://www.reuters.com/article/us-philippines-southchinasea/philippines-calls-for-const ruction-freeze-in-south-china-sea-idUSKBN0ER0LE20140616.

26. Wong and Ansfield, "To Bolster Its Claims."

27. Asia Maritime Transparency Initiative, "Vietnam's Island Building: Double-Standard or Drop in the Bucket?," May 11, 2016, https://amti.csis.org/vietnams-island-building/.

28. Green et al., *Countering Coercion*, 244–45.

29. Cliff Venzon, "Beijing Hints It May Stop Activities in South China Sea If Manila Drops Arbitration," *Nikkei Asia*, August 9, 2014, https://asia.nikkei.com/Politics/Beijing-hints-it-may-stop-activities-in-South-China-Sea-if-Manila-drops-arbitration.

30. Green et al., *Countering Coercion*, 245.

31. Asia Maritime Transparency Initiative, "China Island Tracker."

32. AFP and Minnie Chan, "US Asks China to Stop Building Spratlys Island Which Could Host Airfield," *South China Morning Post*, November 22, 2014, https://www.scmp.com/news/ china/article/1646025/us-asks-china-stop-building-spratlys-island-which-could-host-airfield.

33. Asia Maritime Transparency Initiative, "China Island Tracker."

34. "President Aquino of Philippines Meets China's Xi in APEC Ice-Breaker," NBC News, November 10, 2015, https://www.nbcnews.com/news/world/president-aquino-philippi nes-meets-chinas-xi-apec-ice-breaker-n245981.

35. Batongbacal, "Arbitration 101."

36. U.S. Department of State, Bureau of Oceans and International Environmental and Scientific Affairs, "China: Maritime Claims in the South China Sea," *Limits in the Seas* 143, https:// 2009-2017.state.gov/documents/organization/234936.pdf.

37. Zuraidah Ibrahim and Kristine Kwok, "Beijing Rejects Hanoi's Legal Challenge on Spratly, Paracel Islands Disputes," *South China Morning Post*, December 12, 2014, https://www. scmp.com/news/china/article/1661364/china-rejects-vietnam-claims-arbitration-submiss ion-over-south-china-sea.

38. Position Paper of the Government of the People's Republic of China on the Matter of Jurisdiction in the South China Sea Arbitration Initiated by the Republic of the Philippines, December 7, 2014, https://www.fmprc.gov.cn/nanhai/eng/snhwtlcwj_1/t1368895.htm.

39. Batongbacal, "Arbitration 101."

40. See Permanent Court of Arbitration, *South China Sea Arbitration*, Supplemental Written Submission of the Philippines, 1:89–97, 115–16, https://pca-cpa.org/en/cases/7/.

41. Prashanth Parameswaran, "ASEAN to Intensify South China Sea Response amid China Concerns," *The Diplomat*, January 28, 2015, https://thediplomat.com/2015/01/asean-to-intensify-south-china-sea-response-amid-china-concerns/.

42. Jonathan W. Greenert, *Tenets of a Regional Defense Strategy: Considerations for the Indo-Pacific*, National Bureau for Asian Research Special Report 72 (Seattle: National Bureau of Asian Research, 2018), https://www.nbr.org/wp-content/uploads/pdfs/publications/special_re port_72_regional_defense_strategy_aug2018.pdf.

43. U.S. Senate Committee on Armed Services, "Senators McCain, Reed, Corker, and Menendez Send Letter on Chinese Maritime Strategy," March 19, 2015, https://www.armed-services. senate.gov/press-releases/senators-mccain-reed-corker-and-menendez-send-letter-on-chin ese-maritime-strategy.

44. Rob Taylor, "China's 'Great Wall of Sand' Raises U.S. Concerns," *Wall Street Journal*, March 31, 2015, https://www.wsj.com/articles/u-s-to-move-stealth-destroyers-to-pacific-region-1427784315.

45. Adam Entous, Gordon Lubold, and Julian E. Barnes, "U.S. Military Proposes Challenge to China Sea Claims," *Wall Street Journal*, May 12, 2015, https://www.marketwatch.com/story/us-military-proposes-challenge-to-china-sea-claims-2015-05-12-17103251.

46. Ash Carter, "Reflections on American Grand Strategy in Asia," Belfer Center for Science and International Affairs, October 2018, https://www.belfercenter.org/publication/reflections-american-grand-strategy-asia.

47. Jim Sciutto, "Exclusive: China Warns U.S. Surveillance Plane," CNN, May 20, 2015, https://www.cnn.com/2015/05/20/politics/south-china-sea-navy-flight/index.html.

48. Matthew Rosenberg, "China Deployed Artillery on Disputed Islands, U.S. Says," *New York Times*, May 29, 2015, https://www.nytimes.com/2015/05/30/world/asia/chinese-artillery-spotted-on-spratly-island.html.

49. David Alexander, "Vietnam, U.S. Discuss Land Reclamation in South China Sea," Reuters, June 1, 2015, https://www.reuters.com/article/us-vietnam-usa-defense/vietnam-u-s-discuss-land-reclamation-in-south-china-sea-idUSKBN0OH1L120150601.

50. Green et al., *Countering Coercion*, 251.

51. Asia Maritime Transparency Initiative, "Update: China's Continuing Reclamation in the Paracels," August 9, 2017, https://amti.csis.org/paracels-beijings-other-buildup/.

52. Elina Noor, "Malaysia: Recalibrating Its South China Sea Policy?," Asia Maritime Transparency Initiative, January 8, 2016, https://amti.csis.org/malaysia-recalibrating-its-south-china-sea-policy/.

53. Asia Maritime Transparency Initiative, "Tracking China's Coast Guard Off Borneo," April 5, 2017, https://amti.csis.org/tracking-chinas-coast-guard-off-borneo/; Asia Maritime Transparency Initiative, "Signaling Sovereignty: Chinese Patrols at Contested Reefs," September 26, 2019, https://amti.csis.org/signaling-sovereignty-chinese-patrols-at-contested-reefs/.

54. White House, "Remarks by President Obama and President Xi of the People's Republic of China in Joint Press Conference," September 25, 2015, https://obamawhitehouse.archives.gov/the-press-office/2015/09/25/remarks-president-obama-and-president-xi-peoples-republic-china-joint.

55. See, for example, Morgan Ortagus, "China's Empty Promises in the South China Sea." press statement, U.S. Department of State, September 27, 2020, https://www.state.gov/chinas-empty-promises-in-the-south-china-sea/.

56. Ashton Carter, "US Pacific Command Change of Command," speech, Joint Base Pearl Harbor-Hickam, Hawaii, May 27. 2015, https://www.defense.gov/News/Speeches/Article/606675/; U.S. Department of Defense, "Joint Press Conference by Secretary Carter and Minister of National Defense Thanh, in Hanoi, Vietnam," June 1, 2015, https://www.defense.gov/News/Transcripts/Transcript-View/Article/607052/joint-press-conference-by-secretary-carter-and-minister-of-national-defense-tha/; "Carter Says U.S. Will Sail, Fly and Operate Wherever International Law Allows," Reuters, October 13, 2015, https://www.reuters.com/article/usa-australia-southchinasea-carter/update-1-carter-says-u-s-will-sail-fly-and-operate-wherever-international-law-allows-idUKL1N12D1U120151013.

57. See Chapter 6.

58. See U.S. Department of Defense, "DoD Annual Freedom of Navigation (FON) Reports," accessed October 3, 2020, https://policy.defense.gov/OUSDP-Offices/FON/.

59. Ankit Panda, "After Months of Waiting, US Finally Begins Freedom of Navigation Patrols Near China's Man-Made Islands," *The Diplomat*, October 27, 2015, https://thediplomat.com/2015/10/after-months-of-waiting-us-finally-begins-freedom-of-navigation-patrols-near-chinas-man-made-islands/; Bonnie S. Glaser, Michael J. Green, and Gregory B. Poling, "The US Asserts Freedom of Navigation in the South China Sea," Center for Strategic and International Relations, October 27, 2015, https://www.csis.org/analysis/us-asserts-freedom-navigation-south-china-sea.

60. See Euan Graham, "Innocent Passage: Did the US Just Fumble Its South China Sea Strategy?," *National Interest*, November 4, 2015, http://nationalinterest.org/blog/the-buzz/innocent-passage-did-the-us-just-fumble-its-south-china-sea-14253; Sam LaGrone, "Confusion Continues to Surround US South China Sea Freedom of Navigation Operation," *USNI News*, November 5, 2015, https://news.usni.org/2015/11/05/confusion-continues-to-surro

und-u-s-south-china-sea-freedom-of-navigation-operation; Jeff M. Smith, "An Innocent Mistake: How a Fumbled Freedom of Navigation Operation Set Back US Interests in the South China Sea," *Foreign Affairs*, December 3, 2015, https://www.foreignaffairs.com/artic les/china/2015-12-03/innocent-mistake.

61. Bonnie S. Glaser and Peter A. Dutton, "The US Navy's Freedom of Navigation Operation around Subi Reef: Deciphering US Signaling," *National Interest*, November 6, 2015, http:// nationalinterest.org/feature/the-us-navy%E2%80%99s-freedom-navigation-operation-aro und-subi-reef-14272.

62. For a fuller explanation of this principle, see Chapter 6.

63. "Document: SECDEF Carter Letter to McCain on South China Sea Freedom of Navigation Operation," *USNI News*, January 5, 2016, https://news.usni.org/2016/01/05/document-secdef-carter-letter-to-mccain-on-south-china-sea-freedom-of-navigation-operation.

64. Andrew Shalal and Idrees Ali, "US Navy Plans Two or More Patrols in South China Sea per Quarter," Reuters, November 2, 2015, https://www.reuters.com/article/us-southchina sea-usa-navy/u-s-navy-plans-two-or-more-patrols-in-south-china-sea-per-quarter-idUSKC N0SR28W20151103.

65. Eleanor Freund, "Freedom of Navigation in the South China Sea: A Practical Guide," Asia Maritime Transparency Initiative, August 10, 2017, https://amti.csis.org/freedom-of-navigat ion-practical-guide/.

66. White House, "Joint Statement on the ASEAN-U.S. Strategic Partnership," November 21, 2015, https://obamawhitehouse.archives.gov/the-press-office/2015/11/21/joint-statem ent-asean-us-strategic-partnership.

67. White House, "Joint Statement of the U.S.-ASEAN Special Leaders' Summit: Sunnylands Declaration," February 16, 2016, https://obamawhitehouse.archives.gov/the-press-office/ 2016/02/16/joint-statement-us-asean-special-leaders-summit-sunnylands-declaration.

68. Gregory Poling and Eric Sayers, "Time to Make Good on the U.S.-Philippine Alliance," *War on the Rocks*, https://warontherocks.com/2019/01/time-to-make-good-on-the-u-s-philipp ine-alliance/.

69. Nike Ching, "US, Philippines Agree on Five Locations Covered by Defense Pact," Voice of America, March 18, 2016, https://www.voanews.com/east-asia/us-philippines-agree-five-locations-covered-defense-pact.

70. David Brunnstrom and Andrea Shalal, "Exclusive: U.S. Sees New Chinese Activity around South China Sea Shoal," Reuters, March 17, 2016, https://www.reuters.com/article/us-southchinasea-china-scarborough-exclu-idUSKCN0WK01B.

71. White House, "Remarks by President Obama and President Xi on the People's Republic of China before Bilateral Meeting," March 31, 2016, https://obamawhitehouse.archives.gov/ the-press-office/2016/03/31/remarks-president-obama-and-president-xi-peoples-repub lic-china.

72. Demetri Sevastopulo, Geoff Dyer, and Tom Mitchell, "Obama Forced Xi to Back Down over South China Sea Dispute," *Financial Times*, July 12, 2016, https://www.ft.com/content/ c63264a4-47f1-11e6-8d68-72e9211e86ab.

73. Erik Estrada, "Philippines, U.S. Start Exercise Balikatan 2016," U.S. Department of Defense, April 7, 2016, https://www.defense.gov/Explore/News/Article/Article/715540/philippi nes-us-start-exercise-balikatan-2016/.

74. U.S. Pacific Air Forces, "A-10s Complete Second USPACOM Air Contingent Mission," April 21, 2016, https://www.pacaf.af.mil/News/Photos/igphoto/2001523308/.

75. Minnie Chan, "China to Build Up Atoll in Contested South China Sea, Source Says," *South China Morning Post*, April 25, 2016, https://www.scmp.com/news/china/diplomacy-defe nce/article/1938277/china-build-atoll-contested-south-china-sea-source-says.

76. Sevastopulo, Dyer, and Mitchell, "Obama Forced Xi to Back Down."

77. Zack Cooper and Jake Douglas, "Successful Signaling at Scarborough Shoal?," *War on the Rocks*, May 2, 2016, https://warontherocks.com/2016/05/successful-signaling-at-scarboro ugh-shoal/.

78. Carmela Fonbuena, "U.S. Stopped China's Plan to Build on Scarborough," *Rappler*, March 9, 2017, https://www.rappler.com/nation/us-stopped-china-plan-scarborough-shoal.

79. Prashanth Parameswaran, "US Kicks Off New Maritime Security Initiative for Southeast Asia," *The Diplomat*, April 10, 2016, https://thediplomat.com/2016/04/us-kicks-off-new-maritime-security-initiative-for-southeast-asia/; National Defense Authorization Act for Fiscal Year 2016, S. 1356, Public Law 114-92, November 2015, https://www.congress.gov/bill/114th-congress/senate-bill/1356.

80. Defense Security Cooperation Agency, "Section 1263 Indo-Pacific Maritime Security Initiative (MSI)," accessed October 4, 2020, https://www.dsca.mil/programs/section-1263-indo-pacific-maritime-security-initiative-msi.

81. Ben Bland, "Indonesia Fisheries Chief Hooks Public Imagination," *Financial Times*, January 2, 2015, https://www.ft.com/content/03bc26c0-897b-11e4-ad5b-00144feabdc0.

82. Ankit Panda, "Indonesia Summons Chinese Ambassador after South China Sea Stand-Off Near Natuna Islands," *The Diplomat*, March 21, 2016, https://thediplomat.com/2016/03/indonesia-summons-chinese-ambassador-after-south-china-sea-stand-off-near-natuna-islands/.

83. Ankit Panda, "South China Sea: Indonesian Navy Fires at and Arrests Chinese Fishermen," *The Diplomat*, May 31, 2016, https://thediplomat.com/2016/05/south-china-sea-indonesian-navy-fires-at-and-arrests-chinese-fishermen/.

84. Ankit Panda, "A Third 2016 Natuna Stand-Off Highlights Growing Indonesia-China Tensions," *The Diplomat*, June 21, 2016, https://thediplomat.com/2016/06/a-third-2016-natuna-stand-off-highlights-growing-indonesia-china-tensions/.

85. See David G. Rose, "'China Calls It Fishing, Indonesia Calls It Crime': Pudjiastuti Finds Her Target for Oceans Summit," *South China Morning Post*, October 18, 2018, https://www.scmp.com/week-asia/geopolitics/article/2169153/china-calls-it-fishing-indonesia-calls-it-crime-pudjiastuti.

86. Permanent Court of Arbitration, "The Arbitral Tribunal Commences Hearing on Jurisdiction and Admissibility," press release, July 7, 2015, https://pcacases.com/web/sendAttach/1301.

87. "Full Text: The Philippines' Opening Salvo at The Hague," *Rappler*, July 8, 2015, https://www.rappler.com/nation/philippines-china-hague-opening-statement-full-text.

88. Permanent Court of Arbitration, *The South China Sea Arbitration*, Award on Jurisdiction and Admissibility, October 29, 2015, https://pcacases.com/web/sendAttach/2579.

89. Statement of the Ministry of Foreign Affairs of the People's Republic of China on the Award on Jurisdiction and Admissibility of the South China Sea Arbitration by the Arbitral Tribunal Established at the Request of the Republic of the Philippines, October 30, 2015, https://www.fmprc.gov.cn/mfa_eng/wjdt_665385/2649_665393/201510/t20151030_679419.html.

90. Permanent Court of Arbitration, "The Tribunal Commences Hearing on Merits," press release, November 30, 2015, https://pcacases.com/web/sendAttach/1521.

91. Yann-huei Song, "Taiping Island: An Island or a Rock under UNCLOS," Asia Maritime Transparency Initiative, May 7, 2015, https://amti.csis.org/taiping-island-an-island-or-a-rock-under-unclos/.

92. Asia Maritime Transparency Initiative, "Taiwan Island Tracker," accessed October 3, 2020, https://amti.csis.org/island-tracker/taiwan/.

93. Asia Maritime Transparency Initiative, "Exploring Itu Aba: A Virtual Tour of a South China Sea Islet," March 21, 2016, https://amti.csis.org/exploring-itu-aba-virtual-tour-south-china-sea-islet/.

94. Permanent Court of Arbitration, *The South China Sea Arbitration*, The Philippines' Written Responses on Itu Aba, April 25, 2016, https://pca-cpa.org/en/cases/7/.

95. Asia Maritime Transparency Initiative, "Podcast: Itu Aba and Taiwan's Amicus Brief," April 5, 2016, https://amti.csis.org/podcast/.

96. Permanent Court of Arbitration, *The South China Sea Arbitration*, The Philippines' Written Responses, March 11, 2016, https://pca-cpa.org/en/cases/7/; The Philippines' Written Responses on Itu Aba, April 25, 2016; The Philippines' Written Responses to UKHO Materials, April 28, 2016, https://pca-cpa.org/en/cases/7/; The Philippines' Written Responses on French Archive Materials, June 3, 2016, https://pca-cpa.org/en/cases/7/.

97. White House, "Remarks by President Obama at U.S.-ASEAN Press Conference," February 16, 2016, https://obamawhitehouse.archives.gov/the-press-office/2016/02/16/remarks-president-obama-us-asean-press-conference.

98. Council of the EU, "Declaration by the High Representative on Behalf of the EU on Recent Developments in the South China Sea," press release, March 11, 2016, https://www.consilium.europa.eu/en/press/press-releases/2016/03/11/hr-declaration-on-bealf-of-eu-recent-developments-south-china-sea/.

99. G7 Foreign Ministers' Statement on Maritime Security, April 11, 2016, http://www.g7.utoronto.ca/foreign/formin160411-maritime.html.

100. G7 Ise-Shima Leaders' Declaration, May 27, 2016, https://www.mofa.go.jp/files/000160266.pdf.

101. Asia Maritime Transparency Initiative, "Arbitration Support Tracker," June 16, 2016, https://amti.csis.org/arbitration-support-tracker/.

102. Ministry of Foreign Affairs of the People's Republic of China, "Foreign Ministry Spokesperson Lu Kang's Regular Press Conference," June 14, 2016, https://www.fmprc.gov.cn/mfa_eng/xwfw_665399/s2510_665401/2511_665403/t1372136.shtml.

103. Asia Maritime Transparency Initiative, "Arbitration Support Tracker."

104. Permanent Court of Arbitration, *The South China Sea Arbitration*, Award, July 12, 2016, https://docs.pca-cpa.org/2016/07/PH-CN-20160712-Award.pdf.

105. Asia Maritime Transparency Initiative, "Arbitration Support Tracker."

106. State Council of the People's Republic of China, "Full Text: China Adheres to the Position of Settling through Negotiations the Relevant Disputes between China and the Philippines in the South China Sea," July 13, 2016, http://english.www.gov.cn/state_council/ministries/2016/07/13/content_281475392503075.htm.

107. Council of the EU, "Declaration by the High Representative on Behalf of the EU on the Award Rendered in the Arbitration between the Republic of the Philippines and the People's Republic of China," press release, July 15, 2016, https://www.consilium.europa.eu/en/press/press-releases/2016/07/15/south-china-sea-arbitration/.

108. Government of Montenegro, *Announcement on the Occasion of the Announcement of the Judgment of the Permanent Court of Arbitration in The Hague on the Dispute between China and the Philippines* [Saopštenje povodom objavljivanja presude Stalnog arbitražnog suda u Hagu o sporu između Kine i Filipina], July 12, 2016, https://www.gov.me/naslovna/vijesti-iz-ministarstava/163193/Saopstenje-povodom-objavljivanja-presude-Stalnog-arbitraznog-suda-u-Hagu-o-sporu-izmedu-Kine-i-Filipina.html.

109. Department of Foreign Affairs of the Philippines, "Information Note on the Significance of the 2016 ASEAN Joint Communiqué in Relation to the Arbitral Tribunal Ruling," August 1, 2016, https://www.dfa.gov.ph/newsroom/dfa-releases/10072-information-note-on-the-significance-of-the-2016-asean-joint-communique-in-relation-to-the-arbitral-tribunal-ruling.

110. AP, "Duterte Says He'll Set Aside South China Sea Feud Ruling against Beijing," *South China Morning Post*, December 17, 2016, https://www.scmp.com/news/asia/southeast-asia/article/2055433/duterte-says-hell-set-aside-south-china-sea-feud-ruling.

Chapter 10

1. U.S. Senate Committee on Armed Services, "Senators McCain, Reed, Corker, and Menendez Send Letter."

2. Harold et al., *The Thickening Web*, 293–94; Pia Ranada, "Duterte Wants to Scrap EDCA," *Rappler*, October 25, 2016, https://www.rappler.com/nation/duterte-edca-no-foreign-troops.

3. Bill Chappell, "Philippines' Duterte Says He's 'Separated' from U.S., as He Cozies Up to China," NPR, October 20, 2016, https://www.npr.org/sections/thetwo-way/2016/10/20/498715511/philippines-duterte-says-hes-separated-from-u-s-as-he-cozies-up-to-china.

4. Germelina Lacorte, "Duterte Says America Will Never Die for PH," *Philippine Daily Inquirer*, August 2, 2015, https://globalnation.inquirer.net/126835/duterte-to-military-attaches-ph-not-out-for-war-china-should-just-let-us-fish-in-seas.

5. Marina Koren, "The Philippine President's Vulgar Warning to Obama," *Atlantic*, September 5, 2016, https://www.theatlantic.com/news/archive/2016/09/duterte-obama-extrajudicial-killings/498710/.

6. Jane Perlez and Matthew Rosenberg, "China Agrees to Return Seized Drone, Ending Standoff, Pentagon Says," *New York Times*, December 17, 2016, https://www.nytimes.com/2016/12/17/world/asia/china-us-drone.html.

7. White House, "Remarks by President Trump at APEC CEO Summit," November 10, 2017, https://www.whitehouse.gov/briefings-statements/remarks-president-trump-apec-ceo-summit-da-nang-vietnam/; Gregory B. Poling, "For Lack of a Strategy: The Free and Open Indo-Pacific," *War on the Rocks*, November 13, 2019, https://warontherocks.com/2019/11/for-lack-of-a-strategy-the-free-and-open-indo-pacific/.

8. Kristina Wong, "Exclusive: Trump's Pentagon Plans to Regularly Challenge China in the South China Sea," Breitbart, July 21, 2017, https://www.breitbart.com/national-security/2017/07/20/trump-pentagon-south-china-sea-plan/.

9. Idrees Ali and David Brunnstrom, "U.S. Warship Drill Meant to Defy China's Claim over Artificial Islands: Officials," Reuters, May 24, 2017, https://www.reuters.com/article/us-usa-southchinasea-navy/u-s-warship-drill-meant-to-defy-chinas-claim-over-artificial-island-officials-idUSKBN18K353.

10. Nancy A. Youssef, "Mattis Says China Is 'Out of Step' with International Law," *Wall Street Journal*, May 29, 2018, https://www.wsj.com/articles/mattis-says-china-is-out-of-step-with-international-law-1527636790.

11. Gregory Poling and Conor Cronin, "The Dangers of Allowing U.S.-Philippine Defense Cooperation to Languish," *War on the Rocks*, May 17, 2018, https://warontherocks.com/2018/05/the-dangers-of-allowing-u-s-philippine-defense-cooperation-to-languish/.

12. Claire Jiao and Nick Wadhams, "We Have Your Back in South China Sea, U.S. Assures Philippines," *Bloomberg*, February 28, 2019, https://www.bloomberg.com/news/articles/2019-03-01/pompeo-says-u-s-is-committed-to-keeping-south-china-sea-open.

13. Christia Marie Ramos, "PH Walks Back, Suspends VFA Termination 'Upon the President's Instruction,'" *Philippine Daily Inquirer*, June 2, 2020, https://globalnation.inquirer.net/188098/ph-walks-back-suspends-vfa-termination-upon-the-presidents-instruction.

14. Asia Maritime Transparency Initiative, "A Constructive Year for Chinese Base Building," December 14, 2017, https://amti.csis.org/constructive-year-chinese-building/; Asia Maritime Transparency Initiative, "China's Continuing Reclamation in the Paracels," updated August 9, 2017, https://amti.csis.org/paracels-beijings-other-buildup/.

15. Asia Maritime Transparency Initiative, "An Accounting of China's Deployments to the Spratly Islands," May 9, 2018, https://amti.csis.org/accounting-chinas-deployments-spratly-islands/; Asia Maritime Transparency Initiative, "Exercises Bring New Weapons to the Paracels," May 24, 2018, https://amti.csis.org/exercises-bring-new-weapons-paracels/; Michael R. Gordon and Jeremy Page, "China Installed Military Jamming Equipment on Spratly Islands, U.S. Says," *Wall Street Journal*, April 9, 2018, https://www.wsj.com/articles/china-installed-military-jamming-equipment-on-spratly-islands-u-s-says-1523266320; Amanda Macias, "China Quietly Installed Missile Systems on Strategic Spratly Islands in Hotly Contested South China Sea," CNBC, May 2, 2018, https://www.cnbc.com/2018/05/02/china-added-missile-systems-on-spratly-islands-in-south-china-sea.html; Frances Mangosing, "China Military Planes Land on PH Reef," *Philippine Daily Inquirer*, April 18, 2018, https://globalnation.inquirer.net/165824/china-military-planes-land-ph-reef; Gregory B. Poling, "Illuminating the South China Sea's Dark Fishing Fleets," Center for Strategic and International Studies, January 9, 2019, https://ocean.csis.org/spotlights/illuminating-the-south-china-seas-dark-fishing-fleets/.

16. Bonnie S. Glaser and Gregory Poling, "Vanishing Borders in the South China Sea," *Foreign Affairs*, June 5, 2018, https://www.foreignaffairs.com/articles/china/2018-06-05/vanishing-borders-south-china-sea; Gregory B. Poling and Murray Hiebert, "Stop the Bully in the South China Sea," *Wall Street Journal*, August 28, 2019, https://www.wsj.com/articles/stop-the-bully-in-the-south-china-sea-11567033378; Asia Maritime Transparency Initiative, "Update: Chinese Survey Ship Escalates Three-Way Standoff," April 30, 2020, https://amti.csis.org/chinese-survey-ship-escalates-three-way-standoff/; Asia Maritime Transparency

Initiative, "The Long Patrol: Staredown at Thitu Island Enters Its Sixteenth Month," March 5, 2020, https://amti.csis.org/the-long-patrol-staredown-at-thitu-island-enters-its-sixtee nth-month/; Asia Maritime Transparency Initiative, "Gone Fishing: Tracking China's Flotilla from Brunei to Indonesia," January 30, 2020, https://amti.csis.org/gone-fishing-tracking-chinas-flotilla-from-brunei-to-indonesia/; Asia Maritime Transparency Initiative, "Update: China Risks Flare-Up over Malaysia, Vietnamese Gas Resources," December 13, 2019, https://amti.csis.org/china-risks-flare-up-over-malaysian-vietnamese-gas-resources/; Asia Maritime Transparency Initiative, "China's Most Destructive Boats Return to the South China Sea," May 20, 2019, https://amti.csis.org/chinas-most-destructive-boats-return-to-the-south-china-sea/.

17. Gregory Poling, "South China Sea Code of Conduct Still a Speck on the Horizon," *East Asia Forum*, September 6, 2018, https://www.eastasiaforum.org/2018/09/06/south-china-sea-code-of-conduct-still-a-speck-on-the-horizon/.

18. "ASEAN, China Talk DOC Implementation at 18th SOM Meeting," Vietnam News Agency, October 15, 2019, https://en.vietnamplus.vn/asean-china-talk-doc-implementation-at-18th-som-meeting/162111.vnp; Anh Ngoc, "Vietnam Condemns China's Sovereignty Violations at ASEAN Meeting," *VNExpress*, October 15, 2019, https://e.vnexpress.net/news/news/vietnam-condemns-china-s-sovereignty-violations-at-asean-meeting-3997472.html.

19. Department of State, *A Free and Open Indo-Pacific: Advancing a Shared Vision*, November 4, 2019, https://www.state.gov/wp-content/uploads/2019/11/Free-and-Open-Indo-Pacific-4Nov2019.pdf.

20. See Asia Maritime Transparency Initiative, "Who's Taking Sides on China's Maritime Claims?," September 24, 2020, https://amti.csis.org/whos-taking-sides-on-chinas-maritime-claims/.

21. Michael R. Pompeo, "U.S. Position on Maritime Claims in the South China Sea," press statement, July 13, 2020, https://www.state.gov/u-s-position-on-maritime-claims-in-the-south-china-sea/.

22. U.S. Department of Commerce, "Commerce Department Adds 24 Chinese Companies to the Entity List for Helping Build Military Islands in the South China Sea," press release, August 26, 2020, https://www.commerce.gov/news/press-releases/2020/08/commerce-departm ent-adds-24-chinese-companies-entity-list-helping-build.

23. Michael R. Pompeo, "U.S. Imposes Restrictions on Certain PRC State-Owned Enterprises and Executives for Malign Activities in the South China Sea," press statement, August 26, 2020, https://www.state.gov/u-s-imposes-restrictions-on-certain-prc-state-owned-enterpri ses-and-executives-for-malign-activities-in-the-south-china-sea/.

24. Andrew Erickson and Joel Wuthnow, "Barriers, Springboards and Benchmarks," *China Quarterly* 225 (March 2016): 1–22.

25. "Advanced Policy Questions for Admiral Philip Davidson, USN," Senate Armed Services Committee, April 17, 2018, https://www.armed-services.senate.gov/imo/media/doc/ Davidson_APQs_04-17-18.pdf.

26. For a debate on this topic, see Gregory B. Poling, "The Conventional Wisdom on China's Island Bases Is Dangerously Wrong," *War on the Rocks*, January 10, 2020, https://waront herocks.com/2020/01/the-conventional-wisdom-on-chinas-island-bases-is-dangerously-wrong/; Olli Pekka Suorsa, "The Conventional Wisdom Still Stands: America Can Deal with China's Artificial Island Bases," *War on the Rocks*, February 6, 2020, https://warontherocks. com/2020/02/the-conventional-wisdom-still-stands-america-can-deal-with-chinas-artific ial-island-bases/; J. Michael Dahm, "Beyond 'Conventional Wisdom': Evaluating the PLA's South China Sea Bases in Operational Context," *War on the Rocks*, March 17, 2020, https:// warontherocks.com/2020/03/beyond-conventional-wisdom-evaluating-the-plas-south-china-sea-bases-in-operational-context/.

27. ChinaPower, "How Much Trade Transits the South China Sea?," Center for Strategic and International Studies, accessed October 7, 2020, https://chinapower.csis.org/much-trade-transits-south-china-sea/.

28. Asia Maritime Transparency Initiative, "A Blueprint for Cooperation on Oil and Gas Production in the South China Sea," July 25, 2018, https://amti.csis.org/a-blueprint-for-cooperation-on-oil-and-gas-production-in-the-south-china-sea/.

29. U. Rashid Sumaila and William W. L. Cheung, "Boom or Bust: The Future of Fish in the South China Sea," report, University of British Columbia, November 5, 2015, https://drive. google.com/file/d/0B_oUJE4kCTZrbVI4N2tTVjlpYTA/view.

30. Ibid.

31. McManus, "Offshore Coral Reef Damage."

32. Steven Stashwick, "'Unsafe' Incident between US and Chinese Warships during FONOP," *The Diplomat*, October 2, 2018, https://thediplomat.com/2018/10/unsafe-incident-betw een-us-and-chinese-warships-during-fonop/.

33. Bonnie Glaser and Jeff W. Benson, "Conflict Prevention in the South China Sea Depends on China Abiding by the Existing Rules of Navigation," *South China Morning Post*, February 27, 2020, https://www.scmp.com/comment/opinion/article/3052429/conflict-prevention- south-china-sea-depends-china-abiding-existing.

34. Khanh Vu, "Vietnam Protests Beijing's Sinking of South China Sea Boat," Reuters, April 4, 2020, https://www.reuters.com/article/us-vietnam-china-southchinasea/vietnam-protests- beijings-sinking-of-south-china-sea-boat-idUSKBN21M072.

35. Asia Maritime Transparency Initiative, "Seeking Clues in the Case of the Yuemaobinyu 42212," October 15, 2019, https://amti.csis.org/seeking-clues-in-the-case-of-the-yuemaobi nyu-42212/.

36. See Michael O'Hanlon and Gregory Poling, "Rocks, Reefs, and Nuclear War," Asia Maritime Transparency Initiative, January 14, 2020, https://amti.csis.org/rocks-reefs-and-nucl ear-war/.

37. For examples of how such an arrangement might work, see CSIS Expert Working Group on the South China Sea, *Defusing the South China Sea Disputes: A Regional Blueprint*, Center for Strategic and International Studies, October 2018, https://www.csis.org/analysis/defusing- south-china-sea-disputes.

38. Ministry of Foreign Affairs of China, "Set Aside Dispute and Pursue Joint Development."

BIBLIOGRAPHY

Agence France Press. "Other Nations Must Take Stand on China: PH." *ABS-CBN News*, April 23, 2012. https://news.abs-cbn.com/nation/04/22/12/other-nations-must-take-stand-china-ph.

Agence France Press and Minnie Chan. "US Asks China to Stop Building Spratlys Island Which Could Host Airfield." *South China Morning Post*, November 22, 2014. https://www.scmp.com/news/china/article/1646025/us-asks-china-stop-building-spratlys-island-which-could-host-airfield.

Alexander, David. "Vietnam, U.S. Discuss Land Reclamation in South China Sea." Reuters, June 1, 2015. https://www.reuters.com/article/us-vietnam-usa-defense/vietnam-u-s-discuss-land-reclamation-in-south-china-sea-idUSKBN0OH1L120150601.

Ali, Idrees, and David Brunnstrom. "U.S. Warship Drill Meant to Defy China's Claim over Artificial Islands: Officials." Reuters, May 24, 2017. https://www.reuters.com/article/us-usa-southc hinasea-navy/u-s-warship-drill-meant-to-defy-chinas-claim-over-artificial-island-officials-idUSKBN18K353.

Arreglado, Juan. *Kalayaan: Historical, Legal, Political Background*. Manila: Foreign Service Institute, 1982.

Asia Maritime Transparency Initiative. "An Accounting of China's Deployments to the Spratly Islands." May 9, 2018. https://amti.csis.org/accounting-chinas-deployments-spratly-islands/.

Asia Maritime Transparency Initiative. "Arbitration Support Tracker." June 16, 2016. https://amti.csis.org/arbitration-support-tracker/.

Asia Maritime Transparency Initiative. "A Blueprint for Cooperation on Oil and Gas Production in the South China Sea." July 25, 2018. https://amti.csis.org/a-blueprint-for-cooperation-on-oil-and-gas-production-in-the-south-china-sea/.

Asia Maritime Transparency Initiative. "China Island Tracker." April 11, 2020. https://amti.csis.org/island-tracker/china/.

Asia Maritime Transparency Initiative. "China Quietly Upgrades a Remote Reef." November 20, 2018. https://amti.csis.org/china-quietly-upgrades-bombay-reef/.

Asia Maritime Transparency Initiative. "China's Most Destructive Boats Return to the South China Sea." May 20, 2019. https://amti.csis.org/chinas-most-destructive-boats-return-to-the-south-china-sea/.

Asia Maritime Transparency Initiative. "A Constructive Year for Chinese Base Building." December 14, 2017. https://amti.csis.org/constructive-year-chinese-building/.

Asia Maritime Transparency Initiative. "Exercises Bring New Weapons to the Paracels." May 24, 2018. https://amti.csis.org/exercises-bring-new-weapons-paracels/.

Asia Maritime Transparency Initiative. "Exploring Itu Aba: A Virtual Tour of a South China Sea Islet." March 21, 2016. https://amti.csis.org/exploring-itu-aba-virtual-tour-south-china-sea-islet/.

Asia Maritime Transparency Initiative. "Gone Fishing: Tracking China's Flotilla from Brunei to Indonesia." January 30, 2020. https://amti.csis.org/gone-fishing-tracking-chinas-flotilla-from-brunei-to-indonesia/.

Asia Maritime Transparency Initiative. "The Long Patrol: Staredown at Thitu Island Enters Its Sixteenth Month." March 5, 2020. https://amti.csis.org/the-long-patrol-staredown-at-thitu-island-enters-its-sixteenth-month/.

Asia Maritime Transparency Initiative. "Philippines Island Tracker." April 11, 2020.

Asia Maritime Transparency Initiative. "Podcast: Itu Aba and Taiwan's Amicus Brief." April 5, 2016. https://amti.csis.org/podcast/.

Asia Maritime Transparency Initiative. "Reading between the Lines: The Next Spratly Legal Dispute." March 21, 2019. https://amti.csis.org/reading-between-lines-next-spratly-dispute/.

Asia Maritime Transparency Initiative. "Seeking Clues in the Case of the Yuemaobinyu 42212." October 15, 2019. https://amti.csis.org/seeking-clues-in-the-case-of-the-yuemaobinyu-42212/.

Asia Maritime Transparency Initiative. "Signaling Sovereignty: Chinese Patrols at Contested Reefs." September 26, 2019. https://amti.csis.org/signaling-sovereignty-chinese-patrols-at-contested-reefs/.

Asia Maritime Transparency Initiative. "Slow and Steady: Vietnam's Spratly Upgrades." April 8, 2019. https://amti.csis.org/slow-and-steady-vietnams-spratly-upgrades/.

Asia Maritime Transparency Initiative. "Taiwan Island Tracker." Accessed October 3, 2020. https://amti.csis.org/island-tracker/taiwan/.

Asia Maritime Transparency Initiative. "Tracking China's Coast Guard Off Borneo." April 5, 2017. https://amti.csis.org/tracking-chinas-coast-guard-off-borneo/.

Asia Maritime Transparency Initiative. "Update: China Risks Flare-Up over Malaysia, Vietnamese Gas Resources." December 13, 2019. https://amti.csis.org/china-risks-flare-up-over-malaysian-vietnamese-gas-resources/.

Asia Maritime Transparency Initiative. "Update: China's Continuing Reclamation in the Paracels." August 9, 2017. https://amti.csis.org/paracels-beijings-other-buildup/.

Asia Maritime Transparency Initiative. "Update: Chinese Survey Ship Escalates Three-Way Standoff." April 30, 2020. https://amti.csis.org/chinese-survey-ship-escalates-three-way-standoff/.

Asia Maritime Transparency Initiative. "Vietnam's Island Building: Double-Standard or Drop in the Bucket?" May 11, 2016. https://amti.csis.org/vietnams-island-building/.

Asia Maritime Transparency Initiative. "Washed Away." February 17, 2016. https://amti.csis.org/typhoon-spotlights-island-building/.

Asia Maritime Transparency Initiative. "Who's Taking Sides on China's Maritime Claims?" September 24, 2020. https://amti.csis.org/whos-taking-sides-on-chinas-maritime-claims/.

Associated Press. "China Rejects U.S. Arbitration of Maritime Dispute." *New York Times*, February 19, 2013. https://www.nytimes.com/2013/02/20/world/asia/china-rejects-un-arbitration-of-maritime-dispute.html.

Associated Press. "Duterte Says He'll Set Aside South China Sea Feud Ruling against Beijing." *South China Morning Post*, December 17, 2016. https://www.scmp.com/news/asia/southeast-asia/article/2055433/duterte-says-hell-set-aside-south-china-sea-feud-ruling.

Association of Southeast Asian Nations Foreign Ministers' Statement on the Current Developments in the South China Sea. May 10, 2014. https://asean.org/wp-content/uploads/2012/05/24th-AFMs-Statement-on-SCS.pdf.

Association of Southeast Asian Nations. Singapore Declaration of 1992. January 28, 1992. https://asean.org/?static_post=singapore-declaration-of-1992-singapore-28-january-1992.

Austin, Greg. "Unwanted Entanglement: The Philippines' Spratly Policy as a Case Study in Conflict Enhancement?" *Security Dialogue* 34, no. 1 (March 2003): 41–54.

Batongbacal, Jay. "Arbitration 101: Philippines v. China." Asia Maritime Transparency Initiative, January 21, 2015. https://amti.csis.org/arbitration-101-philippines-v-china/.

Batongbacal, Jay L., and Efren P. Carandang, eds. *Bajo de Masinloc: Scarborough Shoal Maps and Documents.* Taguig City, Philippines: National Mapping and Resource Information Authority, 2014.

Baviera, Aileen S. P., and Jay Batongbacal. *The West Philippine Sea: The Territorial and Maritime Jurisdiction Disputes from a Filipino Perspective: A Primer.* Monograph, University of the Philippines, Manila, July 15, 2013. https://ac.upd.edu.ph/index.php/resources/books-and-monographs/1352-the-west-philippine-sea-the-territorial-and-maritime-jurisdiction-disputes-from-a-filipino-perspective.

Bland, Ben. "Indonesia Fisheries Chief Hooks Public Imagination." *Financial Times,* January 2, 2015. https://www.ft.com/content/03bc26c0-897b-11e4-ad5b-00144feabdc0.

Belmonte, Feliciano, Jr. "P.I. Claim to Spratly Islands in 1946 Bared." *Manila Chronicle,* June 14, 1956.

Bonnet, François-Xavier. *Geopolitics of Scarborough Shoal.* IRASEC Discussion Paper 14. Bangkok: Research Institute on Contemporary Southeast Asia, November 2012.

Bonnet, François-Xavier. "The Spratlys: A Past Revisited." *World Bulletin* 23 (July–December 2004): 13–27.

Bower, Ernest Z. "China Reveals Its Hand on ASEAN in Phnom Penh." *CSIS Commentary,* July 19, 2012. https://www.csis.org/analysis/china-reveals-its-hand-asean-phnom-penh.

Bower, Ernest Z. "U.S.-ASEAN Summit: President Obama Engages Southeast Asia." CSIS Critical Questions, November 9, 2009. https://www.csis.org/analysis/us-asean-summit-president-obama-engages-southeast-asia.

British Broadcasting Corporation. "Vietnam Accuses China in Seas Dispute." May 30, 2011. https://www.bbc.com/news/world-asia-pacific-13592508.

Broder, John M. "U.S. Reaches Accord with Manila, Will Leave Clark Air Base: Philippines: Volcano Causes Abandonment of Field; But Americans Will Keep Subic Naval Base for 10 Years." *Los Angeles Times,* July 18, 1991. https://www.latimes.com/archives/la-xpm-1991-07-18-mn-3381-story.html.

Brummit, Chris. "Vietnam Tries to Stop China Oil Rig Deployment." *USA Today,* May 7, 2014. https://www.usatoday.com/story/news/world/2014/05/07/vietnam-china-oil-rig/8797007/.

Brunei Darussalam. Preliminary Submission concerning the Outer Limits of Its Continental Shelf. May 12, 2009. https://www.un.org/depts/los/clcs_new/submissions_files/preliminary/brn2009preliminaryinformation.pdf.

Brunnstrom, David, and Andrea Shalal. "Exclusive: U.S. Sees New Chinese Activity around South China Sea Shoal." Reuters, March 17, 2016. https://www.reuters.com/article/us-southchinasea-china-scarborough-exclu-idUSKCN0WK01B.

Burt, Richard. "Soviet Ships Arrive at Cam Ranh Bay." *New York Times,* March 29, 1979.

Buszynski, Leszek. *Soviet Foreign Policy and Southeast Asia.* London: Routledge, 1986.

Butcher, John G, and R. E. Elson. *Sovereignty and the Sea: How Indonesia Became an Archipelagic State.* Singapore: NUS Press, 2017.

Cairo Declaration. November 26, 1943. Wilson Center Digital Archive. https://digitalarchive.wilsoncenter.org/document/122101.

Carter, Ashton. *Reflections on American Grand Strategy in Asia.* Cambridge, MA: Belfer Center for Science and International Affairs, October 2018. https://www.belfercenter.org/publication/reflections-american-grand-strategy-asia.

Carter, Ashton. U.S. Pacific Command Change of Command Speech. Joint Base Pearl Harbor-Hickam, Hawaii. May 27, 2015. https://www.defense.gov/News/Speeches/Article/606675/.

Central Intelligence Agency. Freedom of Information Act Electronic Reading Room. https://www.cia.gov/readingroom/.

Centre for International Law, National University of Singapore.

"Documents on ASEAN and the South China Sea." June 2011. https://cil.nus.edu.sg/wp-cont ent/uploads/2011/06/Documents-on-ASEAN-and-South-China-Sea-as-of-June-2011-pdf.pdf.

Chan, Minnie. "China to Build Up Atoll in Contested South China Sea, Source Says." *South China Morning Post,* April 25, 2016. https://www.scmp.com/news/china/diplomacy-defence/arti cle/1938277/china-build-atoll-contested-south-china-sea-source-says.

Chappell, Bill. "Philippines' Duterte Says He's 'Separated' from U.S., as He Cozies Up to China." NPR, October 20, 2016. https://www.npr.org/sections/thetwo-way/2016/10/20/498715 511/philippines-duterte-says-hes-separated-from-u-s-as-he-cozies-up-to-china.

Chemillier-Gendreau, Monique. *Sovereignty over the Paracel and Spratly Islands.* The Hague: Kluwer Law International, 2000.

ChinaPower. "How Much Trade Transits the South China Sea?" Center for Strategic and International Studies. Accessed October 7, 2020. https://chinapower.csis.org/much-trade-transits-south-china-sea/.

Ching, Nike. "US, Philippines Agree on Five Locations Covered by Defense Pact." *Voice of America,* March 18, 2016. https://www.voanews.com/east-asia/us-philippines-agree-five-locations-covered-defense-pact.

Chiu, H., and C. H. Park. "Legal Status of the Paracel and Spratly Islands." *Ocean Development and International Law* 3 (1975): 1–28.

Chongkittavorn, Kavi. "ASEAN-China Tussles: COC Endgame." Presentation at 9th Annual CSIS South China Sea Conference, Center for Strategic and International Studies, Washington, DC, July 24, 2019.

Chubb, Andrew. "PRC Assertiveness in the South China Sea: Measuring Continuity and Change, 1970–2015." *International Security* 45, no. 3 (Winter 2020–21): 79–121.

Chung, Chris P. C. "Drawing the U-Shaped Line: China's Claim in the South China Sea, 1946–1974." *Modern China* 42, no. 1 (January 2016): 38–72.

Clinton, Hillary. "America's Pacific Century." *Foreign Policy,* October 11, 2011. https://foreignpol icy.com/2011/10/11/americas-pacific-century/.

Clinton, Hillary Rodham. Interview with Greg Sheridan of *The Australian.* U.S. Department of State, November 8, 2010. https://2009-2017.state.gov/secretary/20092013clinton/rm/2010/11/150671.htm.

Clinton, Hillary Rodham. Remarks at Press Availability. U.S. Department of State, July 23, 2010. https://2009-2017.state.gov/secretary/20092013clinton/rm/2010/07/145095.htm.

Clinton, Hillary Rodham. Remarks with Secretary of Defense Leon Panetta, Philippines Foreign Secretary Albert del Rosario, and Philippines Defense Secretary Voltaire Gazmin after Their Meeting. U.S. Department of State, April 30, 2012. https://2009-2017.state.gov/secretary/20092013clinton/rm/2012/04/188982.htm.

Cohen, Jerome Alan, and Hungdah Chiuh. *People's China and International Law: A Documentary Study.* Princeton, NJ: Princeton University Press, 1974.

Comptroller General of the United States. "Report to Congress: Military Assistance and Commitments in the Philippines." April 12, 1973.

Constitution of the Republic of the Philippines. February 2, 1987. https://www.officialgazette. gov.ph/constitutions/1987-constitution/.

Cooper, Zack, and Jake Douglas. "Successful Signaling at Scarborough Shoal?" *War on the Rocks,* May 2, 2016. https://warontherocks.com/2016/05/successful-signaling-at-scarborough-shoal/.

Council of the European Union. "Declaration by the High Representative on Behalf of the EU on the Award Rendered in the Arbitration between the Republic of the Philippines and the People's Republic of China." Press release. July 15, 2016. https://www.consilium.europa.eu/en/press/press-releases/2016/07/15/south-china-sea-arbitration/.

Council of the European Union. "Declaration by the High Representative on Behalf of the EU on Recent Developments in the South China Sea." Press release. March 11, 2016. https://www.consilium.europa.eu/en/press/press-releases/2016/03/11/hr-declaration-on-bealf-of-eu-recent-developments-south-china-sea/.

CSIS Expert Working Group on the South China Sea. *Defusing the South China Sea Disputes: A Regional Blueprint.* Washington, DC: Center for Strategic and International Studies, October 2018.

Dahm, J. Michael. "Beyond 'Conventional Wisdom': Evaluating the PLA's South China Sea Bases in Operational Context." *War on the Rocks,* March 17, 2020. https://warontherocks.com/2020/03/beyond-conventional-wisdom-evaluating-the-plas-south-china-sea-bases-in-operational-context/.

Darman, Richard G. "The Law of the Sea: Rethinking U.S. Interests." *Foreign Affairs,* January 1978. https://www.foreignaffairs.com/articles/oceans-seas/1978-01-01/law-sea-rethinking-us-interests?cid=rss-letter_from_newdelhi-the_law_of_the_sea_rethinking-000000.

David, Adrian. "How Malaysia's Five Naval Stations at Spratlys Were Built." *New Straits Times,* March 4, 2019. https://www.nst.com.my/news/nation/2019/03/465854/how-malaysias-five-naval-stations-spratlys-were-built.

Dean, Arthur H. "The Second Geneva Conference on the Law of the Sea: The Fight for Freedom of the Seas." *American Journal of International Law* 54, no. 4 (October 1960): 751–789.

Declaration on the Conduct of Parties in the South China Sea. November 4, 2002. https://asean.org/?static_post=declaration-on-the-conduct-of-parties-in-the-south-china-sea-2.

Del Rosario, Albert. "Statement: The Secretary of Foreign Affairs on the UNCLOS Arbitral Proceedings against China." *Government of the Philippines Official Gazette,* January 22, 2013. https://www.officialgazette.gov.ph/2013/01/22/statement-the-secretary-of-foreign-affairs-on-the-unclos-arbitral-proceedings-against-china-january-22-2013/.

Department of Foreign Affairs and Trade of Australia. "ASEAN Regional Forum." Accessed August 27, 2019. https://www.dfat.gov.au/international-relations/regional-architecture/asean-regional-forum-arf.

Dizon, Nikko. "AFP Uses Couriers to Foil China Spies." *Philippine Daily Inquirer,* April 29, 2014. https://globalnation.inquirer.net/103076/afp-uses-couriers-to-foil-china-spies.

Dumlao, Doris C. "Pangilinan Brings in Chinese to Disputed Recto Bank Oil Exploration Group." *Philippine Daily Inquirer,* June 24, 2012. https://business.inquirer.net/67089/pangilinan-brings-in-chinese-to-disputed-recto-bank-oil-exploration-group.

Entous, Adam, Gordon Lubold, and Julian E. Barnes. "U.S. Military Proposes Challenge to China Sea Claims." *Wall Street Journal,* May 12, 2015. https://www.marketwatch.com/story/us-military-proposes-challenge-to-china-sea-claims-2015-05-12-17103251.

Erickson, Andrew S. "Exposed: Pentagon Report Spotlights China's Maritime Militia." *National Interest,* August 20, 2018. https://nationalinterest.org/feature/exposed-pentagon-report-spotlights-china%E2%80%99s-maritime-militia-29282.

Erickson, Andrew S., and Conor M. Kennedy. *China's Daring Vanguard: Introducing Sanya City's Maritime Militia.* Washington, DC: Center for International Maritime Security, November 5, 2015. http://cimsec.org/chinas-daring-vanguard-introducing-sanya-citys-maritime-militia/19753.

Erickson, Andrew S., and Joel Wuthnow. "Barriers, Springboards and Benchmarks." *China Quarterly* 225 (March 2016): 1–22.

Erlanger, Steven. "Vietnam Promises Troops Will Leave Cambodia by Fall." *New York Times,* April 6, 1989. https://www.nytimes.com/1989/04/06/world/vietnam-promises-troops-will-leave-cambodia-by-fall.html#:~:text=Ten%20years%20and%20three%20months,by%20the%20end%20of%20September.

Esplanada, Jerry E. "Philippines to Seek US Help in Dealing with China over Spratlys Issue—DFA." *Philippine Daily Inquirer,* April 26, 2012. http://globalnation.inquirer.net/34857/philippines-to-seek-us-help-in-dealing-with-china-over-spratlys-issue-dfa.

Estrada, Erik. "Philippines, U.S. Start Exercise Balikatan 2016." U.S. Department of Defense, April 7, 2016. https://www.defense.gov/Explore/News/Article/Article/715540/philippines-us-start-exercise-balikatan-2016/.

Farrell, Epsey Cooke. *The Socialist Republic of Vietnam and the Law of the Sea: An Analysis of Vietnamese Behavior within the Emerging International Oceans Regime.* The Hague: Martinus Nijhoff, 1998.

Felsenthal, Mark. "Obama Says U.S. Commitment to Defend Philippines 'Ironclad.'" Reuters, April 29, 2014. https://www.reuters.com/article/us-philippines-usa-obama-idUSBREA3S02T20140429.

Feuer, A. B. *Commando: The M/Z Unit's Secret War against Japan.* Westport, CT: Praeger, 1996.

Fonbuena, Carmela. "PH Aborts Construction on Pag-asa Sandbar after China Protest." *Rappler,* November 8, 2017. https://www.rappler.com/nation/187690-ph-china-pagasa-standoff-lorenzana.

Fonbuena, Carmela. "U.S. Stopped China's Plan to Build on Scarborough." *Rappler,* March 9, 2017. https://www.rappler.com/nation/us-stopped-china-plan-scarborough-shoal.

Fravel, M. Taylor. *Strong Borders, Secure Nation: Cooperation and Conflict in China's Territorial Disputes.* Princeton, NJ: Princeton University Press, 2008.

Freund, Eleanor. "Freedom of Navigation in the South China Sea: A Practical Guide." Asia Maritime Transparency Initiative, August 10, 2017. https://amti.csis.org/freedom-of-navigation-practical-guide/.

Fu Ying. "Huangyan Dao, and What Happened in 2012: A Witness Account." In Fu Ying, *Kan Shi Jie 2* [*Watching the World 2*]. Beijing: CITIC Publishing Group, 2021.

Garamone, Jim. "Chinese Vessels Shadow, Harass Unarmed U.S. Survey Ship." American Forces Press Service, March 9, 2009. https://archive.defense.gov/news/newsarticle.aspx?id=53401.

Glaser, Bonnie B., and Jeff W. Benson. "Conflict Prevention in the South China Sea Depends on China Abiding by the Existing Rules of Navigation." *South China Morning Post,* February 27, 2020. https://www.scmp.com/comment/opinion/article/3052429/conflict-prevention-south-china-sea-depends-china-abiding-existing.

Glaser, Bonnie S., and Peter A. Dutton. "The US Navy's Freedom of Navigation Operation around Subi Reef: Deciphering US Signaling." *National Interest,* November 6, 2015. http://nationalinterest.org/feature/the-us-navy%E2%80%99s-freedom-navigation-operation-around-subi-reef-14272.

Glaser, Bonnie S., Michael J. Green, and Gregory B. Poling. "The US Asserts Freedom of Navigation in the South China Sea." Center for Strategic and International Relations, October 27, 2015. https://www.csis.org/analysis/us-asserts-freedom-navigation-south-china-sea.

Glaser, Bonnie S., and Gregory B. Poling. "Vanishing Borders in the South China Sea." *Foreign Affairs,* June 5, 2018. https://www.foreignaffairs.com/articles/china/2018-06-05/vanishing-borders-south-china-sea.

Global Times. "Alleged South China Sea Reef Construction Is 'Renovation.'" May 4, 2014. http://english.sina.com/china/2014/0503/697230.html.

GMA News. "Palace: China Expected to Pull Ships Out of Shoal after Exit of PHL Boats." June 17, 2012. https://www.gmanetwork.com/news/news/nation/262228/palace-china-expected-to-pull-ships-out-of-shoal-after-exit-of-phl-boats/story/.

GMA News. "PHL Won't Recognize China Fishing Ban in West Philippine Sea." May 14, 2012. https://www.gmanetwork.com/news/news/nation/258155/phl-won-t-recognize-china-fishing-ban-in-west-philippine-sea/story/.

Gomez, Jim. "Philippines Asks Neighbors to Join Case vs China." *Philippine Star,* February 28, 2014. https://www.philstar.com/headlines/2014/02/28/1295521/philippines-asks-neighbors-join-case-vs-china.

Gordon, Michael R., and Jeremy Page. "China Installed Military Jamming Equipment on Spratly Islands, U.S. Says." *Wall Street Journal,* April 9, 2018. https://www.wsj.com/articles/china-installed-military-jamming-equipment-on-spratly-islands-u-s-says-1523266320.

Government of Indonesia. Declaration by the Government of Indonesia concerning the Exclusive Economic Zone of Indonesia. March 21, 1980. https://www.un.org/depts/los/LEGISLA TIONANDTREATIES/PDFFILES/IDN_1980_DeclarationEEZ.pdf.

Government of Montenegro. *Announcement on the Occasion of the Announcement of the Judgment of the Permanent Court of Arbitration in The Hague on the Dispute between China and the Philippines* [Saopštenje povodom objavljivanja presude Stalnog arbitražnog suda u Hagu o sporu između Kine i Filipina]. July 12, 2016. https://www.gov.me/naslovna/vijesti-iz-ministarstava/163193/Saopstenje-povodom-objavljivanja-presude-Stalnog-arbitraznog-suda-u-Hagu-o-sporu-izmedu-Kine-i-Filipina.html.

Government of the People's Republic of China. Declaration on China's Territorial Sea. September 4, 1958. https://www.documentcloud.org/documents/1341822-declaration-of-the-gov ernment-of-the-prc-on.html.

Government of the People's Republic of China. Declaration on the Baselines of the Territorial Sea. May 15, 1996. https://www.un.org/Depts/los/LEGISLATIONANDTREATIES/PDFFI LES/CHN_1996_Declaration.pdf.

Government of the People's Republic of China. Exclusive Economic Zone and Continental Shelf Act. June 26, 1998. https://www.un.org/Depts/los/LEGISLATIONANDTREATIES/ PDFFILES/chn_1998_eez_act.pdf.

Government of the People's Republic of China. Law on the Territorial Sea and the Contiguous Zone. February 25, 1992. https://www.un.org/depts/los/LEGISLATIONANDTREAT IES/PDFFILES/CHN_1992_Law.pdf.

Government of the People's Republic of China. Position Paper of the Matter of Jurisdiction in the South China Sea Arbitration Initiated by the Republic of the Philippines. December 7, 2014. https://www.fmprc.gov.cn/nanhai/eng/snhwtlcwj_1/t1368895.htm.

Government of the Philippines. Presidential Decree No. 1596. Declaring Certain Area Part of the Philippine Territory and Providing for Their Government and Administration. June 11, 1978. https://www.officialgazette.gov.ph/1978/06/11/presidential-decree-no-1596-s-1978/.

Government of the Philippines. Presidential Decree No. 1599. Establishing an Exclusive Economic Zone and for Other Purposes. June 11, 1978. https://www.officialgazette.gov.ph/1978/06/11/presidential-decree-no-1599-s-1978/.

Government of Malaysia. Proclamation of the Exclusive Economic Zone. April 25, 1980. http://extwprlegs1.fao.org/docs/pdf/mal4799.pdf.

Government of the Socialist Republic of Viet Nam. Statement on the Territorial Sea, the Contiguous Zone, the Exclusive Economic Zone and the Continental Shelf. May 12, 1977. https://www.un.org/Depts/los/LEGISLATIONANDTREATIES/PDFFILES/VNM_1977_Statement.pdf.

Government of the United States. National Defense Authorization Act for Fiscal Year 2016. S. 1356, Public Law 114-92. November 2015. https://www.congress.gov/bill/114th-congr ess/senate-bill/1356.

Government of the United States. Taiwan Relations Act. Public Law 96-8, 22 U.S.C. 3301. January 1, 1979. https://www.congress.gov/96/statute/STATUTE-93/STATUTE-93-Pg14.pdf.

Graham, Euan. "Innocent Passage: Did the US Just Fumble Its South China Sea Strategy?" *National Interest,* November 4, 2015. http://nationalinterest.org/blog/the-buzz/innocent-passage-did-the-us-just-fumble-its-south-china-sea-14253.

Granados, Ulises. "Japanese Expansion into the South China Sea: Colonization and Conflict, 1902–1939." *Journal of Asian History* 42, no. 2 (2008): 117–142.

Green, Michael J. *By More Than Providence: Grand Strategy and American Power in the Asia Pacific since 1783.* New York: Columbia University Press, 2017.

Green, Michael, Kathleen Hicks, Zack Cooper, John Schaus, and Jake Douglas. "Counter-Coercion Series: Scarborough Shoal Standoff." Asia Maritime Transparency Initiative, May 22, 2017. https://amti.csis.org/counter-co-scarborough-standoff/.

Green, Michael, Kathleen Hicks, Zack Cooper, John Schaus, and Jake Douglas. *Countering Coercion in Maritime Asia: The Theory and Practice of Gray Zone Deterrence.* Washington, DC: Center for Strategic and International Studies, May 2017. https://www.csis.org/analysis/counter ing-coercion-maritime-asia.

Greenert, Jonathan W. *Tenets of a Regional Defense Strategy: Considerations for the Indo- Pacific.* Special Report 72. National Bureau for Asian Research, . Seattle: National Bureau of Asian Research, 2018. https://www.nbr.org/wp-content/uploads/pdfs/publications/special_re-port_72_regional_defense_strategy_aug2018.pdf.

Gregor, James A. "The Key Role of U.S. Bases in the Philippines." Heritage Foundation, January 10, 1984. https://www.heritage.org/report/the-key-role-us-bases-the-philippines.

Group of Seven Foreign Ministers' Statement on Maritime Security. April 11, 2016. http://www.g7.utoronto.ca/foreign/formin160411-maritime.html.

Group of Seven Ise-Shima Leaders' Declaration. May 27, 2016. https://www.mofa.go.jp/files/000160266.pdf.

Hagel, Chuck. Remarks at Plenary Session at International Institute for Strategic Studies Shangri-La Dialogue. Singapore, May 31, 2014. https://archive.defense.gov/transcripts/transcript.aspx?transcriptid=5442.

Hagel, Chuck. Statement on the East China Sea Air Defense Identification Zone. U.S. Department of Defense. November 23, 2013. https://archive.defense.gov/releases/release.aspx?releas eid=16392.

Haller-Trost, Renate. "The Brunei-Malaysia Dispute over Territorial and Maritime Claims in International Law." *Maritime Briefings* 1, no. 3 (1994): 1–63. https://www.durham.ac.uk/media/durham-university/research-/research-centres/ibru-centre-for-borders-research/maps-and-databases/publications-database/Maritime-Briefings-(Vol.-1-no.-3).pdf.

Harold, Scott W., Derek Grossman, Brian Harding, Jeffrey W. Hornung, Gregory Poling, Jeffrey Smith, and Meagan L. Smith. *The Thickening Web of Asian Security Cooperation: Deepening Defense Ties among U.S. Allies and Partners in the Indo-Pacific.* Washington, DC: RAND, 2019.

Harris, Harry B. Jr. Remarks at the Australian Strategic Policy Institute. March 31, 2015.

Hartendorp, A. V. H. *History of Industry and Trade of the Philippines: The Magsaysay Administration.* Manila: Philippine Education Company, 1961.

Hayton, Bill. "The Modern Origins of China's South China Sea Claims: Maps, Misunderstandings, and the Maritime Geobody." *Modern China* 45, no. 2 (2019): 1–44.

Hayton, Bill. *The South China Sea: The Struggle for Power in Asia.* New Haven, CT: Yale University Press, 2014.

Hayton, Bill. "When Good Lawyers Write Bad History: Unreliable Evidence and the South China Sea Territorial Dispute." *Ocean Development and International Law* 48, no. 1 (2017): 17–34.

Hollick, Ann L. *U.S. Foreign Policy and the Law of the Sea.* Princeton, NJ: Princeton University Press, 1981.

Hollis, Duncan B. "Treaty Tips from the SFRC Clinton Hearing." *OpinioJuris,* January 15, 2009. http://opiniojuris.org/2009/01/15/treaty-tips-from-the-sfrc-clinton-hearing/.

Huang, Alexander Chieh-cheng. "The Chinese Navy's Offshore Active Defense Strategy." *Naval War College Review* 47, no. 3 (Summer 1994): 1–26.

Ibrahim, Zuraidah, and Kristine Kwok. "Beijing Rejects Hanoi's Legal Challenge on Spratly, Paracel Islands Disputes." *South China Morning Post,* December 12, 2014. https://www.scmp.com/news/china/article/1661364/china-rejects-vietnam-claims-arbitration-submiss ion-over-south-china-sea.

Instrument of Accession to the Treaty of Amity and Cooperation in Southeast Asia by the United States of American. July 22, 2009. https://www.asean.org/storage/images/archive/DOC-TAC-USA.pdf.

International Court of Justice. Territorial and Maritime Dispute (Nicaragua v Colombia). Judgment. November 19, 2012. https://www.icj-cij.org/public/files/case-related/124/124-20121119-JUD-01-00-EN.pdf.

International Crisis Group. *Stirring Up the South China Sea (IV): Oil in Troubled Waters*. Asia Report Number 275. Brussels: International Crisis Group, 2016. https://www.crisisgroup.org/asia/north-east-asia/china/stirring-south-china-sea-iv-oil-troubled-waters.

Jiao, Claire, and Nick Wadhams. "We Have Your Back in South China Sea, U.S. Assures Philippines." *Bloomberg*, February 28, 2019. https://www.bloomberg.com/news/articles/2019-03-01/pompeo-says-u-s-is-committed-to-keeping-south-china-sea-open.

Jürgen Buchholz, Hanns. *Law of the Sea Zones in the Pacific Ocean*. Singapore: Institute of Southeast Asian Studies, 1987.

Karnow, Stanley. *In Our Image: America's Empire in the Philippines*. New York: Ballantine Books, 1989.

Kelly, Todd C. "Vietnamese Claims to the Truong Sa Archipelago." *Explorations in Southeast Asian Studies* 3 (Fall 1999): 27–47.

Kerry, John. Statement on the East China Sea Air Defense Identification Zone. U.S. Department of State, November 23, 2013. https://www.andrewerickson.com/2013/11/statements-by-secretary-of-state-john-kerry-and-secretary-of-defense-chuck-hagel-on-the-east-china-sea-air-defense-identification-zone/.

Kennedy, Conor M., and Andrew S. Erickson. "Model Maritime Militia: Tanmen's Leading Role in the April 2012 Scarborough Shoal Incident." Washington, DC: Center for International Maritime Security, April 21, 2016. http://cimsec.org/model-maritime-militia-tanmens-leading-role-april-2012-scarborough-shoal-incident/24573.

Kishida Fumio. Press Conference. Ministry of Foreign Affairs of Japan. May 9, 2014. https://www.mofa.go.jp/press/kaiken/kaiken4e_000068.html.

Koh, Tommy. *Building a New Legal Order for the Oceans*. Singapore: National University of Singapore Press, 2020.

Koren, Marina. "The Philippine President's Vulgar Warning to Obama." *Atlantic*, September 5, 2016. https://www.theatlantic.com/news/archive/2016/09/duterte-obama-extrajudicial-killings/498710/.

Kreuzer, Peter. *Facing China: Crises or Peaceful Coexistence in the South China Sea*. PRIF Report 134. Frankfurt: Peace Research Institute Frankfurt, 2015.

Lacorte, Germelina. "Duterte Says America Will Never Die for PH." *Philippine Daily Inquirer*, August 2, 2015. https://globalnation.inquirer.net/126835/duterte-to-military-attaches-ph-not-out-for-war-china-should-just-let-us-fish-in-seas.

LaGrone, Sam. "Confusion Continues to Surround US South China Sea Freedom of Navigation Operation." *USNI News*, November 5, 2015. https://news.usni.org/2015/11/05/confusion-continues-to-surround-u-s-south-china-sea-freedom-of-navigation-operation.

Lee, Matthew. "Secretary of State John Kerry Announces $25M in New Aid for Typhoon-Ravaged Philippines." AP, December 18, 2013. https://globalnews.ca/news/1037251/secretary-of-state-john-kerry-announces-25m-in-new-aid-for-typhoon-ravaged-philippine-city/.

Lee, Victor Robert. "Satellite Imagery Shows Ecocide in the South China Sea." *The Diplomat*, January 15, 2016. https://thediplomat.com/2016/01/satellite-images-show-ecocide-in-the-south-china-sea/.

Letter from the Chargé d'Affaires of the Permanent Mission of China to the United Nations Addressed to the Secretary-General. March 28, 1988. A/43/259-S/19694. https://digitallibrary.un.org/record/159645?ln=en.

Letter from the Chargé d'Affaires of the Permanent Mission of China to the United Nations Addressed to the Secretary-General. June 9, 2014. A/68/907. https://undocs.org/pdf?symbol=en/a/68/907

Lin Cheng-yi. "Taiwan's South China Sea Policy." *Asian Survey* 37, no. 4 (April 1997): 323–339.

Lo, Chi-kin. *China's Policy toward Territorial Disputes: The Case of the Spratly Islands*. London: Routledge, 1989; digital printing 2005.

Macias, Amanda. "China Quietly Installed Missile Systems on Strategic Spratly Islands in Hotly Contested South China Sea." CNBC, May 2, 2018. https://www.cnbc.com/2018/05/02/china-added-missile-systems-on-spratly-islands-in-south-china-sea.html.

Mai Thanh Hai. "Gii TrưưTh Sa trưứr tham vvam bá quyyu—Ku 5: Quy Q tt." [Holding the Spratly Islands before Hegemony—Episode 5: Fatal Decision.] *Thanh Nien,* October 25, 2014.

Malaysia and the Socialist Republic of Vietnam. Joint Submission to the Commission on the Limits of the Continental Shelf: Executive Summary. May 6, 2009. https://www.un.org/Depts/los/clcs_new/submissions_files/mysvnm33_09/mys_vnm2009excutivesumm ary.pdf.

Mangosing, Frances. "China Military Planes Land on PH Reef." *Philippine Daily Inquirer,* April 18, 2018. https://globalnation.inquirer.net/165824/china-military-planes-land-ph-reef.

Martinson, Ryan. "Catching Sovereignty Fish: Chinese Fishers in the Southern Spratlys." *Marine Policy* 125 (March 2021): 1–11.

Martinson, Ryan D. "From Words to Actions: The Creation of the China Coast Guard." Paper presented at China as a "Maritime Power" Conference, CNA, Arlington, VA, July 28–19, 2015. https://www.cna.org/cna_files/pdf/creation-china-coast-guard.pdf.

Martinson, Ryan D., and Peter A. Dutton. *China Maritime Report No. 3: China's Distant Ocean Survey Activities: Implications for U.S. National Security.* Newport, RI: U.S. Naval War College, November 2018. https://digital-commons.usnwc.edu/cgi/viewcontent.cgi?article=1002&context=cmsi-maritime-reports.

McCurry, Justin, and Tania Branigan. "Obama Says US Will Defend Japan in Island Dispute with China." *Guardian,* April 24, 2014. https://www.theguardian.com/world/2014/apr/24/obama-in-japan-backs-status-quo-in-island-dispute-with-china.

McDevitt, Michael. *The South China Sea: Assessing U.S. Policy and Options for the Future.* CNA Occasional Paper. Arlington, VA: CNA, November 2014. https://www.cna.org/cna_files/pdf/IOP-2014-U-009109.pdf.

McManus, John W. "Offshore Coral Reef Damage, Overfishing, and Paths to Peace in the South China Sea." *International Journal of Marine and Coastal Law* 32 (2017).

Memorandum of Conversation. Washington, January 23, 1974. In *Foreign Relations of the United States, 1969–1976.* Vol. 18: *China, 1973–1976,* edited by Edward C. Keefer. Washington, DC: United States Government Printing Office, 2007. Document 66. https://history.state.gov/historicaldocuments/frus1969-76v18/d66.

Ministry of Foreign Affairs of the People's Republic of China. "Foreign Ministry Spokesperson Lu Kang's Regular Press Conference." June 14, 2016. https://www.fmprc.gov.cn/mfa_eng/xwfw_665399/s2510_665401/2511_665403/t1372136.shtml.

Ministry of Foreign Affairs of the People's Republic of China. "Foreign Ministry Spokesperson Qin Gang's Regular Press Conference." March 10, 2014. https://www.fmprc.gov.cn/mfa_eng/xwfw_665399/s2510_665401/2511_665403/t1136288.shtml.

Ministry of Foreign Affairs of the People's Republic of China. "Set Aside Dispute and Pursue Joint Development." Accessed May 17, 2020. https://www.fmprc.gov.cn/mfa_eng/ziliao_665 539/3602_665543/3604_665547/t18023.shtml.

Ministry of Foreign Affairs of the People's Republic of China. Statement on the Award on Jurisdiction and Admissibility of the South China Sea Arbitration by the Arbitral Tribunal Established at the Request of the Republic of the Philippines. October 30, 2015. https://www.fmprc.gov.cn/mfa_eng/wjdt_665385/2649_665393/201510/t20151030_679 419.html.

Minutes of the Secretary of State's Staff Meeting. Washington, October 16, 1976. In *Foreign Relations of the United States, 1969–1976.* Vol. E-12: *Documents on East and Southeast Asia, 1973–1976,* edited by Bradley Lynn Coleman, David Goldman, and David Nickles. Washington, DC: United States Government Printing Office, 2010. Document 350. https://history.state.gov/historicaldocuments/frus1969-76ve12/d350.

Minutes of Washington Special Actions Group Meeting. Washington, January 25, 1974. In *Foreign Relations of the United States, 1969–1976.* Vol. 10: *Vietnam, January 1973–July 1975,* edited by Bradley Lynn Coleman. Washington, DC: United States Government Printing Office, 2010. Document 122. https://history.state.gov/historicaldocuments/frus1969-76v10/d122.

Mirski, Sean. "American Paralysis and Troubles in the South China Sea: A Primer on the Philippines-China Arbitration." *Lawfare,* October 13, 2013. https://www.lawfareblog.com/american-paralysis-and-troubles-south-china-sea-primer-philippines-china-arbitration.

Morris, Eric. *Corregidor: The American Alamo of World War II.* New York: Cooper Square Press, 1981.

Muscolino, Micah S. "Past and Present Resource Disputes in the South China Sea: The Case of Reed Bank." *Cross-Currents: East Asian History and Culture Review* 8 (September 2013): 80–106.

Mutual Defense Treaty between the United States and the Republic of the Philippines. August 30, 1951.

Nakamura, David. "Obama at APEC Summit: China Must 'Play by the Rules.'" *Washington Post,* November 12, 2011. https://www.washingtonpost.com/world/obama-at-apec-summit-china-must-play-by-the-rules/2011/11/12/gIQALRu2FN_story.html.

NBC News. "President Aquino of Philippines Meets China's Xi in APEC Ice-Breaker." November 10, 2015. https://www.nbcnews.com/news/world/president-aquino-philippines-meets-chinas-xi-apec-ice-breaker-n245981.

New Straits Times. "World Leaders Outraged by Army Action." June 6, 1989.

New York Times. "Nixon's Report to Congress on Foreign Policy." February 19, 1970. https://www.nytimes.com/1970/02/19/archives/nixons-report-to-congress-on-foreign-policy-introduction-genuine.html.

Ngoc, Anh. "Vietnam Condemns China's Sovereignty Violations at ASEAN Meeting." *VNExpress,* October 15, 2019. https://e.vnexpress.net/news/news/vietnam-condemns-china-s-sovereignty-violations-at-asean-meeting-3997472.html.

Nhung Anh Hung. *Dac Cong Hai Quan Lu Doan 126 [Heroes of the Maritime Special Forces Brigade 126].* Hanoi: Nha xuat ban chinh tri quoc gia, 2016.

Niksch, Larry. "Philippine-U.S. Security Relations." CRS Report for Congress, October 10, 2000. https://www.everycrsreport.com/files/20001010_RS20697_8fcdb8a5e8c9b131e9cd85f17e0c53ee2d56ccb0.pdf.

Noor, Elina. "Malaysia: Recalibrating Its South China Sea Policy?" Asia Maritime Transparency Initiative, January 8, 2016. https://amti.csis.org/malaysia-recalibrating-its-south-china-sea-policy/.

Northwest Atlantic Fisheries Organization. "International Commission for the Northwest Atlantic Fisheries (ICNAF)." Accessed June 20, 2020. https://www.nafo.int/About-us/ICNAF/icnaf-convention#convention.

North Pacific Anadromous Fish Commission. "International North Pacific Fisheries Commission (1952–1992)." Accessed June 20, 2020. https://npafc.org/inpfc/.

Obama, Barack. Remarks to the Australian Parliament. White House. November 17, 2011. https://obamawhitehouse.archives.gov/the-press-office/2011/11/17/remarks-president-obama-australian-parliament.

Obama, Barack. Remarks at U.S.-ASEAN Press Conference. White House. February 16, 2016. https://obamawhitehouse.archives.gov/the-press-office/2016/02/16/remarks-president-obama-us-asean-press-conference.

Oberdorfer, Don. "U.S. Base Rejected in Philippines." *Washington Post,* September 10, 1991. https://www.washingtonpost.com/archive/politics/1991/09/10/us-base-rejected-in-philippines/d580e52d-5060-4cf8-9443-48e689593149/.

Odgaard, Lisolotte. "Between Deterrence and Cooperation: Eastern Asian Security after the 'Cold War.'" *IRBU Boundary and Security Bulletin* (Summer 1998): 69–77. https://www.durham.ac.uk/media/durham-university/research-/research-centres/ibru-centre-for-borders-research/maps-and-databases/publications-database/boundary-amp-security-bulletins/bsb6-2_odgaard.pdf.

O'Hanlon, Michael, and Gregory Poling. "Rocks, Reefs, and Nuclear War." Asia Maritime Transparency Initiative, January 14, 2020. https://amti.csis.org/rocks-reefs-and-nuclear-war/.

Ortagus, Morgan. "China's Empty Promises in the South China Sea." Press statement. U.S. Department of State, September 27, 2020. https://www.state.gov/chinas-empty-promises-in-the-south-china-sea/.

Page, Jeremy. "Vietnam Accuses Chinese Ships." *Wall Street Journal,* December 3, 2012. https://www.wsj.com/articles/SB10001424127887323717004578157033857113510.

Panda, Ankit. "After Months of Waiting, US Finally Begins Freedom of Navigation Patrols Near China's Man-Made Islands." *The Diplomat,* October 27, 2015. https://thediplomat.com/2015/10/after-months-of-waiting-us-finally-begins-freedom-of-navigation-patrols-near-chinas-man-made-islands/.

Panda, Ankit. "Indonesia Summons Chinese Ambassador after South China Sea Stand-Off Near Natuna Islands." *The Diplomat,* March 21, 2016. https://thediplomat.com/2016/03/indonesia-summons-chinese-ambassador-after-south-china-sea-stand-off-near-natuna-islands/.

Panda, Ankit. "South China Sea: Indonesian Navy Fires at and Arrests Chinese Fishermen." *The Diplomat,* May 31, 2016. https://thediplomat.com/2016/05/south-china-sea-indonesian-navy-fires-at-and-arrests-chinese-fishermen/.

Panda, Ankit. "A Third 2016 Natuna Stand-Off Highlights Growing Indonesia-China Tensions." *The Diplomat,* June 21, 2016. https://thediplomat.com/2016/06/a-third-2016-natuna-stand-off-highlights-growing-indonesia-china-tensions/.

Parameswaran, Prashanth. "ASEAN to Intensify South China Sea Response amid China Concerns." *The Diplomat,* January 28, 2015. https://thediplomat.com/2015/01/asean-to-intensify-south-china-sea-response-amid-china-concerns/.

Parameswaran, Prashanth. "US Kicks Off New Maritime Security Initiative for Southeast Asia." *The Diplomat,* April 10, 2016. https://thediplomat.com/2016/04/us-kicks-off-new-maritime-security-initiative-for-southeast-asia/.

Pazzibugan, Dona Z. "Philippines Pulls Spratlys 'Foreign' Posts." *Philippine Daily Inquirer,* June 16, 2011. https://newsinfo.inquirer.net/15230/philippines-pulls-spratlys-foreign-posts.

Pedrozo, Raul (Pete). *China versus Vietnam: An Analysis of the Competing Claims in the South China Sea.* CNA Occasional Paper. Arlington, VA: CNA, August 2014.

Perlez, Jane. "Asian Leaders Fail to Resolve Disputes over South China Sea." *New York Times,* July 12, 2012. https://www.nytimes.com/2012/07/13/world/asia/asian-leaders-fail-to-resolve-disputes-on-south-china-sea-during-asean-summit.html.

Perlez, Jane, and Matthew Rosenberg. "China Agrees to Return Seized Drone, Ending Standoff, Pentagon Says." *New York Times,* December 17, 2016. https://www.nytimes.com/2016/12/17/world/asia/china-us-drone.html.

Permanent Court of Arbitration. "The Arbitral Tribunal Commences Hearing on Jurisdiction and Admissibility." Press release. July 7, 2015. https://pcacases.com/web/sendAttach/1301.

Permanent Court of Arbitration. "Arbitration between the Republic of the Philippines and the People's Republic of China: Arbitral Tribunal Establishes Rules of Procedures and Initial Timetable." Press release. August 2, 2013. https://web.archive.org/web/20210308140742/https://www.pcacases.com/web/sendAttach/227.

Permanent Court of Arbitration. The South China Sea Arbitration (The Republic of Philippines v. The People's Republic of China. Award. July 12, 2016. https://docs.pca-cpa.org/2016/07/PH-CN-20160712-Award.pdf.

Permanent Court of Arbitration. The South China Sea Arbitration (The Republic of Philippines v. The People's Republic of China). Award on Jurisdiction and Admissibility. October 29, 2015. https://pcacases.com/web/sendAttach/2579.

Permanent Court of Arbitration. The South China Sea Arbitration (The Republic of Philippines v. The People's Republic of China). The Philippines' Memorial: Vols. 1–11. March 30, 2014. https://pca-cpa.org/en/cases/7/.

Permanent Court of Arbitration. The South China Sea Arbitration (The Republic of Philippines v. The People's Republic of China). The Philippines' Written Responses. March 11, 2016. https://pca-cpa.org/en/cases/7/.

Permanent Court of Arbitration. The South China Sea Arbitration (The Republic of Philippines v. The People's Republic of China). The Philippines' Written Responses on French Archive Materials. June 3, 2016. https://pca-cpa.org/en/cases/7/.

Permanent Court of Arbitration. The South China Sea Arbitration (The Republic of Philippines v. The People's Republic of China). The Philippines' Written Responses on Itu Aba. April 25, 2016. https://pca-cpa.org/en/cases/7/.

Permanent Court of Arbitration. The South China Sea Arbitration (The Republic of Philippines v. The People's Republic of China). The Philippines' Written Responses to UKHO Materials. April 28, 2016. https://pca-cpa.org/en/cases/7/.

Permanent Court of Arbitration. The South China Sea Arbitration (The Republic of Philippines v. The People's Republic of China). Supplemental Written Submission of the Philippines, Vol. 1. March 16, 2015. https://pca-cpa.org/en/cases/7/.

Permanent Court of Arbitration. "The Tribunal Commences Hearing on Merits." Press release. November 30, 2015. https://pcacases.com/web/sendAttach/1521.

Permanent Mission of Malaysia to the United Nations. Note Verbale HA 24/09. May 20, 2009. https://www.un.org/Depts/los/clcs_new/submissions_files/mysvnm33_09/mys_re_c hn_2009re_mys_vnm_e.pdf.

Permanent Mission of Malaysia to the United Nations, Note Verbale HA 41/09. August 21, 2009. https://www.un.org/Depts/los/clcs_new/submissions_files/mysvnm33_09/mys_re_p hl_2009re_mys_vnm_e.pdf.

Permanent Mission of the People's Republic of China to the United Nations. Note Verbale CML/ 17/2009. May 7, 2009. https://www.un.org/Depts/los/clcs_new/submissions_files/mysv nm33_09/chn_2009re_mys_vnm_e.pdf.

Permanent Mission of the People's Republic of China to the United Nations. Note Verbale CML/ 18/2009. May 7, 2009. https://www.un.org/Depts/los/clcs_new/submissions_files/ vnm37_09/chn_2009re_vnm.pdf.

Permanent Mission of the People's Republic of China to the United Nations. Note Verbale CML/ 8/2011. April 14, 2011. https://www.un.org/Depts/los/clcs_new/submissions_files/ mysvnm33_09/chn_2011_re_phl_e.pdf.

Permanent Mission of the Philippines to the United Nations. Note Verbale No. 000228. April 5, 2011. https://www.un.org/Depts/los/clcs_new/submissions_files/mysvnm33_09/phl_ re_chn_2011.pdf.

Permanent Mission of the Republic of Indonesia. Note Verbale No. 480/POL-703/VII/10. July 8, 2010. https://www.un.org/Depts/los/clcs_new/submissions_files/mysvnm33_09/idn_2 010re_mys_vnm_e.pdf.

Permanent Mission of the Socialist Republic of Viet Nam to the United Nations. Note Verbale No. 86/HC-2009. May 8, 2009. https://www.un.org/Depts/los/clcs_new/submissions_files/ mysvnm33_09/vnm_chn_2009re_mys_vnm_e.pdf.

Permanent Mission of the Socialist Republic of Viet Nam to the United Nations. Note Verbale No. 240/HC-2009. August 18, 2009. https://www.un.org/Depts/los/clcs_new/submissions_ files/submission_mysvnm_33_2009.htm.

Permanent Mission of the Socialist Republic of Viet Nam to the United Nations. Note Verbale No. 77/HC-2011. May 3, 2011. https://www.un.org/Depts/los/clcs_new/submissions_files/ vnm37_09/vnm_2011_re_phlchn.pdf.

Peter, Zsombor, and Kuch Naren. "Cambodia Criticized for Asean Meeting Failure." Reuters, July 13, 2012.

Philippine Daily Inquirer. "Scarborough Shoal Standoff: A Timeline." May 9, 2012. https://globa lnation.inquirer.net/36003/scarborough-shoal-standoff-a-historicaltimeline.

Philippine Star. "DFA Chief Clarifies US Support under Mutual Defense Treaty." May 10, 2012. https://www.philstar.com/headlines/2012/05/10/805080/dfa-chief-clarifies-us-support-under-mutual-defense-treaty.

Plan of Action to Implement the Joint Declaration on ASEAN-China Strategic Partnership for Peace and Prosperity. November 29, 2004. https://asean.org/?static_post=plan-of-act

ion-to-implement-the-joint-declaration-on-asean-china-strategic-partnership-for-peace-and-prosperity.

Poling, Gregory B. "Arguing over Blocks: Do China and the Philippines Both Have a Claim." Washington, DC: Center for Strategic and International Studies, April 16, 2012. https://www.csis.org/analysis/arguing-over-blocks-do-china-and-philippines-both-have-claim.

Poling, Gregory B. "China-Vietnam Tensions High over Drilling Rig in Disputed Waters." Washington, DC: Center for Strategic and International Studies, May 7, 2014. https://www.csis.org/analysis/china-vietnam-tensions-high-over-drilling-rig-disputed-waters.

Poling, Gregory B. "CNOOC Pulls Back the Curtain." Washington, DC: Center for Strategic and International Studies, August 17, 2012. https://www.csis.org/analysis/cnooc-pulls-back-curtain.

Poling, Gregory B. "The Conventional Wisdom on China's Island Bases Is Dangerously Wrong." *War on the Rocks,* January 10, 2020. https://warontherocks.com/2020/01/the-conventional-wisdom-on-chinas-island-bases-is-dangerously-wrong/.

Poling, Gregory B. "For Lack of a Strategy: The Free and Open Indo-Pacific." *War on the Rocks,* November 13, 2019. https://warontherocks.com/2019/11/for-lack-of-a-strategy-the-free-and-open-indo-pacific/.

Poling, Gregory B. "Illuminating the South China Sea's Dark Fishing Fleets." Washington, DC: Center for Strategic and International Studies, January 9, 2019. https://ocean.csis.org/spotlights/illuminating-the-south-china-seas-dark-fishing-fleets/.

Poling, Gregory B. "South China Sea Code of Conduct Still a Speck on the Horizon." *East Asia Forum,* September 6, 2018. https://www.eastasiaforum.org/2018/09/06/south-china-sea-code-of-conduct-still-a-speck-on-the-horizon/.

Poling, Gregory, and Conor Cronin. "The Dangers of Allowing U.S.-Philippine Defense Cooperation to Languish." *War on the Rocks,* May 17, 2018. https://warontherocks.com/2018/05/the-dangers-of-allowing-u-s-philippine-defense-cooperation-to-languish/.

Poling, Gregory B., and Murray Hiebert. "Stop the Bully in the South China Sea." *Wall Street Journal,* August 28, 2019. https://www.wsj.com/articles/stop-the-bully-in-the-south-china-sea-11567033378.

Poling, Gregory B., and Eric Sayers. "Time to Make Good on the U.S.-Philippine Alliance." *War on the Rocks,* January 21, 2019. https://warontherocks.com/2019/01/time-to-make-good-on-the-u-s-philippine-alliance/.

Pomfret, John. "U.S. Takes a Tougher Tone with China." *Washington Post,* July 30, 2010. https://www.washingtonpost.com/wp-dyn/content/article/2010/07/29/AR2010072906416.html?sid=ST2010072906761.

Pompeo, Michael R. "U.S. Imposes Restrictions on Certain PRC State-Owned Enterprises and Executives for Malign Activities in the South China Sea." Press statement. August 26, 2020. https://www.state.gov/u-s-imposes-restrictions-on-certain-prc-state-owned-enterprises-and-executives-for-malign-activities-in-the-south-china-sea/.

Pompeo, Michael R. "U.S. Position on Maritime Claims in the South China Sea." Press statement. July 13, 2020. https://www.state.gov/u-s-position-on-maritime-claims-in-the-south-china-sea/.

Potsdam Declaration. July 26, 1945. National Diet Library. https://www.ndl.go.jp/constitution/e/etc/c06.html.

Quismundo, Tarra. "US Troubled by Ayungin Shoal Incident." *Philippine Daily Inquirer,* March 12, 2014. https://globalnation.inquirer.net/100211/us-troubled-by-ayungin-shoal-incident.

Ramos, Christia Marie. "PH Walks Back, Suspends VFA Termination 'Upon the President's Instruction.'" *Philippine Daily Inquirer,* June 2, 2020. https://globalnation.inquirer.net/188098/ph-walks-back-suspends-vfa-termination-upon-the-presidents-instruction.

Ramos, Marlon, and Tarra Quismundo. "China Building Airstrip on Reef in Philippine Waters." *Philippine Daily Inquirer,* May 15, 2014. https://globalnation.inquirer.net/104333/manila-says-china-reclaiming-land-in-disputed-sea.

Ramzy, Austin. "China's Newest City Raises Threat of Conflict in South China Sea." *Time*, July 24, 2012. https://world.time.com/2012/07/24/chinas-newest-city-raises-threat-of-confl ict-in-the-south-china-sea/.

Ranada, Pia. "Duterte Wants to Scrap EDCA." *Rappler,* October 25, 2016. https://www.rappler. com/nation/duterte-edca-no-foreign-troops.

Rappler. "Full Text: The Philippines' Opening Salvo at The Hague." July 8, 2015. https://www. rappler.com/nation/philippines-china-hague-opening-statement-full-text.

Republic of the Philippines Department of Foreign Affairs. "China's Reclamation on Mabini Reef." May 15, 2014. https://www.dfa.gov.ph/index.php/2013-06-27-21-50-36/dfa-releases/ 2871-china-s-reclamation-on-mabini-reef.

Republic of the Philippines Department of Foreign Affairs. "DFA Statement on China's Allegation That the Philippines Agreed to Pull-out of the Ayungin Shoal." March 14, 2014. https://dfa. gov.ph/index.php/2013-06-27-21-50-36/dfa-releases/2333-dfa-statement-on-china-s-all egation-that-philippines-agreed-to-pull-out-of-the-ayungin-shoal.

Republic of the Philippines Department of Foreign Affairs. "Frequently Asked Questions (FAQs) on the Enhanced Defense Cooperation Agreement." April 28, 2014. https://www.dfa.gov. ph/dfa-releases/2693-frequently-asked-questions-faqs-on-the-enhanced-defense-cooperat ion-agreement.

Republic of the Philippines Department of Foreign Affairs. "Information Note on the Significant of the 2016 ASEAN Joint Communiqué in Relation to the Arbitral Tribunal Ruling." August 1, 2016. https://www.dfa.gov.ph/newsroom/dfa-releases/10072-information-note-on-the-significance-of-the-2016-asean-joint-communique-in-relation-to-the-arbitral-tribunal-ruling.

Republic of the Philippines Department of Foreign Affairs. Note Verbale No. 13-0211. "Notification and Statement of Claim." January 22, 2013. https://dfa.gov.ph/images/UNC LOS/Notification%20and%20Statement%20of%20Claim%20on%20West%20Philipp ine%20Sea.pdf.

Republic of Vietnam Ministry of Foreign Affairs. *White Paper on the Hoang Sa (Paracel) and Truong Sa (Spratly) Islands* (Saigon: Ministry of Foreign Affairs, 1975). https://huongduong txd.com/tshs_whitepaper.pdf.

Reuters. "Carter Says U.S. Will Sail, Fly and Operate Wherever International Law Allows." October 13, 2015. https://www.reuters.com/article/usa-australia-southchinasea-carter/update-1-carter-says-u-s-will-sail-fly-and-operate-wherever-international-law-allows-idUKL1N12D 1U120151013.

Reuters. "Philippines Calls for Construction Freeze in South China Sea." June 16, 2014. https:// www.reuters.com/article/us-philippines-southchinasea/philippines-calls-for-construction-freeze-in-south-china-sea-idUSKBN0ER0LE20140616.

Reuters. "U.S. Cautioned 7th Fleet to Shun Paracels Clash." *New York Times.* January 21, 1974.

Rose, David G. "'China Calls It Fishing, Indonesia Calls It Crime': Pudjiastuti Finds Her Target for Oceans Summit." *South China Morning Post,* October 18, 2018. https://www.scmp.com/ week-asia/geopolitics/article/2169153/china-calls-it-fishing-indonesia-calls-it-crime-pudj iastuti.

Rosenberg, Matthew. "China Deployed Artillery on Disputed Islands, U.S. Says." *New York Times,* May 29, 2015. https://www.nytimes.com/2015/05/30/world/asia/chinese-artillery-spot ted-on-spratly-island.html.

Russell, Daniel. Press roundtable. U.S. Embassy Hanoi. May 8, 2014. https://vn.usembassy.gov/ press-roundtable-with-assistant-secretary-daniel-russel/.

Samuels, Marwyn. *Contest for the South China Sea.* New York: Methuen, 1982.

Schofield, Clive, J. R. V. Prescott, and Robert van de Pol. "An Appraisal of the Geographical Characteristics and Status of Certain Features in the South China Sea." Annex 513. South China Sea Arbitration (Philippines v. China). Supplemental Written Submission of the Philippines. Vol. 9. March 16, 2015. https://pca-cpa.org/en/cases/7/.

Sciolino, Elaine. "U.S. and Philippines Sign Pact on Bases." *New York Times,* October 18, 1988. https://www.nytimes.com/1988/10/18/world/us-and-philippines-sign-pact-on-bases. html?auth=login-email&login=email.

Sciutto, Jim. "Exclusive: China Warns U.S. Surveillance Plane." CNN, May 20, 2015. https://www. cnn.com/2015/05/20/politics/south-china-sea-navy-flight/index.html.

Scott, David. "Conflict Irresolution in the South China Sea." *Asian Survey* 52, no. 6 (2012): 1019–1042.

Security Treaty between the United States, Australia, and New Zealand (ANZUS). September 1, 1951. https://avalon.law.yale.edu/20th_century/usmu002.asp.

Senate Armed Services Committee. "Advanced Policy Questions for Admiral Philip Davidson, USN." April 17, 2018. https://www.armed-services.senate.gov/imo/media/doc/David son_APQs_04-17-18.pdf.

Senate Armed Services Committee. "Senators McCain, Reed, Corker, and Menendez Send Letter on Chinese Maritime Strategy." Press release. March 19, 2015. https://www.armed-services. senate.gov/press-releases/senators-mccain-reed-corker-and-menendez-send-letter-on-chin ese-maritime-strategy.

Senate Foreign Relations Committee. The Law of the Sea Convention. Hearings before the Committee on Foreign Relations. May 23, June 14, and June 28, 2012. https://www.govinfo. gov/content/pkg/CHRG-112shrg77375/pdf/CHRG-112shrg77375.pdf

Senate Foreign Relations Committee. "'24 Star' Military Witnesses Voice Strong Support for Law of the Sea Treaty." Press release. June 14, 2012. https://www.foreign.senate.gov/press/ chair/release/24-star-military-witnesses-voice-strong-support-for-law-of-the-sea-treaty.

Sevastopulo, Demetri, Geoff Dyer, and Tom Mitchell. "Obama Forced Xi to Back Down over South China Sea Dispute." *Financial Times,* July 12, 2016. https://www.ft.com/content/ c63264a4-47f1-11e6-8d68-72e9211e86ab.

Severino, Rodolfo C. "The Philippines and the South China Sea." In *Entering Uncharted Waters? ASEAN and the South China Sea,* edited by Pavin Chachavalpongpun, 166–207. Singapore: Institute of Southeast Asian Studies, 2014.

Shalal, Andrew, and Idrees Ali. "US Navy Plans Two or More Patrols in South China Sea per Quarter." Reuters, November 2, 2015. https://www.reuters.com/article/us-southchina sea-usa-navy/u-s-navy-plans-two-or-more-patrols-in-south-china-sea-per-quarter-idUSKC N0SR28W20151103.

Shen Jianming. "International Law Rules and Historical Evidence Supporting China's Title to the South China Sea Islands." *Hastings International and Comparative Law Review* 21, no. 1 (Fall 1997): 1–75. https://repository.uchastings.edu/cgi/viewcontent.cgi?article=1467&cont ext=hastings_international_comparative_law_review.

Shenon, Philip. "Manila Sees China Threat on Coral Reef." *New York Times,* February 19, 1995. https://www.nytimes.com/1995/02/19/world/manila-sees-china-threat-on-coral-reef.html.

Shenon, Philip. "Philippine Senate Votes to Reject U.S. Base Renewal." *New York Times,* September 16, 1991. https://www.nytimes.com/1991/09/16/world/philippine-senate-votes-to-rej ect-us-base-renewal.html.

Singh, Swaran. "Continuity and Change in China's Maritime Strategy." *Strategic Analysis* 23, no. 9 (December 1999): 1493–1508. https://ciaotest.cc.columbia.edu/olj/sa/sa_99sis01.html.

Smith, Jeff M. "An Innocent Mistake: How a Fumbled Freedom of Navigation Operation Set Back US Interests in the South China Sea." *Foreign Affairs,* December 3, 2015. https://www.for eignaffairs.com/articles/china/2015-12-03/innocent-mistake.

Snyder, Scott, Brad Glosserman, and Ralph A. Cossa. "Confidence Building Measures in the South China Sea." Pacific Forum *Issues and Insights* 2, no. 01 (2001): 1–24. https://pacforum.org/ wp-content/uploads/2019/02/issuesinsightsv01n02.pdf.

Socialist Republic of Vietnam. Submission to the Commission on the Limits of the Continental Shelf: Executive Summary. May 7, 2009. https://www.un.org/Depts/los/clcs_new/submis sions_files/vnm37_09/vnm2009n_executivesummary.pdf.

Song Yann-huei. "The PRC's Peacetime Military Activities in Taiwan's EEZ: A Question of Legality." Paper presented at Peace Forum, Taiwan Security in the Year 2000: Retrospect and Prospects. Taipei, December 15, 2000.

Song, Yann-huei. "Taiping Island: An Island or a Rock under UNCLOS." Asia Maritime Transparency Initiative, May 7, 2015. https://amti.csis.org/taiping-island-an-island-or-a-rock-under-unclos/.

Stashwick, Steven. "'Unsafe' Incident between US and Chinese Warships during FONOP." The Diplomat, October 2, 2018. https://thediplomat.com/2018/10/unsafe-incident-between-us-and-chinese-warships-during-fonop/.

State Council of the People's Republic of China. "China Adheres to the Position of Settling through Negotiations the Relevant Disputes between China and the Philippines in the South China Sea." White Paper. July 13, 2016. http://english.www.gov.cn/state_council/ministries/2016/07/13/content_281475392503075.htm.

Stires, Hunter. "'They Were Playing Chicken'—The U.S. Asiatic Fleet's Gray-Zone Deterrence Campaign against Japan, 1937–40." Naval War College Review 72, no. 3 (Summer 2019). https://digital-commons.usnwc.edu/cgi/viewcontent.cgi?article=8046&context=nwc-review.

Storey, Ian. "China and the Philippines: Implications of the Reed Bank Incident." China Brief 11, no. 8 (May 6, 2011): 6–9. https://jamestown.org/program/china-and-the-philippines-implications-of-the-reed-bank-incident/.

Sullivan, Jacob J. "Subject: Dai." Email to Hillary Clinton. June 17, 2012. http://graphics.wsj.com/hillary-clinton-email-documents/.

Sumaila, U. Rashid, and William W. L. Cheung. "Boom or Bust: The Future of Fish in the South China Sea." Report. University of British Columbia, November 5, 2015. https://drive.goo gle.com/file/d/0B_oUJE4kCTZrbVI4N2tTVjlpYTA/view.

Sun Kuan-Ming. "1995 Policy of the Republic of China towards the South China Sea." Marine Policy 19, no. 5 (September 1995): 401–409.

Suorsa, Olli Pekka. "The Conventional Wisdom Still Stands: America Can Deal with China's Artificial Island Bases." War on the Rocks, February 6, 2020. https://warontherocks.com/2020/02/the-conventional-wisdom-still-stands-america-can-deal-with-chinas-artificial-isl and-bases/.

Swaine, Michael D. "China's Assertive Behavior—Part One: On 'Core Interests.'" China Leadership Monitor 34 (November 15, 2010): 1–25. https://carnegieendowment.org/files/CLM34M S_FINAL.pdf.

Tan, Kimberly Jane. "DFA: 1 of 3 Chinese Vessels in Panatag Shoal Standoff Leaves; Diplomatic Talks Resume." GMA News, April 13, 2012. https://www.gmanetwork.com/news/news/nation/254783/dfa-1-of-3-chinese-vessels-in-panatag-shoal-standoff-leaves-diplomatic-talks-resume/story/.

Taylor, Rob. "China's 'Great Wall of Sand' Raises U.S. Concerns." Wall Street Journal, March 31, 2015. https://www.wsj.com/articles/u-s-to-move-stealth-destroyers-to-pacific-region-142 7784315.

U.S. Department of State, Central Foreign Policy Files, July 1, 1973—December 31, 1979, National Archives, https://aad.archives.gov/aad/series-description.jsp?s=4073&cat=all&bc=sl/ .Terms of Reference of the ASEAN-China Joint Working Group on the Implementation of the Declaration on the Conduct of Parties in the South China Sea. December 7, 2004. https://asean.org/?static_post=terms-of-reference-of-the-asean-china-joint-working-group-on-the-implementation-of-the-declaration-on-the-conduct-of-parties-in-the-south-china-sea.

Thanh Nien News. "Another Vietnamese Ship Disturbed in Territorial Waters: Report." June 1, 2011. http://www.thanhniennews.com/politics/another-vietnamese-ship-disturbed-in-territorial-waters-report-12055.html.

Thayer, Carlyle A. "Analyzing the US-Philippines Enhanced Defense Cooperation Agreement." The Diplomat, May 2, 2014. https://thediplomat.com/2014/05/analyzing-the-us-philippi nes-enhanced-defense-cooperation-agreement/.

Thayer, Carlyle A. "ASEAN'S Code of Conduct in the South China Sea: A Litmus Test for Community-Building?" *Asia-Pacific Journal Japan Focus* 10, no. 34.4 (August 19, 2012): 1–22. https://apjjf.org/2012/10/34/Carlyle-A.-Thayer/3813/article.html.

Thayer, Carlyle A. "South China Sea: Background to ASEAN-China Code of Conduct." Thayer Consultancy Background Brief. Canberra. April 26, 2017. https://seasresearch.wordpress.com/2017/04/27/draft-asean-china-codes-of-conduct-text-and-analysis/.

Tomkins, Damien. "US Reaffirms Asia Role." *The Diplomat,* June 8, 2011. https://thediplomat.com/2011/06/us-reaffirms-asia-role/.

Tønnesson, Stein. "The South China Sea in the Age of European Decline." *Modern Asian Studies* 40, no. 1 (February 2006): 1–57.

Tran Truong Thuy. "Recent Developments in the South China Sea: From Declaration to Code of Conduct." In *The South China Sea: Towards a Region of Peace, Security and Cooperation,* edited by Tran Truong Thuy. Hanoi: Gioi Publishers, 2011.

Treaty of Mutual Cooperation and Security between Japan and the United States of America. January 19, 1960.

Trump, Donald. Remarks at APEC CEO Summit. Danang, Vietnam. November 10, 2017. https://www.whitehouse.gov/briefings-statements/remarks-president-trump-apec-ceo-summit-da-nang-vietnam/.

Tuerk, Helmut. "The 25th Anniversary of the Entry into Force of the United Nations Convention on the Law of the Sea." Paper presented at the Diplomatic Academy of Vietnam's 11th South China Sea International Conference, Hanoi, November 6, 2019.

Tuoi Tre News. "China Moves Illegal Oil Rig to New Area, Still in Vietnam's Waters." May 27, 2014. https://tuoitrenews.vn/society/19907/china-moves-illegal-oil-rig-to-new-area-still-in-vietnams-waters.

Tuyay, Francisco. "BRP Sierra Madre Set to Be Repaired." *Manila Standard,* March 23, 2014. https://manilastandard.net/news/-main-stories/143480/brp-sierra-madre-set-to-be-repaired.html.

U.K. Foreign and Commonwealth Office. "UK Speaks in Support of EU Statement on Tensions in South China Sea." Press release. May 10, 2014. https://www.gov.uk/government/news/uk-speaks-in-support-of-eu-statement-on-tensions-in-south-china-sea.

United Nations. SPLOS/72. Decision regarding the Date of Commencement of the Ten-Year Period for Making Submissions to the Commission on the Limits of the Continental Shelf Set Out in Article 4 of Annex II to the United Nations Convention on the Law of the Sea. May 29, 2001. https://documents-dds-ny.un.org/doc/UNDOC/GEN/N01/387/64/PDF/N0138764.pdf?OpenElement.

United Nations. SPLOS 183. Decision regarding the Workload of the Commission on the Limits of the Continental Shelf and the Ability of States, Particularly Developing States, to Fulfil the Requirements of Article 4 of Annex II to the United Nations Convention on the Law of the Sea, As Well As the Decision Contained in SPLOS/72, Paragraph (a). June 20, 2018. https://documents-dds-ny.un.org/doc/UNDOC/GEN/N08/398/76/PDF/N0839876.pdf?OpenElement.

United Nations Convention on the Continental Shelf. Geneva. April 29, 1958. https://treaties.un.org/doc/Treaties/1964/11/19641122%2002-14%20AM/Ch_XXI_01_2_3_4_5p.pdf.

United Nations Convention on Fishing and Conservation of the Living Resources of the High Seas. Geneva. April 29, 1958. https://treaties.un.org/doc/Treaties/1964/11/19641122%2002-14%20AM/Ch_XXI_01_2_3_4_5p.pdf.

United Nations Convention on the High Seas. Geneva. April 29, 1958. https://treaties.un.org/doc/Treaties/1964/11/19641122%2002-14%20AM/Ch_XXI_01_2_3_4_5p.pdf.

United Nations Convention on the Law of the Sea. Montego Bay, Jamaica. December 10, 1982. https://www.un.org/Depts/los/convention_agreements/texts/unclos/closindx.htm.

United Nations Convention on the Law of the Sea Revised Single Negotiating Text (Part II). Introductory Note. A/Conf.62/WP.8/Rev.1/Part II. May 6, 1976. https://legal.un.org/

docs/?path=../diplomaticconferences/1973_los/docs/english/vol_5/a_conf62_wp8_rev 1_part2.pdf&lang=E.

United Nations Convention on the Territorial Sea and the Contiguous Zone. Geneva. April 29, 1958. https://treaties.un.org/doc/Treaties/1964/11/19641122%2002-14%20AM/Ch_ XXI_01_2_3_4_5p.pdf.

United Nations Division for Ocean Affairs and Law of the Sea. "Preliminary Information Indicative of the Outer Limits of the Continental Shelf beyond 200 Miles." August 15, 2019. https://www.un.org/depts/los/clcs_new/commission_preliminary.htm.

United Nations Division for Ocean Affairs and Law of the Sea. "Submissions, through the Secretary-General of the United Nations, to the Commission on the Limits of the Continental Shelf, Pursuant to Article 76, Paragraph 8, of the United Nations Convention on the Law of the Sea of 10 December 1982." November 21, 2019. https://www.un.org/Depts/los/clcs_new/commission_submissions.htm.

United Nations General Assembly Resolution 2881 (XXVI). December 21, 1971. https://undocs.org/en/A/RES/2881(XXVI).

United Nations General Assembly Resolution 3067 (XXVIII), November 16, 1973. https://undocs.org/en/A/RES/3067(xxviii).

United Nations Treaty Collection. Chapter XXI: Law of the Sea. https://treaties.un.org/pages/ViewDetails.aspx?src=TREATY&mtdsg_no=XXI-1&chapter=21&clang=_en.

United Nations Treaty Collection. Chapter XXI: Law of the Sea. "Declarations and Reservations: China." 1996. https://treaties.un.org/pages/ViewDetailsIII.aspx?src=TREATY&mtdsg_no=XXI-6&chapter=21&Temp=mtdsg3&clang=_en#EndDec.

U.S. Defense Security Cooperation Agency. "Section 1263 Indo-Pacific Maritime Security Initiative (MSI)." October 4, 2020. https://www.dsca.mil/programs/section-1263-indo-pacific-maritime-security-initiative-msi.

U.S. Department of Commerce. "Commerce Department Adds 24 Chinese Companies to the Entity List for Helping Build Military Islands in the South China Sea." Press release. August 26, 2020. https://www.commerce.gov/news/press-releases/2020/08/commerce-department-adds-24-chinese-companies-entity-list-helping-build.

U.S. Department of Defense. "DoD Annual Freedom of Navigation (FON) Reports." October 3, 2020. https://policy.defense.gov/OUSDP-Offices/FON/.

U.S. Department of Defense. "Joint Press Conference by Secretary Carter and Minister of National Defense Thanh, in Hanoi, Vietnam." June 1, 2015. https://www.defense.gov/News/Transcripts/Transcript-View/Article/607052/joint-press-conference-by-secretary-carter-and-minister-of-national-defense-tha/.

U.S. Department of State. Daily Press Briefing. February 19, 2013. https://2009-2017.state.gov/r/pa/prs/dpb/2013/02/204955.htm.

U.S. Department of State. Daily Press Briefing. May 6, 2014. https://2009-2017.state.gov/r/pa/prs/dpb/2014/05/225687.htm.

U.S. Department of State. *A Free and Open Indo-Pacific: Advancing a Shared Vision.* November 4, 2019. https://www.state.gov/wp-content/uploads/2019/11/Free-and-Open-Indo-Pacific-4Nov2019.pdf.

U.S. Department of State. Memorandum of Conversation. "Secretary's Meeting with Philippines Foreign Secretary Romulo." Waldorf Towers, New York. October 6, 1976.

U.S. Department of State. "Treaty Priority List for the 111th Congress." May 11, 2009. https://www.gc.noaa.gov/documents/gcil_bd_2009TreatyPriorityList.pdf.

U.S. Department of State. "U.S.-Vietnam Comprehensive Partnership." December 16, 2013. https://2009-2017.state.gov/r/pa/prs/ps/2013/218734.htm.

U.S. Department of State, Bureau of Intelligence and Research. "Sovereignty Claims in the South China Sea." Report No. 672, January 6, 1977. https://www.cia.gov/readingroom/docs/CIA-RDP08C01297R000300180010-1.pdf.

U.S. Department of State, Bureau of Oceans and International Environmental and Scientific Affairs. *China: Maritime Claims in the South China Sea.* Limits in the Seas No. 143. Washington,

DC: U.S. Department of State, 2014. https://2009-2017.state.gov/documents/organization/234936.pdf

U.S. Department of State, Bureau of Oceans and International Environmental and Scientific Affairs. *Taiwan's Maritime Claims*. Limits in the Sea No. 127. Washington, DC: U.S. Department of State, 2005.

U.S. Department of State, Office of the Historian. "Barbary Wars, 1801–1805 and 1815–1816." June 7, 2020. https://history.state.gov/milestones/1801-1829/barbary-wars.

U.S. Department of State, Office of Intelligence Research. "Islands of the South China Sea." Intelligence Report 7283, August 17, 1956. https://www.cia.gov/readingroom/docs/CIA-RDP08C01297R000300180019-2.pdf.

U.S. Embassy in Indonesia. "Fact Sheet: U.S. Institutional Support for ASEAN." September 2011. https://id.usembassy.gov/our-relationship/policy-history/embassy-fact-sheets/fact-sheet-u-s-institutional-support-for-asean/.

U.S. Embassy Manila. "JTF 505 Disestablished." December 1, 2013. https://web.archive.org/web/20140125090056/http://manila.usembassy.gov/jtf-505-disestablished.html.

U.S. Embassy Manila. "Signing of Enhanced Defense Cooperation Agreement." April 28, 2014. https://ph.usembassy.gov/signing-enhanced-defense-cooperation-agreement/.

U.S. Naval History and Heritage Command. "Darter (SS 227)." January 30, 2017. https://www.history.navy.mil/research/library/online-reading-room/title-list-alphabetically/u/united-states-submarine-losses/darter-ss-227.html.

U.S. Navy Hydrographic Office. *Asiatic Pilot*. Vol. 4. Washington, DC: Government Printing Office, 1915.

USNI News. "Document: SECDEF Carter Letter to McCain On South China Sea Freedom of Navigation Operation." January 5, 2016. https://news.usni.org/2016/01/05/document-secdef-carter-letter-to-mccain-on-south-china-sea-freedom-of-navigation-operation.

U.S. Pacific Air Forces. "A-10s Complete Second USPACOM Air Contingent Mission." April 21, 2016. https://www.pacaf.af.mil/News/Photos/igphoto/2001523308/.

Venzon, Cliff. "Beijing Hints It May Stop Activities in South China Sea if Manila Drops Arbitration." *Nikkei Asia*, August 9, 2014. https://asia.nikkei.com/Politics/Beijing-hints-it-may-stop-activities-in-South-China-Sea-if-Manila-drops-arbitration.

Vietnamese Embassy in Germany. "Viet Nam's International Press Conference." May 7, 2014. http://www.vietnambotschaft.org/viet-nams-international-press-conference-on-7th-may-2014/.

Vietnam News Agency. "ASEAN, China Talk DOC Implementation at 18th SOM Meeting." October 15, 2019. https://en.vietnamplus.vn/asean-china-talk-doc-implementation-at-18th-som-meeting/162111.vnp.

Vietnam News Agency. "Chinese Marine Surveillance Ships Violate VN's Sovereignty." Vietnamese Embassy in the United States. May 27, 2011. http://vietnamembassy-usa.org/news/2011/05/chinese-marine-surveillance-ships-violate-vns-sovereignty.

Vitug, Marites Dañguilan. *Rock Solid: How the Philippines Won Its Maritime Case against China*. Quezon City: Ateneo de Manila University Press, 2018.

Vu, Khanh. "Vietnam Protests Beijing's Sinking of South China Sea Boat." Reuters, April 4, 2020. https://www.reuters.com/article/us-vietnam-china-southchinasea/vietnam-protests-beijings-sinking-of-south-china-sea-boat-idUSKBN21M072.

Vuving, Alexander. "South China Sea: Who Occupies What in the Spratlys?" *The Diplomat*, May 6, 2016. https://thediplomat.com/2016/05/south-china-sea-who-claims-what-in-the-spratlys/.

Wall Street Journal. "Search Hillary Clinton's Emails." March 1, 2016.

Whaley, Floyd. "Clinton Reaffirms Military Ties with the Philippines." *New York Times*, November 16, 2011. https://www.nytimes.com/2011/11/17/world/asia/clinton-reaffirms-military-ties-with-the-philippines.html.

White House. "Joint Statement on the ASEAN-U.S. Strategic Partnership." November 21, 2015. https://obamawhitehouse.archives.gov/the-press-office/2015/11/21/joint-statement-asean-us-strategic-partnership.

White House. "Joint Statement of the U.S.-ASEAN Special Leaders' Summit: Sunnylands Declaration." February 16, 2016. https://obamawhitehouse.archives.gov/the-press-office/2016/02/16/joint-statement-us-asean-special-leaders-summit-sunnylands-declaration.

White House. "Remarks by President Obama and President Xi on the People's Republic of China before Bilateral Meeting." March 31, 2016. https://obamawhitehouse.archives.gov/the-press-office/2016/03/31/remarks-president-obama-and-president-xi-peoples-repub lic-china.

White House. "Remarks by President Obama and President Xi of the People's Republic of China in Joint Press Conference." September 25, 2015. https://obamawhitehouse.archives.gov/the-press-office/2015/09/25/remarks-president-obama-and-president-xi-peoples-repub lic-china-joint.

White House. "The U.S.-Indonesia Comprehensive Partnership." Press release. June 27, 2010. https://obamawhitehouse.archives.gov/the-press-office/us-indonesia-comprehensive-part nership.

Winger, Gregory. "Be Careful What You Wish For: A Historical Retrospective on the Philippines-US Mutual Defense Treaty." Asia Pacific Pathways to Progress Foundation, February 25, 2019. https://appfi.ph/resources/commentaries/2530-be-careful-what-you-wish-for-a-his torical-retrospective-on-the-philippines-us-mutual-defense-treaty.

Wisnumurti, Nugroho. "Legal Regimes of Archipelagic States." Jakarta Post, March 27, 2014. https://www.thejakartapost.com/news/2014/03/27/legal-regimes-archipelagic-sta tes.html.

Wong, Edward. "Chinese Military Seeks to Extend Its Naval Power." New York Times, April 23, 2010. https://www.nytimes.com/2010/04/24/world/asia/24navy.html?login= email&auth=login-email.

Wong, Edward, and Jonathan Ansfield. "To Bolster Its Claims, China Plants Islands in Disputed Waters." New York Times, June 16, 2014. https://www.nytimes.com/2014/06/17/world/asia/spratly-archipelago-china-trying-to-bolster-its-claims-plants-islands-in-disputed-wat ers.html.

Wong, Kristina. "Exclusive: Trump's Pentagon Plans to Regularly Challenge China in the South China Sea." Breitbart, July 21, 2017. https://www.breitbart.com/national-security/2017/07/20/trump-pentagon-south-china-sea-plan/.

Wright, Austin. "Law of the Sea Treaty Sinks in Senate." Politico, July 16, 2012. https://www.polit ico.com/story/2012/07/law-of-the-sea-treaty-sinks-in-senate-078568.

Xue Guifang. "China and the Law of the Sea: An Update." In International Law and Military Operations, edited by Michael D. Carsten, 97–110. International Law Studies vol. 84. Providence, RI: U.S. Naval War College, 1984.

Xinhua. "China Requires Vietnam to Stop Any Form of Disruptions of Chinese Company's Operations." People's Daily, May 9, 2014. http://en.people.cn/90883/8621898.html.

Xinhua. "CNPC Ends Drilling Off Xisha Islands." July 16, 2014. http://www.china.org.cn/busin ess/2014-07/16/content_32963102.htm.

Yabes, Criselda. "Manila Turns Back Coup Bid with Help of U.S. Air Power." Washington Post, December 2, 1989. https://www.washingtonpost.com/archive/politics/1989/12/02/manila-turns-back-coup-bid-with-help-of-us-air-power/62895eef-23e2-4311-bf1b-4da4a 63267f0/.

Yearbook of the International Law Commission 1955. Vol. 2, A/CN.4/Ser.A/1955/Add.1. New York: United Nations, 1960. https://legal.un.org/ilc/publications/yearbooks/engl ish/ilc_1955_v2.pdf.

Yearbook of the International Law Commission 1956, Vol. 2, A/CN.4/SER.A/1956/Add.1. New York: United Nations, 1957. https://legal.un.org/ilc/publications/yearbooks/engl ish/ilc_1956_v2.pdf.

Yoshihara, Toshi. "The 1974 Paracels Sea Battle: A Campaign Appraisal." *U.S. Naval War College Review* 69, no. 2 (Spring 2016): 43–65.

You Ji. "The Evolution of China's Maritime Combat Doctrines and Models: 1949–2001." *IDSS Working Papers* 22 (May 2002): 1–35. https://dr.ntu.edu.sg/bitstream/10356/90547/1/RSIS-WORKPAPER_30.pdf.

Youssef, Nancy A. "Mattis Says China Is 'Out of Step' with International Law." *Wall Street Journal*. May 29, 2018. https://www.wsj.com/articles/mattis-says-china-is-out-of-step-with-international-law-1527636790.

Zhang Yunbi and Qiu Quanlin. "Manila's Attempt to Internationalize Dispute Rejected." *China Daily*, April 19, 2012. http://www.chinadaily.com.cn/china/2012-04/19/content_15084608.htm.

Zou Keyuan. "Scarborough Reef: A New Flashpoint in Sino-Philippines Relations?" *IBRU Boundary and Security Bulletin* (Summer 1999): 71–80.

INDEX

314

INDEX